AMERICA IN LEGEND

ALSO BY RICHARD M. DORSON

America Begins: *Early American Writing*
America Rebels: *Narratives of the Patriots*
American Folklore
Folk Legends of Japan
Buying the Wind: *Regional Folklore in the United States*
American Negro Folktales
African Folklore
The British Folklorists
Bloodstoppers and Bearwalkers:
Folk Traditions of the Upper Peninsula

RICHARD M. DORSON

America in Legend

Folklore from the Colonial Period to the Present

PANTHEON BOOKS

A Division of Random House, New York

Grateful acknowledgment is made to the following for permission to reprint material
that appeared in their publications:

Duke University Press, for "Mose the Far-Famed and World-Renowned," by Richard
M. Dorson, *American Literature,* vol. 15 (1943), pp. 288–300. Copyright 1943,
© 1971 by the Duke University Press.

New England Quarterly, for "The Yankee on the Stage," by Richard M. Dorson, from
vol. 13 (September 1940), pp. 467–93.

American Mercury, for "The Story of Sam Patch," by Richard M. Dorson, from vol.
64 (June 1947), pp. 741–47. American Mercury, Torrance, Calif.

Straight Arrow Publishers Inc., for excerpts from an interview with Jerry Garcia and
Mountain Girl, January 20, 1972. From *Rolling Stone* © 1972 by Straight Arrow
Publishers Inc. All rights reserved. Reprinted by permission.

Again, for Gloria

Contents

Acknowledgments   ix

Foreword: *Identifying Folklore*   xiii

Color Plates   xvi

Introduction: *American Life-styles and Legends*   1

The Colonial Period: *The Religious Impulse*   11
Folklore of the Religious Era   15
Providences   17
Witchcraft   32
The Devil   48
Judgments (Quaker View)   51
Religious Folklore Motifs   54

The Early National Period: *The Democratic Impulse*   57
Folk Heroes of the Democratic Era   60
Davy Crockett the Backwoodsman   64
Mike Fink the Keelboatman   80
Sam Patch the Mill Hand   92
Mose the Bowery B'hoy   99
Yankee Jonathan the Countryman   108

The Later National Period: *The Economic Impulse*   123
Folklore of Economic Occupations   127
Cowboys   128
   The First Cowboy Folklorists   128
   Cowboy Folktales About Cowboys   140
   The Cowboy Code   150
Lumberjacks   153
   Lumberjack Songs   155
   Lumberjack Hero Tales   168

Miners   185
  Coal-Mining Songs   185
  The Molly Maguires   190

Oil Drillers   214
  Tales of Gib Morgan   216
  Oil-Money Legends   228

Railroaders   235
  A Brave Engineer   235
  Other Brave Engineers   242

The Master Workman versus the Businessman   243

The Contemporary Period: *The Humane Impulse*   253

Folklore of the Youth Culture   257

Druglore   260
  Cops and Dopers, Narcs and Heads   260
  Cops as Heads   270
  Paranoia   274
  Owsley, the King of Acid   278
  Freakouts   288
  Druglore Local Legends   291
  Druglore Latrinalia   295
  Druglore Jokes   297
  Drug Games   300

Draft Dodgers   304

Notes   311

Bibliography   324

Index   329

Acknowledgments

To the John Simon Guggenheim Memorial Foundation, thrice my benefactor, I am indebted for a year's grace during which the writing of this book was completed. Its director, Gordon Ray, has given me moral as well as financial support. I am grateful to Roger Abrahams, Alan Dundes, and Barbara Kirshenblatt-Gimblett for making available to me druglore collections in the folklore archives of the University of California, Berkeley, and the University of Texas, and to the students in my American Folklore class at Berkeley in 1968 who introduced me to traditions of the counterculture. Peter Tamony kindly sent me news clippings of the "King of Acid." On the home front, my research assistant, Inta Carpenter, has skillfully nursed me through the gestation of this manuscript.

To Dr. Mehdi Razavi, cardiologist, and Dr. Laurence K. Groves, surgeon, of the Cleveland Clinic Hospital I owe a very special debt. On January 22, 1973, Dr. Groves performed open-heart surgery upon me, with success that enabled me to complete revisions on the manuscript by the March 1 deadline.

A number of individuals and institutions have aided me in the search for illustrations. I particularly wish to thank the following: Joseph C. Hickerson, Archive of Folk Song, Library of Congress; John N. Hoffman, Museum of History and Technology, Smithsonian Institution; Edward D. Ives, director of the Northeast Archives of Folklore and Oral History, University of Maine; Geneva Kiebler, Michigan Historical Division, State of Michigan Archives; Jeanne T. Newlin, Harvard Theatre Collection, Harvard College Library; William A. Owens, professor of English and comparative literature, Columbia University; Earl A. Ross, American Petroleum Institute; William H. Toner, Wyoming Historical and Geological Society, Wilkes-Barre, Pennsylvania; Geneva Warner, Lilly Library, Indiana University; and Neda M. Westlake, Charles Patterson Van Pelt Library, University of Pennsylvania. For allowing me to select from their photographs of the counterculture I am indebted to Sandra Eisert and Bryan Moss. I am also thankful to the editors of *American Literature, American Mercury,* and *The New England Quarterly* for permission to reprint in revised form my articles on Mose, Sam Patch, and the stage Yankee, which originally appeared in their pages.

Illustrations

The Colonial Period

"God's Just Judgment on Blasphemers & A Dreadful Warning to all Wicked and Forsworn Sinners"   p. 21
From John Ashton, *Chap-Books of the Eighteenth Century* (London: Chatto & Windus, 1882)

"The Guilford Ghost"   p. 25
From John Ashton, *Chap-Books of the Eighteenth Century* (London: Chatto & Windus, 1882)

"The Witch of the Woodlands"   p. 34
From John Ashton, *Chap-Books of the Eighteenth Century* (London: Chatto & Windus, 1882)

"A Strange and Wonderful Relation of the Old Woman . . ."   p. 35
From John Ashton, *Chap-Books of the Eighteenth Century* (London: Chatto & Windus, 1882)

"A Terrible and Seasonable Warning to Young Men"   p. 36
From John Ashton, *Chap-Books of the Eighteenth Century* (London: Chatto & Windus, 1882)

"Farther, and More Terrible Warnings from God"   p. 36
From John Ashton, *Chap-Books of the Eighteenth Century* (London: Chatto & Windus, 1882)

"A Timely Warning"   p. 37
From John Ashton, *Chap-Books of the Eighteenth Century* (London: Chatto & Windus, 1882)

"The Miracle of Miracles"   p. 37
From John Ashton, *Chap-Books of the Eighteenth Century* (London: Chatto & Windus, 1882)

"Saducismus Triumphatus"   p. 39
Reprinted by permission of the University of Pennsylvania Library

Conception of a seventeenth-century witch, in an American lithograph of 1892   p. 40
From the Library of Congress Collection of Prints and Photographs

Title page and frontispiece of Richard Boulton's *A Compleat History of Magick, Sorcery, and Witchcraft (1715-16).*   p. 42
Reprinted by permission of the University of Pennsylvania Library

"Witches, Apprehended, Examined, and Executed"   p. 44
Reprinted by permission of the Huntington Library and Art Gallery, San Marino, California

"Witchcraft at Salem Village"   p. 46
From Augustus L. Mason, *The Romance and Tragedy of Pioneer Life* (Cincinnati, Chicago, St. Louis, Dallas: Jones Brothers, 1883)

Cotton Mather praying   p. 48
Taken from *The Encyclopedia of Witchcraft and Demonology* by Rossell Hope Robbins. © 1959 by Crown Publishers, Inc. Used by permission of Crown Publishers, Inc.

The Early National Period

"A Regular Row in the Backwoods"   p. 60

From *The Crockett Almanac 1841* (Boston: published by J. Fischer)

David Crockett   p. 64
By S. S. Osgood, Childs and Lehman, Lithographers, Philadelphia, 1831. Reprinted from Harry T. Peters, *America on Stone* (Garden City, N.Y.: Doubleday, Doran & Co., 1931)

"Fall of the Alamo—Death of Crockett"   p. 66
From *Davy Crockett's Almanack, 1837* (Nashville, Tenn.: published by the heirs of Col. Crockett)

"The Way They Travel in the West"   p. 70
From *The Crockett Almanac 1840* (Nashville, Tenn.: published by Ben Harding)

Cover page of a Crockett almanac   p. 75

James H. Hackett as Nimrod Wildfire   p. 76
By permission of the Harvard Theatre Collection

"Col. Crockett and the Bear and the Swallows"   p. 78
From *The Crockett Almanac 1840* (Nashville, Tenn.: published by Ben Harding)

Davy Crockett   p. 80
By Louis Mauer. Reprinted from Harry T. Peters, *America on Stone* (Garden City, N.Y.: Doubleday, Doran & Co., 1931)

"Mike Fink, the Ohio Boatman"   p. 83
From *Davy Crockett's Almanack, 1838* (Nashville, Tenn.: published by the heirs of Col. Crockett)

"Mike Fink Beating Colonel Crockett at a Shooting Match"   p. 85
From *The Crockett Almanac, 1840* (Nashville, Tenn.: published by Ben Harding)

"The Keel-Boat"   p. 86
From *Harper's New Monthly Magazine* (December 1855)

"A Keel Boat on the Mississippi"   p. 91
From *Davy Crockett's Almanack 1838* (Nashville, Tenn.: published by the heirs of Col. Crockett)

Sam Patch in the fatal leap over the Genesee Falls in 1829   p. 97
From *The Wonderful Leaps of Sam Patch* (McLoughlin Brothers, New York, ca. 1870)

A Glance at New York in 1848 (illustrated playbill)   p. 100
By permission of the Harvard Theatre Collection

The Glance at Philadelphia for the Last Time (illustrated playbill)   p. 101
By permission of the Harvard Theatre Collection

Chanfrau as Mose rescuing a child from the fire   p. 103
By permission of the Harvard Theatre Collection

George H. "Yankee" Hill in Yankee costume   p. 111
By permission of the Harvard Theatre Collection

"Yankee" Hill as Nathan Tucker in *Wife for a Day*   p. 116
By permission of the Harvard Theatre Collection

"Yankee" Hill as Hiram Dodge in *The Yankee*

Pedlar p. 119
By permission of the Harvard Theatre Collection

Dan Marble as Jacob Jewsharp p. 120
By permission of the Harvard Theatre Collection

James H. Hackett as Solomon Swap p. 121
By permission of the Harvard Theatre Collection

The Later National Period

"Storytelling Around the Chuck Wagon" p. 130
By E. Boyd Smith, from Andy Adams, *The Log of a Cowboy* (Boston and New York: Houghton Mifflin Co., 1903)

N. Howard "Jack" Thorp p. 132
From N. H. Thorp, *Pardner of the Wind* (Caldwell, Idaho: Caxton Printers, 1945)

"Riders Were Sent Through the Herd at Break-neck Pace" p. 135
By R. Farrington Elwell, from Andy Adams, *The Log of a Cowboy* (Boston and New York: Houghton Mifflin Co., 1927)

"Cutting Out Cattle from the Herd" p. 141
By Henry Worrall, from Joseph G. McCoy, *Historic Sketches of the Cattle Trade of the West and Southwest* (Kansas City, Mo.: Ramsay, Millett & Hudson, 1874). By permission of the Rare Book Division, The New York Public Library, Astor, Lenox and Tilden Foundations.

The Texas cattle trade p. 144
From *Harper's Weekly Supplement,* May 2, 1874

"Drunken Cowboy on the Warpath" p. 146
By Henry Worrall, from Joseph G. McCoy, *Historic Sketches of the Cattle Trade of the West and Southwest* (Kansas City, Mo.: Ramsay, Millett & Hudson, 1874). By permission of the Rare Book Division, The New York Public Library, Astor, Lenox and Tilden Foundations.

"Cowboys Swimming a Herd Across the Platte River" p. 149
By E. Boyd Smith, from Andy Adams, *The Log of a Cowboy* (Boston and New York: Houghton Mifflin Co., 1903)

"Midnight Storm and Stampede" p. 152
By Henry Worrall, from Joseph G. McCoy, *Historic Sketches of the Cattle Trade of the West and Southwest* (Kansas City, Mo.: Ramsay, Millett & Hudson, 1874). By permission of the Rare Book Division, The New York Public Library, Astor, Lenox and Tilden Foundations.

"Lumbering in Maine and New Brunswick—Drawing the Logs to the Creek" p. 154
From *Harper's Weekly,* September 25, 1858

"Dinner-hour in a Michigan Lumber Camp" p. 156
By Dan Beard, from *Scribner's Magazine,* June 1893

"The Kitchen" p. 156
By Dan Beard, from *Scribner's Magazine,* June 1893

"Sunday in Camp" p. 157
By Dan Beard, from *Scribner's Magazine,* June 1893

Surveying for a logging railway p. 165
From *Frank Leslie's Illustrated Newpaper,* March 3, 1888

Building a railway p. 167
From *Frank Leslie's Illustrated Newspaper,* March 3, 1888

Loading up p. 169
From *Frank Leslie's Illustrated Newspaper,* March 3, 1888

Otto Walta and four fellow lumberjacks p. 171
From Michael G. Karni, "Otto Walta, Finnish Folk Hero of the Iron Range," *Minnesota History,* 1967

Sawyers of the Cutler and Savidge Lumber Company at Douglass, Montcalm County, Michigan p. 173
Courtesy of Michigan State Archives

A load of logs estimated at 100,000 pounds p. 175
Courtesy of Michigan State Archives

Teamsters on a sled load of logs, near Grindstone, Maine, early 1900s p. 176
Gift from M. L. Jordan of Old Town, Maine, to the Northeast Archives of Folklore and Oral History, University of Maine

River drivers on Wassataquoic River, Maine, early 1900s p. 179
Gift from Ludwig K. Moorehead to the Northeast Archives of Folklore and Oral History, University of Maine

The beginning of a spring log drive on the Muskegon River p. 183
Courtesy of Michigan State Archives

Three Maine river drivers working on headworks p. 184
Northeast Archives of Folklore and Oral History, University of Maine

Anthracite coal miner in Pennsylvania p. 186
Courtesy of the Wyoming Historical and Geological Society, Wilkes-Barre, Pennsylvania

Coal miners at entrance to mine, Schuylkill County, Pennsylvania, 1897 p. 188
Courtesy of the Smithsonian Institution

Miners setting up timber supports underground, Schuylkill County, Pennsylvania, 1907 p. 191
Courtesy of the Smithsonian Institution

Mollies kidnap a miner who has refused to go on strike with them p. 192
From Allan Pinkerton, *The Molly Maguires and the*

Detectives (New York: G. W. Carleton & Co., 1877)

The Pinkerton detective James McParlan   p. 192
From Allan Pinkerton, *The Molly Maguires and the Detectives* (New York: G. W. Carleton & Co., 1877)

Coal miners of Pennsylvania in the Honey Brook Mines   pp. 195-7
Sketched by Theo. R. Davis for *Harper's Weekly*, September 11, 1869

The Avondale mine disaster   pp. 200-201
From *Frank Leslie's Illustrated Newspaper*, September 25, 1869

Two Molly Maguires murder a mine superintendent   p. 203
From Allan Pinkerton, *The Molly Maguires and the Detectives* (New York: G. W. Carleton & Co., 1877)

A Molly Maguire shoots Gomer James   p. 209
From Allan Pinkerton, *The Molly Maguires and the Detectives* (New York: G. W. Carleton & Co., 1877)

Mollies murder Thomas Sanger   p. 210
From Allan Pinkerton, *The Molly Maguires and the Detectives* (New York: G. W. Carleton & Co., 1877)

A savage battle between the Molly Maguires and the Sheet Irons   p. 212
From Allan Pinkerton, *The Molly Maguires and the Detectives* (New York: G. W. Carleton & Co., 1877)

Gilbert Morgan   p. 216
From Mody C. Boatright, *Gib Morgan, Minstrel of the Oil Fields,* (Dallas Texas: Southern Methodist University Press, 1945)

Drake Well, Pennsylvania, 1859   p. 217
Courtesy of the Library of Congress Collection of Prints and Photographs

The first oil wells pumping in the United States, Titusville, Pennsylvania, 1860   p. 218
Courtesy of the Library of Congress Collection of Prints and Photographs

Seminole, Oklahoma, in 1927   p. 221
Courtesy of American Petroleum Institute, Washington, D.C., from the Exxon Corporation

"Implements Used in Boring"   p. 222
From *Harper's New Monthly Magazine*, April 1865

The spring-pole method of drilling   p. 223
Courtesy of American Petroleum Institute, Washington, D.C.

A "borer" at work   p. 224
Courtesy of American Petroleum Institute, Washington, D.C.

William A. (Uncle Billy) Smith at Titusville, Pennsylvania, 1859   p. 225
Courtesy of American Petroleum Institute, Washington, D.C.

A rotary rig in the Sour Lake oilfield, Texas, about 1905   p. 226
The Oral History of Texas Oil Pioneers, University of Texas Library

Drillers with tools used in the early oil fields of western Pennsylvania   p. 228
Courtesy of American Petroleum Institute, Washington, D.C.

Coal Oil Johnny   p. 231
From John Washington Steele, *Coal Oil Johnny: The Story of His Career as Told by Himself* (Franklin, Pa.: 1902)

The famous Lucas well at Spindletop, Texas   p. 233
Courtesy of American Petroleum Institute, Washington, D.C. from the Standard Oil Company of Ohio

A farm family made wealthy by an oil well   p. 234
From Boyce House, *Oil Boom* (Caldwell, Idaho: Caxton Printers, 1941)

Casey Jones   p. 236
Frontispiece in Fred J. Lee, *Casey Jones, Epic of the American Railroad* (Kingsport, Tenn.: Southern Publishers, 1939)

The famous No. 638   p. 238
From Fred J. Lee, *Casey Jones, Epic of the American Railroad* (Kingsport, Tenn.: Southern Publishers, 1939)

The Contemporary Period

Woodstock   p. 254
Baron Wolman

Demonstrator and troops at the Pentagon demonstration march, 1967   p. 256
Marc Riboud, Magnum

Allen Ginsberg   p. 256
Roger Lubin

A late afternoon swim in Connecticut   p. 258
Mark Haven

Girl in Haight-Ashbury   p. 259
Baron Wolman

Janis Joplin   p. 264
Courtesy of Columbia Records

On the street in Haight-Ashbury   p. 266
Wayne Miller, Magnum

Hitchhikers   p. 267
Bryan Moss

Plastic marijuana plants   p. 270
Baron Wolman

An arrest in Berkeley   p. 277
Roger Lubin

The Grateful Dead   p. 282
Mary Anne Mayer, and J. L. Overlook, courtesy of Rock Scully

Drop City, Colorado   p. 303
Dennis Stock, Magnum

War resister David Harris with Joan Baez   p. 304
UPI Telephoto, Compix

March on Washington, 1965   p. 305
Charles Harbutt, Magnum

The Democratic Convention, Chicago, 1968   p. 307
Charles Harbutt, Magnum

Indiana University student protest, 1969   p. 309
Sandra Eisert

Foreword

Identifying Folklore

American history as written by historians is largely a story of the elite. With the best will in the world, the chroniclers of our past cannot personalize the "common man" about whom they speak in large statistical generalities. "Dead men tell no tales and fill out no questionnaires," moans one historian of the New Left, endeavoring to rewrite American history from the bottom up.[1] Allan Nevins has declared that the most fascinating part of history but the most difficult to obtain is the record of how plain men and women lived and were affected by the social, economic, and cultural changes of their times. Other historians complain about the preoccupation of their colleagues with all-too-familiar events and personalities presented within the framework of federal government. Yet when they turn to neglected areas of American history, say of the blacks, they repeat their elitist formulas, merely changing the names of George Washington, Abraham Lincoln, and Franklin D. Roosevelt to those of Booker T. Washington, Frederick Douglass, and W. E. B. Du Bois.

One means of redressing the inattention to the common folk in American life and history is through the use of folklore sources. In the materials of folklore dead men do tell tales, and leave behind them a wake of traditions that illuminate thoughts and emotions never confined to writing. But using folktales and folksongs for historical ends is a tricky business. Oral items of folklore do not carry a publisher's imprint, and their genealogies may extend back to Egypt of the Pharaohs or the China of Confucius. Does folklore collected today reflect the past of which it speaks or the present in which it is recorded? There is also the problem of locating folk traditions in bygone times before the day of tape recorders and the concept of field collecting. "Folklore" as a term was coined only in 1846. For these reasons, and because very few of them are historically trained, American folklorists have for the most part shied away from attempts at historical treatment.

These questions about possible historical uses of folklore can be met. In lieu of live informants, printed sources may be combed with care and caution as repositories of folkstuff in past centuries. The difficulty of pinning down even by approximate dates the elusive, floating, perhaps long-ancestried tales, ballads, and sayings vanishes when folklore is recognized as an expression of its times. This is a rather heretical viewpoint, for the fathers of folklore studies, such as Jacob and Wilhelm Grimm in Germany and the antiquaries and anthropological folklorists in England, notably Edward B. Tylor, regarded folk traditions as survivals from pagan and prehistoric eras. But they associated folklore with the peripheral rather than the mainstream culture, with the peasant rather than the shopkeeper. Currently folklorists are beginning to explore folklore of the living, not the dying, culture, to penetrate the city as well as the countryside and modern industry as well as traditional crafts. It is the thesis of this book that the vital folklore and especially the legends of a given period in American history reflect the main concerns and values, tensions and anxieties, goals and drives of the period. We may well find in the folk legends a statement of the common man's outlook denied us in conventional documents. The pulsating folklore that mirrors the philosophy of one period becomes the ossified "superstition" of a later period. While in the seventeenth century Americans of the central culture exchanged tales of witches and the Devil with thorough conviction, in the twentieth century these legends pass muster only in such marginal subcultures as the Ozarks, the Mississippi Delta, Little Egypt in southern Illinois, and urban ethnic pockets. Whether or not a given piece of folklore may be traced far back in time or far out in space matters less, in this instance, than its adaptability and suitability to the needs of a particular period.

The four bodies of legendary traditions here presented reflect the main thrust in four large sequences of American history. The attempt is not by any means to discuss the total folklore of a period—even if that were possible—but the folklore of the new sector, the cutting edge of a changing society.

And what do we mean by "...lklore," a term used, misused, and abused in an endless variety of ways? Let me begin with an example or two rather than with a rigid definition. In addressing a university audience today, if I ask who has heard the tale of the man with the hook, half a dozen hands will go up, mainly those of coeds, there will be squeals of recognition and anxiety, and then various tellings will follow. In essence, the story relates how an alarm has gone out that an escaped lunatic with a hook in place of an arm is on the rampage. Girls in the dormitory bolt their doors in terror, but late in the evening the coeds in one room hear a scratching, scratching, scratching on the outside of their door. They wait through the night in panic, and only in the morning when the scratching has ceased do they summon the nerve to open the door, and find slumped on the corridor in a pool of blood, not the madman with the hook, but their roommate, who had dragged herself from his clutches and was seeking to gain entry to her room.

In this same audience, there will be some black students who will not have responded to this account, but when I mention "playing the dozens," they will nod and chuckle appreciatively. They recognize at once the ritualistic game of the ghetto street culture in which youthful combatants seek to outcap each other in a stream of powerfully charged, electrically obscene insults.

Now if I inquire of this same American audience who knows what the *kappa* is, not a single glint of recognition will appear. Yet every member of any group of Japanese people you might encounter in Japan will know the *kappa* as well as their own names. In Japanese tradition the *kappa* is a boyish goblin with an inverted, saucerlike cavity on his head containing a magic fluid that gives him supernatural powers; if the fluid is spilled, he is reduced to impotence.

In each of these instances a number of individuals—the number may vary from a few hundred to many millions—share a tradition intimately known to themselves but alien and bizarre to the outsider. These esoteric traditions constitute the items referred to as folklore. They fall into various categories, such as folk narratives, folksongs, proverbs, riddles, folk speech, folk festivals, traditional games, and folk beliefs, and these categories are further refined into subdivisions. Under folk narrative, for instance, we speak of the *Märchen* as a fiction filled with magical notions, the *legend* as a purportedly true happening, and the *anecdote* as a brief incident supposedly attached to a historical personality. Under folksong, we allude to *ballad* as a sung verse narrative and to *lyric* as a traditional song describing emotions rather than unfolding a story. Increasingly, folklorists are recognizing that they should consider traditional ideas and values which may be expressed within tale and song and other genres or in ordinary conversation. These codes of values reveal the drives and goals of a given subculture.

Identifying and defining folklore becomes a technical matter for scholars, whose methods may prove irritating to the layman impatient to savor the folkstuff. Yet the issue cannot be skirted or minimized, for it involves the falsifying and distortion of cultural materials. In 1950 I coined the word "fakelore" to designate the spurious, synthetic, and cloying packages of pseudofolklore foisted on the public. Most Paul Bunyan books fall under the heading of fakelore.

Their authors have invented the stories or repeated earlier literary renditions, but asserting that Paul Bunyan is a folk hero does not make him one. Only the folk who spin legends, relate anecdotes, and sing ballads about a figure who has captured their imagination can provide the evidence. Folklorists who have actually gone into the field to speak with lumberjacks report very few or no tales about Old Paul, although woodsmen possess considerable hoards of folklore on other subjects. Furthermore, the contents of the Paul Bunyan books greatly distort the actual nature of folk tradition, by presenting a saccharine superman, suitable for a Walt Disney production but not for the raw, coarse nature of much folkstuff. To ensure the folkloric character of his items, the folklorist applies certain tests: evidence of oral circulation; identification in the great indexes and catalogues of folktale motifs and types, ballad texts, and proverb and riddle forms; and close parallels in existing field collections. If he does his homework properly, he can speak with some confidence about folklore and legends.

Color Plates

1. Two scenes from Thomas A. Gunn, *Mose Among the Britishers, or The B'hoy in London,* a rare twenty-page booklet of hand-colored lithographs depicting Mose's adventures on a visit to London. Shown are the title page, with Mose in a characteristic pose, and Mose starting a "muss" (a fight) at a masked ball in London. The booklet is dedicated to Francis S. Chanfrau, who created the character of Mose on the stage.

2. "The Trial of George Jacobs"
A painting of the 1692 witchcraft trials in Salem Village done in 1868 by Tompkins H. Matteson, a New York painter of historical scenes from the colonial and Revolutionary periods. Courtesy of the Essex Institute, Salem, Mass.

3. A scene from Thomas A. Gunn, *Mose Among the Britishers, or The B'hoy in London.* Mose is shown back home again among the fireboys.

4. "Hello, Friend, Don't Forget That Vote"
An engraving by Howard Alken (1774–1850), an English illustrator of hunting and sporting books, based on a scene from *The Life of David Crockett*

5. Forty years after Sam Patch jumped to his death over Genesee Falls in 1829, an illustrated children's book presented his now legendary feats to a new generation. The pictures reproduced here show *The Wonderful Leaps of Sam Patch* (McLoughlin Brothers, New York, circa 1870).

6. Sheet-music cover of the famous song written in 1909 that made the name of Casey Jones a household word. Courtesy of Lilly Library, Indiana University.

7. "We Gave the Wagon No Time to Sink"
An illustration by R. Farrington Elwell, from Andy Adams, *The Log of a Cowboy* (Boston and New York: Houghton Mifflin Co., 1927).

8. The round-up was the occasion on which cowboys drove together a large herd of cattle so that the ranchman could select out stock to fulfill his contract, or so they could "cut out" cows to brand their calves. This scene may have appeared on a cigar-box cover. Courtesy of the Library of Congress Collection of Prints and Photographs.
The illustrations surrounding "A Round Up" depict scenes from the Texas cattle trade drawn for *Harper's Weekly Supplement,* May 2, 1874.

9. Bob Dylan poster, by Milton Glaser. Courtesy of Columbia Records.

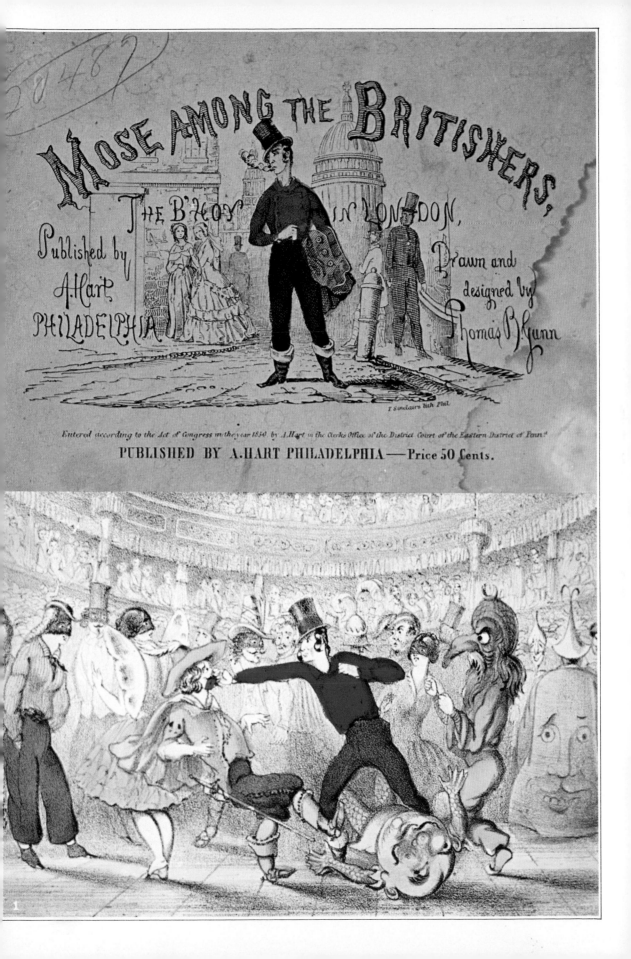

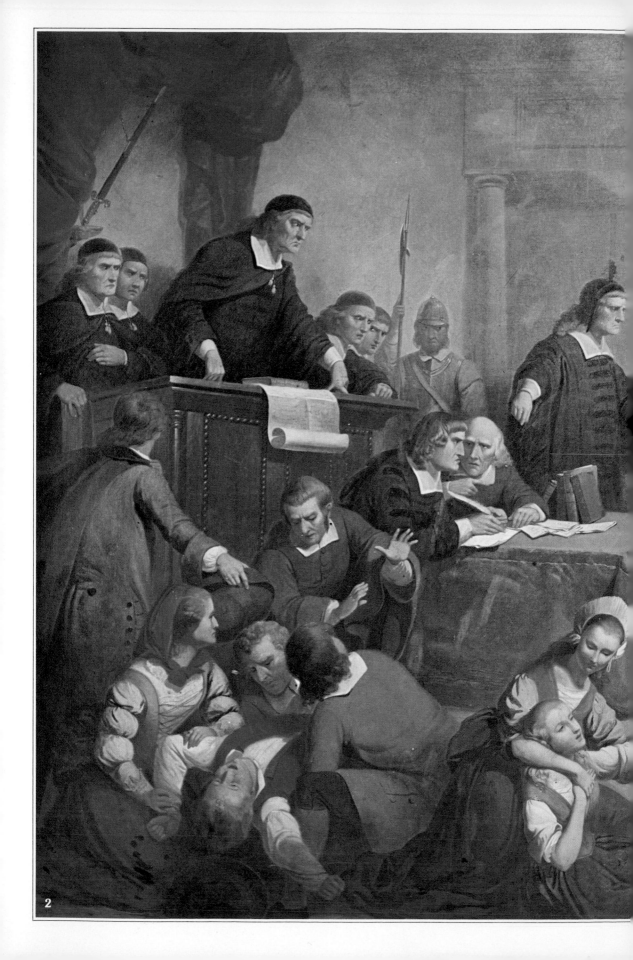

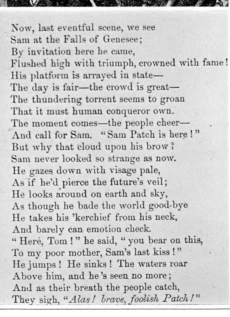

Now, last eventful scene, we see
Sam at the Falls of Genesee;
By invitation here he came,
Flushed high with triumph, crowned with fame!
His platform is arrayed in state—
The day is fair—the crowd is great—
The thundering torrent seems to groan
That it must human conqueror own.
The moment comes—the people cheer—
And call for Sam. "Sam Patch is here!"
But why that cloud upon his brow?
Sam never looked so strange as now.
He gazes down with visage pale,
As if he'd pierce the future's veil;
He looks around on earth and sky,
As though he bade the world good-bye
He takes his 'kerchief from his neck,
And barely can emotion check.
"Here, Tom!" he said, "you bear on this,
To my poor mother, Sam's last kiss!"
He jumps! He sinks! The waters roar
Above him, and he's seen no more;
And as their breath the people catch,
They sigh, "*Alas! brave, foolish Patch!*"

1877 AR

D UP. 1887

DYLAN

9

Introduction

American Life - styles and Legends

American history may be viewed as falling into three periods dominated by particular life-styles, to use a term currently in vogue, with the 1960s marking a convulsive transition into a fourth. Each life-style reflects the dominant goals and aspirations of the period, and it is reflected in turn in the prevalent social philosophy, in the educational institutions, in the landmark writings, in the culture heroes and popular heroes, and in legends and folklore. Characteristically, the American life-style has sought to express a freedom of action and belief against an enemy of freedom, against the Establishment of its day.

The first life-style was that of the Religious Man, and his oppressor was the Established Church of England. This style dominated the seventeenth century and prevailed perhaps halfway through the eighteenth, when revivalism on one side and Arminian rationalism on the other choked off the Puritan thrust. Religious Man, in his Protestant reforming guise of Puritan, Quaker, or Mennonite, concentrated on the salvation of his soul. He came to America to place himself in a stronger position to attain this priceless end, free from the medieval shackles of a hidebound Anglican Church, still close to Rome, which mixed saints and sinners. The covenant or federal theology of Calvinistic Puritanism controlled the public and private lives of New Englanders with its formidable dialectic of covenants, election, predestination, congregationalism, perseverance of the saints, justification by faith, and preparation to receive God's predetermined grace. In the Massachusetts Bay commonwealth, all magistrates must be saints, for sinners could never govern God's elect. Harvard College, first of American universities, was founded in 1636, the precursor of other denominational colleges intended to train ministers in the exegesis of Scripture and to graduate a laity capable of understanding such exegesis. Culture heroes in the colonial era are godly men. The leaders of the first settlements—William Bradford, John Winthrop, Francis Daniel Pastorius—bent their energies to safeguarding their new, autonomous religious societies. Aboard the *Arbella* in 1630 as it sailed for New England, John Winthrop lectured to his fellow emigrants on their mission, "The end is to improve our lives to do more service to the Lord." Samuel Eliot Morison wrote of him, "His ideal was to devote every waking moment to God."[1] Cotton Mather is the greatest of the mid-colonial culture heroes—splenetic, unquenchable, oracular, preaching on every event and issue within reach, from Salem witchcraft to smallpox inoculation, and finding God's providence behind every act. His crowning work, the *Magnalia Christi Americana* (1702), celebrated the achievements of Christ in the American wilderness, according to His general providential design and His specific providential judgments. Coupled

1

with the *Magnalia* in influence and fame is the colonial bestseller, *The Day of Doom,* written in 1662 by a Puritan divine, Michael Wigglesworth, and narrating in wooden rhyme the "Great and Last Judgment" when idolaters and saints learn their eternal fates.

In their somber dress, austere meeting-houses, and strict biblical code of conduct, the Puritans molded their daily life-style on their theology. Protected from its external enemy, the repressive Church of England, by three thousand miles of ocean, the Puritan state developed its own orthodoxy and bred its own internal enemies. These were heretics and schismatics, such as the antinomians, who set grace above the law, the Arminians, who set piety above grace, false-faced sinners in the Puritans' midst who practiced bestialities, Indian savages who worshipped the Devil, and ranting Quakers who defiled Christian doctrine. Jonathan Edwards in the 1730s and 1740s is the last of the religious culture heroes, fighting with all his genius of intellect and fervor of spirit to down these enemies and recapture the glory of God in an enlightened age when man exalted his own reason. Vernon Louis Parrington called Edwards an anachronism, and Perry Miller called Parrington misguided for not perceiving that Edwards reasoned with the concepts of the eighteenth century. But Edwards *was* anachronistic in trying to preserve the religious life-style that had become outmoded.

The folklore of the colonial period echoes its life-style. It is first and foremost a religious folklore, strewn with tales of remarkable providences, devilment and witchcraft. One of the most hair-raising books in American folklore is Increase Mather's *An Essay for the Recording of Illustrious Providences* (1684), contrived by the New England clergy to preserve and thence to study God's marvelous actions in the New World through which He communicated His satisfaction or His wrath to His saints. So Increase and his fellow divines gathered in the unfathomable accounts of remarkable escapes from storms at sea and from savages on land; of preternatural phenomena, such as demon-possessed houses and bloody apparitions; of blasphemers struck down by lightning, thunder, tempests, and earthquakes. In effect, they collected local legends. The wars of the Lord, whether against the Indians of the forests or Satan's witches within the gates, bred legends of red sorcerers and goodwives versed in the black arts. Balanced against these hell-fiends are the popular heroes and heroines delivered by God's grace from Indian captivities and yawning whirlpools. Cotton Mather enlarged his father's work into one of the six books of the *Magnalia,* where it has remained a quarry for legend revivers to the present day.

The Religious Man was succeeded along about the 1760s by the Democratic Man, when agitation of the colonists against the Coercive Acts of King and Parliament mounted to the point of revolution. Now the foe is the state, acting on an irrational theory of divine-right monarchy that permits a tyrant to injure and destroy his subjects. The patriots espouse the philosophy of natural rights, with its principle of government based on a social compact among sovereign individuals, each inalienably entitled to life, liberty, and the pursuit of happiness. Democracy replaces salvation as the goal to be achieved and promises secular salvation through citizenship. With democracy comes political freedom to reinforce the religious freedom already won.

The culture heroes are statesmen, wedded to the democratic faith: Franklin, apostle of the common man; Washington, father of his country; Jefferson, architect of the Declaration of Independence; Jackson, called The Hero by the people; Lincoln, savior of the republic. Once they had launched the republican ship of state, they encountered stormy waters. Internal enemies threatened to sink the craft, Federalist aristocrats and Southern slavocrats on the right, Jacobinical revolutionaries on the left. As a bulwark against antirepublican ideologies emerges a new educational ideal, state support of free public schools to train a citizenry for the responsibilities of participation in the democratic process. As secretary to the Massachusetts state board of education from 1837 to 1848, Horace Mann hammered away at the "absolute right" of every human being to an education and the "correlative duty" of republican government to provide that education and so enable its citizens to discharge their duties.

The classic writing of the period celebrated the grand theme in its very title, *Democracy in America*. Written in four thick volumes, published in 1835 and 1840 by a young Frenchman, Alexis de Tocqueville, who toured the embryonic republic for ten months in 1831 and 1832, the treatise exhaustively analyzed American political institutions and contrasted the novel society of American democracy with the established patterns of European aristocracy. "So while the rulers of aristocracies sometimes seek to corrupt, those of democracies prove corruptible" was a typical aphorism. Judging Tocqueville's work, Henry Steele Commager wrote, "By common consent his *Democracy*

in America is the most illuminating commentary on American character and institutions ever penned by a foreigner, the one which, a century after its appearance, seems best assured of immortality."[2]

Through the period the democratic style gathered momentum. The patrician Jefferson, friend of the people, but still a Virginia aristocrat with his shiny pumps, velvet breeches, white waistcoat, and powdered wig, gave way to the commoner Jackson, himself a wealthy slaveowner but ushering in the reign of King Mob, it was feared, and attracting to himself much popular symbolism—Old Hickory, they dubbed him. At the end of the line came the true man of the people, Honest Abe, log-cabin-born in Kentucky, ungainly and ugly like the butts of many frontier tales, full of salty sayings and apt stories, the most legendary of our presidents.

Folk heroes even more than the culture heroes emphasized the manners of democracy. In this second period, his life and legends spanning it neatly from the close of the Revolution to the signals of Civil War, arises David Crockett, frontiersman, congressman, legendary hero in a new style that shocked and excited the nation. The historical Crockett is not much of a figure, a Jacksonian turncoat exploited by the Whigs, but he is above all a political personality, electioneering from the stump in a democratic fashion, arguing the issues of the national bank and paper currency with frontier saws, lending his name and personality to political writings. Crockett, like Lincoln, is the backwoods humorist, and his tall tales catch the spirit and soaring rhetoric of Manifest Destiny. Other legendary heroes who emerge in these buoyant years of early American nationalism share Crockett's home-spun manners, roughhewn speech, and daredevil outlook: Mike Fink, Mose, Sam Patch, Yankee Jonathan, and in the subliterature of the frontier, Simon Suggs, Sut Lovingood, and Jim Doggett—all shaggy heroes of a democratic folk, mocking the genteel dandies of the drawing room.

A new mood and a changed set of historical conditions usher in the period of Economic Man in the hundred years from the close of the Civil War to the 1960s. The latter decades of the nineteenth century witnessed the spectacular growth of American industry and the shift of wealth and power from farm to factory, from country to city. Wealth now looms as the great desideratum for American youths and oldsters. Well-being, or material success, is their target and their dream. Happiness lies, not in a state of grace nor in free suffrage, but in property and income. The right to vote counts for little in the jungle of competitive warfare, and reformers like Henry George sought formulas to distribute more equably the goods of the land. Now the external enemy to the good life made possible by the free-enterprise system appears as the bogey of communism, conjuring up an alien ideology and an international conspiracy, insidious and subversive, threatening every cherished American ideal, especially the goal of individual wealth. In his famous essay, *The Gospel of Wealth,* Andrew Carnegie opposed the sacredness of property civilization to the barbarousness of communism and the "capable, industrious workman" of the one society to the "incompetent and lazy fellow" of the other. The philosophy of social Darwinism buttresses the status of the millionaires, who represent the bloom of civilization. Fair competition, the survival of the fittest, and the laissez-faire role of government, whose only obligation is to protect property, are the rules for Economic Man laid down by the Creator of an evolutionary world. Internal enemies arose to plague free-enterprise capitalism, which found itself crunched between the stifling power of monopolistic trusts on the right and the reacting violence of radical labor on the left.

The underlying myth of this era is the rags-to-riches career attainable by every hard-working, thrifty, patriotic American boy. Horatio Alger's badly written and immensely popular novels related the rise of Ragged Dick the bootblack to chairmanship of the board. In the realm of fact the great culture heroes of the period, businessmen all, illustrate the plausibility of the myth. The poor immigrant lad from Scotland, Andrew Carnegie, ended up king of the United States steelmakers and sold his steel company for $250 million. Beginning as clerk and bookkeeper, John D. Rockefeller formed the Standard Oil Company, earned more money than any man who ever lived, and retired a billionaire. Born on a farm near Detroit, Henry Ford worked in a machine shop, designed an automobile, and organized the Ford Motor Company, whose assets came to exceed a billion dollars. Simplicity and hard work characterized all three, who inspired feverish adulation as benefactors of humanity and savage obloquy as exploiters of the people. All emphasized the ethic of work and never indulged themselves in their wealth. "Work! Persevere! Be honest! Save! You won't have a happy life if you don't work," admonished John D. "The paramount right is the right to work," echoed Ford.

It remained for Carnegie to write the

most influential piece of his time, *The Gospel of Wealth,* published in the *North American Review* in 1889 and expounding the doctrines of social Darwinism in a context of Presbyterian Calvinism. A wealthy industrialist deserved the fortune he had acquired by his merits, but as a steward of God's bounty he should supervise its disbursal during his lifetime to ensure maximum benefits to society. Two other classics of the period also dealt with problems of Economic Man. In *Progress and Poverty* (1879), Henry George sought to restore equality of economic opportunity with his single tax on the unearned increment accruing to land speculators. Conspicuous consumption and keeping up with the Joneses characterize the acquisitive life-style, Thorstein Veblen mordantly explained in *The Theory of the Leisure Class* (1899), in which he caricatured the honorific displays and useless learning of the rich.

In the 1880s and 1890s the graduate school entered the educational scene, exemplified by Johns Hopkins University, and changed the college into the modern university with its emphases on doctoral degrees, specialized research, and scholarly productivity. The university came to mirror the corporation, as a departmentalized organization of experts governed by a public-relations-minded board of businessmen.

An ambivalence toward the industrial corporation runs through this third period. Populists, progressives, and socialists challenge the social Darwinists, but to regulate, not destroy, the giant trusts. Jack London vacillated between individualism and socialism, Nietzsche and Marx; he himself was the virile, handsome culture hero who loves, hates, defeats, and is defeated by competitive capitalism. Were the robber barons despoilers or empire builders? Allan Nevins changed his mind and in his later years wrote eulogistic biographies of Rockefeller and Ford.

Folklore, now for the first time deliberately collected from taletellers and ballad singers, depicts Economic Man in a series of occupations connected with outdoor industries of the period: cattle raising, coal mining, white-pine lumbering, oil drilling, railroading. In the early days of these industries, before the streamlining of modern technology, the strength, skill, and courage of the individual worker counted for more than machine tools, and cycles of folk narratives and folksongs recall homely and heroic incidents of men at work in the forests, on the prairies, and underground. The legendary type to emerge from these occupational lores is the master workman, an updated version of Davy Crockett, still a commoner and a mighty fellow but not the eccentric nor the braggart, rather a laconic, no-nonsense figure dedicated to his work, a proud and independent wage earner. He is the cowboy, the lumberjack, the miner, the driller, the engineer.

Half a century after these types began generating folk traditions, a pseudofolklore, reflecting the ambivalence and ambiguity of the period, burst on the scene. In the 1920s and 1930s writers created a series of jolly giants, at first taken seriously by an unwitting public, to represent various American occupations. In an age of gigantic productivity, why should not these demigods illustrating American size and might be manufactured for a ready market? The Red River Lumber Company adopted Paul Bunyan as a trademark, and United States Steel sponsored Joe Magarac as a supersteelworker. In its puerile way fakelore as well as folklore lauded the master workman.

We appear to be struggling today toward a new life-style. One commentator after another speaks of the "revolution" overtaking American society, a cultural, social, sexual, musical, educational, and youth revolution. All see a collision of cultures between the inherited and the rebellious modes of life, and employ terms now become commonplace to denote the "youth culture," "alternate culture," "counterculture," "underculture," "hip drug culture," "street culture," and "new culture." The full-scale eruption of the new culture can be dated in 1964, when the Free Speech Movement on the Berkeley campus triggered off a series of assaults and take-overs of hallowed American universities by radical student dissenters. As always with historical boundaries one can see anticipatory waves—in the civil rights movement in the South in the 1960s, in the ennui of Jack Kerouac and the beatniks—but 1964 was the year of decision and Berkeley the launching pad. While a decade into the new era permits only tentative surmises as to its directions, already one can perceive the cutting edge of new values and goals that correspond to the thrusts of earlier periods.

The current life-style may be designated that of the Humane Man. On all sides the demand is heard for a more human quality of life, for a humanizing of technology—even, in the words of Stewart Udall, for a more human automobile: in short, for an assertion of humane over materialistic values. The editor of the *Harvard Crimson,* Nicholas Gagarin, who took part in the capture of Harvard's administration building on April 9, 1969, expressed the new spirit in his account of the take-over from "Mr. Big, Harvard U," and of the "carnival, open, free-wheeling life-style" that evolved inside the building. He reached this conclusion:

What is really at stake—and what I think that small apolitical group of us was sitting in at University Hall for—is not a political revolution, but a human one. And if we could bring that about, if we could bring ourselves into the beautiful human togetherness that existed inside the Hall, if we could end the inhumanity, competitiveness, and alienation that the University teaches us so that we may fit neatly into an inhuman, competitive, alienated society—then such things as the war, ROTC, and slumlandlording would be inconceivable.[3]

As his goal Humane Man seeks liberation. What salvation signified to colonial Americans, liberation implies to Americans of the new culture. In the broadest sense radicals and dissenters want the liberation of body, mind, and spirit from the shackles and taboos of a fiercely competitive, dehumanized society. In more specific senses, the young want liberation from the business models furnished by the over-thirties; the blacks want liberation from white racism; wo-

6

men want liberation from male chauvinism; gays want liberation from heterosexual norms; Indians and Chicanos join the blacks in seeking liberation from Whitey's dominance. The desire for liberation, often cast in flaming, bitter rhetoric, expresses its scorn and rejection of the old culture in various ways: beards and long hair, public use of tabooed words, drug taking, amplified rock music, sexual acts performed on screen and stage, disregard of marriage by young couples, open marriage of homosexuals, communal living, eating of organic foods, psychedelic sensations.

These patterns of behavior all attempt to undermine the enemy without, by consensus called "the System." This enemy embraces "Amerika" itself, and subsumes the Establishment, the power structure, the status quo, all the mechanisms that sustain and perpetuate what the counterculture brands a business civilization, an acquisitive society, and a repressive state. Paul Goodman commences *Growing Up Absurd* by castigating the "Organized System of semi-monopolies, government, advertisers" and praising disaffected youth "whose main topic is the 'system' with which they refuse to co-operate."[4] Charles Reich in *The Greening of America* disavows the "liberal because he will accept defeat without questioning the system; the student will fight the system and therefore cannot be ignored."[5] Abbie Hoffman titled one of his books *Fuck the System.*

A governing social philosophy of the Movement, equivalent to the covenant theology, the natural rights philosophy,

and social Darwinism in the three earlier periods, remains to be formulated, but the seeds exist for what might be called radical humanism. All the theoreticians of the counterculture—Herbert Marcuse, Norman O. Brown, Allen Ginsberg, Paul Goodman, Charles Reich, Christopher Lasch, Kenneth Keniston, Dave Dellinger—take a radical stance and espouse a humanist creed. The radicals vigorously repudiate the liberals of the Old Left who wish simply to reform and tinker with the System. Rather, these revolutionaries seek to replace the System—through radical politics or, as Reich prefers, a radical change of consciousness—with a new world based on humane values of love, peace, co-operation, respect for the individual, and care for the environment.

Already an internal enemy has mounted a threat to the idealists of the counterculture, in the form of hard-drug addicts and pushers. In their quest for liberation from the System, youthful dissenters relied heavily on the smoking of marijuana and the swallowing of LSD tablets as a means of expanding their consciousness and transcending the regular, conventional, confining perceptions of the straight world. But they have drawn a firm philosophical line between the mind-expanding soft drugs and the hard drugs of speed (the amphetamines) and junk (heroin). Users of hard drugs sought instant kicks; they robbed and murdered for money to gratify their cravings, and opened themselves to the inroads of big-time dealers, of the Mafia and the CIA and the whole network of the international narcotics scene as documented by Alfred W. McCoy in *The Politics of Heroin in Southeast Asia* (1972). Yet ultimately, the hard-drug scene of addicts and pushers drove the flower people out of Haight-Ashbury.

The demand by the new culture for a new educational philosophy has found expression in the concept of the free university. In 1964 the rolling cry "a free university in a free society" first sounded over college campuses, and five years later some three hundred had come into existence. Free universities stood opposed to the forms of the grad-uate-school-oriented universities that young radicals regarded as intolerable: the authoritarianism of teachers, the com-petition for grades, the abstruseness of course content, the research preoccu-pations of professors. Consequently the free university, which grew up under the shadow of the Establishment univer-sity, offers no-credit, no-grade courses on any subject anyone wishes to teach that anyone else wishes to take. A num-ber of status quo universities now spon-sor student-directed free universities.

We can speak already of landmark writings celebrating values of the coun-terculture. In 1968 Tom Wolfe—and a generation of older Americans had to learn that Tom was not Thomas — published *The Electric Kool-Aid Acid Test,* a book without precedent in Ameri-can literature. It is narrative, partici-pant-observer history of the Bay Area acid heads in the highlight years 1965 to 1967, featuring Ken Kesey as the hero-leader of the Merry Pranksters in their madcap cross-country trip in a Day-Glo bus and their antic put-ons in California. At the same time it is intro-spective history in the author-reporter's endeavor to look at these events through the perceptions and sensations of his strung-up, tuned-in, freaked-out cast of characters, and he sets down his chron-icle with a whirring whizbang of verbal effects that marvelously convey the vibra-tions of the new drug scene. Charles Reich in *The Greening of America* praised Kesey's actions described in the *Test* as a "purposeful . . . under-taking that represented a serious search for awareness and new knowledge." Reich's own controversial book, issued by five book clubs in 1970, advocated Consciousness III as a coming revolu-tion that promised "a more human community, and a new and liberated individual."

As for culture heroes—and heroines, themselves symbolic of the new mood — a number have achieved high visibility but must await the screening of time to determine their staying power. These personalities are united by their op-position to the System; they are anti-heroes and anti-heroines, mocking the values of the old culture, from cleanli-ness to affluence to patriotism. To cor-relate them with godly men, statesmen, and businessmen in the earlier periods, we may call them men and women of spirit, using spirit in a double sense, of activism and energy on the one hand, and the possession of spiritual convic-tions, of soul, on the other. Various candidates for the pantheon, coming out of diverse constituencies in litera-ture, folk music, politics, philosophy, films, come promptly to mind: Ken Kesey and Allen Ginsberg, Bob Dylan, Herbert Marcuse, Eldridge Cleaver and Bobby Seale, Tom Hayden, Abbie Hoff-man and Jerry Rubin, and Ralph Nader. On the female side one thinks of Kate Millett, Gloria Steinem, and Angela Davis, Janis Joplin and Joan Baez, and Jane Fonda. You can add your own choices. Each has his or her constituency and vehement detractors, as necessary to the legend-building process as the adulators. The position of the anti-hero is a tricky one, for if he becomes too favored he enters the Establishment of media celebrities. Michael Rossman criticized Jerry Rubin in a public letter: ". . . you're into the Leadership Heresy; Yippie is a hippy bureaucracy that decrees. Look around you at the structure: already a central permanent office, regional chapter contacts, regular weekly meetings, press conferences, proclamations."[6] An anti-hero must stay lean and hungry.

The folklore and folk heroes of the counterculture synchronize with its culture heroes and social values. To a large extent the folklore is a druglore, and this is fitting, for the illegal consumption of drugs has become the focal point of the revolution against the System. How extensive is the body of legends, anecdotes, jokes, sayings, customs, and games associated with drug-lore becomes evident in the examples published here for the first time, and collected by students in folklore classes who were themselves participants in the youth culture. Pill peddlers who confound the narcs and draft dodgers who hoodwink the induction officers take on the laurels of anti-hero folk heroes. Acid heads and potheads succeed the tricksters and outlaws of earlier narrative cycles as defiers of an unjust Establishment. This fresh corpus of circulating oral legendry may strike the reader as unconventional and contrary to the stereotyped notions of what folklore is, but the discovery of each new vein of lore in changing periods of American life has aroused astonishment and shock.

The Colonial Period
The Religious Impulse

*e*xtending from the first permanent settlement at Jamestown, Virginia, in 1607 to the Declaration of Independence by the thirteen colonies in 1776, the colonial period witnessed the birth of an American civilization. At the end of the period a French settler, de Crèvecoeur, wrote his famous essay "Who then is the American, this new man?" suggesting that a new culture had indeed evolved on the north Atlantic coast. The interplay of English, French, Dutch, German, Spanish, and other nationalities, the influence of the Indian, the effects of a novel environment, and the isolation from European centers of civilization enforced by three thousand miles of ocean all contributed to the formation of the American character and the shaping of American habits and institutions. Did a separate American folklore also develop during the seventeenth and eighteenth centuries?

The answer, somewhat surprisingly, is no. Folk legends and folk beliefs did germinate in North America and they did reflect American energies and experiences, yet they prove to be for the most part carbon copies of the folklore in Tudor and Stuart England. Religious issues preoccupied colonial Americans, and in affairs of the church they stayed close to English and Continental models. Perry Miller has traced the hardening of the first generation of New England

Puritan dissenters from the Anglican Church into a Presbyterian orthodoxy of their own, and Daniel Boorstin has sketched the slippage of Virginian Anglicans into loose Congregational forms as a result of frontier conditions. But the colonies produced no new churches. Innovative American faiths such as Mormonism and Christian Science grew out of the nineteenth century. On theological matters the settlers remained on the whole conservative. Dissenting Protestant sects like the Puritans, the Quakers, and the Anabaptists crossed to America, not to evolve new creeds and forms, but to protect and maintain those already conceived, while the established churches—Anglican, Roman Catholic, Dutch Reformed—kept a hold on their New World communicants tight enough to prevent schisms or defections.

What was true for institutional religion proved even truer for its underside, the folk supernaturalism that helped order the universe for seventeenth-century man. American colonists faithfully retained the folk beliefs they had inherited from their English and Continental forebears. We may set colonial and Tudor-Stuart spectral narratives side by side and find virtual duplication. Divine judgments and providences, witches and witchcrafts, ghosts and poltergeists, a personalized Devil and his train of invisible demons, provided the themes of countless anecdotes, legends, and cautionary tales on both sides of the Atlantic. Puritans in England and America kept diaries laden with providential incidents. Court records of witchcraft cases in both countries contained similar accounts of *maleficium.* Clergy and common folk in the mother country and in the colonies feared the Devil in his shapes of a suave gentleman, a black man, a black dog, and other guises. Such excellent studies as Katharine Briggs's *Pale Hecate's Team,* Alan Macfarlane's *Witchcraft in Tudor and Stuart England,* and Keith Thomas's *Religion and the Decline of Magic,* which present in full detail the religious folk beliefs of sixteenth- and seventeenth-century England, could readily extend their coverage to the North American colonies. George Lyman Kittredge did indeed title his older, classic work *Witchcraft in Old and New England* to indicate the transatlantic continuity of credence in witches.

The providence as a supernatural sign of God's will and intent convinced Englishmen and Americans equally. Calvin had stated in his *Institutes* (1536) that supernatural events occurred daily, and Calvinistic Puritans on both sides of the ocean noted them in their journals as evidence of God's disposition toward saints and sinners. A scholar in England, Matthew Poole, conceived the idea for recording remarkable providences that Increase Mather executed successfully in Massachusetts. When William Turner, vicar of Walberton in Sussex, assembled in 1697 *A Compleat History of the most remarkable Providences, both of Judgment and Mercy, which have hapned in this present age,* he levied impartially upon English and American examples. The themes of providences recorded by the Mathers follow those observed in the mother country: monstrous births, judgments upon sinners, armies seen in the skies. When John Winthrop listed the acts of retribution that had befallen the critics of New England, he was emulating a strategy common in the land he had left, where God's elect publicly paraded the misfortunes that had destroyed their political and religious enemies. Even the providential concept of history that led Cotton Mather to write the *Magnalia Christi Americana* as a chronicle of God's favors toward His saints in the New World echoed the theme of writers in England, who beheld the English nation as fulfilling a special destiny to which they were elected by the Lord.

Ranged against the Lord, sharing His powers, and fighting with Him for souls was that fallen angel the Devil, whom Englishmen and Americans sighted in various forms, often as a black man. "The Devil, the great Enemy of Mankind, was constantly present in men's thoughts in the seventeenth century," Katharine Briggs has written. "Thoughtful and learned men of all shades of opinion believed, no less than the man in the street and the man behind the plough, in the constant presence of the Devil. . . ."[1] Keith Thomas generalizes in the same way for the sixteenth century, saying that the efforts of organized religion over the centuries to press home the notion of a personal Satan gave the devil-figure "a reality and immediacy which could not fail to grip the strongest mind."[2] Thomas then sets down anecdotes of loose talkers who invoked the Devil in their daily conversation with such phrases as "Devil take me!" and were indeed visited by Satan with fatal effect. Exactly the same fates overtook blasphemers in Boston.

Witches in America shared a sisterhood with witches in England rather than with those on the Continent, who specialized in such sophisticated magic as the Black Mass, sexual orgies, and aerial flights. On a simpler level, the Anglo-American crones cursed and maimed pious men and their domestic animals and transformed themselves into cats, dogs, or the shapes of their enemies. The com-

munity of attitudes between parent country and colonies is seen in the case of the woman in Huntingdonshire who sold herself to Satan for a gift of persuasive prayer which caused ministers from far and near to attend and admire her praying, but she was uncovered, moved to New England, and was there executed as a witch.[3] That witches obtained powers from the Devil was a commonplace on both sides of the water. Not only were the surface actions of alleged witches identical in Essex and Massachusetts, but so were the social mechanisms that led to the stereotyping of the witch. In his detailed study of witchcraft in Essex villages, Macfarlane reports that gossip, rumor, and suspicion, pooled among villagers over a considerable period of time, fastened suspicion on a generally disliked hag. Mishaps and accidents were attributed to her ill will, and eventually the latent fear of witchcraft in the community found its confirmation in accusation, trial, and execution of the suspect.[4] This train of events clearly operated in Salem Village in 1692 in the trial of Susanna Martin, long a target of her neighbors' opprobrium.

Yet if America shared with the mother country the same folk beliefs, they possessed a special intensity in the New World setting. For the American Puritans had dedicated their energies and fortunes and souls to erecting a Bible commonwealth in New England, and they regarded with extra foreboding the threats of the invisible world and the powers of darkness.

Was colonial American folklore, then, nothing more than transplanted English folk beliefs? Not quite. Some minor variations may be noted. The covenant theology developed by American Puritans came to include covenanting relations between devils, witches, and sinners as well as between God and His saints. In effect New England theologians extended the covenant idea to cover the figures of folk supernaturalism.

Tribal Indians presented a wholly novel element that distinguished the American scene from the English. Yet the Indians, whose odd manners and customs were described in repetitive detail by colonial writers, rapidly became incorporated into the existing religious folklore of the settlers. Believing in magicians and demons, they readily credited the preternatural feats and marvels claimed by the Indian powaws. In 1621 Robert Burton, musing in his *Anatomy of Melancholy* over the state of magic in England, complained that "Sorcerers are too common, Cunning men, Wisards and white-witches . . . in every village."[5] These "cunning folk" occupied an ambiguous position in English society. They practiced the beneficent white magic of fortunetelling, healing, finding lost goods, and combatting witchcraft, but they also used their powers for harm, depending on which client they were serving, and some were themselves indicted as witches. The same ambiguity cloaks the powaws, who today would be called shamans or medicine men. Cotton Mather told of an Indian on Martha's Vineyard, sick and tormented from witchcraft, who was cured by the very powaw who had enchanted him.[6] In another like case a greater powaw relieved the suffering of a woman bewitched by a lesser powaw through a fervent prayer to his god. The prayer effected the release of the spirit of a drowned Englishman that had entered the woman, and the powaw trapped it in a deerskin. He advised the woman to move away, for the spirit being English, he could not contain it long. On another occasion a settler wishing to recover stolen goods repaired to a powaw, who insisted as a prerequisite that his client place faith in the Indian god. As with the "cunning folk" of English villages, so the powaws offered advice primarily on matters of health and lost property.

From Maine to the Carolinas, settlers and planters reported wondrous eyewitness tales of Indian conjurations. Uniformly they ascribed the magic of the powaws to their traffic with the Devil. Writing of the red men, Edward Johnson, who led a westward trek from Boston to Woburn, Massachusetts, in 1640, sneered, "As for any religious observation, they were the most destitute of any people yet heard of, the Devil having them in very great subjection, not using craft to delude them, as he ordinarily doth in most parts of the world, but keeping them in a continual slavish fear of him." Johnson added that the powaws sometimes recovered their sick folk through charms used with help from the Devil, whom they consequently esteemed all the more.[7] Instead of contributing a new element to folklore in the colonies, the Indians were fitted into the world-view and supernatural concepts of the Englishman.

If colonial folklore borrowed most of its content from the mother country, it did not borrow all that was available. A notable omission in North American legendry from the major folk traditions of Tudor and Stuart England is the fairy belief. The generic term "fairy" covered a host of unnatural creatures: imps, elves, brownies, bogles, sprites, pixies, boggarts, hobgoblins, changelings, Robin Goodfellows. These beings cavorted and made mischief throughout the isles of Britain, but failed to take passage with the emigrants sailing for

America. One explanation may be that they were absorbed in the new environment by the stronger figures of witches, ghosts, and devils with which they were closely associated in the folk mind. In Chaucer's day house hauntings had been attributed to fairies, by the time of Shakespeare they were being credited in good part to demons, and the Mathers spoke only of demons and evil spirits when reporting the sensational occurrences that afflicted certain New England domiciles. Cotton Mather conceived of armies of demons or devils inhabiting the invisible world, and such catchall terms easily swallowed up individualized imps and fairies.

But a still more compelling reason exists for the nonmigration of fairy beings. No European, African, or Asian people entering American shores have brought with them the folk creatures of their *Heimat*, the spirits rooted in the soil—as Devil, witch, and ghost were not—of the homeland. The water nymph, the mountain troll, the garden gnome, belong irrevocably to the old culture and the Old Country.

Folklore of the religious era

The folklore that the Puritans and other colonists accepted—providences, judgments, apparitions, specters, witchcrafts, poltergeists, compacts with the Devil—have been known in other times and places, but for the first generations of Americans they carried a special urgency. Clerical and civic leaders of the Massachusetts Bay Colony pressed this circulating folklore into their service. Their dedicated purpose lay in establishing a holy society, a covenanted community of saints, in the wilderness where a host of enemies threatened them from without and within. Followers of false doctrines, from Anglicans to Quakers, the savages of the forest, sinners and heretics in their midst camouflaged as pious brethren, and of course Satan and his army of demons and crew of witches, all sought to destroy the Puritan state.

Accordingly, the Massachusetts theocrats endeavored to demonstrate that the Lord supported them in this continuous battle against His and their enemies, and in this light interpreted the various supernatural manifestations (which we today call legends and folklore) commonly discussed by men and women of the seventeenth century. So John Winthrop and John Cotton, Edward Johnson and Mary Rowlandson, Increase and Cotton Mather, explained, or strove to explain where the evidence was cloudy, spectral ships and haunted houses and Indian magicians in terms of a diabolical conspiracy to subvert the Bible commonwealth. Frequently they could make the connection clearly and directly. Governor Winthrop pointed out the string of disasters that befell critics of the New England way, obviously God's judgments on those who scorned His elect. Cotton Mather beheld in the corpse of John Sausaman that gushed blood at his murderer's touch a confirmation, through God's providence, of the planned uprising of King Philip against the New Englanders. One of King Philip's followers had slain Sausaman, a Christian Indian friendly to the whites, to keep his lips sealed, but God had willed that His saints learn of the plot. In the activities of witches, culminating in the Salem Village outbreak in 1692, ministers and magistrates saw the Devil's carefully laid scheme to sow dissension in their goodly company and bring it to ruin.

Individuals could of course interpret providences and other marks of God's and the Devil's doings to accommodate their needs. When a dreadfully deformed baby was born in 1638 to a follower of Anne Hutchinson, the antinomian troublemaker who had denounced the clergy for lack of grace and would be exiled to Rhode Island, the saints promptly recognized God's judgment on a rank heretic. But a curious side-issue developed. An elder, hearing of the monster, asked Mrs. Hutchinson why the birth had not been chronicled, in accord with the strict practice of the Bay Colony requiring public registration of all births, marriages, and deaths. She replied that the concealment was on the advice of the Reverend John Cotton. The leading divine of the first generation of Puritan settlers, Cotton had already tarnished his reputation by too close an association with the notorious Anne, who had excluded him from her charges and declared that here was one clergyman in a state of grace. Governor Winthrop inquired about the matter from Reverend Cotton, who explained that he saw a "providence of God" in the fact that at the time of the birth the mother was alone, all her women attendants coming and going at the time of her travail being absent. Hence he judged that God intended the instruction primarily of the parents. Cotton repeated this apology in public and it was well accepted.[8] In effect, by playing one providence against another, he had gotten himself off the hook in a ticklish situation that was gravely dividing the infant colony.

The providences were a two-edged sword. The Lord kept His saints on their toes with judgments and puzzling prodigies directed at themselves, so that they would not wax too confident about their own state of grace. Their enemies too could quote providences against them, as did the Quakers of Pennsylvania and the Dutch Calvinists of New Netherlands. Religious folklore in the seventeenth century lit up issues of individual salvation and damnation, of the public weal, of the destiny of New England and America, and it should be read in that light.

Providences

The covenant theology of the Puritans bred a folklore genre of distinctive properties, the "remarkable," "memorable," or "illustrious" providence. A providence was an event, possibly a great matter encompassing the whole community of the saints, perhaps a small incident affecting only a given individual. Since in the Puritan and Reformation concept, God willed every event, from the black plague to the sparrow's fall, all events held meanings for errant man. The Lord worked chiefly through natural or secondary causes, or He might intervene directly in the processes of the world, as a first cause, but whichever the case, He guided every occurrence. When the Lord was pleased, events ran smoothly and regularly, and the saints could take comfort. But since the customary state of man found him in perpetual struggle against the dark powers of Satan and his army of infernal spirits, life seldom moved for long on an even keel. The untoward, the inexplicable, the dramatic happening threaded the days of the saints to give them pause and doubt, or, when they surmised the intent, either comfort or consternation.

These happenings they called providences, an easy glide from the use of Providence as a synonym for the Lord to a designation of the acts He caused. Providences flourished in America. Because the first generation of New England Puritans represented those elect who had consciously come together in old England and sailed away to the New World, the better to live in covenant with each other and with God, unhampered and uncontaminated by sinners within or without the Church of England, they were highly providence-minded. Zealous to assure themselves of their collective and individual state of grace, they searched the providences for continuous evidence of God's favor or wrath. They had tried every human means to assure themselves and each other of their election, but tainted always with some remnant of original sin, they could never be entirely certain of having achieved a state of grace. A margin of error could never be discounted. Hence the providences played a signal role in providing clues to God's will concerning their destinies.

The providences meet all the requirements of folklore. Being remarkable and out-of-the-ordinary transpirings, they were stories twice-told. People talked about the spectral ships, the monstrous births, the demon-haunted houses that eventually fell into the net of the Mathers. Since these were events and phenomena actually observed, a critic today might ask, how could they be folklore? The answer is that because they were so much talked about, they acquired legendary aspects. It is an axiom of the folklore process that oral repetitions of startling incidents take on legendary form. We can test this theorem by indicating how many international motifs of folklore turn up in the providences. The seemingly localized event proves to have a long ancestry in folk tradition. Like Unidentified Flying Objects today, spectral vessels in the air were sighted by persons familiar with their outlines and shapes and manner of appearance. The poltergeist who inhabits a family residence and causes kitchen utensils and furniture to spin about madly was known to medieval man and still plagues twentieth-century man; when he surfaced in Puritan New England he was promptly fitted into the typology of providences. Furthermore, a large portion of providences incorporated supernatural beliefs—in ghosts, witchcraft, powers of the Devil—already firmly planted in the minds of seventeenth-century people, the intellectuals as well as the folk.

Not only do providences meet the tests of folklore but many were collected much in the manner that folklorists go about their business today. While Increase and Cotton Mather lacked tape recorders (as did folklore sleuths until after World War II), pen or pencil and paper and a willing ear can effectively capture word-of-mouth traditions. Increase set in motion a whole network of skilled collectors by enlisting his fellow clergymen in his project. In the preface to *An Essay for the Recording of Illustrious Providences,* published in 1684, he tells how he chanced on a manuscript, author unknown, issuing from a "Design for the Recording of Illustrious Providences" that a group of eminent ministers in England and Ireland had discussed a quarter of a century earlier. They had never consummated their plan, but the examples of providences in the manuscript, and the accompanying rules for the enterprise, stimulated Increase to present at a general meeting of ministers in Massachusetts on May 12, 1681, "Some Proposals concerning the Recording of Illustrious Providences." The eight brief proposals stressed that only *re-*

markable providences be recorded and published, "for God's glory and the good of posterity"; that the "ministers of God" and the elders, both in the Bay Colony and in neighboring colonies, "diligently enquire into and record such illustrious providences" and transmit them to the individual designated to assemble them (who proved of course to be Increase); and that the final manuscript be read and approved at a meeting of the elders. The key proposal spelled out the nature of the prizes: "Such Divine judgements, tempests, floods, earthquakes, thunders as are unusual, strange apparitions, or whatever else shall happen that is prodigious, witchcrafts, diabolical possessions, remarkable judgements upon noted sinners, eminent deliverances, and answers of prayer, are to be reckoned among illustrious providences."[9] This would be a fair set of guidelines today under the heading "Religious Folklore" in a field collector's manual.

Increase published his *Essay* "as a specimen of a larger volume" in hopes that the work would continue, and Cotton quoted this phrase in his own preface to the extension of his father's project, book six of his *Magnalia Christi Americana,* "Remarkables of the Divine Providence Among the People of New England." The *Magnalia* appeared in 1702, and in the meantime Increase had issued, in 1694, under his signature as president of Harvard College, another set of "Certain Proposals, Made by the President and Fellows of Harvard College, to the Reverend Ministers of the Gospel in the several Churches of New-England." Cotton signed his name with that of the six other Fellows. The definition and description of the "more illustrious discoveries of Divine Providence" employ somewhat different and a little fuller wording: "The things to be esteemed *memorable,* are especially all *unusual accidents,* in the heaven,

or earth, or water: all wonderful *deliverances* of the distressed: *mercies* to the godly; judgments on the wicked; and more glorious fulfilment of either the *promises* or the *threatenings* in the Scriptures of truth; with *apparitions, possessions,* inchantments, and all extraordinary things wherein the existence and agency of the *invisible world* is more sensibly demonstrated."[10] The addition of the phrase "invisible world" would seem to be Cotton's touch, as he wrote a tract on the Salem witchcraft trials in 1692 under the title *The Wonders of the Invisible World.* In book six — *"Thaumaturgus,* The Wonder-Worker, or Book of Memorable Events," as he also called it — he lamented how few providential histories the churchmen had delivered to the Harvard committee, even though they were promised "some singular *marks of respect."* Still he amassed enough to fill one of the *Magnalia's* seven books, and all of it based on New World observations. Cotton incorporated his father's firsthand providences into *Thaumaturgus,* but for the most part discarded Increase's derivative passages that considered remarkables known to the ancients or to foreign authors. The same providences written in Increase's relatively straightforward style become touched with fire and gall when revised by Cotton. Since in effect the entire *Magnalia* is a providential history, individual providences are scattered throughout the other six books as well as being grouped in *Thaumaturgus.* The celebrated spectral ship sighted over New Haven harbor in 1648 by a large crowd, and described in close detail by the minister of New Haven

in a letter to Cotton, appears in book one, "Antiquities," within an account of colony founding in Connecticut. In effect, the Mathers and other Puritan divines were collecting legends of the supernatural, for God's glory and their own reassurance that they were indeed His elect.

A number of mythological motifs in the providences deal with lightning and thunder dispatched by the Lord to warn or awe or mystify mortals. These are universal themes. North American Indians identified their tutelary deities with the thunders. The voice of God the Creator spoke in thunder to the Jews and the Chinese. In different parts of India thunder is construed as the sound of God's gun, or the clatter of horses' hooves as the gods play ball, or the noise of a waterskin dragged along the sky floor by the rain god. In black Africa, thunder is the drumming of the dead. To the Jews, lightning was God's messenger; the ancient Greeks thought thunder was made by a god; the early inhabitants of India believed heavenly horses struck their hooves against stars to create claps of thunder.

Increase Mather devoted an entire chapter of the *Illustrious Providences* to cases "Concerning Remarkables about Thunder and Lightning." He made the point that while "terrible lightnings with thunders" had been seen ever since "the English did first settle in these American desarts," they had never injured man or beast until recent years, when "fatal and fearful slaughters have in that way been made amongst us."[11] And he was reminded how the Lord overthrew Sodom and Gomorrah. Commencing with the year 1654, he set down in minute detail the circumstances of thunderstorms and lightning bolts that had burned dwellings, stunned whole families, and killed predetermined individuals and animals. How closely the Mathers identified God with these heavenly phenomena is seen in their choice of metaphors: "Heaven's arrows," "the fire of God," "God, the high thunderer."[12] The meaning of these deaths and near-deaths was usually plain enough. As a fellow clergyman wrote Increase from Connecticut in 1682, after listing fatalities to oxen, swine, and a dog, "What are these but warning pieces, showing that men's lives may go next?"[13]

The execution of Richard Goldsmith by thunder and lightning left little doubt as to God's intent. Here is Increase's account:

On the 18th of May (being the Lord's day) A.D. 1673, the people at Wenham (their worthy pastor, Mr. Antipas Newman, being lately dead) prevailed with the Reverend Mr. Higginson of Salem to spend that Sabbath amongst them.

The afternoon sermon being ended, he, with several of the town, went to Mr. Newman his house. Whilst they were in discourse there about the word and works of God, a thunder-storm arose. After a while, a smart clap of thunder broke upon the house, and especially into the room where they were sitting and discoursing together; it did for the present deafen them all, filling the room with smoke, and a strong smell as of brimstone. With the thunder-clap came in a ball of fire as big as the bullet of a great gun, which suddenly went up the chimney, as also the smoke did. This ball of fire was seen at the feet of Richard Goldsmith, who sat on a leather chair next the chimney, at which instant he fell off the chair on the ground.

As soon as the smoke was gone, some in the room endeavoured to hold him up, but found him dead; also the dog that lay under the chair was found stone dead, but not the least hurt done to the chair. All that could be perceived by the man, was, that the hair of his head, near one of his ears, was a little singed. There were seven or eight in that room, and more in the next; yet (through the merciful providence of God) none else had the least harm.

This Richard Goldsmith, who was thus slain, was a shoemaker by trade, being reputed a good man for the main; but had blemished his Christian profession by frequent breaking of his promise; it being too common with him (as with too many professors amongst us), to be free and forward in engaging, but backward in performing; yet this must further be added, that half a year before his death, God gave him a deep sense of his evils, that he made it his business, not only that his peace might be made with God, but with men also, unto whom he had given just offence.

He went up and down bewailing his great sin in promise-breaking; and was become a very conscientious and lively Christian, promoting holy and edifying discourses, as he had occasion. At that very time when he was struck dead, he was speaking of some passages in the sermon he had newly heard, and his last words were, *Blessed be the Lord.*[14]

References to the thunderstorm and the presence of God are intertwined throughout this passage, and every Puritan who talked about the judgment on errant Richard Goldsmith could quickly see the providential message. Goldsmith had erred, but he had recog- nized his sin, and sought the grace of God—thus serving as an object lesson for his fellow sinners.

Cotton Mather inserted a sermon into the *Magnalia* titled "The Voice of the Glorious God in the Thunder," filled with meditations on the mes-

Title pages of eighteenth-century English chapbooks narrating examples of God's judgments on sinners

From John Ashton, *Chap-Books of the Eighteenth Century*

A Dreadful Warning

To all Wicked and Forsworn
SINNERS.

Shewing the sad and dreadful Example of Nicholas Newsom and David Higham, who were drinking in a Public House in Dudley near Birmingham on Thursday; the 5th day of March 1761. Giving an Account, how they laid a Wager, whether could swear the most blasphemous Oaths, and how they were struck Deaf and Dumb, with their Tongues hanging out of their Mouths.

To which is added a Sermon, preached on this Occasion, by the Rev. Dr. Smith from the following Text. Matt. 5. 34. 35. Swear not at all neither by Heaven for it is God's Throne; nor by the earth for it is his Footstool.

GOD'S JUST JUDGMENT ON

BLASPHEMERS,

Being a Terrible Warning Piece to repining Mur- murers, set forth in a dreadful Example of the Almighty's Wrath, on one Mr. Thomas Freeburn a Farmer, near Andover in Wiltshire, who utter'd those horrid and blasphemous Expressions, That God never did him any good in his Life, and he believed did not know what he did himself; with other words too monstrous and devilish to be re- peated: Upon which he was immediately struck Speechless, Motionless and almost without sign of Life, and fell down as in a dead Sleep; and no strength of Men or Horses, has been able hitherto to remove him from the ground.

Also an Account of his wicked Life and Actions for 24 Years before this just Judgment fell upon him, with his coming to his Speech again, in four Months and twenty Day's time, and the terrible Sights he saw in the other World, which he has discover'd to some thousands of Spectators.

LICENSED AND ENTERED ACCORDING TO ORDER.

sages of the Lord expressed in His thunderous communications. Cotton was quick to point out that thunder was a "natural production," resulting from the laws of matter and motion, as "divers weighty clouds" clashed against each other, and lightning too, issued from the "subtil and sulphureous vapours" taking fire in this combustion, which were "fulminated with an irresistible violence upon our territories."[15] But still he recognized that God was the "first mover" of these causes, that the Scripture continually referred to the "thunder of God," which was wonderfully evident at the creation, and that even at the present time the thunder did sometimes directly execute the purpose of God. Cotton further conceded that the Devil, as Prince of the Air, could by God's leave and through his own nefarious armies make thunders. Conjuring popes in covenant with evil spirits brought down thunder and lightning on their enemies, and in New England too devils had vented their thunderous spite especially against churches. The notion that the Devil attacks churches with storms has a long tradition in England, where at various times the Prince of the Powers of the Air has left his clawprints on church bells and walls after wreaking havoc on the buildings and the worshippers inside.[16]

A number of providences connect bloodstains or bleeding corpses to deaths by foul and sinful means. Lashing out against English traders, non-Puritans who sold liquor to the Indians, Cotton Mather warned that the "blood of souls" would be found upon their skirts, and related a case where eight Indians coming home from a drunken orgy drowned crossing a little ferry. Three months later, in March, a dead body floated to shore near the spot of the orgy "and lying on the shore, it bled so plentifully, as to discolour the water and sand about it."[17] Cotton added that spectators thought of the biblical passage saying the stone shall cry out of the wall against him that gives his neighbor drink, and they felt this sign was crying out "Blood! blood!" against some wicked English.

A sheaf of New England colonial legends share this idea that guilty blood stains the earth permanently. The British corvette *Alden,* which had been ravaging the Maine coast in 1770, struck a ledge on a stormy night, and was forced to lower boats into the raging sea. Only one made shore on Matinicus Isle, but the twenty-four seamen aboard froze to death and were buried on the beach. Every spring thereafter when the sun warmed the sand, dark crimson pools splotched the shore. An islander commented, "Blood that is spilled on the ground always leaves its stain, and it never comes out never!"[18] In this tradition the blood on the sand is of the English evildoers rather than of their victims. Other local stories tell of annually recurring blood marks: of white moss on Chebeague Island near the site of an Indian massacre that turns blood red once a year; of an apple tree in West Farms, Connecticut, whose fruit bore a red globule at the center ever since a peddler was murdered beneath its branches; of rhododendrons growing in Mast Swamp in eastern Connecticut that display blood-red hearts on the anniversary of the death in 1637 of a Pequot chief slain by the English.[19] The ineradicable bloodstain that marks floors, the soil, fruit, and plants following a bloody accident or tragedy runs through English and American folk legendry.

Murder had another way of speaking out, when blood gushed from a corpse touched by the murderer. The *Magnalia* records two instances of this revelation, and refers to one of them twice: the judgment on Mary Martin, who in 1646 yielded to the seduction of a married man and bore a child, delivering it herself and then putting it to death. According to Cotton, "God made the infant bleed afresh before her, for her confusion."[20] In this case the bleeding corpse has exposed a sinner among the saints, one of the Devil's tools against New England.

The belief that a corpse bleeds at the murderer's touch was held throughout Western Europe, and found its way into the English and Scottish popular ballads. In his note to the ballad of "Young Hunting," Francis James Child comments: "That the body of a murdered man will emit blood upon being touched, or even approached, by the murderer is a belief of ancient standing, and evidence of this character was formerly admitted in judicial investigations."[21] And he cites a string of references. In the ballad the test is applied to stricken Earl Richard by his lady, who swears her innocence, and her maid, whom she has accused:

The maiden touched the clay-
  cauld corpse,
 A drap it never bled;
The ladye laid her hand on him,
 And soon the ground
     was red.[22]

Speaking in the *Magnalia Christi Americana* of wonders of the invisible world, Cotton Mather brushed aside premonitions of death as common matters throughout history, but lingered over ghostly apparitions after death as stranger happenings. He noted that "they have been often seen in this land: particularly, persons that have died abroad at sea have, within a day after their death, been seen by their friends in their houses at home. The sights have occasion'd much notice and much discourse at the very time of them; and records have been kept of the time, (reader, I write but what hath fallen within my own personal observation;) and it hath been afterwards found that very time when they thus appear'd."[23] Elsewhere he affirmed that ghosts, through God's will, might disclose murderers. "'Tis a thousand pitties, that we should permit our Eyes, to be so *Bloodshot* with passions, as to loose the sight of many wonderful things, wherein the Wisdom and Justice of God, would be Glorify'd. Some of those things, are the frequent *Apparitions* of Ghosts, whereby many Old *Murders* among us, come to be considered."[24]

He then volunteered a case in point, documented through a letter shown Cotton in 1692 by his friend Samuel Sewall, the famed diarist who was one of the judges in the Salem witchcraft trials. Sewall had received the letter from a resident of Salem Village, Thomas Putnam, whose wife and daughter had accused some of the alleged witches. Putnam wrote Sewall presenting evidence obtained from an apparition that later was used in the proceedings of the Salem court against Giles Corey, the first man in New England ever to be pressed to death, when he refused to undergo trial by jury on the charge of witchcraft.

The Last Night my Daughter Ann, was grievously Tormented by Witches, Threatning that she should be *Pressed* to Death, before *Giles Cory*. But thro' the Goodness of a Gracious God, she had at last a little Respite. Whereupon there appeared unto her (she said) a man in a Winding Sheet, who told her that *Giles Cory* had Murdered him, by *Pressing* him to Death with his Feet; but that the Devil there appeared unto him, and Covenanted with him, and promised him, *He should not be Hanged.* The Apparition said, God Hardned his heart; that he should not hearken to the Advice of the Court, and so Dy an easy Death; because as it said, *It must be done to him as he has done to me.* The Apparition also said, That *Giles Cory,* was carry'd to the Court for this, and that the Jury had found the Murder, and that her Father knew the man, and the thing was done before she was born.

Now Sir, This is not a little strange to us; that no body should Remember these things, all the while that *Giles Cory* was in Prison, and so often before the Court. For all people now Remember very well, (and the Records of the Court also mention it,) That about Seventeen Years ago, *Giles Cory* kept a man in his House, that was almost a Natural Fool: which Man Dy'd suddenly. A Jury was impannel'd upon him, among whom was Dr. Zorobbabel Endicot; who found the man bruised to Death, and having clodders of Blood about his Heart. The Jury, whereof several are yet alive brought in the man Murdered; but as if some Enchantment had hindered the Prosecution of the Matter, the Court Proceeded not against *Giles Cory,* tho' it cost him a great deal of Mony to get off. Thus the Story.[25]

The ghost story of Ann Putnam touched a crucial nerve in the colony's affairs. As accusations of witchcraft and executions of witches mounted, the judges and the community grew increasingly disturbed. Giles Corey, a sturdy, uncowed farmer who pleaded not guilty and then stood mute before the court to accept a dread penalty of *peine forte et dure,* especially aroused sympathy. Heavy stones were placed on his chest, and when his tongue protruded, the sheriff pushed it back in his mouth with his cane as Giles lay dying.

At this juncture an apparition of a village idiot, presumably pressed to death by Giles Corey years before, appeared to Ann Putnam, as the quoted story explains. The apparition was making known to Ann the circumstances of his death, so that she could remind the people of Salem Village of Corey's foul deed and true character. God and the Devil had both entered the case. According to his covenant with the Devil, Corey escaped hanging. But God's greater power ensured that Corey met a just retribution, by dying in the same manner as his victim.

This ingenious apparition tale was calculated to shift public sentiment against Corey. Instead of being an innocent farmer accused of witchcraft by hysterical girls, he was a murderer

in covenant with the Devil. The tale also accounted for Corey's choice of death by pressing over the quicker death by hanging. Believing in revenants, Salem judges William Stoughton and Samuel Sewall certified the authenticity of Thomas Putnam's letter, as one of the documents presented in Boston on October 11, 1692, by Cotton Mather in his report of the trials.

Ghosts of murdered men that visit the living to make known the circumstances of their deaths, and bring retri-

Title page of an eighteenth-century chap-book describing the appearance of the ghost of a man executed on July 9, 1709, for the alleged murder of his sweetheart, although he proclaimed his innocence to the end
From John Ashton, *Chap-Books of the Eighteenth Century*

THE

GUILFORD GHOST.

Being an Account of the Strange and Amazing Apparition or Ghost of Mr. Christopher Slaughterford; with the manner of his Wonderful Appearance to Joseph Lee his Man, and one Roger Voller, at Guildford in Surrey, on Sunday and Monday Night last, in a sad and astonishing manner, in several dreadful and frightful Shapes, with a Rope about his Neck, a flaming Torch in one hand and a Club in the Other, crying Vengeance, Vengeance. With other amazing particulars.

LONDON: PRINTED FOR J. WYAT IN SOUTHWARK, 1709.

bution to the malefactors, are thick in Anglo-American folklore. The ghost of Hamlet's father has a long lineage. Yet most ghosts reported today are not vengeful! Certain laws rule ghostly behavior; thus a ghost cannot speak until spoken to.[26] In Cotton Mather's narrative of Joseph Beacon, where the dialogue is transcribed, Joseph initially addressed the transatlantic apparition of his murdered brother. Although the revenant of a murdered man is so familiar a belief, obtaining exact field texts of such a tradition is not simple, since they involve a charge of murder. When texts are recorded, the proper names have usually dropped out. In the Schoharie Hills of New York, early in the present century, a hillman told how his mother, sitting by the fire with her Bible, petted a big black dog that suddenly appeared and as suddenly vanished. Then a headless man came along. "What, in the name of the Lord, do you want?" she asked him. "To be decently buried, and to have my murderer hung," the ghost answered. "You will find my body buried under the cellar stairs. Take it up, give it decent burial; then have the owner of this house arrested, and when the trial comes off, I will be there." The owner was an old man suspected of foul play toward peddlers and travelers. The trial was duly held and, according to the tale, the headless man did come to testify that he had been murdered.[27]

A Tennessee tale collected in 1923 also involves a ghost seeking court action. An Irishman who emigrated to America was told he could stay all night in a deserted house where nobody dared live. After he went to bed a woman came in his room holding a candle. "Well, what do you want?" asked the Irishman. She replied that she had been killed by a neighbor man, and requested, "You go make oath of it and if he denies it, I'll appear the day of the trial." The Irishman did make oath, and the murderer was arrested, confessed, and was destroyed.[28]

In these fragmentary legends the ghost of the murdered person seeks, successfully in both cases, to present evidence in court. Often this type of ghost story remains sketchy because of its libelous implications. Various persons witnessed a headless ghost called "Old Raw Head" in Morgan County, Missouri, as far back as 1850. In modern times one John Hannay claimed to have seen it sitting on a haystack in the moonlight, and said that his grandparents too had seen the specter. Hannay knew of many cold-blooded murders committed in the vicinity after the Civil War, but he did not wish to mention any names, because relatives and descendants were still living.[29] Such qualms did not trouble the Bay colonists, who regarded murder as the work of demons and witches operating through weak mortals, and who trusted apparitions and ghosts to identify murderers.

The high point in folkloric content in book six of the *Magnalia* comes with chapter seven, *"Thaumatographia Pneumatica,* Relating the Wonders of the Invisible World in Preternatural Occurrences." Here is a dense sheaf of poltergeists, apparitions, witchcrafts, ghosts, demons, and specters. All are linked together by Cotton Mather in a prefatory discussion of Azazel, or the Devil, who buffeted Christ in the wilderness. Cotton reasons that the Christians driven into the American wilderness see the operations of Azazel frequently displayed, probably because the devils

of the invisible world deeply resent the invasion of their precincts by the saints. Many of these "true" and "strange" occurrences have been allowed to slip into oblivion, Cotton mourns, but others have been preserved by veracious men, and he sets down fourteen such "remarkable histories." They constitute one of the most familiar kinds of folklore in the English-speaking world, the believed tales of evil spirits harassing and possessing mortals.

A variety of noxious spirits plagued the New England settlers. One that still turns up today in Western Europe and North America is called by folklorists the poltergeist, defined as an invisible spirit (sometimes identified as a ghost or witch) responsible for all sorts of mischief in or around a household. This house demon played havoc in several homes. In the house of William Morse of Newbury, in 1679, an invisible hand hurled bricks, sticks, and stones about; threw a cat at the woman of the house; caused a long staff to dance up and down the chimney and to resist the efforts of two persons to place it on the fire; whirled an iron crook about; tossed a chair on the dining table in the midst of the meat; scattered ashes over the suppers, heads, and clothes of the family; beat a bag of hops taken from a chest; hit the man of the house with several instruments, one being a besom, while he was at prayer; and threw foul corn in with the clean while the people were winnowing. An invisible hand snatched an inkhorn from the man of the house while he was writing; clapped a shoe on his head which pulled him backward to the floor; threw frozen clods of cow dung at him; and stuck his awls and needles and bodkins into his body. Once when he was writing, a dish jumped into a pail and threw water over him. A little boy in the family had his bedclothes pulled from him and his bed shaken, while the bedstaff leaped backward and forward. When he sat in a chair, it fell to dancing and nearly threw him into the fire. At different times bystanders, hearing the boy cry out that he had been pricked, pulled forks, pins, knives, iron spindles, and a spoon out of his back. One spoon seemed to come out of his mouth. Several times the lad was thrown into the fire. For a while he barked like a dog and clucked like a hen, and had his tongue pulled out of his mouth. At length he complained that a man called P—l had carried him over the top of the house and thrown him against a cart wheel in the barn. This specter made the meat fly out of the boy's mouth and forced him instead to eat ashes and sticks and yarn. When his parents took the youngster to bed with them for safety, the specter emptied a chamber pot upon all three. Of a sudden the demon took on some visibility. His fist was seen beating the man and an apparition of a "blackamoor" child came into view. Persons in the house heard a drumming on the boards and a voice singing "Revenge! revenge! sweet is revenge!" The terrified people called upon God, who was pleased "mercifully to shorten the *chain of the devil.*" A mournful voice sounded several times, "Alas! alas! we knock no more, we knock no more!" Then all ended.[30]

In Portsmouth, New Hampshire, in 1682, an invisible hand showered stones which landed softly upon the people going in and out of the house of George Walton. Strangely, the stones broke windows from the inside of the house. The spit was carried up the chimney and came down point first in the backlog.

A hollow whistling and the snorting of a horse were heard. Walton fled the house and rowed up the bay in a boat to a farm he had, but the stones and a stirrup iron came jingling after him, and the anchor leaped overboard several times. Cocks of hay were hung upon trees, a cheese was taken from the cheese press and crumbled upon the floor, and a kettle was hung upon a piece of iron stuck in the wall. Walton was a Quaker. He attributed these machinations to a widow who had charged him with unjustly withholding land from her. Cotton skimped this point, perhaps because he wrote after the Puritans' loss of their charter for intolerance to the Quakers, but Increase, writing earlier on the same affair, called upon the Quaker to reflect if guilt lay upon his conscience and to confess to God.[31]

These phenomena belong to the familiar outlines of the poltergeist tradition, already well known in the Mathers' day. Increase juxtaposes with the American examples similar reports he had read in Joseph Glanvil's *Collections of Relations* (continued by Henry More) and Clark's *Relations.* He explains these house disturbances as caused either by witches or directly by the Devil—always under the permission of Providence—and usually as punishment for a murder or some other heinous sin. We can distinguish poltergeists from ghosts and witches in several ways. They are invisible or partly visible. They do not interact primarily with one person but with a household: the whole family, the domestic animals, the furnishings and possessions. They engage in mischievous pranks resulting

27

in injury, discomfiture, alarm, but usually not in fatalities. In this respect they resemble such domestic tricksters as Tyl Eulenspiegel, Robin Goodfellow, and Friar Rush. In the nineteenth century their satanic molestations were associated with spiritualistic mediums, who presumably enjoyed power to enter the invisible world.

In the Puritan universe, the poltergeist was construed as a judgment. True, the malefactor could not always be detected, but in all likelihood he was the man of the house. In one case given by the Mathers, the spectral voice calling for revenge insinuated evildoing on the part of some member of the family, and the wife was tried for witchcraft against her husband a year after the disturbances there.

Of all the kinds of illustrious providences they recorded, the New England Puritans seem to have most relished divine judgments. In these acts of punishment the Lord turned His dreadful power on the enemies of the saints and the followers of Satan. As the favored elect of God, the Puritans found reassurance in God's vengeance against their critics on the outside and the sinners within their ranks. Increase Mather included a whole chapter "Concerning Remarkable Judgements" in his *Essay for the Recording of Illustrious Providences,* and Cotton Mather in the *Magnalia* similarly allotted a chapter, with much new material, to the topic, calling it "*Historia Nemesios,* Relating Remarkable Judgments of God, on several sorts of Offenders, in several scores of instances." As he had done with the kindred topics of witchcraft and the Devil, Cotton spiced doctrinal exegesis with concrete examples.

True to his schematic bent, he divided classes of divine judgments into those contained in the Bible, those forthcoming on the Day of Judgment, and those dispensed in the world. For earthly judgments he laid down a set of seven rules. In the first rule Cotton was quick to cover himself against the charge of evaluating judgments for personal ends without proper evidence. He cautioned against "injudicious interpretation," and warned the "rash expositors" of God's judgments that they might well be the first to feel His true judgments. There must be "some convincing circumstance and character . . . something in the time of it, or in the place of it, or in its resemblance to the fault for which it comes, or in the confession of the person chastised" to indicate the event is God's punishment for sin. Cotton's other rules set forth a series of admonitions to the saints: they should pay heed to remarkable judgments in former ages, in other nations, to malefactors at home, to the righteous themselves, to pious pretenders falling under the Devil's spell, and to young people among them consumed in wars, epidemics, shipwrecks, and strange casualties across the globe. All these targets for God's punishments carried warning for all mankind. The evils that He dealt with in one age or one land He would surely deal with again elsewhere. Ungodly sinners should fear the Lord's judgments against His own people, for judgments begin in the house of God and may afflict whole churches of Christians. Cotton reserved his most fervent alarms for the young men of New England. "Behold, vain youths! behold how the waisting judgments of God have been upon you, till we cry out, 'The curse has devoured the land, and few young men are left.'"[32]

In a second sermon on the same subject, incorporated into the *Magnalia,* Cotton pinpointed the dire consequences of specific sins in an "entertaining recapitulation of the divine judg-

ments." He divided his extensive bag of judgments into neat categories correlated with the Ten Commandments and the power structure of the Puritan Church. There was, first, the sin of contempt of the gospel, which provoked the "God of heaven" to breathe "hot lightnings of death out of his *nostrils.*" When the powerful Narragansett Indians rejected the gospel of our Lord Jesus Christ and engaged in hostile acts against the saints, an inferior force of the settlers laid their city in ashes, killed twenty of their chief captains, and decimated the nation.

So too when Philip, prince of the Wampanoags, spurned the Reverend John Eliot while he was preaching the gospel, by pulling a button off Eliot's coat and saying *"he did not value what he preached any more than that,"* the Lord smote the Indians, who fell in a rebellious war against the English. Just as Philip was telling his counselors a dream that he had fallen into his enemy's hands, one of his own nation led the English to him in a thicket, and an Indian shot him through the heart.

But it was not simply the savages who traduced the gospel. Cotton was quick to point out that angry men in the churches who criticized the ministers of the gospel died miserably crying on their deathbeds for their pastors. Getting down to cases, he alluded to a mechanic in a Connecticut town who, when asked by the godly minister to substitute for him one day and read a sermon from a good book, audaciously preached a sermon the mechanic had written himself. For his text he took the phrase "Despise not prophecyings,"

and developed the idea that the clergy envied those of the Lord's people who could serve as prophets without benefit of theological training. Here was heresy indeed, the heresy of antinomianism and a lay clergy that would level the ministry and exalt any self-proclaimed apostle. Cotton reported happily that God struck the offender right in the pulpit with a raving madness from which he never fully recovered. Even more explicitly, when one town cut the salaries of their two eminent ministers to thirty pounds apiece, the Lord immediately caused the town to lose three hundred pounds in a disaster to their cattle. Surely, interjected Cotton, God abhorred such an abominable sacrilege wherein the ministers of Christ were defrauded of their dues.

Whoremongers and adulterers and all who lived uncleanly composed another group of sinners to fall under God's sentence. Many young women secretly murdered their bastard infants, and of their number Mather singled out Mary Martin as the dire example. In 1646 her father sailed from Boston to England, leaving her in the house of a married man, who coveted her. She yielded, but begged God that if she were overtaken again, He would make of her a public example. She sinned twice again, conceived, delivered the infant herself in a dark room, murdered it, and hid the little corpse in a chest. The babe's body being found, the mother was brought to trial, and when she touched its face before the jury (according to the belief that blood flows from a corpse at the murderer's touch), it bled. "The blood of the child cried, when the cry of the child itself was thus cruelly stifled." The mother confessed and was sentenced. The renowned minister John Cotton preached a sermon for her from Ezekiel: "Is this of thy whoredom a small matter, that thou hast slain my children?" At her hanging Mary Martin acknowledged that she had twice tried to kill her babe before succeeding, and the unskilled executioner twice turned her off the ladder before she died.[33]

Adulteries were bad enough, but New England was also the scene of "damnable bestialities." A New Haven church member named Potter, outwardly a devout and pious Christian, satisfied his lusts by buggering his domestic animals, before the eyes of his wife and son. Heaven sent him warnings; his daughter dreamed that she had seen him being hanged before a great multitude. And so it came to pass, for he was hanged on June 6, 1662, along with a cow, two heifers, three sheep, and two sows with whom he had conversed. Before his execution he admitted that he never used secret prayer in his life, and frequently omitted family prayer too. The case of Potter cut across several of Mather's categories: secret sinners posing as professing Christians, men who omit their prayers to God, and those who live in uncleanness.

Cotton Mather was but the most zealous of many collectors of judgments among Puritans and other Protestants and Catholics in all the colonies. John Winthrop, the long-time governor of Massachusetts, recorded a string of disasters that befell critics of the country as clear instances of the Lord's displeasure against New England's enemies. There was the Bristol ship full of "profane scoffers," the *Mary Rose,* which blew up in Charlestown harbor in 1640 when her own powder caught fire. The master and company had spoken very ill of the saints because

the market for their commodities fell below their expectations. There was the well-to-do settler, one Austin, who after coming to Quinnipiac with his family in 1638, grumbled that he could not subsist there, and took ship back to England. But the ship was taken by the Turks, and Austin and his family were sold in Algiers for slaves. There was the group of four magistrates, a minister, and a schoolmaster, unhappy with the fall of prices for land and cattle, who also endeavored to return. A tempest battered their ship in the English Channel, whereupon three of the ministers and the schoolmaster humbled themselves before the Lord and admitted He was dealing justly with them for speaking ill of New England. But since one of them, Mr. Phillips of Wrentham, had spoken well of the colony, the Lord turned aside the wind so that the ship reached the Isle of Wight. On shore He still followed them. Plague took away two children of the schoolmaster. The daughter of another went mad, and two of her young sisters were abused. All these distant judgments the governor kept track of in his personal journal.[34] He had no need to stifle dissent if the Lord punished His critics. Fortunate the governing official who could count on Providence to chastise the malcontents!

The small as well as the great felt God's wrath for their sins. Two blasphemous manservants of one John Moody, who came to New England in 1633, went gathering oysters against their master's will. The tide carried out their boat, and they drowned before help could come. "A dreadful example of God's displeasure against obstinate servants," wrote John Eliot, missionary to the Cape Cod Indians.[35] In 1639 a barber-chirurgeon was overtaken by a snowstorm on his way from Roxbury to Boston and froze to death. This barber had used his occupational advantage when cutting his customers' hair to talk at great length on heretical matters, noted Edward Johnson in his providential history of Woburn, Massachusetts.[36]

Colonists outside New England also made note of divine judgments. John Smith recorded how "the great God of heaven," being angered at actions of the Bermuda settlers in 1617, sent down a swarm of rats that overran the islands and ate every growing thing upon them.[37] So too did God visit a plague of weevils upon the godless planters of Maryland and Virginia at the time of the Anglo-Dutch war over New Netherlands in 1664. The weevils ate up all the grain and other crops of the reckless planters, who had squandered their means on the wine and brandy brought by ship from England. So great a famine did the Lord cause that a mother killed her own child and ate it, and then called on her neighbors to see the remains. She was arrested and condemned to be hanged. On the scaffold, she cried out to the people, in the presence of the governor, that he should bear the guilt for the delirium of hunger that had caused her to kill and eat her baby. God had sent the weevils as a visitation upon the governor, she exclaimed, for warring against the Dutch and burning an abundant harvest of their wheat and other crops and fruits, when he failed to pierce their defenses. Thereby, the governor had sinned against God and His goodness, against the Dutch, who lost their

grain, and against the English, who needed it even more than the Dutch. So protesting before the crowd and the governor, she was swung up.

Noteworthy here is the interpreting of a providential judgment by an Englishwoman, with her last breath, against the English governor for attacking his Dutch neighbors and laying waste their fields. But we notice that a Dutch traveler, Jasper Danckaerts, is the source. Dutch Protestants could invoke providential judgments against English Anglicans as vigorously as did the Puritans against their various enemies.[38]

The instances of divine judgments assembled by the Puritans and other colonists contain some of the most pervasive motifs in world folklore. Punishment by God or the gods for the errant actions of mortals has always provided a favorite theme for the folk narrator who places himself on the side of the angels, and for the cleric in the pulpit who intersperses moral stories, or exempla, in his sermons. So ubiquitous a folk motif as "Adultery punished" is known on every continent and is found in the collections of the Grimms and Boccaccio and in the myths of the ancient Celts and Greeks, of Buddhists and Jews, of North and South American Indians. Judgments have persisted in byways of folk tradition throughout most of American history. Seventeenth-century Americans accepted them as routine demonstrations of God's wrath toward the enemies of His elect.

Witchcraft

Witchcrafts, being complex episodes rather than single events, did not fit readily into the typology of providences, but the Puritan divines and magistrates had no hesitation in interpreting them providentially. They regarded the Lord as actively combatting the armies of the Devil and his covenanted witches who tormented the saints, and showing His hand against them by numerous providential acts. Cotton Mather recounted some of these in a London tract of 1689, reprinted in 1691, which he titled *Late Memorable Providences Relating to Witchcrafts and Possessions, Clearly Manifesting, Not only that there are Witches, but that Good Men (as well as others) may possibly have their Lives shortned by such evil Instruments of Satan*. After describing bewitched persons whom he had closely observed, Mather appended "A Discourse of the *Power* and *Malice* of the DEVILS" and a "Discourse on Witchcraft" in which he explained the operation and strategy of the dark powers. A prefatory note "To the Reader" stated that "the following Account will afford to him that shall read with Observation, a further clear Confirmation, That, There is both a GOD, and a Devil, and Witchcraft." Cotton recounted the behavior of possessed individuals, and then announced categorically, "But I am resolv'd after this, never to use but just one grain of patience with any man that shall go to impose upon me, a denial of Devils, or of Witches."[39] As proof he related some of the strange and evil acts perpetrated by witches.

Belief in demons and witches and narratives illustrating their magical and diabolical deeds lie at the heart of folklore. The Mathers and their fellow Puritans accepted this folklore and incorporated it into their covenant theology. They did not swallow wholesale the old wives' tales and notions freely circulating among the folk, with which they were fully acquainted, but rather endeavored earnestly to screen out "superstitions" and "fabulous" elements from genuine evidences of sorcery and diabolism. The New England Puritan fathers took a median position on witchcraft lore, rejecting at one extreme the skeptics who denied the actuality of witches, and at the other the gullible who thought witches could transform themselves into beasts and birds.

In the Puritan cosmology, devils and witches fitted into the covenant structure of the universe as logically as did saints and angels. The devils entered into a "*Covenanting* with the *Witches*" in a "most hellish *League* made between them, with various *Rites* and *Ceremonies*." In this covenant, the witches promised to serve the devils, and the devils promised to help the witches. Cotton Mather drew a picture of a "vast *Power,* or Army of *Evil Spirits,* under the Government of a Prince who employs them in a continual Opposition to the Designs of GOD." This army dwelt in the atmosphere, commanded by Beelzebub, the "Grand Seignior of Hell," who instructed them in their myriad mischiefs. As the law of God and Christ is challenged by the sinful code of witchcraft, so "the *sure Mercies* of the New Covenant, and all the *just Duties* of it, are utterly abdicated by that *cursed Covenant* which *Witchcraft* is Constituted with. ... *Witchcraft,*—What shall I say of it! It is the furthest Effort of our Original Sin. . . ." When Cotton Mather remonstrated with a witch, he attempted to reason with her in terms of covenant relationships: "I set before her, the *Ne-*

cessity and *Equity* of her breaking her *Covenant* with *Hell,* and giving her self to the Lord Jesus Christ, by an everlasting Covenant. . . ."[40] In a similar vein, Increase exhorted against using "herbs or plants to preserve from witchcrafts," for they are doing the very thing they profess to abhor, by trying to improve the Devil's work. "Now, for men to submit to any of the devil's sacraments is implicitly to make a covenant with him."[41]

The Devil's covenant was regarded as a tangible document and not a figure of speech. In his Preface to *An Essay for the Recording of Illustrious Providences,* Increase recounted a "marvelous relation" concerning a young French scholar who signed a contract in blood with the Devil for money, then repented and decided to commit suicide. But ministers fasted and prayed with him in the field where he had met the Devil, and asked the Lord to make known His power over Satan by releasing the contract. After some hours a cloud appeared over them, and from it dropped the blood-signed contract. The young scholar promptly tore it into pieces. This providence was related in Normandy by a minister of attested character.

In short, all covenanting outside God's grace between devils, witches, ghosts, and sinners was suspect and fraught with hellish consequences. Increase castigated those well-meaning persons who attempted folk remedies against witchcraft such as destroying wax images pricked with needles, or drawing blood from suspected witches, or bottling the urine of witches, or nailing horseshoes over the door, for having "fellowship with that hellish covenant" between the Devil and his witches. These widely practiced folk charms he dismissed as superstition, but at the same time he recognized the malevolent force of the dark covenants. So he quoted the "excellent Sennertus" as saying, "They that force another to do that which he cannot possibly do but by vertue of a compact with the devil, have themselves implicitly communion with the diabolical covenant."[42] The art of "unbewitching persons" could only be learned from magicians and devils themselves, insisted Increase, and to practice this art in effect served the Devil's ends and worked for his salvation. Increase used the term "white witches," commonly employed by the folk in the sense of helpful magic makers who can counter the harm effected by the black witches, but he considered both species equally culpable. Such heathen notions were, he felt, on a par with papist veneration of icons and relics of the cross.

Evil covenanting played a role in the Salem witchcraft upheaval of 1691–1692. In the account in the *Magnalia Christi Americana,* Tituba, the African servant who baked a cake with a bewitched girl's urine in an attempt to discover the witch, expressed penitence that she herself had covenanted with the Devil. Others at the Salem trials also confessed to having "covenanted with Satan."[43] John Hale, whose manuscript is quoted in the *Magnalia* by Cotton Mather, sought to refute the "mistaken principles" that the Devil acts regularly in covenant with a witch, and that "proof of such a covenant" can be seen in the fits into which a supposedly

Witch of the Woodlands;

COBLER'S NEW TRANSLATION.

Here Robin the Cobler for his former Evils,
Is punish'd bad as Faustus with his Devils.

The Witch of the Woodlands.

HERE the old Witches dance, and then agree,
How to fit Robin for his Lechery;
First he is made a Fox and hunted on,
'Till he becomes an Horse, an Owl, a Swan.

At length their Spells of Witchcraft they withdrew,
But Robin still more hardships must go through;
For e'er he is transform'd into a Man,
They make him kiss their bums and glad he can.

This is the argument of the story, which is too broad in its humour to be reprinted, but the following two illustrations show the popular idea of his Satanic Majesty and his dealings with witches.

Title page, passages, and illustrations from an eighteenth-century English chapbook recounting in verse the transformations imposed by witches on a lascivious cobbler, and depicting the witches with their familiars and the Devil
From John Ashton, *Chap-Books of the Eighteenth Century*

bewitched person falls when looked upon by a suspected witch. Often the Devil can act alone, Hale contended, and throw suspicion of witchcraft on innocent people, just to create turmoil and recrimination.[44] Earlier Cotton Mather had argued that witches sometimes injured those against whom they harbored no ill will, once ensnared in the covenant. "The witches, which by their covenant with the Devil are become owners of the specters, are oftentimes by their own specter required and compelled to give their consent for the molestation of some whom they had no mind otherwise to fall upon. . . ."[45]

So the ministers debated over the implications of the Devil's covenant. But as to its reality all were fully agreed.

Stories about witches fill a large and tenacious sector in Anglo-American folk belief and folk narrative. They are still heard in the Ozarks, in southern Illinois, on the Maine coast, among Southern Negroes, and elsewhere in the United States where the English tradition has persisted or infiltrated. In the seventeenth century, the intellectuals and elder statesmen at the center of power talked about witches as much as did the folk. The Dutch traveler Jasper Danckaerts, who visited America in 1679-1680, observed that he had never heard more talk about witchcraft and witches anywhere than in Boston. In the eyes of the Puritans, witches in covenant with the Devil and his army of demons threatened the fabric of their holy commonwealth with their black magic aimed at demoralizing the saints and subverting the true church. Hence they listened carefully to tales about alleged witches, and where the evidence seemed overwhelming, tried and executed them.

Yet the same kind of evidence might lead the observers to opposite conclusions, so tenuous was the distinction between the magic of the true witch and the behavior of innocent victims deluded by demons. In two cases juxtaposed in the *Magnalia*, those of Ann Cole of Hartford in 1662 and Elizabeth Knapp of Groton in 1671, the women displayed similar symptoms. They were taken with fits and spoke with the voices of demons, sometimes unintelligibly, sometimes clearly, accusing people in the town of evil doings. One mentioned by Ann Cole, Goody Greensmith, sat in prison, already charged with witchcraft, and readily confessed to all of Ann Cole's accusations, even to admitting familiarity with the Devil, who had appeared to her as a skipping deer. Goody Greensmith was executed. But in the case of

Title page of an eighteenth-century English chapbook, reprinted by John Ashton, who writes, "The frontispiece has nothing whatever to do with the book, but it is curious and valuable, as giving a representation of the ducking-stool." The ducking-stool was used to punish the witch by immersing her repeatedly.
From John Ashton, *Chap-Books of the Eighteenth Century*

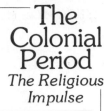

A Strange and Wonderful

RELATION

OF THE

OLD WOMAN

WHO WAS DROWNED AT

RATCLIFFE HIGHWAY

A Fortnight ago.

TO WHICH IS ADDED

THE OLD WOMAN'S DREAM,

A little after her Death.

PART THE FIRST.

PRINTED AND SOLD IN LONDON.

A Terrible and seasonable Warning to young Men.

Being a very particular and True Relation of one *Abraham Joiner* a young Man about 17 or 18 Years of Age, living in *Shakesby's* Walks in *Shadwell*, being a Ballast Man by Profession, who on *Saturday* Night last pick'd up a leud Woman, and spent what Money he had about him in Treating her, saying afterwards, if she wou'd have any more he must go to the Devil for it, and slipping out of her Company, he went to the *Cock* and *Lyon* in *King Street*, the Devil appear'd to him, and gave him a Pistole, telling him *he shou'd never want for Money*, appointing to meet him the next Night at the *World's End* at Stepney ; Also how his Brother perswaded him to throw the Money away, which he did ; but was suddenly taken in a very strange manner ; so that they were fain to send for the Reverend Mr. Constable and other Ministers to pray with him ; he appearing now to be very Penitent ; with an Account of the Prayers and Expressions he makes use of under his Affliction, and the prayers that were made for him to free him from this violent Temptation.

The Truth of which is sufficiently attested in the Neighbourhood, he lying now at his mother's house, etc.

Title page of an eighteenth-century English chapbook showing the Devil appearing to a lecherous youth and ministers praying for the young man

From John Ashton, *Chap-Books of the Eighteenth Century*

Elizabeth Knapp, who blasphemed against the minister and a respected and devout woman in town, blame was laid on the demon that possessed her. The pious woman (not named by Cotton) visited Elizabeth, who announced that she had been deluded by an apparition of Satan.

Witches could harm, torment, and eventually kill human beings and animals. Because they sought to decimate the saints, a natural target of their malice, Puritans especially feared the witches. Cotton Mather described how an exemplary man of Hadley, Philip Smith, age fifty, son of virtuous parents, deacon of the church, member of the General Court, justice in the county court, selectman of the town, lieutenant in the militia, was in 1684 "murder'd with an hideous witchcraft." As part of his office he ministered to the poor, and was threatened by one "wretched woman" in the town, dissatisfied with his treatment of her. Philip fell ill with sciatica, and warned his brother that the woman was enchanting him, saying,

Title page and accompanying illustration from an eighteenth-century English chapbook reporting a divine judgment on a whole community in the form of an earthquake

From John Ashton, *Chap-Books of the Eighteenth Century*

Farther, and more Terrible Warnings from God.

Further and more Terrible Warnings from God.

Being a sad and dismal Account of a dreadful
Earthquake or Marvelous Judgments
of God.

That happen'd between Newcastle and Durham on Tuesday the 24th day of August last ; which burst open the Earth with such Violence, that near an Hundred Souls, Men, Women and Children were Kill'd and Destroy'd ; being Buried Alive in the sad and dreadful Ruins thereof. Besides great Damage to many Houses and Persons for several Miles round. With the Names of some of the Persons Destroy'd thereby. With a Sermon Preach'd on that deplorable Occasion, and of the late dreadful Thunder and Lightning.

BY THE REVEREND MR. SALTER MINISTER OF THE GOSPEL
AT HARETIN NEAR NEWCASTLE.

LONDON, PRINTED BY J. NOON. NEAR FLEET STREET 1708.

A

𝕮imely 𝖂arning

To Rash and Disobedient

CHILDREN.

Being a strange and wonderful RELATION of a young Gentleman in the Parish of *Stepheny* in the Suburbs of *London*, that sold himself to the Devil for 12 Years to have the Power of being revenged on his Father and Mother, and how his Time being expired, he lay in a sad and deplorable Condition to the Amazement of all Spectators.

EDINBURGH : PRINTED ANNO 1721.

Title page of an eighteenth-century English chapbook concerning a youth who sold himself to the Devil, out of malice against his parents.

From John Ashton, *Chap-Books of the Eighteenth Century*

THE

𝕸iracle of 𝕸iracles.

Being a full and true Account of *Sarah Smith*, Daughter of *John Symons* a Farmer, who lately was an Inhabitant of Darken Parish in Essex, that was brought to Bed of a Strange Monster, the Body of it like a Fish with Scales thereon : it had no Legs but a pair of great Claws, Tallons Like a Liands, it had Six Heads on its Neck, one was like the Face of a Man with Eyes Nose and Mouth to it, the 2d like the Face of a Cammel, and its Ears Cropt, Two other Faces like Dragons with spiked Tongues hanging out of their Mouths, another had an Eagles Head with a Beak instead of a Mouth at the end of it, and the last seeming to be a Calves head. Which eat and fed for some time, which Monster has surprised many Thousand people that came there to see it. Daily, Spectators flock to view it, but it was by Command of the Magistrates knock'd on the Head, and several Surgeons were there to dissect it. Also you have a Funeral Sermon on the Woman who brought it forth, a very wicked Liver, and disobedient to her Parents, and one that was mightily given to Wishing, Cursing and Swearing. With a Prayer before and after the said Sermon. It being very fit and necessary to be had in all Families for a Warning to Disobedient Children. This strange and unheard of Monster was brought into the World in May last, and if any doubt the truth thereof, it will be certify'd by the Minister and Church-Wardens of the said Parish of Darkins in Essex as aforesaid.

ENTRED IN THE HALL BOOK ACCORDING TO ORDER.

Title page of an eighteenth-century English chapbook relating an account of a monstrous birth, interpreted as a divine judgment on a sinful woman. A similar birth, to a heretic, was reported on October 17, 1638, in Massachusetts.

From John Ashton, *Chap-Books of the Eighteenth Century*

"But be sure to have a care of me; for you shall see strange things. There shall be a wonder in Hadley! I shall not be dead, when 'tis thought I am!" Smith shortly became delirious, spoke in various languages, and complained of pins pricking him. A strange musky smell pervaded the room in which he lay, scratchings were heard, gallipots of medicine were unaccountably emptied, fire appeared on the bed, and people felt something as big as a cat which they could not grasp stir on the bedsheets. All the while Smith complained of the woman, and when some of his young neighbors disturbed her, he slept comfortably, but only then. Finally he died, and the jury that examined his corpse found his privates burned and his back full of bruises and holes seemingly made with an awl. Cotton Mather added that he could give other instances of similar tragical deaths attended with preternatural manifestations.[46]

So involved did Cotton become with the invisible world that when a "very stupendous witchcraft" erupted in Boston in 1688, he made personal observations on the affair, took one of the afflicted persons into his house, and wrote about the matter in a pamphlet and later in the *Magnalia.* This was the *cause célèbre* of John Goodwin's four children, all of excellent character, who became possessed by demons and fell into extraordinary fits:

Sometimes they were *deaf,* sometimes *dumb,* sometimes *blind,* and often this at once. Their tongues would be drawn down their throats, and then pull'd out upon their chins, to a prodigious length. Their mouths were forc'd open to such a wideness, that their jaws went out of joint; and anon clap together again, with a force like that of a spring lock; and the like would happen to their shoulder-blades and their elbows, and hand wrists, and several of their joints. They would lie in a benumb'd condition, and be drawn together like those that are ty'd neck and heels; and presently be stretch'd out—*yea, drawn back* enormously. They made piteous out-cries, that they were cut with *knives,* and struck with *blows;* and the plain prints of the *wounds* were seen upon them.[47]

Investigators soon ran down the culprit, a "scandalous" Irishwoman named Glover, mother of the laundress of the Goodwins, who once had defended her daughter in an argument with the eldest Goodwin child over some missing linen. At the trial she spoke only in her native Irish, a situation requiring the use of interpreters, who believed that another witch had laid a spell on Goody Glover to prevent her telling tales. As it turned out, she admitted freely and even boasted of her guilt, and so was condemned to death. A number of themes commonly associated with witches turn up in the Goodwin affair. Searchers of the Glover house found "images" or "poppets" or "babies" made of rags and stuffed with goats' hair, which she would stroke with her fingers dipped in her spittle to torment her enemies. She repeated the experiment in court, and when she stroked an image, one of the Goodwin children present promptly fell into a fit. Cotton Mather knew of similar doings in New England. The Reverend George Burroughs, accused of wizardry, brought poppets to witch meetings along with thorns to stick into them, and searchers in Bridget Bishop's cellar found rag poppets with headless pins in them, the points sticking outward.[48]

Image magic has a long history, dating from classical times and documented in England from Chaucer up to the twentieth century. George Lyman Kittredge devoted a whole chapter to the subject in *Witchcraft in Old and New England.* As late as 1916, in his examples, a woman in West Sussex showed her vicar a figure cut out of a turnip, supposed to represent herself, with two pins stuck in the chest. Her husband had made it, to torment her. She complained of chest pains, and eventually died of diabetes.[49] Describing witchcraft in the Ozarks today, Vance Randolph explains poppets as contrivances of the witch masters who sought to put the witches out of commission. The witch master would make an image out of mud or beeswax to resemble the witch, cover it with cloth she had worn, then drive nails into the image and beat it with a hammer or burn it, to paralyze and kill the witch, thus throwing her own artifices back upon her.[50]

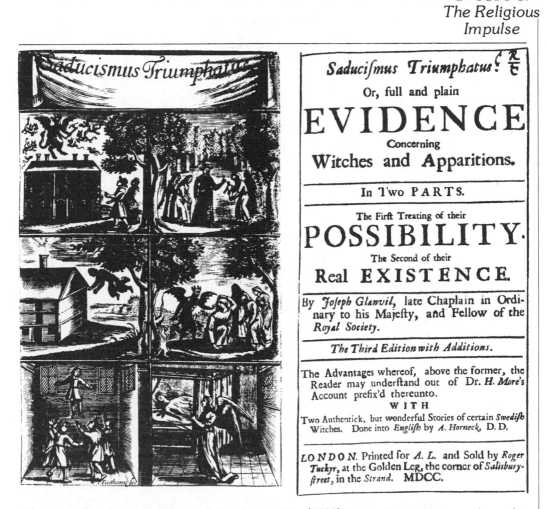

Title page and first frontispiece of the third edition (1700) of one of the most popular and influential books in the seventeenth century asserting the reality of witches and apparitions, the *Saducismus Triumphatus* of Joseph Glanvil, an Oxford graduate who became chaplain to Charles II. First published in 1681, it was often cited by Increase and Cotton Mather.

"The boxes represent the Drummer of Tedsworth, the Somerset Witch (Julian Cox), levitation of Richard Jones at Shepton Mallet, the rendezvous of witches at Trister Gate (Wincanton), Margaret Jackson, a Scottish witch devoting herself to the devil, and a celestial apparition at Amsterdam" (Rossell Hope Robbins, *The Encyclopedia of Witchcraft and Demonology*, New York: Crown, 1959, p. 225).

The relation of witches and the bewitched to good and evil books—by which the Puritans meant of course their own writings versus those of their theological opponents—is another hardy folklore theme surfacing in the Goodwin case. Witches obtained power from magic books and were weakened and rendered powerless by the Bible. Goody Glover, who professed herself a Roman Catholic, could repeat her paternoster readily except for one phrase, which she said she could not master for all the world. The eldest Goodwin girl, a thirteen-year-old under Cotton Mather's surveillance in his home, could not glance into the Bible, nor could anyone else in the room read it, even without her knowledge, without her falling into torments. Yet she could easily read a Quaker's book, save for the words "God" and "Christ." (In the Ozarks, a witch is unable to say "For God's sake.")[51] While allowing the girl to read Quaker and Popish books, her demons sent her into convulsions if she tried to read an edifying work, and when she looked at her catechisms they tossed her about the house "like a foot ball."

In her enchantment the Goodwin girl rode an invisible horse before the astonished eyes of Cotton Mather. Her unseen cohorts brought her the steed; she sprang upon it and rode at various gaits, now ambling, now trotting, now galloping furiously, often without her feet touching the ground. Sometimes the horse threw her violently, especially if anyone stabbed the air beneath her.

The animal carried her from her chair to other rooms and even up the stairs, but when she rode into a study—presumably Cotton's—where the Word of God prevailed, she returned to her normal pious self. When she went downstairs, the horse was waiting for her. Many other wonders and vexations did Cotton endure before a three-day vigil of prayer and fasting by a fellow minister finally delivered the Goodwin children from the demons.

The affair of the Goodwin children slid inevitably—it now seems—into the affair of the children of Salem Village and the witchcraft outbreak of 1691-1692. Cotton Mather assigned his fourteenth and last example of "Thaumatographia Pneumatica" to the Salem witches, presenting a firsthand account by John Hales [sic.].[52] In 1692 the Mas-

Conception of a seventeenth-century witch in an American lithograph of 1892

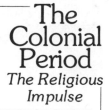

sachusetts Bay Colony was nervous; they had lost their charter, they feared the pagan Indian enemy without, the Satanic enemy within, and their critics in England overseas. About this time John Evelyn noted in his diary, "Unheard-of stories of the universal increase of Witches in New England; men, women and children devoting themselves to the devil, so as to threaten the subversion of the government," and in the next breath mentioned a conspiracy discovered among the Negro slaves in Barbados to murder all their masters.[53] The two uprisings were equally feared. A defendant in prison confessed in writing that the Devil appeared to him as a black man, made him sign his book, and took him to a sacrament, after which the Devil brought his shape to Salem to afflict people there. "And the design was to destroy Salem Village, and to begin at the minister's house, and to destroy the churches of God, and to set up Satan's kingdom, and then all will be well," glossed Cotton Mather.[54]

Actually Cotton gave relatively little space to the Salem witchcraft business in the *Magnalia,* since he had covered it in such detail in *The Wonders of the Invisible World* (1693). In the earlier work, written in the heat of the trials, Cotton expressed passionately and fearfully his conviction of a subversive conspiracy engineered by the Devil against the Bay Colony. He said so in plain words. Satan, appearing as a small black man, had gathered proud, ignorant, envious, and malicious creatures into his service, enticing them to sign his book, whereupon they became witches. They then met in "hellish

rendezvous" at which, according to confessors, they imitated the rites of baptism and the Lord's Supper with "diabolical sacraments." At these meetings they plotted *"to destroy the kingdom of our Lord Jesus Christ in these parts of the world."*

How would they do this? Cotton explained in specific terms. By their covenant with the Devil the newly initiated witches came into possession of specters or devils, whom they commissioned to torment and bewitch innocent people throughout the country. The devils bit, scratched, disjointed, and stuck pins into their victims and carried them over trees and hills in the effort to make them sign the Devil's laws in a spectral book. Once signed up, these sufferers then loosed their specters on other unfortunates. To complicate matters, the demons used their nefarious powers to assume the likeness of harmless and virtuous people. Since spectral evidence—the sighting of specters by the injured in the shape of living persons—was fully admissible in court, the judges, the ministers, and the community had to discriminate between true and false specters. Devils had power to take on the shapes of the innocent and in those shapes to afflict others. How could one discriminate between the witch's real specters and the Devil's false impositions? In his quandary Cotton cried out, quoting Jehoshaphat, *"We know not what to do!"*

Another power of the witches and demons that agitated Cotton Mather was their facility to make "themselves and their tools invisible." Third parties saw plainly enough the marks and

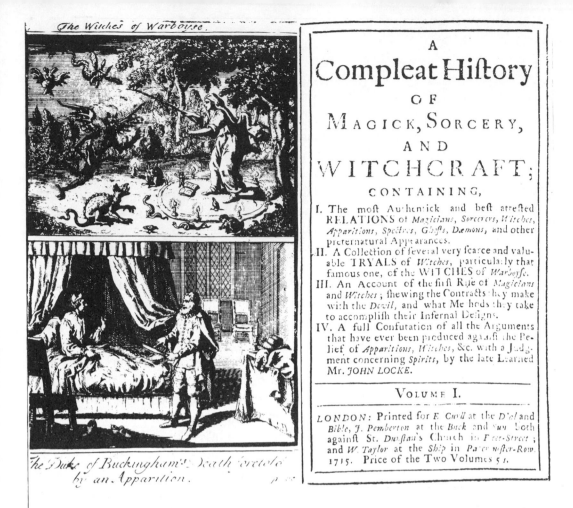

A
Compleat History
OF
MAGICK, SORCERY,
AND
WITCHCRAFT;
CONTAINING,

I. The moſt Authentick and beſt atteſted RELATIONS of *Magicians, Sorcerers, Witches, Apparitions, Spectres, Ghoſts, Dæmons,* and other preternatural Appearances.

II. A Collection of ſeveral very ſcarce and valuable TRYALS of *Witches,* particularly that famous one, of the WITCHES of *Warboyſe.*

III. An Account of the firſt Riſe of *Magicians* and *Witches;* ſhewing the Contracts they make with the *Devil,* and what Methods they take to accompliſh their Infernal Deſigns.

IV. A full Confutation of all the Arguments that have ever been produced againſt the Belief of *Apparitions, Witches,* &c. with a Judgment concerning *Spirits,* by the late Learned Mr. *JOHN LOCKE.*

VOLUME I.

LONDON: Printed for E. Curll at the Dial and Bible, J. Pemberton at the Buck and Sun both againſt St. Dunſtan's Church in Fleet-Street; and W. Taylor at the Ship in Paternoster-Row. 1715. Price of the Two Volumes 5 s.

The Duke of Buckingham's Death foretold by an Apparition. p.

Title page and frontispiece of volume one of a two-volume work, Richard Boulton's *A Compleat History of Magick, Sorcery, and Witchcraft* (1715–16), which staunchly upheld the existence of magicians and witches and included the Salem witchcraft cases among its examples.

bruises left by pins and iron instruments on the bodies of their victims, but they could not see the weapons nor the specters. Cotton cited two cases where tortured persons grabbed at the demons tormenting them and made visible an iron spindle and a corner of a sheet, which remained in their hands. But except for such rare lucky snatches, the hapless human pincushions could not see who or what was attacking them. The sorcery of witches for "invisibilizing of the grossest bodies," and the ability of demons to impersonate pious people confounded the Puritan divines.

In this atmosphere of consternation and dread, old wives' tales bloomed and some were related to judges sitting in court. The trial of Susanna Martin for witchcraft, held at the court of oyer and terminer in Salem, June 29, 1692, brought into the open a cycle of whispered narratives such as folklorists tape-record today. Farmers and a farmwife appeared to testify to the evil doings of their neighbor.

John Allen of Salisbury gave testimony that when he had refused to carry some staves for Goody Martin because his oxen were weak, she threatened him, saying his oxen would never do him much more service. Allen replied, "Dost thou threaten me, thou old witch?" (Apparently he knew her character already.) "I'll throw thee into the brook." Off she "flew" over the bridge. Allen

led his oxen to Salisbury Beach, a customary resting place, but they all ran off into the Merrimack River and swam out to sea, and only one swam back and was finally found in the woods near Amesbury.

This is a pure example of what Kittredge calls the essential witchcraft document. There are no learned elements of a black man, a book to sign, a covenant with Satan, hellish revels — although these came in a later testimony. What is present is the threat and its fulfillment: *damnum minatum et malum secutum.*[55]

After John Allen came other villagers to the Salem court, each with his grievance to tell, each striving to outdo the other in his memoir of Susanna Martin's enchantments. The testimonies took the form of what folklorists call today a memorat, an individual encounter with a well-known supernatural creature or mortal with dark powers, in this case the witch or her specter. Details of time, place, and injury varied in the memorats, but the outlines followed a common pattern. The farmers were telling folktales in court.

Those who followed John Allen echoed his complaint of how Susanna rendered cattle distraught, a customary grievance among the farmer folk who depended heavily on the milk of their cows and the strength of their oxen. John Atkinson testified how Goody Martin muttered darkly when he exchanged a cow of his own with one belonging to her son. The cow her son had swapped changed suddenly from a tame to a wild beast and broke all the ropes with which she was tied. John Kembal re-

called how Susanna in a spite had threatened that a certain cow *"should never do him any more good,"* and soon after it was found "stark dead" on the ground, with no trace of distemper. Other of his cattle also strangely died. So did the cattle of Bernard Peache. John Pressy was minded how, twenty years before, when he had given evidence against the Martin woman, she had cursed him with foul words, saying he never should prosper more, and particularly that he never should have more than two cows. And in all that time, he never did own more than that number.

The affinity between witches and cows has long been remarked. Kittredge devoted a whole chapter to "The Witch in the Dairy" in his *Witchcraft in Old and New England,* and gave a sequence of examples reported from the fifteenth to the twentieth century of witches drying up cows and keeping the butter from coming. Some farmers believed that the spirit of the witch possessed the cow, and that her body received whatever injury was visited on the beast. A number of tales collected in the Schoharie Hills of New York by Emelyn E. Gardner in the second decade of the present century reflect this belief in sympathetic magic. When a cow whom the local witchwoman had admired suddenly lay down and frothed at the mouth for three days, its owner decided to knock it on the head with his axe and put it out of its misery. Before he could act, the witchwoman's children appeared, saying their mother had had a vision the cow would be up on its feet eating grass in twenty minutes.

43

And so it proved. In another case, the farmer did kill a sick heifer, and a reputed witch showed a lump on her temple just where he had struck the animal. In the case of a cow who did not give milk properly, the owner tried milking it into a pailful of coals. A great stench arose from the sizzling milk. The next day a strange old woman of the neighborhood was seen about with her hair burned off, while the cow began giving her milk again normally.[56]

In my own collecting on the Maine coast in 1956, I tape-recorded a conversation from local people about a woman they called Mother Hicks the witch. Mother Hicks coveted a cow on Beals Island and bewitched it, so that it jumped

Title page of an English pamphlet of 1613 depicting the ordeal by swimming the year before of an accused witch, Mary Sutton. The right thumb of the accused was tied to the left big toe. It was believed that an innocent person would sink and a guilty one float. Such trials by water reached their peak in the first half of the seventeenth century, were approved by King James I, and were conducted in America as late as 1706.

Witches Apprehended, Examined and Executed, for notable villanies by them committed both by Land and Water.

With a strange and most true triall how to know whether a woman be a Witch or not.

Printed at London for *Edward Marchant*, and are to be sold at his shop over against the Crosse in Pauls Church-yard. 1 6 1 3.

about and bit itself. An onlooker recommended that the owner build a fire, kill the cow, throw the cow's innards into the fire, and then deny the request of whoever came asking for something. The islander did as told, and sure enough two boys appeared asking for an article from the house, while the innards tried to leap out of the fire. The family sent the boys back empty-handed, and Mother Hicks died of internal burns.[57]

Goody Martin assaulted people as well as cattle, according to the tale testimony. She tormented William Brown's "most pious and prudent wife" with birds that pecked her and a bunch in her throat that choked her and frightened her by disappearing before her eyes. Only when the church appointed a day of prayer in Goodwife Brown's behalf did the troubles cease. But later, after Goody Brown testified against Goody Martin (the plaintiffs were apparently practiced in telling judges their stories about Susanna), the witch came upon her as she milked her cow and cursed her, saying, "For thy defaming me at court, I'll make thee the miserablest creature in the world." And shortly after, Goody Brown fell into and remained in a frantic distemper, which the physicians called preternatural. In a similar episode reported from Devonshire about 1601 or 1602, Alice Trevisard jeered at John Beddaford, saying he would lose his wits, and within three weeks he was witless.[58]

Several times Susanna came at night to the farmers as they lay abed. She appeared as a cat in the bedroom of Robert Downer, seized him by the throat, and nearly strangled him. Downer remembered that the day before when she was being prosecuted in the court for witchcraft, he had told her he thought she was a witch, and she had threatened *"that some she-devil would shortly fetch him away!"* So with great effort he cried out, "Avoid, thou she-devil! In the name of God the Father, the Son, and the Holy Ghost, avoid!" Thereupon the cat leaped out the window. In like manner the Martin woman threatened John Kembal when he rejected one of her puppies, saying, "If I live, I'll give him puppies enough." Some days later as Kembal was coming home from the woods, a coal-black puppy jumped on him, eluded his axe, and leaped at his throat, whereupon Kembal invoked the name of Jesus Christ, and the dog vanished. (In popular belief, uttering aloud the name of the Lord acts as an effective counterspell against a demon.) Another time Susanna came scrabbling at the window of Bernard Peache on Lord's day night, jumped down on the floor, seized Peache's feet, drew his body intó a heap, and lay on him for nearly two hours. When finally he could stir, he bit three of her fingers and she departed. The same business happened to Jervis Ring, except that Susanna bit him on the finger as he lay oppressed at night, and long after, the mark still showed. Here Susanna takes the role of the "nightmare witch" whom Kittredge calls "eminent among haunting creatures."[59]

Even though the witch could maim and kill, her enemies still could strike back if they kept up their courage, and indeed sometimes they did draw blood on the she-devil. When Susanna and another pursued Bernard Peache, after he had refused to attend a cornhusking at her house and she had threatened him, he lunged at them with a quarterstaff. The roof of the barn broke one of his blows. About this time a rumor

went around town that Susanna had a broken head. Equally valiant was John Pressy, who found himself bewildered near the Martins' field, where he saw a "marvelous light, about the bigness of a half bushel," which he struck at mightily forty times with a stick, and felt a substance. As he left, his heels went out from under him and he slid on his back into a pit, although afterwards he could find no such pit. Recovering, he walked on, and saw Susanna Martin standing on his left hand, but they exchanged no words. Next day he heard that she was in miserable condition from pains and bruises.

The beleaguered farmer in England and America has frequently attempted to break a witch's spell by striking, shooting, cutting, or burning other bewitched objects or shapes. He may put a hot iron in the cream when the butter does not come, shoot a hovering bird or a black cat with a silver bullet, boil his own urine, whip barnyard animals or burn them alive, and hope that the witch suffers accordingly. Customarily he learns that she is scalded, crippled, burned, or unable to urinate. In the Schoharie Hills, a boy out hunting found he was continually missing partridges, which would shake their feathers and talk partridge talk after each shot. His uncle shot a bent sixpenny piece at the birds and they disappeared in a clap of thunder, while Witch Schermerhorn was seen standing in the path with crossed hands. Ever after she had holes in her wrists that never healed. Even mills and steamboats were bewitched and had to be chastised.[60]

To return to Susanna Martin. The most

startling testimony, from Joseph Ring, placed Susanna at a "hellish rendezvous" to which he had been transported through the air by demons. At these witch meetings one demon tried to get him to sign a book with pen and blood-like ink, on promise of many bounties, and when Ring refused, the pack let out dreadful screeches. Here is the learned element of witch lore, contrasting with the simple farm tales of clear-cut enchantment. Churchmen formulated the notions of the witches' Sabbath in the fourteenth and fifteenth centuries as a profane parody of the Mass, at which recruits signed the covenant with the Devil and received a demon of their own to assist them in nefarious designs. Participants flew to the Sabbaths on broomsticks or the backs of demons. So Joseph Ring's testimony elevated Susanna Martin from traditional folk notions to intellectualized concepts of witchcraft. For Cotton Mather this was the climactic accusation, coming at the end of the more commonplace charges. Yet the witches' Sabbath touched English folk belief much more lightly than did the drying up of a neighbor's cow. Kittredge shows that the Black Mass never became a charge in English trials until 1612 and concludes that it was a learned importation from the Continent.[61]

Comparative and historical evidence demonstrate clearly enough that the accusers of Susanna Martin were telling folk legends. But interior evidence in the testimony also indicates that these were oft-repeated tales. Some witnesses— Robert Downer, John Kembal, and "several testimonies" in support of Downer —agreed that the alleged witch had known and talked to her family and neighbors about the accidents she had caused before they had said a word to anyone on these matters. The nearly identical language of these allegations,

and the nature of the allegation itself, must be based on excited talk. We can imagine Edmond Eliot rushing to tell John Kembal that the Martin woman had just mentioned to him that Kembal had been scared by puppies the night before, and Kembal replying that he had never breathed a word of it to anyone, not even his wife, for fear of frightening her. Edmond Eliot turns up twice in Kembal's testimony, for Kembal stated in court that Eliot told him Goody Martin

had threatened to give Kembal "puppies enough," a few days before Kembal saw the specter dogs. There are also the disclosures by William Brown, Robert Downer, and John Pressy that some of them had testified against Susanna years before. In his remarks Bernard Peache spoke of a "rumor about the town that Martin had a broken head" the day after Peache had struck at her shape. All these indicators point to eddies of storytelling and rumormongering

"Witchcraft at Salem Village" as conjectured by an artist in the late nineteenth century
From Augustus L. Mason, *The Romance and Tragedy of Pioneer Life*

"When I prayed in the room . . . her postures were exactly such as the chained witch had before she died."—Cotton Mather (1688).

An artist's conception of Cottom Mather praying with a woman believed to be bewitched

From Rossell Hope Robbins, *The Encyclopedia of Witchcraft and Demonology*

by the settlers of Salisbury, Newbury, and Amesbury about the evil powers of the Martin woman. The depositions at the trial of Susanna Martin were fragments of a legendary cycle of witch tales that had percolated through the villages north of Boston. Magistrates, clergymen, and physicians as well as farmer folk believed these tales. When William Brown's wife fell into a distemper, the physicians declared that her illness resulted from bewitchment by some devil.

For the leaders of New England, the case of Susanna Martin held a peculiar terror. It depicted the nature of the subversives in their midst. Cotton Mather called her "one of the most impudent, scurrilous, wicked creatures in the world." The likes of her were seeking to overthrow the Bible commonwealth forged in the wilderness by God's elect.

The Devil

The magic of the witches stemmed from their covenanting partner, the Devil, Satan, the Prince of Darkness, the Evil One, his Sable Majesty. In the folklore of the Western world, the Devil commands the most attention and the largest slice of folk motifs.

He made his appearance in colonial New England, not as the comic, dull-witted figure of thousands of folk anecdotes told after the Devil had lost his potency, but in the prime of his virulent powers. Cotton Mather described him visiting his human prey "ordinarily as a small black man,"[62] who cozened proud, envious, ignorant, and malicious

mortals into signing his book. But he could assume many guises. From learned sources Increase Mather quoted instances of the Devil taking the likenesses of good Christians, of the Virgin Mary, of Jesus Christ.[63] A "lewd and ignorant woman," Goody Greensmith, found guilty of bewitching Ann Cole of Hartford in 1662, confessed that the Devil had come to her "in the form of a deer or fawn, skipping about her," becoming gradually more familiar, talking with her, and carnally knowing her.[64] Mercy Short, bewitched at Salem Village in 1692, gave Cotton Mather an elaborate sketch of a demon:

There exhibited himself unto her a Devil having the figure of a Short and a Black Man; and it was remarkable that altho' she had no

sort of Acquaintance with Histories of what has happened elsewhere, to make any Impressions upon her Imagination, yet the
Devil that visited her was just of the same Stature, Feature, and
complexion with what the Histories of the Witchcrafts beyond-sea
ascribe unto him; he was a wretch no taller than an ordinary Walk-
ing-Staff; he was not of a Negro, but of a Tawney, or an Indian
colour; he wore an high-crowned Hat, with straight Hair; and had
one Cloven-foot.[65]

If Mather's statement that Mercy Short had read no learned histories of witchcraft is correct, and there is no reason to assume that an ordinary goodwife read widely, the inference follows that the learned tradition had by this time seeped into the folk traditions, as we have seen in the deposition of Joseph Ring that Susanna Martin had participated in a Black Mass. Thousands of legends scattered through Christendom delineate the appearance of the Devil, who may take the form of a monster, an ugly man, a priest, a handsome knight, a pilgrim, a peasant, a beautiful black wench, a Jew, a shoemaker, an angel, various animals and birds, a ball of fire, a stream of water, a whirlwind, a wagon wheel. The cloven foot or hoof regularly marks the Devil of popular tales. In colonial New England the white settlers credited sights by their Indian neighbors of a grotesque and hideous figure to the appearance of Satan. Edward Johnson heard that they had seen the Devil in a bodily shape, sometimes very ugly and terrible, sometimes like a white boy, inhabiting hideous woods and swamps. John Josselyn was told by "two Indians and an Indess" who came running into his house that Cheepie, their

Devil, had passed over the field gliding in the air with a long rope hanging from one of his legs, looking like an Englishman, dressed in a hat and coat, shoes and stockings, and portending death. William Wood related that some Indians once saw a Negro slave—a "blackamoor"—atop a tree, and came running to the English asking them to conjure away their Devil.[66]

From "an honest and useful English man," a preacher of the gospel to the Indians (probably his uncle John Cotton), Cotton Mather received the story of a Christian Indian, himself a preacher, who while making tar in the woods was accosted by the Devil in the shape of "a Black-Man, of a Terrible aspect, and more than humane dimensions." The dark stranger then threatened to kill the Indian unless he stopped preaching to his countrymen and refrained from mentioning Jesus Christ. Courageously the Indian replied, "I will in spite of you go on to Preach Christ more than ever I did, and the God whom I serve will keep me that you shall never hurt me." Thereupon the apparition calmed down and offered the Indian a thick book and pen and ink with which to sign it, promising to trouble him no further if he signed. But the Indian refused, knelt down in fervent prayer to God, and so caused the demon to vanish.[67]

This story had obviously traveled, from the lips of the "praying Indian" to those of at least two eminent Puritan ministers. The Indian recognizes and stands up to the visible Devil, rising above his fears with the strength of God behind him—according to the interpretation of John Cotton and Cotton Mather. Here is an oral legend incorporating widely known folklore motifs: the Devil as a black man; the Devil in the woods; the Devil departing at the mention of God's name; and the bargain with the Devil, in this case averted by the Indian's fortitude. How thoroughly the Indian preacher was Christianized, and Puritanized, is evident in his relaying to his white friends their own version of Satan and Satan's behavior.

Such allusions reveal the joint acceptance by red man and white of the Devil incarnate, often possessing the coloring of the other race: white or black to the Indian, tawny to the English. While the colonists readily labeled the savages as superstitious and barbarous, they fully accepted the red men's relationship with the Devil and indeed found in this relationship the explanation for the Indians' benighted condition. In Edward Johnson's view, the Devil had so subjugated and reduced the Indians to slavish fear that he had no need to use craft upon them as he did in other parts of the world.[68] Only the Indian powaws enjoyed familiar intercourse with the Devil, much as did witches, and used his black arts for their acts of conjuration and therapy.

Sightings of the Devil occur throughout the colonial period and are still talked about in the nineteenth and twentieth centuries. An enduring legend of the Ozarks claims that the Devil appeared to two youths, John Chesselden and James Arkins, near the Mississippi on May 24, 1784, in the daytime, first as a beast with flaming eyes and smoking nostrils, then as a headless man with a cloven foot, then as a dazzling demon who attempted to lure them to his realm. When they refused, the Devil seized Arkins, tore out half the hair of his head, and wounded him about his body. Thereupon Chesselden fell to his knees and cried out to the Lord for preservation from the fallen angel. Hearing these prayers, the demon vanished. Chesselden carried the injured Arkins to town on his back, and the two pointed to Arkins's wounds to convince the skeptics that they had indeed seen the Evil One.[69]

This tradition resembles Cotton Mather's story of the praying Indian in several respects: the Devil in human form emerging from the woods, seeking to entice mortals, and disappearing at the mention of the Lord's name.

The visible Devil in multiple forms—human, animal, and insect—is still common in Negro folk belief today, an inheritance from the religious doctrine slaves absorbed in an earlier time. Frequently he walks the earth as a fancy gentleman with silk tophat and frock coat, an ambrosial curl in the center of his forehead to hide his horn, and cloven feet.[70]

The purpose of the Devil in visiting mortals is to purchase their souls by a compact in which he proffers them riches and success for the rest of their lives. American as well as European folk legends dwelt on the compact, in the tradition associated in literature most prominently with Faust. As supernaturalism dwindled, the Devil became a clownish dolt in popular tales, cheated out of his souls by cleverer human beings. But in the seventeenth century the compact with Satan was deadly

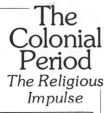

serious, for it was the hellish counterpart of God's covenant with His saints.

The Devil is still a real personality in the twentieth century. In his vast compendium of *Folk-lore from Adams County, Illinois,* Harry M. Hyatt sets down half a dozen "Devil Tales" in which people repeated to him their experiences, or experiences of those close to them, with the Devil.[71] In the twentieth century a folklorist ferrets out these diabolical encounters from the hidden corners of American life. In the seventeenth century the Devil could plainly be seen anytime, anywhere, by saints and sinners alike.

Judgments (Quaker view)

While the New England Puritans subscribed to a particularly rich body of religious folklore, other sects in the colonies accepted many of the same ideas. For example, the Quakers challenged the Puritans on their own providential ground.

In the divine judgment Puritan ministers and magistrates possessed an effective weapon with which to discredit their enemies and critics, but it was a weapon that could be turned against them. The Quakers shared enough of the Puritans' reforming principles, and differed enough on the degree to which the Reformation should be carried, to believe equally in judgments and to interpret them in their own behalf. A battle of judgments ensued, between the followers of George Fox in Pennsylvania and John Calvin in Massachusetts.

The Quakers pushed reforming Protestantism to the ultimate extreme. They eliminated all distinctions between clergy and laity, they downgraded Scripture in favor of the direct revelation of God, they eliminated the two remaining Puritan sacraments of baptism and communion, and they rejected the church as a physical and organizational structure. At the same time they retained the central concept of personal salvation through God's grace, available to all who would cultivate the Inner Light within themselves. Militant in their belief in lovingkindness, the Quakers descended on Massachusetts from other colonies, particularly from their haven at Rhode Island, to endure whippings, unheated jails, mutilation, and in 1659, the death of two Friends by hanging. A female companion, Mary Dyer, waiting alongside them on the gallows, was given a last-minute reprieve and banished, but within a year she had returned to Boston to seek, and receive, the execution she had been denied. The Quakers attacked the dark dogmas of election, predestination, and original sin to spread a new creedless gospel of open-ended salvation assured all men who would link their hearts to a God of love.

In addition to the corporal punishment they inflicted on meddlesome Quakers, the Puritans also sought out evidence of the Lord's vengeance against these defiers of His law. In his *Illustrious Providences* Increase Mather took occasion to cite the "blasting rebukes of Providence upon the late singing and dancing Quakers," and recorded specific instances that transpired in 1681. A young merchant of Boston named Thomas Harris fell in with some "mad Quakers," and like them began to dance and sing and ascribe his extraordinary raptures to joy, while calling those who opposed him, even his father, devils. The next day his body was found by the seaside, with three holes in his throat, his tongue missing, one of his eyes hanging down on his cheek, the other sunk deep in the socket. Mather gives no surmise as to the cause of death, but makes it plain that diabolical forces were involved, for the two nights following Harris's burial the high sheriff heard the voice of Harris calling at the window and by his bedside, demanding that justice be done him.

The Quakers were quick to respond. George Bishop in *New England Judged* (1667) and George Keith in *The Presbyterian and Independent Visible Churches in New-England and Else-Where* (1691) countered with examples of God's judgments against their Puritan persecutors. The long subtitle of Bishop's work listed sufferings of individual Quakers at the hands of the people of Massachusetts, and concluded with "the remarkable judgments of God in the death of John Endicot, Governour, John Norton, High Priest, and Humphry Adderton, Major General." In the body of the book Bishop described how the persecutor Major General Adderton, after passing sentence of death against Mary Dyer, and taunting another Quaker, Wenlock Christian, at his trial that "the Judgments of the Lord God [predicted by Wenlock] are

not come upon us yet," was thrown from his horse and had his brains dashed out as he was riding home one night. A cow crossing the path startled the horse, just at the place where the Friends, who had been arrested and whipped in Boston, were turned loose from the prisoners' cart. Adderton lay on the ground with "*his* Eyes being started out of *his* Head like Sawcers, *his* Brains out of *his* Nose, *his* Tongue out of *his* Mouth, and *his* Blood out of *his* Ears. . . . And thus *he* . . . came to be . . . as a *Flag* of Warning, by *his* dreadful example, to *all* that dare to persecute and make sport at the shedding of *Innocent* blood, and the most cruel sufferings of the *Innocent,* and to tempt the Lord concerning *his* Judgments. So lie *thou* there, *thou Adderton,* as an Ensign for *New Englands Blood-suckers;* and so let all thine Enemies, O *God,* perish."[72] Keith also referred to this retribution as a relation he had heard from New Englanders, who had in turn heard it from Quaker prophets, an indication of how widely the matter had been bruited.[73]

Between the printing of Bishop's and Keith's volumes there had appeared Increase Mather's *Essay for the Recording of Illustrious Providences* with its judgments against cavorting Quakers. So Keith included in his work "A brief Answer to some gross Abuses, Lies and Slanders" fomented by Mather. Keith made much of an episode told him by people in Barnstable, Massachusetts. A Quaker in that town, Ralph Jones, owned four cows and some calves, which the Puritan preacher claimed in wages. The "said Priest" killed a calf and sent part of the meat to his daughter lying in childbirth. As soon as she tasted a piece she cried out, "Return home the Man's Cows, I hear a great noise of them," and so saying, died. The "Priest" charged the

Quakers had bewitched his daughter. Nevertheless he killed another cow and ate of its meat to see if the Quakers could bewitch him, and soon after he too died. "The passage is so fresh in that Town," wrote Keith, "that it is acknowledged by divers of the Neighbours to be true."[74] He commented further that the Puritan congregations in Barnstable, Sandwich, and neighboring towns were greatly exercised over the affair and ready to wreak havoc on the Quakers, had not the king's "granting an Indulgence to all tender Consciences" at that time spared them.

Here is a clear illustration of a colonial local legend, attached to specified persons and places but incorporating international folk motifs, and interpreted by both Quakers and Puritans according to their biases. This was a living not a literary tale, talked about heatedly by townspeople, who were prepared to take action against Ralph Jones. Puritans believed him a witch, in covenant with the Devil, who had poisoned the cattle rightfully taken from him by a minister of God's elect. Quakers believed the death of the minister and his daughter to be divine judgments against the "Priest" who had wrongfully seized the property of an honest, innocent man.

George Keith also cited approvingly the judgment befalling repressive Governor John Endicott, who had raised the storm against the Quaker intruders of 1659. As Keith told it, "one of these persecuted Servants of the Lord, called *Quakers,* did plainly fore-tell, *that the House of Governor* Indicot, a greater Persecutor, *should be left desolate,*

and become a Dunghil, as did accordingly come to pass, and hath been observed by divers, to have been a real Prophecy, divine Justice and Providence did so bring it about."[75] The Quakers outdid the Puritans by linking prophecies to their judgments.

Besides these signs of divine punishment meted out against individuals, the Quaker chroniclers such as Keith pointed out "many signal and manifest Judgments of God, that came upon the People of *New-England* in general . . . for that horrible persecution they raised against that honest People called *Quakers,* and putting to death four of the Lord's Servants, for which the Name of these Actors and Abettors, are a stink over many places of the World."[76] Keith listed a series of catastrophes overtaking the Puritans after their execution of the four Friends: the blasting of their wheat, Indian wars (King Philip's War broke out in 1675), a plague of smallpox forewarned by a Quaker woman named Margaret Brewster come from Barbados, and the revocation of the Massachusetts Bay charter in 1684. It was true enough that the loss of the colonial charter and the converting of Massachusetts into a royal colony did result in good part from the Puritan intolerance toward Quakers, but the modern historian would broaden the explanation to a general displeasure of King William of Orange at the theocratic rule in the Bay Colony. The Quaker critics saw the king's decision as an instrument of the Lord's will. So did the Puritan self-critics, who were quick to recognize when Jehovah's punishments applied to themselves. The point of difference lay in the interpretation of the judgment. None of the elect would have seen in their severity toward Quakers a cause of the judgment. Some slackening of their faith must be the reason, but to chastise Quakers was a manifestation of faith.

Religious folklore motifs, according to Stith Thompson, *Motif-Index of Folk Literature,* 6 vols. (Bloomington: Indiana University Press, 1955-58), and Ernest W. Baughman, *Type and Motif-Index of the Folktales of England and North America,* Indiana University Folklore Series no. 20 (The Hague: Mouton & Co., 1966).

Motifs	Page
A184 "God as founder and protector of certain peoples"	15-16
A285.1 "Lightning weapon of the gods"	20
D1318.5.2 "Corpse bleeds when murderer touches it"	16, 23, 29-30
D1766.1 "Magic results produced by prayer"	50
D1810.8 "Magic knowledge from dream"	29, 30
D1812.3.3.11 "Death of another revealed in dream"	30
D2141.0.3 "Storms produced by devil"	22
E231 "Return from dead to reveal murder" (Baughman)	23-24
E234.0.1 "Ghost returns to demand vengeance" (Baughman)	25-26
E281.0.3* "Ghost haunts house, damaging property or annoying inhabitants" (Baughman, who comments, "It is very difficult to tell whether the haunters under this category are ghosts, witches, or familiar spirits")	26-28, 37
E422.1.11.5.1 "Ineradicable bloodstain after bloody tragedy" (Baughman)	22
F471.1 "Nightmare"	44
F473 "Poltergeist" (Baughman)	26-28
G211.1.7 "Witch in form of cat"	44-45
G211.1.8 "Witch in form of dog"	45
G224.4 "Person sells soul to devil in exchange for witch powers"	33, 41, 50
G241.3 "Witch rides on horse"	40
G243.2 "Parody of church ceremony at witch's sabbath"	46
G262 "Murderous witch"	36-37, 52-53
G262.3.2 (a) "Witch as wildcat presses person to death by sitting on person's chest at night" (Baughman)	44
G263.4.2 "Witch causes victim to have fits"	37, 38

Motifs	Page
G265.4.0.1 "Witch punishes owner for injury or slight by killing his animals"	42-43
G265.4.1.1* "Witch causes death of cattle" (Baughman)	43, 53
G265.6.2.1 "Witch causes cattle to run about wildly"	42-43
G269.4(b) "Witch curses person for injury or insult, the person becomes ill" (Baughman)	44
G269.17 "Invisible witch sticks victim with pins"	38, 42
G271.4.5 "Breaking spell by beating the person or object bewitched"	45
G303.3.1.6 "The devil as a black man"	48, 49
G303.3.3.2.8 "Devil in form of deer"	48
G303.4.5.3 "Devil has horse's foot"	49, 50
G303.8.13 "Devil in the woods"	49
G303.16.8 "Devil leaves at mention of God's name"	45
G303.25.21.1* "Blasphemous mother bears monster child" (Baughman)	16
M210 "Bargain with devil"	41, 50
Q220.1 "Devil plagues impious people"	50-51, 52
Q225 "Punishment for scoffing at religious teachings"	29-30, 31, 52
Q235 "Cursing punished"	30, 52
Q241 "Adultery punished"	29-31
Q253.1 "Bestiality punished"	30
Q300 "Contentiousness punished"	30
Q413.4 "Hanging as punishment for murder"	30, 31
Q551.7.1.1 "Heretic suddenly becomes tongue-tied"	29
Q558.4 "Blasphemer stricken dead"	52
Q582 "Fitting death as punishment"	30, 52
V52 "Miraculous power of prayer"	50

The Early National Period
The Democratic Impulse

*T*he American Revolution and the Civil War provide two giant markers of a historical period that saw colonial Americans acquire political independence and develop national traits. Religious zeal yielded to political drives. The dissenting sects having won their battle for recognition, the arena shifted, and the electorate now fought for representative institutions. This is the era of the Constitutional Convention, the establishment of the republic, the initiation of political parties, the Louisiana Purchase, the Monroe Doctrine, Manifest Destiny, the issue of slavery in the territories, the struggle for preservation of the union. The great policy questions hinged on the management of a young nation run on democratic principles. An age of reason and practical common sense had replaced an age of supernatural faith.

In this period an indigenous American folklore buds and flowers. As American political processes had departed from English precedents, so Yankee folklore now breaks sharply from English patterns. One main ingredient of post-Revolutionary legends proves to be folk humor, of a special American hue. In contrast to the somber, God-fearing, anxiety-laden supernatural tales repeated by the colonists, citizens in the new republic enjoyed telling and listening to realistic anecdotes and extravagant tall tales. The mobile, expansive atmosphere of the westward-shifting nation fostered yarns of scenes, incidents, and characters across the land. Raconteurs spun stories about bear and coon hunts, scrapes with Indians, travel by stagecoach and steamboat, the bench and bar in the backwoods, politicking, quarter-racing, gambling, rough-and-tumble fights, shooting contests, Yankee peddlers, doctoring in the swamps, rustics agape in the city, courtships and weddings in the back country, horse trades, camp meetings, tricks on merchants, frolics and country dances, itinerant actors, small-town newspaper editors, "darkies" on the plantation—the whole panorama of a lusty, gregarious frontier society. This fund of yarns edged its way into print in the decades following the War of 1812, when the republic turned its attention inward to concentrate on internal growth and the conquest of the continent. Somewhere in the 1820s the newspapers of the day commenced to carry entertaining sketches and anecdotes clearly derived from oral sources, and they maintained this fare for appreciative readers, who often doubled as contributors, until the Civil War.

A folklorist combing these newspaper files, or the books in which some of the sketches were reprinted, can identify a number of folktales. Stock stories written with an air of truth prove to be variants of oft-told narratives. A yarn-spinner or newspaper correspondent would never see any need to distinguish between a description of an episode he had observed and a good yarn he was repeating or a fiction he was composing. All three forms might deal with the same subject, and they could flow one into another, as an original oral anecdote caught the attention of one audience and was relayed to other listeners to become a folktale, or a correspondent contrived a sketch of his own invention suggested by tall tales he had heard. Since the daily newspapers and sporting weeklies like the New York *Spirit of the Times* and the Boston *Yankee Blade* regularly reprinted each other's choice items, an appealing yarn flew across the country in print and undoubtedly entered the oral repertoires of local narrators.

These spoken and written narratives accented the humorous. They drew their fun from character quirks and eccentricities, clever tricks and "sells," and Münchausen lies. The trickster, the braggart, and the "original" played the central roles, sometimes coalesced into the same figure. This was a humor of democracy, portraying common folk in their pursuits and pastimes, catching their local idioms, depicting them pictorially—as in the woodcuts of the Crockett almanacs, the lithographs of Mose the Bowery b'hoy, and the book illustrations of Felix O.C. Darley— in all their oddity of costume and physiognomy. The spirit of a shaggy equalitarianism pervades this oral and journalistic subliterature, and holds up to ridicule the manners and foibles of monocle-wearing English travelers, or dandified French dancing masters, or effete dudes from Eastern cities. The heroes that emerged from loosely strung cycles of anecdotes never shed their comic postures.

The formation of regional and urban character types in various sections of the United States through two centuries of history determined and shaped this folk humor. Inhabitants of the new Western states in particular reflected the democratic style, as Frederick Jackson Turner would point out in his famous essay of 1893 on the influence of the frontier in American history. Removed from Eastern centers of high culture, the frontiersmen developed their own peculiar roughhewn ways, talk, and dress, and received generic nicknames to indicate their backwoods qualities: the Puke from Missouri, the Sucker from Illinois, the Buckeye from Ohio, the Wolverine from Michigan, the Red Eel from Kentucky. But it was not only the West that produced characters. From the hillside farms of New England evolved the Yankee, by turns crotchety and sassy, gullible and wily. Middle Atlantic cities, too, cradled eccentrics cut from a similar cloth, as we shall see in the cases of Mose, the New York fireboy, and Sam Patch, the cotton spinner from Pawtucket, Rhode Island, and Paterson, New Jersey.

First attracting attention as clownish figures in local legends, some of these slattern characters ascended toward heroic or at least mock-heroic stature. American comic mythologizing began with the Revolutionary War, a seedbed for symbols and traditions needful for the new nation. Ethan Allen, the Green Mountain boy, astounded the British at Fort Ticonderoga by demanding their surrender in the name of Jehovah and the Continental Congress. Later, a prisoner at whom English visitors stared, aghast to see a real live Yankee, he astonished them again by chewing an iron tenpenny nail fastening the bar of his handcuffs. "Damn him, can he eat iron?" cried one of the spectators, according to the tale. A now largely forgotten naval hero of the Revolution, Nathaniel Fanning, born in Stonington, Connecticut, helped create his own legend in his *Narrative of the Adventures of an American Navy Officer* (1806). Imprisoned in the hold of a British frigate on starvation rations, he and his fellow prisoners opened a crawlspace into the captain's storeroom and lived high throughout the voyage. When the frigate arrived in England many of her crew had died from scurvy, but the American prisoners looked hale and hearty, causing a general on board to exclaim, "Damn them, there is nothing but thunder and lightning will kill them." In a later adventure, freed on exchange and in command of a privateer, Fanning found himself headed directly toward the English Channel Fleet. Unabashedly he hauled up an English ensign and pendant and sailed through the entire fleet, announcing himself as His Majesty's cutter *Surprize,* before being discovered and pursued, in vain. In this maneuver Fanning both played a "Yankee trick," as he described it, and exhibited a cheeky bravado, the combination of cunning and daring that would characterize American folk heroes.[1]

The Revolutionary tradition yielded a harvest of personal memoirs written by veterans of struggles on land and sea, but it did not bequeath enduring folktypes to American lore. Two candidates appeared in a drama of 1821, *The Pedlar* by Alphonso Wetmore, himself an army officer, presenting a whole gallery of native comic types: Mike Fink the boatman, Opossum the frontier roarer, Nutmeg the Yankee peddler, Old Prairie the settler, along with a Revolutionary veteran, Old Continental, who reminisces about Bunker Hill, and a roving tar, Harry Emigrant, who won't give up the ship. These last two character types faded from the

"A Regular Row in the Backwoods"
From *The Crockett Almanac 1841*

American scene, in which military and naval traditions would not take root until late in the twentieth century. But Wetmore's half-dozen homespun characters all reflected the same legend-building tendencies. In the early national period local comic types attained general prominence, through the media of stage, press, and travelers' tales, and took on mythological dimensions, without ever betraying their democratic origins.

Folk heroes of the Democratic era

Davy Crockett, Mike Fink, Sam Patch, Mose the Bowery b'hoy, and Yankee Jonathan all sprang to eminence from the people. Each exemplified a regional or urban type prominent on the American scene in the 1820s, 1830s, and 1840s. They made too deep an impact on the national imagination to vanish completely after the Civil War, and oral legends about all five linger into the twentieth century. But today they are curiosities for the scholar, antiquary, or romancer. Walt Disney's Crockett of the 1950s was a grown-up boy scout who bore little resemblance to the frontier original of a century earlier. Humorists, buffoons, and clowns, they also inspired admiration and awe at their daredeviltry and cocksureness. All breathed the spirit of American destiny, in the name of *demos*. "There's no mistake in Sam Patch," said Sam. "Be sure you're right, then go ahead," proclaimed Davy, and in a moment of triumph he announced, "I've got the world by the tail with a downhill pull." Crockett stands first as a figure of political and social democracy. The young republic chose for its folk heroes, not a general, a president, a justice, a poet, an explorer, but a backwoods hunter, a Western boatman, a hillside farmer, a cotton spinner, and a volunteer fireman.

These figures provoke a number of questions. How can such eccentrics be

called folk heroes? Crockett is a well-known historical personality. Fink has but a slight anchorage in history and little is positively known about him, although, like Davy, he became the subject of many tales. The real-life daredevil jumper Sam Patch, the most obscure of millworkers, reaped reams of newspaper publicity for three years until he jumped to his death in 1829, and he continued to attract attention in the popular media for years afterward. As for Mose the Bowery b'hoy and Jonathan the Yankee, they represented character types, one from the city, the other from the countryside. Mose was individualized, but the Yankee remained a generic portrait.

These characters received a good deal of criticism, scorn, and ridicule in their day as ruffians, fools, and windy show-offs. Since collectors of folklore would not begin their activities until much later, legends of the period, if they existed, must be culled from printed sources, plays, and the graphic arts, and this evidence may fall short of satisfactory proof that our motley company deserve the status of folk or legendary heroes. No project equivalent to the Mathers' scheme for the recording of illustrious providences was carried out in the early national period. And it has been claimed that Sam Patch cannot properly be designated a folk hero, on the grounds that egomaniac Patch stood for nothing larger than himself and certainly not for Jacksonian democracy, and that no oral legends about Patch are known.[2]

All these objections can be readily disposed of. To appeal to his following,

a folk hero must embody traits and values they applaud, but whether he is historical or fictional does not affect the issue. Paul Bunyan gets disqualified as a genuine folk hero of north-woods lumberjacks, not because he never existed as a flesh-and-blood person, but because folklore collectors—including myself—have discovered that lumberjacks very rarely tell Bunyan tales. Rather they spin anecdotes about the lumber-camp bosses, who are their real folk heroes. Whether the folk hero is launched from a historical or an imaginary base, he ends up with fairly uniform lineaments. Legends alter and reshape the personage from history to suit the folk imagination, while a historical setting forms around the created figure who will be regarded by the folk as a real-life superman. Scholars themselves disagree on whether the great heroes and demigods of the world's mythologies ever lived.

Crockett, Fink, Patch, Mose, and Jonathan each embodied a generic class that had evolved in the young republic: Crockett the backwoodsmen, Fink the keelboatmen, Patch the mill hands, Mose the city toughs, Jonathan the New England rustic farmers. Impersonators of these characters studied the environments from which they grew to ensure the accuracy of their portrayals. Francis Chanfrau, the actor who scored such a success with his characterization of Mose, based the role on an actual Bowery b'hoy, Moses Humphreys. Celebrated Yankee actors such as George H. "Yankee" Hill and Dan Marble visited New England towns to mingle with and observe the speech and behavior patterns of Down East originals. All five folk personalities attracted attention, not because of their uniqueness, but because of their representativeness of hitherto unrecognized American types, anonymous democrats who had developed their own peculiar ways and talk. As the drama reviewer of the *New York Herald* commented after seeing a Mose play, Mose perfectly depicted a certain class of person in New York known to the general public only through the records of the Court of Sessions.

As for the popularity of the folk hero, we must recognize that it begins with his own constituency, whose viewpoint he expresses. The outside world may know little of him, and what it knows may be inflamed by third-hand rumor and the coloring of hostile or threatened reporters. To take two outlaw heroes from the late nineteenth century, Jesse James and Billy the Kid, we perceive a sharp clash of opinion as to their merits. Midwest farmers liked Jesse because he only robbed banks and gave to the poor, and they hated Billy the Kid as a sadistic gunman and pariah. Southwest cowpunchers admired the Kid because he fought for the open range, and they despised Jesse as a money-mad robber. Or take today's generations, among whom Abbie Hoffman and Jerry Rubin attract a cult following of hippies and Yippies and at the same time receive choice opprobrious epithets from Middle America. For the folk hero to really make his mark he must broaden his support to include other than his own immediate constituency, and this is what happened in the 1830s, 40s, and 50s with our quintet of potential demigods. Their feats, escapades, and mannerisms appealed to ever-widening audiences. Theatrical touring companies presented farces and melodramas around the

country that introduced these local and regional types to the American people. We can appreciate the ripples of apprehension that preceded the arrival of Mose in the hinterland, the moment of truth when an audience faced him for the first time, and its enthusiastic reception of the Bowery buffoon, in a series of Louisville, Kentucky playbills (quoted below) announcing the coming and conquest of Mose. The advance bills seek to allay alarms about the character of Mose, whom they praise as a goldenhearted hero in spite of his rough exterior, and notices subsequent to the first performance report that the theatergoers have indeed appreciated Mose's sterling qualities. In the Yankee plays we see Jonathan ascend from secondary roles as a comical servant to stage center as a doughty and heroic swashbuckler. After his death Sam Patch reappeared in larger outlines on stage in the re-enactments of Dan Marble, not as an oddity, but as a daring spirit worthy of attention and emulation.

In the United States of the decades between the War of 1812 and the Civil War the sense of nationalism had overtaken the pull of localism. Her citizens, more mobile now thanks to turnpikes, steamboats, and the railroad, knit together by the waging of two wars, and looking ever more to the federal government rather than the state governments, welcomed a knowledge of regional characters from other parts of the land. They relished common elements in these novel character types: the good-humored metaphoric brag, the tall-tale deeds, the sly trickery, the idiom, the costume, the perkiness of slattern democrats thumbing their noses at Establishment aristocrats. So regional characters acquired national support, although the supercilious would always sneer.

Finally there is the question of oral legendry. In the cases of Crockett and

Fink, observers did set down anecdotes and legends about them, and Davy had a hand in autobiographical writings in which he retold some of his own personal narratives. The folklorist can test these literary and subliterary versions and determine their traditional nature, and they are indeed traditional, clearly derived from oral sources. For the Yankee, while I have relied here mainly on the plays that portrayed him as a comic hero, there exists also in similar vein a large body of newspaper yarns and sketches, which I have tapped elsewhere, in my *Jonathan Draws the Long Bow,* and they are demonstrably close to spoken oral anecdotes. Yankee comedians often engaged in humorous monologues between the acts in which they related Yankee stories, after the fashion of raconteurs in country stores and taverns.

As for Mose and Sam Patch, their legends lie in old files of newspaper publicity and in flimsy dramas, which do not satisfy the folklorist. But the itinerant theatrical troupes and grassroots newspaper editors of pre-Civil War days often drew from and fed directly into folk tradition. When media so close to the people gave so much attention to these characters drawn from the people, we can be sure their antics and sayings traveled on many lips. Indeed, the sources say so. Hawthorne and Howells knew of Patch, and newsboys talked of Mose. No folklore collectors noted tales about Sam Patch and Mose in the 1830s and 1840s, but they did in the twentieth century. Gathering material for a book on New York's underworld at the time of World War I, Herbert Asbury heard fabulous legends about Big Mose from old Bowery bums, which he subsequently printed. Herbert Wisbey, in the *New York Folklore Quarterly,* states that he has heard many oral anecdotes about Sam, who is yet today "bigger than life to the common folk of upstate New York."[3] No more dramatic testimony could be produced than this evidence of the continuing oral vitality of the Patch and Mose legends among their constituencies. So too with the others: Ozarkers still yarn about Davy Crockett, Pennsylvania rivermen about Mike Fink, back-country farm folk about Yankee characters.

These are the trickles of a once gushing torrent of twice-told legendary anecdotes about America's first folk heroes sprung from the people.

Davy Crockett the backwoodsman

In the fall of 1821 a tall, black-haired hunter and trapper from the canebrake country of west Tennessee took a seat in the Fourteenth General Assembly of the Tennessee state legislature, convening at Murfreesboro. The newcomer, David Crockett, soon acquired the cognomen of the "gentleman from the cane" and a reputation for storytelling to make his point. On one occasion, the legislators were debating a bill to create a county, and Crockett became locked in controversy with the author of the bill over where to run the boundary line. Finally the gentleman from the cane rose and delivered the following speech:

"David Crockett, with signed endorsement: 'I am happy to acknowledge this is to be the only correct likeness that has been taken of me.'"

S. S. Osgood, from Harry T. Peters, *America on Stone*

Mr. Speaker,—Do you know what that man's bill reminds me of? Well, I 'spose you don't, so I'll tell you. Well, Mr. Speaker, when I first come to this country, a blacksmith was a rare thing; but there happened to be one in my neighborhood: he had no striker, and whenever one of the neighbors wanted any work done, he had to go over and strike till his work was finished. These were hard times, Mr. Speaker, but we had to do the best we could.

It happened that one of my neighbors wanted an axe, so he took along with him a piece of iron, and went over to the blacksmith's to strike till his axe was done. The iron was heated, and my neighbor fell to work, and was striking there nearly all day; when the blacksmith concluded the iron wouldn't make an axe, but 'twould make a fine mattock. So my neighbor wanting a mattock, concluded he would go over and strike till his mattock was done. Accordingly, he went over the next day, and worked faithfully; but towards night the blacksmith concluded his iron wouldn't make a mattock but 'twould make a fine ploughshare. So my neighbor wanting a ploughshare, agreed that he would go over the next day and strike till that was done. Accordingly, he again went over and fell hard to work; but towards night the blacksmith concluded his iron wouldn't make a ploughshare, but 'twould make a fine *skow*. So my neighbor, tired working, cried, "A skow let it be." And the blacksmith taking up the red hot iron, threw it into a trough of water near him, and as it fell in, it sung out *"skow."*

And this, Mr. Speaker, will be the way with that man's bill for a county. He'll keep you all here doing nothing, and finally his bill will turn out a *skow,* now mind if it don't.[4]

This anecdotal speech appeared in 1833 in a book that solidified Crockett's reputation as a character and an "original," *The Life and Adventures of Colonel David Crockett of West Tennessee,* published in Cincinnati but reprinted the same year in New York under its best-known title, *Sketches and Eccentricities of Col. David Crockett of West Tennessee.* Stories attributed to Crockett lard the work, and their narration formed a vital part of his electioneering and legislative technique, for he would relax his listeners with a good yarn, capture their attention, and sometimes apply the moral of his tale to the political issue at hand. Lincoln would employ this technique with still greater effectiveness. From where did the backwoods congressman obtain his stories? In good part from the floating store of anecdotal legends to which master storytellers everywhere have access. Often the folkloric nature of a given tale is not immediately apparent, and only in recent years has the pattern of the skowmaker narration come to light.

Curiously, the analogue to the skowmaker surfaced in World War II in a "true" incident that was widely repeated in variant forms. A navy recruit signs up as a kleshmaker. None of the navy brass want to admit their ignorance of his function, so he goldbricks comfortably until one day an officer requests that he make a klesh. The recruit asks for an iron rod four inches square and twelve feet long, locks himself in the ship's foundry, and pounds away for a full day. At length he cries out "Gangway," staggers up the deck holding the white-hot iron rod in front of him, beaten into the shape of a giant pretzel, and tosses it over the railing, where it lands in the sea with a hissing noise—"Kallesh!"[5]

In my folklore classes at Michigan State University from 1951 to 1954, students, reporting versions of the "skow" tale known to them, told of a galoop, gleek, glug, kaplush, daswish, sloosch, lush, spooch, and squish maker.[6] Some of these navy specialists display considerable ingenuity. The squishmaker requests that a tank half a mile in diameter be filled with water and that a crane be constructed big enough to lift an airplane. Then he orders the crane's crew to hoist and suspend the airplane over the tank, and upon his signal to release the flying machine into the water. In it falls—"Squish!" By contrast, the galoop maker, who eventually gets promoted to vice-admiral, opens a box he has kept close to his person, inside which is another box and inside that a smaller box, until he reaches a matchbox. He opens the matchbox, which is lined and padded so that nothing can happen to the contents. Inside the box are two steel balls the size of marbles. The admiral lifts them out and drops them over the side of the ship one at a time: "Galoop, galoop."

Clearly this series of hoax-tales and Crockett's skowmaker yarn belong to the same family of folk narratives. They deal with a charlatan who associates an object he pretends to be making with the sound that object produces when dropped into water. The World War II version elevates the charlatan into a trickster-hero who gulls the navy brass, whereas Crockett exposes the duplicity of the blacksmith and likens his false promises to the claims being made by his legislative opponent. In the scene in the Tennessee legislative chamber we see foreshadowed the elements that would coalesce to help create a new model for the American folk hero, a man sprung from the people, participating actively in the democratic process, and larding his speeches with jokes, stories, and salty sayings in the popular idiom, rather than in pompous rhetoric, to win support for his issues. In short order Crockett became a subject as well as a vendor of humorous tales.

David Crockett was born in east Tennessee in 1786, on the edge of the American frontier. His grandparents had been killed by Creek and Cherokee Indians nine years before. John Crockett, David's father, tried his hand with little success at running a mill, homesteading, and keeping a tavern. In 1811 David began the moves that would land him in the forests of west Tennessee, forty miles from a settlement, the region with which he would be identified politically. He tried farming but preferred hunting deer, elk, raccoon, wolf, panther, turkey, and bear, and fought Indians under Andrew Jackson in the Creek Wars of 1813–1814. In 1816 he was appointed justice of the peace, in 1821 he was elected to the state legislature, and in 1827 he ran on a dare for the national Congress, winning and being re-elected in 1829 and 1833. When he broke with Jackson in 1829 by proposing a bill to make public land available cheap to poor squatters, the Whigs adopted him enthusiastically, but Crockett lost a portion of his constituency. After his defeat in the campaign of 1834 he went to Texas to fight in its cause against Mexico and was killed at the siege of the Alamo in 1836.

Writing in 1893 on "The Signifi-

"Fall of the Alamo—Death of Crockett"
From *Davy Crockett's Almanack, 1837*

cance of the Frontier in American History," Frederick Jackson Turner hailed the frontier as the seedbed of American democracy. David Crockett perfectly exemplifies the democratic qualities of the frontier in both its political and its social sides. With little schooling, he relied on "natural-born sense instead of law learning" and quoted homely proverbs rather than legal precedents to buttress his position. When he emerged from the canebrakes into the halls of the Tennessee legislature and was twitted by a fashionably dressed legislator, David pinned a cambric ruffle, which had been torn off the shirt of his ridiculer, onto his own coarse tow shirt, and appearing this way in the House, dissolved the membership in laughter and compelled his critic to retire in confusion.[7] The incident typified Crockett's disdain of aristocratic values and determination to "stand up to his lick log, salt or no salt," that is, to insist on his egalitarian rights and merits. "Democracy and the 'far-west' made Colonel Crockett," an English observer noted in 1839. "He is a product of forests, freedom, universal suffrage, and bear-hunts."[8]

Turner emphasized the democratic values and behavior stimulated by the frontier environment, where each man stood on his own feet and asked no questions about his neighbor's past, but a corollary of the Turner thesis can stress the legend-building tendencies of frontier settlements. Lacking the educational institutions of the settled East—colleges, printing presses, urban centers—the backwoods country developed a largely oral culture, with analogies to the heroic ages of civilizations with long histories. From these heroic ages evolved, as the Chadwicks have documented in their great comparative study *The Growth of Literature,* illustrious champions who would be celebrated in lays, legends, and folk epics. Davy Crockett and Mike Fink belong to the same heroic company as Achilles, Beowulf, Siegfried, and Grettir.

The canebrake country in which Crockett lived and hunted was locally known as the Shakes, from shattering earthquakes and hurricanes that had struck this land east of the Mississippi, particularly between 1811 and 1813. These blows of nature had dammed rivers, created giant fissures in the earth, and splintered forest trees in all directions. Forbidding to man, this tangle of fallen trees, undergrowth, and ravines attracted game of all sorts, and proved to hardy backwoodsmen a hunter's paradise.[9]

Conditions for a heroic age and an oral culture may exist, but at some point a bard or Boswell must write down the saga. In Crockett's case, newspapers first carried choice anecdotes attributed to him, then publications issued in his name captured them in more permanent form.

The best evidence for the oral folk tradition surrounding Crockett lies in the book that confirmed his national celebrity, *The Life and Adventures of Colonel David Crockett of West Tennessee.* Published anonymously in 1833 as a campaign document to aid him in running for Congress on the Whig ticket, the *Life* appealed hugely to an audience already familiar with the backwoods politician through newspaper and word-of-mouth stories. The author is conjectured to be Mathew St. Clair Clarke, who was clerk of the House of Representatives from 1832 to 1833, a writer as well as a staunch Whig, and an intimate of Crockett.[10] Actually Clarke served less as an author than as a compiler of tales allegedly told by the "colonel" and quoted in his own words, and of anecdotes circulating about the backwoodsman.

The *Life* was a nonbook, and is best understood as a partial transcript of the comic legend that grew around Crockett. It shares the legend with *The Lion of the West,* the play written in 1830 by James K. Paulding around the character Nimrod Wildfire, a stage representation of Crockett; with the *Autobiography* written in 1834 by Thomas Chilton, a Whig congressman from Kentucky, in collaboration with Crockett; and with the series of Crockett almanacs issued annually from 1835 to 1856. All dipped into the same body of oral frontier tradition and used the same themes and even the same tales, sayings, and boasts. But the *Life* reproduced most faithfully the spoken yarns that stimulated subliterary extensions.

The *Life* merely pretended to give a life story of Crockett. Initial chapters present in stilted and artificial language some episodes of Crockett's boyhood. Only when the adult Crockett comes to view and starts narrating in the first person does the work begin to breathe. The yarns Crockett tells fall into three groups: realistic and spine-tingling relations of bear, elk, and panther hunts; comic pieces in "Dutch" (actually German) dialect; and humorous fiction, both anecdotes and tall tales, of the frontier. In addition Clarke alludes to and paraphrases stories being told about Crockett that stress his original

and fabulous characteristics. Clarke often makes the point that Crockett was a natural raconteur and employed his gift (like Lincoln) for political ends. "While electioneering, the colonel always conciliates every crowd into which he may be thrown by the narration of some anecdote"; "He has lived almost entirely in the woods, and his life has been a continued scene of anecdote to one fond of hairbreadth escapes and hunting stories"; "He was ever the humorous hero of his own story. . . ."[11] Not only could Crockett narrate with flair and relish, but he would also portray himself triumphing over his detractors, or falling into predicaments, as have other folk storytellers who have fostered their own legends.

The hunting stories were not folktales, although some stretched credulity. They described crisply and suspensefully Crockett's trailing a tough bear with his dogs for hours in the cold of night, finally cornering the beast up a tree or down a hole, and giving him the *coup de grâce* with his knife. A sportsman or even an indoorsman tingles at these narrations, and they appealed to a staunch audience in the ante-bellum decades. Correspondents in the Old Southwest sent in many factual hunting sketches to the New York *Spirit of the Times,* the best-known sporting weekly of its day. Although realistic enough, these yarns did contribute to the legend of Crockett in providing the basic character of the backwoodsman as a hunter and sharpshooter. One hunting narrative does contain a hint of supernaturalism out of keeping with the realism and comedy of backwoods yarnspinning. David hunted bear instead of turkey because he had dreamed the night before of "a hard fight with a big black nigger, and I knowed it was a sign that I was to have a battle with a bear; for in a bear country, I never know'd such a

dream to fail."[12] In the *Life* Clarke delineated a shooting match in the Western country of the sort that delighted the hunters of Kentucky and Tennessee, a match in which Crockett manifested an easy skill and poise. From extraordinary truth to fabulous untruth in hunting and shooting stories was an easy step for the almanac and newspaper writers. The supreme fiction of the Southern humorists, Thomas Bangs Thorpe's "The Big Bear of Arkansas," raised the bear-hunt story to the plane of extravaganza. "In b'ar hunts I am numerous," said Jim Doggett, the backwoods Arkansawyer regaling the steamboat crowd, and launched into his tale of an unhuntable bear, much like the hunts of Crockett, but fantasized still further.

The Dutch dialect stories, inserted into the *Life* without any special justification, puzzle the modern historian and critic, but they are readily explained by the folklorist. When making a field trip to the Upper Peninsula of Michigan in 1946 I encountered a ubiquitous form of oral storytelling which depended for its humorous effect upon the mispronunciation and malapropisms of immigrants to the United States speaking English as a late second language. Each prominent ethnic group generated its own brand of dialect story. The Finns, the French Canadians, the Cornish, the Swedes, the Italians, talked in distinctive ways, according to the relation of their mother tongue to English. Native-born Americans mimicked these lingoes and built them into anecdotes, short and long, incorporating not only language mistakes but also cultural mishaps. A favorite story, known in several lingoes, deals with the immigrant who goes to his first baseball game and is mystified by what he observes. The dialect story is a characteristic American phenomenon, because of the juxtaposition of ethnic minorities within the dominant English-speaking population. So the Jewish story in the East, the Mexican story in the Southwest, the Pat and Mike story that burgeoned after the Irish immigration of the 1850s, all represent the same folktale pattern. To an audience familiar with the particular speaking style of the immigrant group, the dialect mimicry is hilarious. Clearly a German lingo had caught on in Davy Crockett's backwoods (the Germans were called Dutchmen from their own word for themselves, *Deutsche*). The Hans Breitmann ballads of Charles Godfrey Leland, first issued in 1857, exploited the same vein.

The *Life* presents three of Crockett's Dutchman stories in excellent texts that reproduce phonetically the comic verbal errors. In one a Dutchman tells how he set a fox trap to catch a "tam harricoon" (damn raccoon) that had picked the hair out of the backs of his "hinkles" (hens). The Dutchman catches the animal, and finds he is black and white and spotted, "an I hits him a lick and if he lif he tail up, and don't you tink I smelt him?" The raccoon was a skunk. This is the true dialect yarn, with the humor both of speech and mishap, linked to an ethnic fool character. The printed page can only suggest the oral delivery of the dialect story, or of any story for that matter, and it is further evidence of the oral tradition behind these texts that the *Life* describes Crockett as telling one anecdote in the "loud swelling language of the young Dutchman."[13]

Besides the hunting and the dialect stories, Crockett related, and others related about him, humorous fictions popular in the back country: tall tales, trickster anecdotes, Yankee yarns. These veins of frontier comedy formed a new body of American folk humor coming into view in the early years of the republic and reflecting the naturalistic, secular, and regional characteristics of the trans-Appalachian West.

The best-known anecdote attached to Crockett concerns his deception with a coonskin. Even the author of the *Life* admits he does not altogether credit its truth. While electioneering the colonel, as was his wont, offered to treat the company. In lieu of hard or paper money, animal skins served as common currency in the backwoods. A coonskin purchased a quart of whiskey, but when he was alone Crockett, frugal in his spending, carried hareskins to buy half-pints. On this occasion he threw the one coonskin he possessed on the counter and liberally called for its value in whiskey. The merchant measured out the whiskey and threw the skin up into the loft. Seeing space between the logs, the colonel pulled out his ramrod and, when the merchant's back was turned, twisted the coonskin out and put it back in his pocket. He kept repeating this trick until the crowd was well liquored up.[14]

This slight incident becomes considerably elaborated in the *Autobiography,* and is credited with securing Crockett his first election to Congress, when he was still pro-Jackson. David tells how he started off to the Cross Roads, dressed in his hunting shirt, with his rifle on his shoulder. His opponent had already attracted a crowd with his "speechifying" and treating, but Crockett's appearance drew off a number who congregated around the colonel as he mounted a stump and began to "bush-

"The Way They Travel in the West"
From *The Crockett Almanac 1840*

whack." But soon his constituents drowned out his oratory with pleas for "thirst quenchers." The colonel led them to a shanty erected by one Job Snelling, "a gander-shanked Yankee, who had been caught somewhere about Plymouth Bay, and been shipped to the west with a cargo of codfish and rum."[15]

The unidentified merchant of the *Life* takes on mythological detail in the *Autobiography.* Job Snelling is the sly Yankee peddler of a thousand tavern yarns, knockabout farces, and homespun aphorisms in the first half-century of the republic. Taking his gimcrackery and his wiles to the Western clearings, he confronts the Salt River roarer in a clash of young America's two most prominent regional types, the crafty Down Easter and the ebullient Westerner. The *Autobiography* gives a thumbnail sketch of Job Snelling that synopsizes the legend of the peddling Yankee and his breed:

Job was by no means popular; he boasted of always being wide awake, and that any one who could take him in was free to do so, for he came from a stock, that sleeping or waking had always one eye open, and the other not more than half closed.

The whole family were geniuses. His father was the inventor of wooden nutmegs, by which Job said he might have made a fortune, if he had only taken out a patent and kept the business in his own hands. His mother Patience manufactured the first white oak pumpkin seeds of the mammoth kind, and turned a pretty penny the first season. And his aunt Prudence was the first to discover that corn husks, steeped into tobacco water, would make as handsome Spanish wrappers as ever came from Havanna, and that oak leaves would answer all the purpose of filling, for no one could discover the difference except the man who smoked them, and then it would be too late to make a stir about it.

Job, himself, bragged of having made some useful discoveries; the most profitable of which was the art of converting mahogany sawdust into cayenne pepper, which he said was a profitable and safe business; for the people have been so long accustomed to having dust thrown in their eyes, that there wasn't much danger of being found out.[16]

This was the character with whom the aspiring politician from the cane now had to deal. The indigent colonel entered the shanty, followed by his constituents hollering "Huzza for Crockett" and "Crockett forever," and ordered a quart of Job's best rum. Job, who was busy with other customers, simply pointed to a sign over the bar, *"Pay to-day and trust to-morrow."* Discomfited, for ready money in the West was then "the shyest thing in all natur," the colonel withdrew and his fickle followers left him. Walking into the woods with his rifle on his shoulder, he shot and skinned a fat coon and returned with it to Job's shanty. Jauntily he threw the skin on the counter, ordered his quart of liquor, and soon had the crowd drinking and laughing at his stories. When the quart ran out, one constituent moved that Crockett postpone the balance of his speech until after the crowd had washed down the first part with more of Job Snelling's "extract of cornstalk and molasses." In this predicament, Crockett caught sight of one end of the coonskin sticking out between the logs that supported the bar. He jerked it up and slapped it on the counter again. In the course of the day he obtained ten quarts of rum the same way.

The surge in Crockett's popularity that resulted came, so he claimed, not from the satisfaction of the immediate crowd whose thirst he had slaked, but from the larger body of his constituents who were delighted to hear that Crockett had outwitted the Yankee "in fair trade." If he could handle Job Snelling, he could take on Old Nick himself, they believed. Crockett wrote that after the election he offered to pay Job for the price of the rum but Job refused payment, saying it sharpened his ideas to be taken in occasionally, and that in any case he had added the bill to the account of Crockett's opponent at the hustings.

There are several noteworthy aspects to this story. It links Crockett to electioneering, and to the most grass-roots, democratic kind of electioneering. To get liquored up, to tell yarns, and then to debate the issues: such was the spirit of the American *demos,* and Crockett epitomized it perfectly. Further, this

was the most popular and the most characteristic story attached to Crockett. It was told about him, he told it on himself, and it has been told on others; it is a widespread American folktale, in the form of a legendary anecdote. Among all the variant texts, the case of Crockett is the only one that ties the deception to political campaigning. Otherwise the story recounts a good-natured jape played by a local wag on an unsuspecting storekeeper.

The anecdote of the coonskin trick has traveled around America. A version antedating Crockett's by a year amused soldiers in Fort Brooke, Georgia, where a Negro lad sold the same pair of terrapins ten times to the same officer.[17] Mark Twain attached the sell to Tom Blankenship, the original Huck Finn, in Hannibal, Missouri.[18] The tale lives on today in various back corners of the nation. In the Ozarks two brothers named Turner rode into a trading post at Poncey, in the days when cash was scarce and storekeepers traded for furs and bear oil and ginseng roots. They threw a coonskin on the counter, ate its worth in sardines and crackers and cheese, and left. Later they came in again with another coonskin, consumed some whiskey, and picked out candy and tobacco. And still a third time they returned with a coonskin, and drank it up in nightcaps. After they left, the storekeeper went to the back room and found only one coonskin, and when he noticed a loose board and a piece of wire, he realized how the Turners had conned him. Yet, like Job Snelling, the Ozark storekeeper harbored no ill will, saying the Turners could have lifted his far more valuable mink skins, and he laughed at the joke as part of the games people played on tradesmen.[19]

In the rural region of southern Illinois known as "Egypt," the coonskin deception has lived orally for a century and a half. One story dates back to the War of 1812 when frontiersmen traded at general stores with pelts of raccoon, mink, deer, and other animals. A crowd of convivial spirits in Bond County tricked the tipsy grocery keeper very much as had Crockett, except that a whole group was involved in the chicanery. The same incident supposedly transpired also in Saline and Williamson counties.[20] Local people in Carrier Mills in Saline County refer to the town as "Catskin" in memory of the dodge of a thirsty citizen who first palmed off a catskin as a mink skin on the merchant and then retrieved the catskin and repeated the sell. Carrier Mills then consisted solely of a country store, which the pioneers thereafter called Catskin.[21] The substitution of a catskin for a mink skin to dupe a storekeeper has its own anecdotal history.[22] In some tellings an object other than an animal skin is repeatedly traded for drinks. A Wisconsin version has a woodsman entering a saloon with a bundle of laths, which he gives the bartender in exchange for liquor. Leaving, he takes the bundle with him surreptitiously and deposits it outside, whereupon another bully boy picks it up and enters to quench his thirst, and so on until the whole group has drunk well.[23] In a related deception told in Alberta, Canada, a man collects bounty on the same pack of stray dogs day after day.[24]

And here in my own newspaper, the *Indianapolis Star* for May 12, 1971, a front-page headline reads, "Donkey Dealer Denies Dirty Dealings," and a smaller, equally enigmatic caption teases the reader: "Same Steed Said Sold 9 Times." Reprinted from the *Los Angeles Times,* and originating in Rio de Janeiro, the story runs as follows:

E verybody knew that Silvio Deolindo De Carvalho—known as "he of the donkeys"—sold some of the best horses and donkeys you could find.

The trouble was, say police, he sold them again and again and again—the same donkeys and horses. He reportedly even sold one donkey nine times—twice to the same buyer!

De Carvalho has denied the charges, but police will go ahead with the case. They say he stole at least 50 horses and donkeys and resold them.

When he was charged officially, more than 20 people turned up at the local police office where he was being held to press the charges against him.

One of De Carvalho's top moneymakers, police charge, was a donkey called Ioio (pronounced Yo-Yo). This donkey was so fond of De Carvalho it would follow him everywhere.

All he had to do was sell it, and then pass by the house of the man to whom he had sold it. He did not have to steal Ioio back. It recognized him and came trotting after him.

One man told police he bought the donkey, which was a very fine animal, but it disappeared soon afterward.

A long time later, De Carvalho told him he had another animal for sale, again a fine animal. But after he had bought it, the man realized it was the same animal he had bought the first time.

Now of course De Carvalho could have perpetrated the resale of the same donkey, and Davy Crockett could have bought drinks with the same coonskin, and all the other tricksters could have sold the same animals back to their owners. They *could have,* but the folklorist knows they never did.

An incident less publicized than the coonskin trick which shows Crockett in the same trickster role enabled him to defeat his opponent for Congress, Adam Huntsman, in 1833. "Peg-leg" Huntsman had one wooden leg, a fact that Davy put to his own advantage one night when the two were campaigning together. They had stopped at the house of a well-to-do farmer who was pro–Andrew Jackson and for Huntsman, since Davy by this time had broken with the president. After all had retired, Crockett rose from the shed room in which he and Huntsman were sleeping, opened the door, and carrying a chair, walked stealthily the length of a porch to another shed room where the farmer's daughter snoozed. He then seemingly attempted to force the door. The noise awoke the girl, who screamed lustily. Crockett grasped the chair by the back, placed his foot on the lower crosspiece, and using the chair as a leg, thumped his way back to his room, dropped the chair, scrambled into bed, and began snoring at high volume.

In a moment the farmer burst into the room and threatened to murder Huntsman, who vehemently protested his innocence to no avail. "Oh, you can't fool me," shouted the farmer. "I know you too well, and heard that darned old peg leg of yourn too plain."

Consequently the farmer, and a number of others to whom he reported the incident, switched their votes from Huntsman to Crockett, who won the election. Huntsman might not have run again had not Davy considered the joke too good to keep.[25] So Huntsman did electioneer in 1835 and defeated Crockett, who allegedly then said his constituents could go to hell and he would go to Texas.

In perpetrating the coonskin and the simulated peg-leg tricks, Crockett exhibited the trait of craftiness and deception ordinarily associated with the Yankee, his opposite number in the newly burgeoning pantheon of democratic folk heroes. The backwoodsman was reputedly a hunter, an Indian fighter, a marksman, a boaster; the Yankee was supposedly "cute," cunning, wily, scheming, artful, traditionally a peddler. Yet their characters partially overlapped, and the backwoodsman could deceive while the Yankee could brag. In another much-talked-about episode that Crockett related on himself, he retrieved a situation in a shooting match in which, after having scored with a bull's-eye on the first round, he completely missed the target on the second. The colonel then risked loss of face before the electorate of Little Rock, Arkansas, who were tendering him a public dinner and had come to see his vaunted marksmanship: As usual in his personal accounts of his

They examined it [the target] all over, and could find neither hair nor hide of my bullet, and pronounced it a dead miss; when says I, "Stand aside and let me look, and I warrant you I get on the right trail of the critter." They stood aside, and I examined the bull's eye pretty particular, and at length cried out, "Here it is; there is no snakes if it ha'n't followed the very track of the other." They said it was utterly impossible, but I insisted on their searching the hole, and I agreed to be stuck up as a mark myself, if they did not find two bullets there. They searched for my satisfaction, and sure enough it all come out just as I had told them; for I had picked up a bullet that had been fired, and stuck it deep into the hole, without any one perceiving it. They were all perfectly satisfied, that fame had not made too great a flourish of trumpets when speaking of me as a marksman; and they all said they had enough of shooting for that day, and they moved that we adjourn to the tavern and liquor.[26]

exploits, Crockett emerges the victor, but he is the clever Odysseus rather than the powerful Achilles. The colonel could perform a Yankee trick as well as any Down Easter.

The legendary career of Davy Crockett moved through several phases. It began in his role of backwoods storyteller-politician. In this phase he attracted attention from his constituency by his gift for telling anecdotal folktales of the kind appreciated in that region and era. Master narrators bloom in every culture, but their reputation as storytellers does not confer on them the status of folk heroes. But if the raconteur is also a character and a personality in his own right, he may well move toward stardom. He inserts himself into the folktale and tells it as a personal adventure, as did Baron Münchausen and Gib Morgan,

Vol. I. "*Go Ahead!*" No. 3.

Davy Crockett's
1$ ALMANACK, 37
OF WILD SPORTS IN THE WEST.
Life in the Backwoods, & Sketches of Texas.

O KENTUCKY! THE HUNTERS OF KENTUCKY!!!
Nashville, Tennessee. Published by the heirs of Col. Crockett.

Cover page of a Crockett almanac

the minstrel of the oil fields, and so stimulates his own legend. Other raconteurs repeat the tales he broadcasts about himself (as also happened with the Baron and Gib). Finally, a separate body of legends can be told about and attributed to the colorful figure. In most of the world's folklore, heroes inspire rather than relate tales. All three processes operated in the case of Crockett.

In the books and almanacs relating his supposed adventures, we see the double perspective, as Davy is now the storyteller and again the story subject. After his death in action, the oral and written traditions about him multiplied, in the series of Crockett almanacs (1835-1856) with their woodcuts of Davy in backwoods scenes, and in humorous songs brought together in 1839 in *Crockett's Free-and-Easy Song Book*. Meanwhile James H. Hackett kept impersonating Davy as Nimrod Wildfire in *The Lion of the West* through the 1840s and 1850s, and Chicagoans saw the play as late as 1858. Here is the third phase of Crockett's folkloric history: popular literature written about him, rather than folk anecdotes told by him, or told by others about him. A shift takes place from oral tradition to popular culture, and in the character of Crockett from the backwoods trickster-humorist-stump orator to an all-conquering and globe-circling ringtailed roarer. In this shift, while the legend becomes more grandiose, its folk basis diminishes. Hack writers in Eastern cities hammered out fanciful escapades for the annual almanac issues. Davy climbs the lightning and greases it with a bottle of rattlesnake tallow; he sails up Niagara Falls on the back of an alligator; he outdives pearl divers off

"Come back, stranger! or I'll plug you like a watermillion!"
James H. Hackett as Nimrod Wildfire, the stage likeness of Davy Crockett
From the original painting by A. Andrews

the Japanese coast and dances a Kentucky hornpipe on the oyster beds; he climbs the peak of Daybreak Hill, greases the earth's frozen axis with bear's fat, and snatches a piece of sunrise to take back down as fuel for cooking his bear steaks. And everywhere he fights, wrestles, shoots, and conquers men—Injuns, blacks, squatters, Pukes, Mexicans, dandies, cannibals—and beasts—b'ars, panthers, snakes, moose, wolves. The almanac yarns constitute a subliterature rather than a folklore. But they represent a transition, not a sharp break. Crockett of the *Sketches* and the *Autobiography* had delivered frontier boasts, and after his death Westerners kept repeating these boasts. An English traveler, Captain R. C. A. Levinge, noted some when he visited Louisville in 1839:

E verything here is Davy Crockett. He was a member of Congress. His voice was so rough it could not be described—it was obliged to

be drawn as a picture. He took hailstones for "Life Pills" when he was unwell—he picked his teeth with a pitchfork—combed his hair with a rake—fanned himself with a hurricane, wore a cast-iron shirt, and drank nothing but creosote and aquafortis. . . . He could whip his weight in wildcats—drink the Mississippi dry—shoot six cord of bear in one day—and, as his countrymen say of themselves, he could jump higher, dive deeper, and come up dryer than any one else. . . . he could slide down the slippery end of a rainbow, and was half-horse, half-alligator and a bit of snapping turtle.[27]

In the realm of hunting narratives, the *Crockett Almanac* for 1840 carried the following adventure of Davy with a bear, which presents a possible, if out of the ordinary, kind of scrape:

COLONEL CROCKETT AND THE BEAR AND THE SWALLOWS

People tell a great many silly stories about swallows. Some say that if you kill one your cows will give bloody milk, and others tell as how they fly away in the fall and come back again in the spring, when the leaves of the white oaks are jest as big as a mouse's ear. Again, there are some that tell how they keep Christmas and New Year's among the little fishes, at the bottom of some pond; but you may tell all them that sez so they are dratted fools and don't know nothing about the matter. Swallows sleep all winter in the holler of some old rotten sycamore, and I'll tell you how I come to find it out.

I was out early in the spring with my rifle on the banks of the Tennessee, making up my opinion about matters and things in general, when all of a sudden I heard a clap of thunder, and that set me a-thinking. "Now," sez I, "if I were to go home and tell of that the boys would think me a d——d liar, if they didn't dare to call me so; for who ever heard of such a thing as thunder under a clear sky of a bright spring day." And with that I looked up, and again I heard the thunder, but it was not thunder anyhow I could fix it; for a hull swarm of swallows come bodily out of an old hollow sycamore, and it was the noise they made with the flapping of their wings.

Now I thought to myself that them ar little varmints were doing some mischief in the tree, and that it were my duty to see into it. For you see just then I felt hugeously grandiferous, for the neighbors had made me a justice of the peace.

So I cut down a sapling with my knife and set it agin the tree and clum up like a squirrel; for you know a sycamore has a smooth bark. As I were bending over the edge of the holler to look down, the sapling broke under me, and trying to catch at something I lost my balance and fell down into the tree head foremost. When I got to the bottom I found myself a little the nastiest critter ever you saw, on account of the swallow's dung, and how to get out I didn't know; for the hole was deep, and when I looked up I could see the stars out of the top.

Presently I put my hand into some thing as soft as a feather bed, and I heard an awful growling, so that I thought it was the last trump sounding to fall in and dress to the right for the day of judgment. But it was only an old b'ar I woke out of his winter nap, and I out "Butcher" [Crockett's knife] to see which were the best man. But

"Col. Crockett and the Bear and the Swallows"
From *The Crockett Almanac 1840*

the critter was clean amazed and seemed to like my room better than my company and made a bolt to get out of the scrape, most cowardly.

"Hollo, stranger!" sez I, "we don't part company without having a fair shake for a fight." And so, saving your presence, I clenched hold both his posterities. But finding the hair was like to give way I got hold of his stump of a tail with my teeth, and then I had him fast enough. But still he kept on climbing up the holler, and I begun to sorter like the idea; for you know he couldn't get up without pulling me up after him. So when he begun to get tired, I quickened his pace with an awful fundamental poke with my Butcher, jest by way of a gentle hint. Before long we got to the top of the tree, and then I got to the ground quicker than he did, seeing he come down tail foremost. I got my shooting iron to be ready for him.

But he kinder seemed to got enough to my company, and went off squealing as if something ailed his hinter parts, which I thought a kind of curious; for I've no opinion of a fellow that will take a kick, much less such usage as I give him. However, I let him go; for it would be unmanly to be unthankful for the service he done me, and for all I know he's alive yet. And it was not the only thing I had to thank him for, I had a touch of the toothache before, and the bite I got at his tail cured me entirely. I've never had it since, and I can recommend it to all people that has the toothache to chew two inches of a bear's tail. It's a certain cure. There are a wicked sight of virtue in bear's grease, as I know by my own experience.[28]

This exploit of the colonel's is no hack writer's invention but a version of an international folktale, "How the Man Came Out of a Tree Stump," which has found a congenial home in the United States. Field collectors have reported variants from Kentucky, Illinois, Indiana, Missouri, New Mexico, New York, North Carolina, and Wisconsin. In a short story he published in 1870, titled "How Sharp Snaffles Got His Capital and Wife," William Gilmore Simms sets the episode in the Tennessee mountains and makes it the hinge of a boy meets girl, boy loses girl, boy gets girl plot.

Another connection with folk tradition occurs in the opening paragraph of the narrative dealing with beliefs about swallows. These are traditional beliefs. Vance Randolph reports the conviction among Ozarkers that shooting a barn swallow brings bad luck and makes cows give bloody milk.[29] In England good luck is portended when swallows build under eaves.[30] Davy may have derided stories about swallows, but he knew them closely.

Crockett of the almanacs is the rustic, he is the hunter, and he is the republican democrat. One farfetched almanac story finds him in Haiti in the presence of the black emperor Soulouque, who is astride a black horse and resplendent with feathers, stars, gilt, and breastpins. All his subjects fall down groveling on their hands, knees, and stomachs, but Crockett remains erect, saying, "I am Col. Davy Crockett, one of the sovereign people of Uncle Sam, that never kneels to any individual this side of sunshine." [31] While plainly contrived and blatantly racist, the narrative does echo a sentiment accredited to Crockett in a traditional anecdote written down in a history of Memphis by a close acquaintance, James B. Davis. In the spring of 1836 eleven recruits appeared at Nacogdoches, Texas, to enlist in the Texas army. Colonel John Forbes swore them in, but when he reached the portion of the oath requiring allegiance "to the Republic of Texas, or any other government that might be established," one recruit stepped forward and declared he could not subscribe to such wording.

"I am a republican," he stated firmly, "and believe in a republican form of government, and if any other kind of government results from this revolution, I will never support nor defend it."

Colonel Forbes immediately conceded the point and offered to substitute for the offending phrase "or any other republican government that might be established." The change proved satisfactory to the recruits, who were all mustered into service.

The speaker who thus upheld the republican ideal was David Crockett. [32]

"A Sketch of Davy Crockett, made by Louis Mauer a few days before his 99th birthday, in 1930; a portrait lithograph"
From Harry T. Peters, *America on Stone*

Mike Fink the keelboatman

Well, I walk tall into varmint and Indian, it's a way I've got, and it comes as natural as grinning to a hyena. I'm a regular tornado, tough as a hickory withe, long winded as a nor'-wester. I can strike a blow like a falling tree, and every lick makes a gap in the crowd that lets in an acre of sunshine. Whew, boys! [33]

So bragged Mike Fink to his fellow keelboatmen of the half-horse, half-alligator breed as they sailed and poled their craft down the Mississippi sometime early in the 1800s. How exact a transcript of Mike's boast was set down by the journalist Thomas Bangs Thorpe, author of the classic fiction in the humor of the Old Southwest, "The Big Bear of Arkansas," when he wrote a sketch about Fink, we can only surmise. But clearly the various writers who contributed traditional incidents about Mike to periodicals, newspapers, almanacs, and annuals from 1828 into the 1850s were drawing upon a yeasty corpus of anecdotal legends that floated up and down the river cities of the Ohio and Mississippi from Pittsburgh to New Orleans.

Some shadowy facts are known about Mike. He was born around 1770 at Fort Pitt, site of the future Pittsburgh, probably of Scotch-Irish ancestry, although a claim has been made for a Pennsylvania German origin. In his early youth he served as scout and Indian fighter in the fiercely contested area around Fort Pitt, the gateway to the West. After the Treaty of Greenville in 1795 removed the Indian menace, many of the restless and independent scouts joined the hardy crews of

flatboatmen and keelboatmen who transported produce to markets downriver. The keelboatmen, who disparaged the flatboatmen and fought with them at every opportunity, poled their pointed crafts upriver, a task requiring the greatest stamina and strength, while the covered flatboats were knocked up for lumber at their Southern terminuses. With the coming of the steamboat to Western waters in 1815 the era of the keelboatmen drew to a close, and in 1822 Mike signed up with the group of scouts and trappers employed by Major Andrew Henry and William H. Ashley in their historic enterprise to ascend the Missouri River to its source and open up the Rocky Mountain country for the fur trade. Within the year Mike was shot to death by an associate in a quarrel that initiated new legends about the brawling boatman.

Many observers marveled at the stalwarts who poled the broadhorns. A Crockett almanac for 1838 describes succinctly the Mississippi keelboatmen among whom Mike reigned:

Of all the species of mankind existing under heaven, the western boatmen deserve a distinct and separate cognomen. They are a sort of amphibious animal—kind-hearted as a Connecticut grandmother, but as rough as a Rocky Mountain bear. In high water they make the boat carry them, and in low water they are content to carry the boat—or in other words, they are ever ready to jump in and ease her over the sand-bar, then jump on board and patiently wait for the next.

Spending the greater portion of their time on the water, they scarce know how to behave on shore, and feel only at home upon the deck of their craft, where they exercise entire sovereignty.[34]

Other accounts stress their hardihood and splendid physique (except for balding heads from constant exposure to sun and wind), their vast knowledge of river lore, their forceful slang, their open manner, their boastfulness, courage, delight in drink and fighting, and exuberant animal spirits.[35] Among these bully boys Fink gained renown as a marksman and humorist, although he was less the cunning trickster and more the crude practical joker than Davy Crockett. Various testimonies acclaimed his reputation as kingpin of the ferocious boatmen:

He was the hero of a hundred fights, and the leader in a thousand daring adventures.

He was also a wit; and on that account he gained the admiration and excited the fears of all the fraternity of boatmen; for he usually enforced his wit with a sound drubbing, if any one dared to dissent by neglecting or refusing to laugh at his jokes. . . .

"There ar'nt a man," said Captain Jo, "from Pittsburgh to New Orleans but what's heard of *Mike Fink;* and there ain't a boatman on the river, to this day, but what strives to imitate him. Before them 'ere steamers come on the river, Mike was looked up to as a kind of king among the boatmen. . . ."

Among the flat-boatmen, there were none that gained the notoriety of *Mike Fink:* his name is still remembered along the whole of the Ohio as a man who excelled his fellows in every thing—particularly in his rifle-shot, which was acknowledged to be unsurpassed. Probably no man ever lived who could compete with Mike Fink in the latter accomplishment.

Mike was the tallest, strongest, longest winded fellow in the section, carried the truest rifle, knew more "Ingin ways," was the wildest hand at a frolic, and, withal, was the greatest favorite in the country.

You've all on you, heered of Mike Fink, the celebrated an self-created, an never to be mated, Mississippi roarer, snag-lifter, an flatboat skuller.

The celebrated Mike Fink, the great admiral of flat-boatmen on the Western rivers, the William Tell of marksmen on land, and the most daring of all wild-forest adventurers, was the Prince of moose-catchers.

Among the most celebrated of these [the boatmen], every reader of history will at once remember MIKE FINK, the hero of his class. So many and so marvellous are the stories told of the man that numbers of persons are inclined altogether to disbelieve his existence.[36]

"Mike Fink, the Ohio Boatman"
From *Davy Crockett's Almanack, 1838*

From 1828 to 1852, the periodicals, newspapers, and almanacs of a day that purveyed choice yarns and sketches toasted Mike in this fashion. In shooting with the long rifle, rough-and-tumble eye-gouging fighting, and consuming rotgut liquor on the large scale, Mike excelled his hardy peers and attained among them a hero's status. But more staid members of society regarded him as a vicious desperado. An earnest young Ohioan who poled on Mike's keelboat about 1815 for fifty cents a day described him as "a very noted character" and "one of the most wild and reckless rowdying men of his class." A Western historian writing in a Cincinnati newspaper in 1845 called Mike

"worthless and vile," and a correspondent, corroborating that judgment, added that "Mike was one of the very lowest of mankind, and entirely destitute of any of the manly qualities which often were to be found among the bargemen of his day."[37]

In appearance, dress, and behavior Mike exemplified the half-horse, half-alligator genus of Western boatmen that astonished travelers and river passengers. Observers and writers pictured Mike as herculean in build, sunburned and weatherbeaten to the color of a mulatto, garbed in a loose blue jerkin with a white fringe, red flannel shirt, coarse linsey-woolsey trousers fastened around his waist by a leather belt in which a sheath held a long hunting knife, moccasins on his feet, and a cap of animal skin on his head of raven-black hair. His air was assured, relaxed, and jaunty. Other boatmen hailed him as "Snapping Turtle" on the Ohio and "The Snag" on the Mississippi, envious hunters dubbed him "Bang-All," and the intelligentsia called him a "Western Lion." Mike himself spoke in the metaphorical imagery characteristic of the boatmen and backwoodsmen. Vaunting his skill with his rifle "Betsy," he crowed, "Jest pint out a musketeer at a hundred yards, and I'll nip off his right hinder eend claw at the second jint afore he kin hum, 'Oh, don't.'" In high spirits he bragged, "I am a salt river roarer; and I love the wimming, and how I'm chock-full of fight." In Emerson Bennett's melodramatic novel, *Mike Fink: A Legend of the Ohio* (1848), Mike bangs on the door of old Mother Deb the fortuneteller and cries, "Open, Deb, or by all the fishes of the Dead Sea, I'll snag this old door in less time nor a Massassip alligator can chaw up a puppy!" After getting knocked down by the Methodist circuit-riding preacher Peter Cartwright, he shook his hand admiringly and said, "By golly, you're some beans in a bar-fight. I'd rather set to with an old he bar in the dog-days. You can pass in this 'ere crowd of nose-smashers, blast your picture!"[38]

How did the deeds of Mike Fink match up with his vainglorious words? They fall into three groupings: his shooting feats, his rough tricks, and his fisticuffs. A thread that runs through many of his stunts is a cocky independence of custom and law. Mike refused to stand in awe of any man, whether a savage Indian or a pretentious judge, and he showed his disdain with daredevil pranks.

Anecdotes smacking of legend related Mike's wizardry with the rifle. As a scout in the Pennsylvania forests, he spied a deer and was about to shoot from his cover when he beheld an Indian also aiming at the deer from another vantage point. Mike redirected his aim, and at the instant the savage shot the deer he shot the Indian. Once while sailing up the Mississippi, Mike spied a sow and her pigs on the riverbank and was about to shoot one when a companion protested. Mike fired nevertheless at a distance of forty or fifty yards and shaved off their tails. This incident is elaborated in a Crockett almanac tall tale in which Mike bested Davy in a shooting match. Davy first shot the ears off a tomcat sitting on a fence a hundred and fifty yards away. Mike then let fly at a sow and her litter "till he hadn't left one of them are pigs enough tail to make a tooth-pick on." Davy next shot off one inch left on the tail of one piglet. Irate, Mike fired at his wife and knocked half the comb out of her hair, and challenged

Davy to shoot away the other half. But now Davy gave up beat, for he said his hand would be sure to shake if he pointed his gun at a female.

Two audacious shots contributed to Mike's renown and also show his contempt for the red and the black man and for the law. One ball from his rifle clipped off the prized scalp lock that adorned the head of a degenerate Cherokee Indian who stood outlined against the riverbank. Mike then leaped from his keelboat into the Ohio and swam from the pursuit of an outraged group of onlookers to the opposite shore. Similarly he shot from his boat at a Negro standing on a bluff whose protuberant heel presented a target that Mike could not resist. This time Mike did not escape the law, and was taken to the magistrate's office in St. Louis. In the account written by John S. Robb, one of the corps of talented newspaper humorists of the Old Southwest, the magistrate is a French settler and so fits into the comic stereotype of the dialect-speaking, dimwitted Frenchman of frontier society. Mike at once took the offensive and demanded the justice pay him a small bill.

"You shall collect ze bill from me?" inquired the justice. "What for you do the city good to de amount of von bill? Ah, ha! You kick up your *heel* and raise de batter and de salt of de whole town wiz your noise so much as we nevair get some sleep in de night!"

Mike had his answer ready. "You jest hit the p'int, Squire," he responded, "when you said that thar word *heel!* I want you to pay me fur trimmin' the heel of one of your town niggers! I've jest altered his breed, and arter this his posterity kin warr the neatest kind of a boot!"[39]

At this effrontery the boatmen howled, the justice frothed, and Mike departed airily. Robb's sketch reveals Mike in the role of trickster as well as marksman, and also softens the seeming crudity of Fink's action by having him give money both to the officer who arrested him and to the unfortunate Negro whose heel he trimmed. (In the same way, Davy Crockett offered to pay the Yankee merchant whom he had tricked with the coonskin.) The shooting episode seems based in fact, and one commentator claims to have seen the circuit court record and the jury verdict of guilty, with Mike's defense "that the fellow's long heel prevented him from wearing a genteel boot."[40]

Of all Fink's shooting feats, the one that most captured the popular imagination was the boatmen's practice, when well liquored up, of placing tin cups filled with whiskey on each other's heads and drilling rifle balls through them at a distance of thirty yards. The half-horse, half-alligator roarers indulged in this pastime to show their mettle, to astonish onlookers, to win wagers, and to demonstrate their fraternal bonds and trust. One would stand unmoved and unblinking while a fellow carouser took aim and splintered the cup two inches above his head, causing the whiskey to spurt over his face, perhaps even leaving the riddled cup still standing on the boatman's head. Some traditions reported variations on this theme. When penned on the broadhorn and unable to get to land, a boatman in the stern would hold up a tin cup, and another in the bow would knock out the bottom with a rifle shot, but if he missed he had to stand a quart for the crew. A story barely hinted at in print has Mike testing the fidelity of his girl friend by shooting at a tin cup held between her knees or thighs. Shooting the cup led to the most vigorous of the Fink legends, the one surrounding his death.

Before this final episode, other scenes helped swell the anecdotal talk about the bully of the broadhorns. At times he displayed a brash roguery, as in the piece

"Mike Fink Beating Colonel Crockett at a Shooting Match" From *The Crockett Almanac 1840*

a correspondent wrote to the *Western General Advertiser* about Mike's stratagem of "stilling." While boating down the Ohio, in 1819, an observer overheard Mike say during the night, "Well, boys, who's going to *still* tonight?" Watching, he saw Mike on an adjacent keelboat carry a tin bucket, into whose bottom a small pipe had been inserted, up to a cask of wine or brandy, make a hole in the cask, insert the pipe, and fill the bucket with a couple of quarts of water. The "still" then commenced to operate, as Mike drew the spirits from the head of the cask until the water emptied in the bucket, to replace the wine or brandy that would enter the throats of Mike and his boon companions. So did Mike help himself to the cargo he was presumably guarding.[41] This ruse suggests one of the celebrated tricks in American folklore, getting rum (or other liquor) without credit. In the fictional newspaper serial of Joseph M. Field, "Mike Fink: 'The Last of the Boatmen,'" published in the *St. Louis Reveille* of 1847, Mike, in his last year with the mountain men at Fort Henry on the Yellowstone River, demanded liquor at the fort but was refused. He raised his rifle and sent a ball crashing through the head of a liquor barrel at the far end of the storeroom, then picked up a large vessel, walked coolly over to the gushing stream, caught the flow in his receptacle, and quaffed it thirstily. This incident, which might have come from the oral yarns Field heard in river towns, belongs to the getting-liquor-without-credit family of tales, although it portrays Mike as marksman and bully rather than as trickster.

In another trickster narrative with many affiliates in tradition, Mike cozens a sheep owner out of some sheep. As his boat idled downstream, Fink eyed with longing a handsome flock of sheep grazing on the riverbank. He needed provisions, but on principle scorned to purchase them. Accordingly he landed his boat, opened a bladder of Scotch snuff from his cargo, stepped ashore, caught half a dozen of the sheep, and rubbed the snuff over their faces. Then he returned to the boat and dispatched one of his men to the sheep owner's house to tell him something was the matter with his sheep. When the old gentleman hastened to the pasture, he beheld some of

"The Keel-Boat"

From *Harper's New Monthly Magazine*, December 1855, illustrating an article, "Remembrances of the Mississippi," by Thomas Bangs Thorpe, who writes (p. 29): "The keel-boat was long and narrow, sharp at the bow and stern, and of light draft. From fifteen to twenty hands were required to propel it along. The crew, divided equally on each side, took their places upon the 'walking-boards,' extending along the whole length of the craft, and, setting one end of their pole in the bottom of the river, the other was brought to the shoulder, and with body bent forward, they *walked* the boat against the formidable current."

his flock leaping, bleating, rubbing their noses against each other and on the ground, and engaging in similar strange antics. Dismayed, he asked Mike, innocently standing by, if he knew the cause of the trouble. "The black murrain," Mike replied with a straight face. "All the sheep upriver's got it dreadful. Dyin' like rotten dogs—hundreds a day." Mike warned the sheepman that the murrain would surely infect the whole flock if the infected sheep were not promptly shot and disposed of, and with a show of reluctance agreed to undertake the task, upon promise of two gallons of peach brandy. After dark, his men recovered the sheep from where Mike had thrown them in an eddy, packed them aboard the boat, and at dawn glided happily away.[42]

This yarn belongs with the large group of folk anecdotes in which a rascal through some ingenious deception separates a property owner from his possessions. It was also told of a bargeman on the James River named William Creasy, and probably transferred from the lesser to the greater folk personality. Mike the keelboatman shares the trickster propensity with Crockett the backwoodsman and Jonathan the Yankee.

Fink also displayed a darker, coarser, and brutal side, as in his shooting of the Indian's scalp lock and the Negro's heel. This sadistic streak—or robustly humorous one, depending on one's point of view—comes to the fore in an anecdote set in November 1820 near the mouth of the Muskingum River, where several keelboats had landed for the night. Without informing the other boatmen what he was up to, Mike scraped together

dried leaves blown to the ground by the early autumn frost, piled them up to the height of his head, arranged them in an oblong shape, and lay down inside, as if to test a possible bed-space. Then he strolled back to his boat, secured and primed his rifle, and called his wife Peg to follow him to shore. "Get in there and lie down," he commanded her, with an oath.

"Now, *Mr.* Fink" (the term she addressed him with in his angry moments), "what have I done, I don't know, I'm sure—"

"Get in there and lie down, or I'll shoot you," Mike shouted with another oath, raising his rifle to his shoulder.

Peg crawled inside the pile of leaves and Mike spread them over her. He then split a flour barrel into pieces, which he lit from the fire aboard the boat, and set fire in four places to the leaves. Immediately the pile blazed up, fanned by a fresh wind. Peg stood the heat for a few moments, in fear of grinning Mike and his poised rifle, then dashed to the river, hair and clothes aflame, and plunged in. "There," said Mike, "that'll larn you to be winkin at them fellers on the other boat."[43]

The unidentified contributor of this anecdote presents it as evidence that "Mike was one of the very lowest of mankind" and devoid of the manly qualities that characterized his fellow boatmen. Yet the tale can be read another way. Peg may have deserved chastisement for her flirtatious behavior, as Mike's final words suggest, and he was teaching her a lesson in a fashion reminiscent of an international folktale, "The Taming of the Shrew," that has enjoyed considerable American repetition in the form of an anecdotal legend.

One imaginative picaresque legend shows Mike doing a good deed while having his fun with the law. On this occasion he allowed himself to be arrested in Louisville in order to benefit a constable, an old friend, who pleaded the poverty of his family and his need to benefit from taking Mike into custody. Mike consented to the arrest, but as usual turned the situation into farce, by insisting that he be accompanied in court by his men and his boat:

Accordingly a long-coupled wagon was procured, and with oxen attached to it went down the hill at Third Street for Mike's yawl. The road, for it was not then a street, was very steep and very muddy at this point. Regardless of this, however, the boat was set upon the wagon, and Mike and his men, with their long poles ready, as if for an aquatic excursion, were put aboard, Mike in the stern. By dint of laborious dragging the wagon had attained half the height of the hill, when out shouted the stentorian voice of Mike calling to his men—SET POLES!—and the end of every long pole was set firmly in the thick mud—BACK HER!—roared Mike, and down the hill again went the wagon, yawl, men and oxen.

Mike had been revolving the matter in his mind and had concluded that it was best not to go; and well knowing that each of his men was equal to a moderately strong ox, he had at once conceived and executed this retrograde movement. Once at the bottom, another parley was held and Mike was again overpowered. This time they had almost reached the top of the hill when *Set Poles!—Back Her!* was again ordered and again executed. A third attempt, however, was successful and Mike reached the court house in safety; and as his friend, the constable, had endeavored to induce him to believe, he was acquitted for lack of sufficient evidence.

Other indictments, however, were found against him, but Mike preferred not to wait to hear them tried; so, at a given signal he and his men boarded their craft again and stood ready to weigh anchor. The dread of the long poles in the hands of Mike's men prevented the posse from urging any serious remonstrance against his departure. And off they started with poles "tossed." As they left the court house yard Mike waved his red bandanna, which he had fixed on one of the poles, and promising to "call again" was born back to his element and launched once more upon the water.[44]

In this vignette, written in 1852 by Ben Cassedy, historian of Louisville, the literary touches do not conceal the rollicking sportiveness of a choice yarn. Here is Mike in his favorite role of trickster and strong man, in his boat surrounded by his bully boys, but on dry land, in the most incongruous of physical situations, complying with yet thumbing his nose at the law and the Establishment.

And we have yet another sight of Mike as the jovial prankster sporting with his fellow roarers, but this time in the unfamiliar posture of the ballad maker and ballad singer. According to Joseph M. Field, Fink wrote and sang a ditty called "Neal Hornback," about another boatman whose kegs of whiskey Mike surreptitiously stole and then sat back and laughed to see Neal blame another. Field states that the publisher of the *St. Louis Reveille*, Colonel Charles Keemle, copied down the words directly from Mike's singing on the Missouri, the last year of his life:

NEAL HORNBACK

"My name it are Neal Hornback
  I sail-ed from Mudford shore,
And ven-tur-ed up the Poll-ing fork,
  Where Indians' rifle roar.
Oh, the matter it are conclu-di-ed,
  It are hard for to unbin-d
I waded the forks of Salt Riviere,
  And left my kegs behind.

"An hour or two before day,
  I pick-ed up my gun,
Returned to my periogue,
  And saw the mischief done.
I laid it on Tom John-sti-on,
  Who were innercent and clear,
But for to destroy my charac-ture,
  It plainly did appear.

"I call-ed my friends er-round me,
  And thus to them did s-a-a-a-y,
Macdannilly and Tom John-sti-on,
  Have stoled my kegs er-way."
"Oh, if they are the lads whot stoled your kegs
  They have done the verri thing,
And if your kegs are miss-ing,
  You'll not see them er-gin."

Neal's body it were enormer-ous,
  His legs were long and slim,
Good Lord, it would make you sor-ri,
  Was you to look on him.

He were crook'd back'd hump'd shoulder-ed
  And with thick lips is blessed,
And for to make him ug-i-ly,
  The Lord has done his best.[45]

"Fink used to sing the song with a rich sobriety, enjoying it fully," noted Field. As a home-made local ballad it rings true to indigenous American minstrelsy, with its account of a small personal incident and characters known only to the immediate circle, and the caricaturing of hapless Neal Hornback in the style of the solemnly intoned mock ballad. Lumberjacks, sailors, and cowboys have written and sung similar pieces. So Mike was a bard in his own right as well as a subject for bardic compositions.

In heroic saga, the death of the hero always plays a prominent role, since his legend will scarcely benefit if he dies in bed of arthritis or gets killed in a fair fight by one doughtier than he. Davy Crockett profited from his death at the Alamo, fighting in a siege against overwhelming odds. Mike, like Davy, went West to die on a new frontier, where he met his end under mysterious and enigmatic circumstances that provide a fitting climax to his shadowy, daredevil career. At least a hundred accounts of his death reached print between 1823 and 1955, according to his biographers Walter Blair and Franklin Meine, accounts that reflect the ceaseless variations of detail associated with a far-flung oral legend. On one kernel all agree, that the death episode resulted from the last instance of Mike's most celebrated and distinctive feat, shooting at the tin cup on a friend's head. But this time Mike missed his aim, deliberately so in most versions, and sent his bullet between the eyes of his companion. In revenge, a friend of the deceased shot Mike. Thus the bare bones of the affair. But as to the whereabouts of the scene,

the reason for the killing, and the identity of Mike's victim and assassin, the traditions offer a host of options. Several accounts place the shooting on the banks of the Missouri River, and others at the mouth of the Yellowstone River. The date is usually 1822 or 1823. A number name Mike's victim as Carpenter, a friend of his on the Ashley-Henry expedition of boatmen, hunters, and trappers up the Missouri to the Rockies in 1822. Some versions pass off the fatal shot as an accident, perhaps resulting from Mike's being corned—but he was always corned when he shot the tin cup. More intriguing are the reports of a quarrel over a squaw, or of darker insinuations about the relations between the two men. In the circumstantial narrative of Joseph M. Field, Fink prevailed on the youth Carpenter to withdraw from the fort during the winter and reside with him in a cave in the riverbank, well stocked with whiskey. The trappers in the fort sought to separate Carpenter from Fink by ridiculing the young man as a mere slave to the former keelboatman, with other "foul insinuations" (of homosexuality?). Carpenter remained with his mentor, but their relations deteriorated. Finally the two sallied forth for a frolic in the spring with the boys from the fort, and to celebrate the occasion Carpenter and Fink agreed to shoot the tin cup. The youth shot first, and his ball creased Mike's scalp. Mike then fired, and laid Carpenter dead on the ground. Fink retired sullenly to his cave, and while the men at the fort muttered their suspicions, none took action until a gunsmith named Talbott, who had denounced Fink, in panic shot and killed the boat-

"A Keel Boat on the Mississippi"
From *Davy Crockett's Almanack, 1838*

man as he entered Talbott's gunshop. In other tellings, an onlooker shoots Fink on the spot after he commits the presumed murder. One unusual variation has Mike shooting an apple from Carpenter's hand at eighty yards for a gallon of whiskey, and then, after a quarrel with Carpenter, deliberately aiming for his friend's head. At the time Mike pretended that his rifle had hung fire, but later, when in his cups, he admitted he had fired intentionally at Carpenter. To escape the law he traveled far up the Missouri, but was followed and stabbed to death by one of Carpenter's comrades.

So Mike met his death, violently, on the far Western frontier, and the legends about him began to seep into print. The first known reference to Fink appears in the last line of a play produced in St. Louis in 1821, *The Pedlar*, by Alphonso Wetmore, paymaster of the United States Army. In the farce a whole pantheon of democratic folk types take the boards: the Yankee peddler, the Revolutionary veteran, the Western roarer, the boatman in red shirt and tow trousers, whom at the play's end the roarer names as Mike Fink. The *St. Louis Republican* carried the news of Mike's death on July 16, 1823; a Pittsburgh editor, Morgan Neville, in 1828 wrote an extended sketch of "The Last of the Boatmen" in a gift-book annual, *The Western Souvenir;* a comparable vignette appeared the next year in the *Western Monthly Review;* and Mike's posthumous career in literary legend was fairly launched. The high period came in the years between 1842 and 1860, when twenty-three fresh stories or sketches about Mike were published, while only four were printed between 1828 and 1841 and four more between 1861 and 1883. If reprintings, which helped to swell Mike's popularity, are included, the count runs ten items from 1828 to 1840, twenty-four in the

1840s, and twenty-three in the 1850s, and then tails off sharply for the rest of the century.[46] Although he died twelve or thirteen years before Crockett, Fink's apotheosis coincides closely with Davy's and they were coupled together in comic fictions.

What kind of a figure emerged from these thirty-odd narratives that captured segments of a seemingly vigorous oral tradition? Some observers called Mike harsh names, for his heavy drinking, savage fighting, and coarse practical jokes. After 1850 a reaction against Mike becomes evident in the newly printed traditions that show Mike being bested in fights by Peter Cartwright, the muscular Methodist circuit-riding preacher, and Jack Pierce, the pugnacious flatboatman renowned for his butting head and promises to his mother to behave. When faced with Christian morality, the boatman's rowdy secularism had to take second place. Yet the strongest note that recurs in this subliterature sounds in support of Mike's basic good humor, good heart, and good sense, along with his recognized strengths of eye and arm. "There was nothing malevolent about Mike's heart," wrote Joseph M. Field. "His huge frame was animated by a nature warm, generous, impulsive—full of the milk of human kindness, and only terrible and dangerous when roused by treachery and wrong."[47] The historian of Louisville, Ben Cassedy, remarked that in all his "little tricks, as Mike called them, he never displayed any very accurate respect to the laws either of propriety or property, but he was so ingenious in his predations that it is impossible not to laugh at his crimes."[48] Refusing subservience to the petty laws and decorum of aristocratic society, Mike nevertheless did nothing evil; he was the jolly picaro, having fun at the expense of the spluttering justice or the dull-witted sheep owner. When he shot the protuberance off the Negro's elongated heel, he did send the lamed lad a pocket of silver to ease his pain. To the straights of his time Mike Fink was a ruffian, but his sympathizers eulogized him as king of the boatmen.

Sam Patch the mill hand

TO THE LADIES AND GENTLEMEN OF WESTERN NEW-YORK AND OF UPPER CANADA

All I have to say is, that I arrived at the Falls too late, to give you a specimen of my Jumping Qualities, on the 6th inst.; but on Wednesday, I thought I would venture a small Leap, which I accordingly made, of Eighty Feet, merely to convince those that remained to see me, with what safety and ease I could descend, and that I was the TRUE SAM PATCH, and to show that Some Things could be Done as well as Others; which was denied before I made the Jump.

Having been thus disappointed, the owners of Goat Island have generously granted me the use of it for nothing; so that I may have a chance, from an equally generous public, to obtain some remuneration for my long journey hither, as well as affording me an opportunity of supporting the reputation I have gained, by Aero-Nautical Feats, never before attempted, either in the Old or New World.

I shall, Ladies and Gentlemen, on Saturday next, Oct. 17th, precisely at 3 o'clock, P.M. LEAP at the FALLS OF NIAGARA, from a height of 120 to 130 feet (being 40 to 50 feet higher than I leapt before), into the eddy below. On my way down from Buffalo, on the morning of that day, in the Steam-Boat Niagara, I shall, for the amusement of the Ladies, doff my coat and Spring from the Mast head into the Niagara River.

SAM PATCH
Of Passaic Falls, New Jersey.

Buffalo, Oct. 12, 1829.

So boasted Sam Patch in posters distributed only a month before the leap that terminated his mortal life and ensured him a legendary existence. Few persons in the United States of the 1830s and 1840s could have avoided all the poems, ballads, rhymes, anecdotes, reminiscences, tall tales, and theatrical farces that celebrated this braggart jumper of history, fantasy, and hoax. A century later the myth is as dead as the man, and like Mike Fink, Davy Crockett, and Mose the Bowery b'hoy, Patch must be reintroduced to his present legatees.

The biographical data about Samuel Patch prior to his first public jumping exploit in 1827 are extremely slight. He spent his early years in Pawtucket, Rhode Island, where he worked in Samuel Slater's cotton mill and made running jumps into the Pawtucket River from nearby roofs, thus earning the plaudits of his townsmen. Moving to Paterson, New Jersey, still a cotton spinner, Sam eluded the constables and jumped seventy feet from the highest cliff overlooking the scenic Passaic Falls to steal the show from Timothy Crane, who was then pulling the first bridge across the chasm. Exhilarated by the notoriety he received, Patch took to electrifying crowds in New Jersey and New York with descents from bridges, until Niagara Falls provided his crowning conquest.

Apparently plans to blast off a portion of Table Rock, treacherously overhanging the chasm from the Canadian bank, suggested to Buffalo citizens the idea of securing an additional attraction. They invited the Jersey jumper to perform, and also decided to send the shallow-draught schooner *Superior* careening over the falls. (Two years earlier the unseaworthy brig *Michigan* had floated down the rapids with an animal crew of bears, foxes, geese, and a buffalo, plus an effigy of Andrew Jackson, before fascinated thousands.) Patch accepted, but as the handbill quoted above indicates, he missed the festival day, and the throngs saw a ship fall and smash, rather than a man leap and live. On the next day Sam did demonstrate his powers to a limited audience with a preliminary plunge of some seventy feet from the lower end of Goat Island. Robbed of his rightful turnout, however, Patch publicized a second and greater leap for the following week. For these exhibitions, the wooded islet splitting the cataract in an uneven half between the American and the Horseshoe Falls provided a logical springboard. Observers congregated on the island and lined the American and Canadian shores. For this second leap the platform on Goat Island stood about two-thirds the elevation of the 160-foot-high neighboring banks, a fearful height when scanned from the depths below.

On a rainy Saturday, Sam boldly climbed the perpendicular ladder to the scaffold, ignoring tearful farewells and protestations from persons at the foot. Before ascending, he shed his shoes and coat and tied a handkerchief about his neck. Atop the ladder, which had been built from four trees spliced together and fastened by ropes running back upon Goat Island, he mounted the narrow, reeling platform. It was barely large enough for a man to sit upon, and for ten minutes he displayed his poise and tested the stand, while the spectators repeatedly cheered. At length he rose upright, took the handkerchief from his neck, tied it about his waist, waved his hand, kissed the American flag which flew over his head, and stepped off steadfastly in the swirling flood. A general cry of "He's dead, he's lost!" swept through the crowd, according to one account; a second reports a benumbed silence, broken only by joyous congratulations when Sam's head burst out of the waters. While handkerchiefs waved and huzzas roared, the Jumping Hero swam briskly to the shore, to inform his first onrushing admirer, "There's no mistake in Sam Patch!" Unanimously the surrounding group exclaimed, "This is the real Sam Patch!" The *Buffalo Republican* commented: "The jump of Patch is the greatest feat of the kind ever effected by man. He may now challenge the uni-

verse for a competitor."

Flushed with the publicity of press notices and the public excitement, Sam turned to Rochester and the Genesee Falls for a new conquest. By now the newspapers of the nation were playing up Sam enthusiastically, and his sponsors determined to provide a still greater, climactic feat, by erecting a twenty-five-foot scaffold on the rock's brow to extend the jump to a distance of 125 feet. In the posters Sam announced, with unwitting irony: "HIGHER YET! SAM'S LAST JUMP. SOME THINGS CAN BE DONE AS WELL AS OTHERS. THERE IS NO MISTAKE IN SAM PATCH." Monroe and Ontario counties poured out for the November 13 leap; schooners and coaches ran excursions; betting ran high in the local bars as to the outcome; nearby roofs and windows and both banks swarmed with the curious. But when Sam walked out on the grassy, tree-covered rock that divided the greater and lesser branches of the cataract, at two P. M. (his pet bear was to jump at three), and climbed up to the platform, some spectators thought he staggered and lacked his usual aplomb. Some assert that the jumper was reeling drunk; others stoutly deny that he took more than a glass of brandy to counteract the chilly day. Sam made a brief speech: Napoleon was a great man and conquered nations, Wellington was a greater and conquered Napoleon, but neither could jump the Genesee Falls—that was left for him to do. Then he jumped. But this time the descent lacked its usual arrowy precision. One third of the way down his body began to droop, his arms parted from his sides, he lost command of his body and struck the water obliquely with arms and legs extended. He did not reappear before the horror-stricken assemblage. Dragging for the body proved unsuccessful, perhaps because of pinioning branches on the river bed. Nor was it found until the following March 17, when a farmer broke the ice to water his horses at the mouth of the Genesee near Lake Ontario. The black kerchief was still tied about the waist. An autopsy revealed a ruptured blood vessel and dislocation of both shoulders. The body was buried in a nameless grave and lay long forgotten in the Charlotte cemetery, until it was finally identified by a board head-marker reading, "Here lies Sam Patch; such is Fame." Since the removal of the marker, controversy has arisen as to Sam's real whereabouts.

Torrents of rhetoric, moralizing, editorial comment, elegy, rumor, and speculation washed over the lifeless high jumper in a volume to match the waters of Genessee Falls. One reaction took the form of sermons: it was emphasized that vain and mortal man should not carelessly attempt, nor the curious encourage, trifling with divine Providence. "Shall we wantonly precipitate ourselves from the cataract of Niagara, trusting in God's mercy to preserve us, or plunge into the burning crater of the mountain, vomiting forth melted lava, hoping that God will sustain us?" Other interpreters read a selfless heroism and sublime grandeur into the tragedy. But the most general note avoided both preachment and panegyric for jocose commentary, in prose and verse, which was probably more appropriate to the clownish daredevil. One editor bluntly remarked that the whole editorial corps would regret his "precipitate" loss, since he had previously supplied so many sparkling paragraphs, and it was also announced that Patch had imitated the pig who a week before had jumped the falls to its death, by "going the whole hog of the leap and forfeiture." Punning doggerel provided a spurious epitaph, with each atrocious double meaning italicized: "*divers* times, a *drop* too much, untimely *bier*, this sad *fall*." It concluded:

There's none alive
  will ever match him—
Ah, cruel Death,
  thus to *dis-PATCH* him!

Many refused to believe that Sam had really died. Knowing his propensity for stunts, one faction accepted the surmise that Sam had previously discovered an eddy that ran under a shelving rock, where he had hidden a suit of dry clothes, a bottle of Santa Cruz, and something to eat. Following his jump he swam to the spot, remained there till dark, and then traveled eastward incognito. A man in Albany had seen and talked with him; another in Rochester bet one hundred dollars that Sam would reappear in that city before the first of January; a notice posted prominently in Rochester stated that Patch would recount his adventures at Acker's Eagle Tavern the forenoon of December 3; reports spread that he had been sighted at Pittsford, Canandaigua, and other places on his way to New Jersey. One widely printed newspaper story, signed by "Sam Patch," declared the Genesee jump to be a capital hoax, with a man of straw and paint, sand and stones, substituting for the Jumping Hero.

Even after the finding of the body the jumper continued to be seen: there were those who at twilight perceived Sam sporting at the falls, and repeating his fearful feat to a concourse of sea gulls and fishes.

To American poets and rhymesters of the 1830s searching for native themes, the heroics, tragedy, and humors of the Last Leap proved magnetic. In a heavily humorous mock elegy Robert Sands, a New York lawyer, dabbler in letters, and classicist, compared Sam to aerialists famed in mythology—to Leander, Sappho, Icarus, Helle, Empedocles—and found his bravery, loneliness, and mother love not too inferior hero stuff. A lengthy narrative poem by Thomas Ward, a Newark doctor, made an elegant Byronic hero of "The Great Descender, mighty PATCH—Spurner of heights—great Nature's overmatch!" and unblushingly likened him to Columbus, Franklin, Newton, Galileo, and Nelson in what must be accounted an overlooked curiosity of American literature. Humbly born Patch, "half dust, half deity," belonged to the immortal class who combined "Th' heroic body with th' inventive mind," and died a true "martyr of science." In a protracted Shakespearean soliloquy he perceives the path to fame in a meteor's downward descent, which fires his mind with the glories in the setting sun, diving bells, parachutes, and waterfalls. Daring the challenge of the boiling Passaic, he triumphantly flings himself down the water-flooded vale, pausing only to quaff a draught of the nectar heroes ever love—whiskey. In Boston a printer ran off an anonymous news-ballad on the Last Leap, with a picture of Sam careening downward. Seba Smith, who wrote the Jack Downing letters and the folksong about Fair Charlotte, felt inspired to compose a brisk ballad chronicle on the saga of Patch; in Smith's

mock epic the ecstatic mob votes to change the scurvy name of Patch to "Squire Samuel O'Cataract" after his triumphant Niagara splash. One odd effusion presented a Burns-like ballad in Scottish dialect:

The cattle-show was over
   and past,
Sam advertis'd to loup his last,
Whilk gar't town bodies
   stand aghast,
Whan in he jump'd
For there were nane to
   cry avast!
Whan in he plump'd.

A decade and a half later a popular jingle had distilled the essence of the tragedy:

Poor Samuel Patch—a man
   once world renounded,
Much loved the water,
   and by it was drownded.
He sought for fame,
   and as he reached to pluck it,
He lost his ballast, and
   then kicked the buck-it.

If the versifiers mourned for Patch, the humorists promptly restored him to life and glory. Remolded by fabulists, he took on the outlines of the American mock hero. A Yankee whaler sighted the Jumping Hero in the South Seas. Amazed, he asked him, "Why, Sam, how *on airth* did you get here? I thought you was drowned at the Canadian lines." "Why," said Sam, "I didn't get *on earth* here at all, but I came slap *through* it. In that Niagara dive I went so everlasting deep, I thought it was just as short to come up t'other side, so out I came in these parts. If I don't take the shine off the sea serpent when

I get back to Boston, then my name's not Sam Patch."

A spurious autobiography, riddled with misspellings and puns, narrated sensational feats of the superjumper for comic-annual readers. At the age of six months Sam jumped from Nanny's arms into a washtub of soapsuds; as a boy he was attracted to leapfrog; in school he would always skip over hard words; before he was four-and-a-half feet tall he jumped from the masthead of a piragua into Hell Gate; at Niagara he bobbed about in the froth like a huckleberry on top of a pail of fermented beer. Since Sam, like Davy Crockett, could not write after his demise, an editor supplied the concluding paragraph and the moral, "Look before you leap." The nation's youth learned about the illustrious aerialist in a brightly illustrated nursery book, *The Wonderful Leaps of Sam Patch,* tracing the saga in rhyme from precocious springs to

An artist's conception, forty years later, of Sam Patch's fatal leap over the Genesee Falls in 1829

adult transatlantic leaps between Washington and London.

In 1836 an aspiring comedian, already known for his Yankee roles, portrayed Sam Patch in Buffalo, and found himself heir to the fame bestowed on the original. In Western cities, and then in New York and Boston, Dan Marble exhibited *Sam Patch, or The Daring Yankee,* and its sequel, *Sam Patch in France, or The Pesky Snake,* year after year before enthusiastic audiences. After various Yankee capers, involving a courtship, an encounter with Mrs. Trollope, and a discussion of Steam Doctors, the stage Patch leaped tremendously over Niagara Falls, from a height estimated at between forty and seventy feet, to bob up triumphantly in a pool of spray and foam. The bills proudly announced, "Mr. Marble will leap from the extreme height of the Theatre, a feat never attempted by any one but himself, and prove that *'Cold Water won't drown love.'*" An open trap behind the water set, containing a spring bed piled with bags of shavings, caught Marble when he jumped from the flies, a performance that frequently cost him minor bruises and at least once a serious injury. On one occasion a substitute was obliged to jump. The victim fortified himself as Patch had before the Last Leap, with almost identical consequences, for he came down fast and lopsidedly and broke his leg. The jumping mania affected the audiences. Clerks jumped counters, farmers jumped fences, boys and old folks vied in "doing" Sam Patch. Marble and his fellow actors, Addams, McVicker and "Yankee" Locke, presented a Yankee roarer to American audiences already conditioned to stage Jonathans and half-alligator heroes.

In its fruition, the Patch legend was taken note of by the literary great, and provided the masses with a proverbial reference. Nathaniel Hawthorne, always receptive to somber American traditions, stirred eagerly to this one on viewing the Genesee Falls in the dusk, and immediately extracted its implications for one of his tales. "How stern a moral may be drawn from the story of poor Sam Patch! . . . Was the leaper of cataracts more mad or foolish than other men who throw away life, or misspend it in pursuit of empty fame, and seldom so triumphantly as he?" He knew, too, of the superstition that Sam still lived. But the projected tale, so surely framed in his mind and so easily visualized by the reader, remained a synopsis.

In a novel with a good deal of factual description of western New York, William Dean Howells revealed a close familiarity with the legend, and caused one of his characters to be shocked at a wife's ignorance of Patch: "Isabel, your ignorance of all that an American woman should be proud of distresses me." On the level of popular allusion, "Sam Patch" gained household currency, like "Sam Hill": "Afore you could say *Sam Patch*"; "Why did you play *Sam Patch,* and jump into the river?" In 1891 a senator from Vermont illustrated his point on the floor of Congress by quoting the overeager Patch.

Although the eccentric adventurer had disappeared from the national purview by mid-century, he retained, in local histories and feature articles, a traditional prestige in communities with special claims to him—Pawtucket, Paterson, and, most faithfully, Rochester, which accorded him a float in its jubilee pageant. On the centennial of the Last Leap, the public-minded, recalling that "George Eastman's town" had once been "Sam Patch's town," proposed christening a park for the hero, to be dominated by a bronze effigy of Sam diving. Since Sam always jumped rather than dove, the nonfulfillment of this suggestion may be approved.[49]

Mose the Bowery b'hoy

Across a Broadway stage one night in 1848 strutted and swaggered an elegant tough, who flicked his cigar daintily before spitting and spoke with jerky emphases a peculiar lingo. A hush of wonder greeted his entrance, and then a roar of recognition burst from the pit that echoed for more than a decade and pealed across the nation. For this was Mose the Bowery b'hoy, unique compound of gutter bum, East Side swell, and volunteer fire laddie evolved by some curious alchemy from the swirling currents of the melting pot, and in a moment of theatrical genius snatched from the waterfront alleys and thrust onto the boards in living likeness.

"B'hoy" signified to New Yorkers in the years from 1846 to 1866 a gay rowdy of the town, and specifically a loafer-dandy familiar on New York's Chatham Street and Centre Market Square down in the Bowery. The Bowery b'hoy was distinguished by his rolling gait, surly manner, slangy talk, and extravagant costume, to wit, a shiny stovepipe hat tipped over the forehead, soaplocks plastered flat against the temple, a "long nine" cigar uptilted at a forty-five-degree angle, bright red shirt, heavy pearl-buttoned pea jacket, and rolled-up trousers tucked into the boots. A city folktype, in the figure of Mose he became America's first urban folk hero.

The play that introduced Mose, *A Glance at New York in 1848,* opened at the Olympic Theater on February 15, 1848, and became one of the greatest successes in the history of the New York stage and of the American theater,

since traveling companies carried the Mose dramas to audiences all over the nation. *A Glance* delighted the Centre Market b'hoys who patronized the Olympic and recognized their image onstage. Their contagious enthusiasm soon spread across the city; further scenes and characters were added on March 15, and the play enjoyed a record run of seventy-four performances, soon to be followed by melodramatic sequels.

Several elements came to happy synthesis in *A Glance at New York.* Its playwright, Benjamin A. Baker, conceived the idea of adapting an enormously popular English play of 1821, *Life in London,* to the American scene by substituting New York for London in its plot frame, a tour of the seamy side of a metropolis by a visiting yokel. Its main actor, Francis S. Chanfrau (1824–1884), modeled the part of Mose on an actual character, Moses Humphreys, a printer on the *New York Sun,* a fireboy on Lady Washington engine number 40, and a notorious Bowery brawler. Frank's brother Hen supposedly worsted Humphreys in the only fight he ever lost and caused his retreat in disgrace to the Sandwich Islands. Just beginning an enduring connection with the American theater as actor and manager, Frank Chanfrau had attracted Baker's attention by his handsome appearance and extraordinary mimetic gift. Conflicting accounts have Chanfrau importuning Baker to write him a fireboy role, and spurning the proposal when suggested by Baker. In any case the part made him famous, and in spite of at least twelve competitors he became identified with Mose in the public mind throughout his career. At one time Chanfrau acted Mose at the Olympic in the *Glance,* then threw a cloak over his costume and took a cab to the Chatham to play in its sequel, and ended the evening with a third performance at Newark after a ferry trip and a nine-mile ride by horse and buggy. On tour in the 1850s Chanfrau played Mose over a thousand times in major theatrical cities from the East Coast to the West: Albany, Atlanta, Augusta, Baltimore, Boston, Buffalo, Charleston, Chicago, Cincinnati, Denver, Louisville, Lowell, Memphis, Mobile, Montreal, Nashville, New Orleans, Newark, Philadelphia, Pittsburgh, Providence, St. Louis, San Francisco, Savannah, Wheeling, Worcester. Chanfrau always attempted to promote American themes. "There are no American playwrights because there are no American managers wanting American plays," he declared in an interview in 1877.

In the decade following the first performance of the *Glance* Mose cavorted through a series of interlocking skits, all rowdy and hectic, riotous and comical, and spiced by city folkways. (Only the *Glance* was ever printed, and its sequels must be reconstructed in part from playbills and reviews.) In addition to the *Glance,* Chanfrau enacted Mose in such favorites as *New York As It Is!, The Mysteries and Miseries of New York, Mose in California!* and *Linda, the Cigar Girl.* A scurvy pantheon gathered around Mose: Lizey, his gallus g'hal; diminutive Sykesy, his Sancho Panza; Master Mose, his offspring and literally spitting image, for he too sported a cigar; Porgy Joe, a tatterdemalion loafer; and Jakey, a Philadelphia compeer. As his career expanded, the b'hoy moved out of the New York slums for escapades in California, France, China, and Arabia. The New York *Spirit of the Times* remarked in its issue of July 6, 1850: "We should not be surprised to hear of him in the moon, and to see the stars doing him homage. He is one himself, although sublunary." Various theatrical forms, from ballet to the circus, borrowed the intrepid fire laddie. *Mose's Dream* was advertised as a "Dramatic, Spectacular, Extravagantic, Pantomimic Ballet."

Before long Mose, who had originated on the sidewalks, moved outside the theater proper into channels of popular idiom, humor, and graphic art. Commenting on the excitement created by *A Glance at New York,* a contemporary account reported that "the catch phrases were in the mouths of the newsboys, bootblacks and city sparrows generally,

Mr. F. S. Chanfrau as Mose and Miss M. Taylor as Lize in *A Glance at New York in 1848*
"Lize, will you go to Vauxhall tonight? All our Bo'hoys are going."
"Yes, Is Sykesy going to be there?"
"What Sykesy? I go in for Sykesy because he runs wid our Machine, but he ain't a-goin' to come it around my gal."
From a contemporary lithograph

they crept into newspaper reports, even appeared in editorials. The Park might bring out the best London star and the star played to empty benches, while all New York flocked to see the Olympic *Mose*." Schoolboys quoted such choice Mose utterances as "Sykesy, take de butt" and "Get off dem hose or I'll hit yer wid a spanner." Mose humor sprouted in newspapers, jokebooks, ephemeral publications. A twenty-page booklet of hand-colored lithographs, *Mose Among the Britishers,* by Thomas Gunn (1850), followed Mose on shipboard to London where he viewed the sights—Westminster Abbey, Trafalgar Square, the British Museum—got himself in a "muss" at a masked ball, and ended up in the stationhouse. The *Union Jack* carried a series of comic letters in 1848 ostensibly written by Mose in various cities. An advertisement in 1848 for a work titled *Asmodeus! or, The Iniquities of New York* mentioned a scene, "Mose in a Muss," with the comment, "It is now impossible to write or talk of life in New York without a Mose." Artists and illustrators depicted Mose in his flaming shirt and stovepipe hat in garish posters, lithographs, and drawings.

The local dramas that established Mose as a figure of popular legend ignored the artistic amenities and concentrated on giving their customers action and excitement. Metropolitan landmarks and underworld hide-outs provided backdrops for scabby scenes of city folkways that fulfilled the playbills' promise to show "Crime, Robbery and Violence in these worst shapes." Playgoers saw such New York sights

THE
GLANCE AT PHILADELPHIA
FOR THE LAST TIME.

MR. DE BAR as Sykesy,
MISS A. FISHER as Susey,
MR. RADCLIFFE as Peter Simple

Received nightly with the
☞ GREATEST APPROBATION ☜
AND
SHOUTS OF LAUGHTER AND APPLAUSE.

An illustrated playbill announcing a Mose play

as the Battery, the Astor House, Vauxhall Gardens, the American Museum, and St. Paul's Church, and the Catherine Fish Market and Walnut Street wharf in Philadelphia. They were further titillated by scenes in a ladies' gymnasium, a gamblers' flash crib, the Soup House (soup one penny a bowl), a mendicants' den, an elegant saloon, and a mock auction room. Action jammed the pieces, in the form of frequent brawls and set-tos, bustling close-ups of dancehall and wharf-front hangouts, eruptions into song and dance as raffish groups resolved into chorus and solo or surged to a garden ball, and grand climaxes of the fire laddies at work extinguishing a burning building. An unexpected development, the rise to eminence of Mose, shifted the focus of the pieces from general panorama to individual saga, and intruded an element of myth-making into routine drama construction. Originally introduced as a type example of local oddity, but one of many exhibits in the Cook's tour of urban wonders and terrors, the fireboy ran away with the show. But the primary impulses of urban local color, melodramatic heroics, and moral fable remained constant in the threefold role of Mose—buffoon, champion, and guardian angel of the Bowery.

Comedy was a major element in the legend, and Mose the prankster, clown, and "original" provoked laughs with his ludicrous actions and speech. Entering a ladies' bowling parlor in female disguise, he promptly kisses a fair bowler; prospecting for gold in California, he spars with a bear and parleys hopelessly with the Indians; in London he marvels at the mummies in the British Museum but considers "They ain't of no good to nuthin," dons the gloves with Lord Brougham, and, presented at court, hopes that the Queen's children are "pretty bright and sassy." Unconventional expressions and vulgarisms studded his talk. "Blow your horn," he says to his g'hal Lizey, requesting a song, and after its completion compliments her with, "Well, I'm blowd if that ain't slap up. Lize, you can sing a few." "Gallus" was a favorite adjective of emphasis; "de butt" signified the hose and "de machine" the fire engine; to "make a muss" was to start a row; "foo-foos" represented outsiders "wot can't come de big figure," i.e., three cents for a glass of grog and a night's lodgings. Some of Mose's sayings acquired classic standing. "Sykesy, take de butt," signified a command to his vassal to hold the end of the hose, and was later applied to the stub of a cigarette. "Bring me a plate of pork and beans," Mose orders the waiter at Vauxhall Gardens, and then, perhaps with the notion of impressing Lizey, adds the afterthought that delighted New York for years— "Say, a large piece of pork, and don't stop to count de beans." (Legend has Chanfrau overhearing Moses Humphreys actually deliver this order in a Bowery restaurant.)

The comic blended into the heroic in the second side of Mose, the champion who conquered men with his fists and fires with the machine. "I'm bilin' over for a rousin' good fight with someone somewhere," reiterates the b'hoy mournfully, ". . . if I don't have a muss soon, I'll spile." He didn't spile. In *A Glance at New York* Mose creates a general row in Loafers' Paradise, wipes up the Peter Funks at a phony auction, and leaves the stage at the end to aid Sykesy in a muss. In *New York As It Is* he raises a "plug-muss" in the Soup House with a "candidate for Sing Sing," then engages in a "general fight," in which we are informed "Mose does his share of the work." At a Dutch ball in *The Mysteries and Miseries of New York*, Mose and Sykesy participate in "A regular rush-in and drag-out." *Mose in California* allows its hero to display his prowess in a "desperate rough and tumble" with the Indians. Musses explode everywhere in *Mose, Joe and Jack*, in the Tombs, on the Jersey City ferry, down in The Cellar of Forty Steps where "Mose floors the rowdies." In all these rows, brawls, and free-for-alls, "the hero of a hundred musses" emerges of course victorious, if occasionally crestfallen by demands for his appearance at the stationhouse.

Fisticuffs might be the b'hoy's hobby, but fighting fires was his business, and

supplanted even his love for a muss. "I did think yesterday I'd leave de machine," he admits sheepishly, "but I can't do it; I love that ingine better than my dinner; last time she was at de corporation-yard, we plated de brakes, and put in new condensil pipes; and de way she works is about right, I tell you. She throws a three-inch stream de prettiest in town." In the line of duty the daredevil fireboy combines matter-of-fact valor with a streak of sentiment and a rude chivalry. Mose recalls one time he had hold of the pipe in the midst of burning shanties when a sobbing woman approached him:

Seys I, "What's de matter, good woman?" Seys she, "My baby's in de house, and it's burnin'!" Seys I, "What!"—I turned my cap hindside afore, and buttoned my old fire-coat, and I went in and fetched out dat baby. I never forgot dat woman's countenance wen I handed de baby to her. She fell down on her knees and blessed me. *(Wipes his eye with sleeve.)* Ever since dat time I've had a great partiality for little babies. The fire-boys may be a little rough outside, but they're all right here. *(Touches breast.)* It never shall be said dat one of de New York boys deserted a baby in distress.

Hearing about Mose's rescues was obviously far less satisfactory than seeing them. Consequently the bills tantalized with MOSE SAVING A HELPLESS CHILD FROM THE FLAMES or BUILDING IN FLAMES, MOSE ARRIVES AND SETS DE MASHINE AT WORK, and the pieces vied with each other in reproducing elaborate fire scenes, of the Old Brewery, in Philadelphia's Spring Garden, on board the good ship *Humbug* California-bound. Triumphantly the machine would trundle across the stage; fireboys manned the hose, set up the ladder, mounted the roof, and began chopping with their axes; up to a flame-framed window clambered the b'hoy in answer to a piteous wail; down the teetering ladder he tenderly bore an inert body through the sweeping tongues of death. Blessed and commended, Mose would shrug

Chanfrau as Mose rescuing a child from the fire
From a contemporary lithograph

his shoulders: "I ain't no engine house pirate, so there's no use o' gassing."

Heroism fused with sentiment in the character of Mose to provide his third role, the guardian daemon of the Bowery. This protective function did not stop with saving babies from the blaze; Mose had from the first sided with honest virtue, when in *A Glance at New York* he befriended the greenhorn duped by sharpers and foo-foos. Playbills and reviews of the subsequent sketches outline a list of knightly acts. Mose interposes between Linda the Cigar Girl and her molesters—"The persecutors felled to the ground by Mose"; he assists a distressed outlander—"Mose undertakes to see the Countryman righted"; he protects an old gentleman "with a Heart full of sympathy and a Pocket full of Money"—"Precise saved from death by Mose"; he intercepts a designing libertine—"the generous-hearted Mose foils his base purposes." Through the slums and vice lairs of Gotham moved a strange, uncouth avenger, a gutter scamp turned knight errant.

Yet the taint of tawdry associates and tenement breeding clung to the Bowery's Robin Hood. Even *America's Own, or, The Fireman's Journal* savagely criticized the stage portrayal as a sham, degrading in its effects on youth and a stigma to the profession. So widely did suspicion root that a Louisville playbill, announcing the coming of *New York As It Is,* went to considerable pains to reassure back-country patrons of the rightful nobility of its besmirched hero:

Mose, the far-famed, and world-renowned, presents himself at our Theatre this evening. In all the pieces of this class, there is scarcely a single incident that is not calculated to warn the unwary against the arts of the designing, and prepare the adventurer for the trials he must expect to encounter. All the spirit, fun and knock situations, are rendered prominent; but in this, as in every other MOSE piece, produced by MR. CHANFRAU, the hero is always found defending right against wrong; protecting the weak against the assaults of the strong; and invariably siding with innocence, helplessness, and distress. No two characters have been more misunderstood than MOSE and LIZEY. This hero and heroine of humble life have been too often considered perfect rowdies and profligate outcasts, while the very reverse is the case. MOSE, it is true, is one of the fire b'hoys, full of fun, frolic and fighting, but without one vicious propensity in his nature; and LIZEY is a good-hearted, worthy and virtuous woman, attached to MOSE, with no other prominent fault than the very excusable one of striving to imitate the peculiarities of the man of her heart.

Any lingering doubts about the integrity and pure motives of the b'hoy must assuredly have been dispelled by the last and most resplendent Mosedrama, modestly referred to in the bills as "the best dramatic production of modern times." *Linda, the Cigar Girl; or, Mose Among the Conspirators* (1859) dressed up the routine local sketch in the romantic conventions of the day's sentimental literature, and exhibited Mose at his sterling best.

A lengthy synopsis has preserved the flavor of the piece. Impoverished but virtue-clinging Linda implores the aid of God—"Heaven help me and direct me, for on earth I have no guide"—while proudly rejecting that of man—"I am most helpless, but the sun that rises on my ruin shall set upon my grave." Confronted on the street by her persecutor, Chowles, she breathes a ringing defiance: "Remember the magic words that make my heart leap with exultation, life for my unknown mother's sake; but death before dishonor." Meanwhile Mose in disgrace stands trial at the stationhouse; genuine sentiment likewise gushes from his manly breast: "I should have tried to be something more if my mother had lived; but, when she was gone, there was no one left to care for me, so I never tried to raise myself higher; though oftentimes there's something here [tapping the manly breast] that tells me I might have done it if I had." Mose is honorably discharged.

Finding Linda adrift on the streets on an "inclement" night, he bears her into a splendid mansion. Apparently Linda was coolly received, because her customary lament now becomes strongly class-conscious. "I thought when a poor girl was perishing in the streets, the proudest mansion in the land was a hospital to succour her. You call her a pauper; look well upon her, and then tell me if her form is not as fair as the proudest of you here; clasp on her arms the gems that glitter there on yours, and tell me if they lose their lustre. No! they fade in brightness only when worn by one whose heart-streams are so corrupted she cannot feel a throb of pity for one of her own sex who lies dying at her feet." The first act ends when the woman of the corrupted heart-streams recognizes Linda as her lost daughter. All during the second act, however, Linda continues to be persecuted, and Mose continues to attempt her rescue; in the guise of an Irish watchman he penetrates her beggar's den. At length the plot coil leaves Linda firmly in the power of the blackguard Russell, who mocks her misery and supplications; she then looses her feverish wail full upon him: "When we meet at yonder awful tribunal, mine shall be the voice to hurl your shivering spirit down the steps of horror and perdition." Linda renders that tribunal imminent by setting fire to the apartment, and gloats over Russell's terror. She herself is thrillingly rescued from the chamber window by the gallant fireboy, who in response to the cheers of the crowd modestly inquires, "AIN'T I DOOIN MY DOOTY?"

Perhaps it required the more delicate insights of a female playwright to expose to the full the moral lining of the East Side tough. In allying the fireboy with the bedeviled heroine of the feminine fifties, Louise Reeder placed the pedestal under the guardian saint of the Bowery; Mose had been called to the cause of chaste womanhood that so deliciously obsessed the littérateurs of the age. The protector of flophouse bums and country greenhorns had been assigned to the fairest flower of the literary landscape, the constant virgin. Mose had come of age.

Time caught up even with the indomitable fireboy. By the 1860s the robust drama-cycle had subsided to a vestigial skit. Friends asked Chanfrau why he did not revive his major triumph, and he explained, "There is really nothing in the play. It is a conglomeration of scenes—a piecemeal affair altogether—and the local hits and slang phrases, while they were understood by everybody who heard them when the play was new, are utterly incomprehensible to the present run of playgoers. When *Mose* was born, he was simply a representative of a well-known class in New York. The era of steam fire engines changed all that, and *Mose* no longer exists." Nevertheless, Chanfrau did yield to the urging of stage veterans to play the role once more. An observer wrote its obituary:

The audience sat stolidly wondering what the devilish old trumpery was about. When Mose came on and said: "He wasn't going to run wid der macheen any more," there wasn't a smile in the house. Nobody seemed to know or care what he was talking about. But that line used to wake the echoes at the Olympic and the Chatham.

So Mose died on the stage. Of all the plays, only one saw print, and the hobo hero slipped into oblivion. But the image had penetrated too deeply into the American imagination to be summarily erased, and it rose again in a newer form and more fanciful conceit. Underworld stories sprang up around a fabled Bowery giant, twelve feet tall, with hands as big as hams reaching down almost to the ground; he wore a red shirt and a red helmet as big as a tent. When Big Mose charged into battle against the New York gangs, he carried an uprooted lamppost in one hand and a butcher's cleaver in the other; wrathfully he hurled paving blocks ripped from the streets at the Plug Uglies and the Dead Rabbits. For sport he drank drayloads of beer at a sitting, or jumped from Manhattan to Brooklyn, or blew ships back down the East River with the fumes of a two-foot cigar, or unhitched a horsecar and ran with it pell-mell the length of the Bowery. When his girl turned him down, Big Mose fled the Bowery for the South Seas, where he married an island princess, became king of the Sandwich Islands, and raised forty half-breed children. But even today when a bum picks up a cigarette stub he says, "Big Mose must of dropped it."

The tall tales of Big Mose are the discovery of the prolific historian of America's urban underworlds, Herbert Asbury, who published them in his books on *The Gangs of New York* (1928) and *Ye Olde Fire Laddies* (1930). In a letter to me of October 4, 1941, he wrote: "I shall be glad to tell you what I can about the origin of Old Mose, or Big Mose, the legendary hero of the Bowery b'hoys, and am sorry that few definite sources of material can be cited. The stories about Mose grew up as did those of Paul Bunyan. I started collecting them when I first came to New York in 1915, when I used to spend considerable time on the Bowery talking to the old-timers in the saloons and lodging-houses. Some of these old men professed to remember the Bowery in the days before the Civil War, and from them I got most of the stories about Mose."

Mr. Asbury went on to state his belief that the Bowery brawler Moses Humphreys was the actual prototype of Big Mose. After being licked by Frank Chanfrau's brother Hen, Moses departed for

the Sandwich Islands (now Hawaii). "He never returned to New York, but memories of his prowess remained, and all the fantastic legends that gradually grew up about the bowery b'hoy clustered about him. I think it fairly certain that Moses Humphrey[s] was thus the original Big Mose, but it is doubtful if he would have become a legendary hero had it not been for Baker's playwriting and Chanfrau's acting."

So a fabulous oral tradition did take root in the Bowery and perpetuate a legend of Mose long after the cycle of plays about him had vanished from the stage. But the national legend of the Bowery b'hoy belongs to the decade after *A Glance at New York* opened at the Olympic in 1848 and overnight brought the theater to the people.

The Mose plays sounded a popular, realistic note in the American theater that did not appeal to certain custodians of the drama. A critic of the period, William K. Northall, called the *Glance* an "unmitigated conglomeration of vulgarity and illiteracy . . . low in design, vulgar in language and improbable in plot." Worst of all in his eyes, "the boxes no longer shone with the elite of the city; the character of the audiences was entirely changed, and Mose, instead of appearing on the stage, was in the pit, the boxes, and the gallery."

True, the folk swarmed to the playhouse to see their favorite. The drama reviewer for the *New York Herald* of September 5, 1848, commented on the phenomenon:

The announcement of the new local piece of the *Mysteries and Miseries of New York* attracted a tremendous audience last evening. At an early hour . . . the steps and vicinity of the theatre were crowded; and, within a short time from the opening of the doors, the house was found to be so filled, that the further sale of tickets was stopped. The interior . . . presented an animated appearance—tier upon tier, all filled, the lower circle had its due proportion of ladies, and the remainder of the house was completely filled, the lobbies as well, every inch of space, in fact, from whence even a glimpse of the stage could be had. . . .

This reviewer could see merit as well as popular appeal in the production, and praised its social documentation that presented "a perfect picture of a certain class of liver in this great city, whose existence is scarcely known to the mass of our citizens, save through the records of the Court of Sessions."

In the end Mose touched many phases of the national mythmaking. The catchpenny portrait of the Bowery b'hoy expanded along familiar lines of American popular creation—the chesty rough, the comic boor, the Robin Hood picaro, nature's nobleman, the Yankee abroad, the crime-fighting Superman, the Paul

Bunyan demigod. The artistically despised vehicles that launched his career reflect the throb and thrum of a spawning metropolis and portray the urban culture, not of the drawing room, but of the streets and alleys and dives. At stage center is the b'hoy, America's first urban folktype.[50]

Yankee Jonathan the countryman

In the cases of the Tennessee hunters, the Ohio riverboatmen, and the Bowery b'hoys, a single hero-clown came to symbolize the breed. With the Down East rustic, "verdant," and "original," favorite terms for the Yankee farmer, no one individual emerged to typify the species, but the Yankee as an immediately recognizable type achieved high visibility in the decades before the Civil War. He began to take shape in the years after the American Revolution, as a comic character in yarns, plays, illustrations, and songs. The Down Easter represented the New England version of the American genus that took its place in the family of national stereotypes with the establishment of the republic. By contrast with the cultured European, the newly decolonialized American seemed a boor and a lout, ignorant of the amenities and refinements of civilized living.

The Yankee on the hillside farm fell still further behind the cosmopolitan population of the seaboard towns in his innocence of modern ways. His visit to the city became a staple theme of humorous lore. Sharpers and merchants gulled him until, with pockets empty, he fled back to the safety of his pasture and woodlot. Yet there was another side to the Yankee, his low cunning and craft when conducting a horse trade or peddling his notions. On the road vending gimcracks the Yankee peddler enticed his customers with the Devil's tongue. To "play a Yankee trick" became a stock phrase indicating a sly triumph in some petty transaction.

Thousands of risible anecdotes about Yankees swirled through the taverns and countinghouses of early America and found their way, with some literary touches, into the breezy newspapers of the 1830s and 1840s. First and foremost, the Yankee was a country bumpkin, a sight to behold, an oddity to listen to—if the one observing and listening was a sophisticated city type. The following portrait, which appeared in the Exeter, New Hampshire, *News Letter* for June 15, 1841, the New York *Spirit of the Times* for December 23, 1843, and no doubt other papers, catches Jonathan the Yankee as he had crystallized into a folktype after two centuries of New England back-country existence:

AN ORIGINAL CHARACTER

Whoever travels through any of the New England States, and twigs, as he journeys, the eccentricities of some of the natives, cannot but be amused with the following graphic sketch, and may derive many new ideas in respect to etymology and diversity of character.

Some years since an acquaintance of ours set out on horseback from the eastern part of Massachusetts for the Green Mountains in Vermont. While travelling through the town of New Salem his road led into a piece of woods some five miles in length, and long before he got out of which, he began to entertain doubts whether he should be blest with the sight of a human habitation; but as all things must have an end, so at last the woods, and the nut brown house of a farmer greeted his vision. Near the road was a tall, rawboned, overgrown, lantern-jawed boy probably seventeen years of age, digging potatoes. He was a curious figure to behold. What was lacking in the length of his tow breeches was amply made up for behind; his suspenders appeared to be composed of birch bark, grape vine, sheepskin; and as for his hat, which was of dingy felt—poor thing, it had once evidently seen better days, but now, alas! It was only the shadow of its glory . . . and through the aperture red hairs in abundance stood six ways for Sunday. In short, he was one of the roughest specimens of domestic manufacture that ever mortal beheld. Our travelling friend, feeling an itching to scrape an acquaintance with the critter, drew up the reins of his horse and began:

"Hallo, my good friend, can you inform me how far it is to the next house?"

Jonathan started up—leaned on his hoe handle—rested one foot on the gamble of his sinister leg, and replied—

"Hullo yourself! how'd dew? Well I jess can. 'Taint near so fur as it used to be afore they cut the woods away—then 'twas generally reckoned four miles, but now the sun shrivels up the road and don't make more'n tew. The fust house you come to, though, is a barn, and the next is a hay stack; but old Hobsin's house is on beyant. You'll be sure to meet his gals long afore you get there; tarnil rompin' critters, they plague our folks more'n little. His sheep git in our pasture every day, and his gals in our orchard. Dad sets the dog arter the sheep and me arter the gals—and the way we makes the wool and the petticoats fly, is a sin to snakes."

"I see you are inclined to be facetious, young man—pray tell me how it happens that one of your legs is shorter than the other?"

"I never 'lows any body to meddle with my grass tanglers, mistur; but seein' it is you, I'll tell ye. I was born so at my tickler request, so that when I hold a plough, I can go with one foot in the furrer, and t'other on land, and not lop over; besides, it is very convenient when I mow round a side hill."

"Very good, indeed—how do your potatoes come off this year?"

"They don't come at all; I digs 'em out and there's an everlastin' snarl of 'em in each hill.". . .

"You have been in these parts some time, I should guess."

"I guess so tew. I was borned and got my bro'tin up in that 'ere house; but my native place is down in Pordunk."

"Then you said that it is about three and half miles to the next house?"

"Yes, sir; 'twas a spell ago, and I don't believe it's grow'd much shorter since."

"Much obliged. Good bye."

"Good bye to ye—that's a darn slick horse of yourn."

There, reader—there is a Jonathan for you of the first water. You don't find his equal every place.[51]

Here is Jonathan full-size. He never gives a straight answer—and outside New England on his travels he pesters strangers with inquisitive questions as vexing as his circuitous responses on his home soil. His speech abounds with barnyard similes and tall-tale snatches. Jonathan's allusion to his short leg marks the first known appearance in American folklore of the trait that distinguishes the sidehill gouger, a mythical beast of the lumberwoods come to light in the twentieth century, who wore one leg down traveling the same route around mountainsides.

Although a native of one of the six New England states, Jonathan—the Yankee's most frequent sobriquet—turned up all over the country, and we have encountered him in Davy Crockett's clearing as Job Snelling the merchant. In his dual roles, as the gawking dolt or the crafty trader, Jonathan seems to have little of the stuff from which heroes are made, but he does develop heroic lineaments, particularly in his theatrical appearances. Impersonators of all the folk heroes of the Democratic Life-style appeared on the stage, which in Jacksonian times closely followed the currents of the popular

and folk imagination, and the spate of plays depicting the Yankee show clearly his ascent from an amusing booby into a defender of the democratic faith and democratic mores.

After humble beginnings as a boorish servant, the stock Yankee expands and inflates until he takes on the proportions of a comic Odysseus, moving through a series of ludicrous situations that carry him to far parts of the globe. In spite of the wide range and duration of the Yankee plays, the type-figure they contain adheres consistently to set formulas and conventions associated with the mythical Yankee in the mind of the folk.

The stage Yankee was never an individualized character; he was always a stereotype. In the first plays only brief glimpses were afforded of him; in later ones, in the 1830s, 40s, and 50s, when the vogue of frontier humor was at its height, his eccentricities, instead of providing mere comic interludes, became the basis of the plot structure. But whether it was the subordinate or the dominant part, the main features of the stereotype did not change; the play could not make of the Yankee a creature of flesh and blood. Sometimes where such a stricture hampered the playwright, he put a Yankee mask on one of his characters to supply the comedy and removed it to fulfill the plot requirements. This use of disguise is one very clear recognition of the existence of a mythical Yankee who was properly the property of the folk; another is the repeated references by other characters to "a real live Yankee," "an original," "a perfect natural," that emphasizes the oddity of the type;[52] a further is the tendency to give individual examples of the genus a common name, Jonathan. What, then, are the characteristics that made distinctive this half-mythical Jonathan, the real live Yankee as he appeared on the stage?

The traditional Yankee, in his red wig, bell-shaped hat, and striped coat and trousers, was a country bumpkin. To him the big city was a source of awe and bewilderment. "Well, I swan to man," he declared, "this is the tarnallest place—this ere New York. All sorts of folks here tu—niggers, a nation on 'em—foreigners by the bushel. Guess Europe are unpopulated, now—anyhow all come here to see New York." "What tarnal comical creturs these towns are. I'll be darned but I guess I've lost my way, though I chalked the corners of the streets as I went along." "No, I don't know where anybody lives in this big city, not I; for my part, I believe how they all lives in the street, there's such a monstrous sight of people a scrouging backards and forards." "This must be Broadstreet, and broad nough tis tewe, by gum! I've been walken up it this good fifteen minutes, and darn'd 'f I've got a crost it yit. I must keep tewe eyes bout me, or I shall be intewe Kingstreet, and

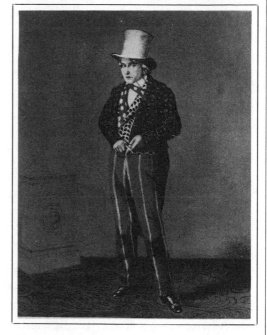

George H. "Yankee" Hill in Yankee costume, whittling a stick

the black barded jews'll shave the hair off my teeth. Folks say they're keener than yankees for all they aynt hafe the wit; yit a poor lubberly country cracker stands no more chance with um, 'thout he's a brother Jonathan, than a leetle Tomy cat in hell 'thout claws, or a fly skippen bout in a hot glew pot."[53]

The rustic Yankee, adrift in the big city, refuses to pay the porter or the cab driver. He gapes at outdoor statues and indoor statuettes, shocked at their nudity.[54] He is considerably startled at seeing his first play; the original Jonathan of *The Contrast* thought when the curtain was raised that he was being given a peep into his neighbor's house.

Even though his naiveté was a subject for ridicule, and his role was that of a dependent, Jonathan admitted inferiority to none and proudly vaunted his

American independence. "Yankee Doodle," whistled, sung, or recited, was continually on his lips, the badge of his jingoism; it was so closely identified with the eccentric countryman that it gained a substantive use as a nickname for him. Any imputation of servitude he was quick to resent:

Jonathan. I've no master,
  I calculate.
Rust. No! I beg pardon,
  I thought you served the young aboriginal gentlemen?
Jonathan. May be, so I do—but serving a man don't make him my master, by a darn'd sight.[55]

The assertion became a refrain: "Sarvant!!! By jingoes! Sarvant! I wonder where's the being on a pair of legs, that I'd call master! I'm mad!"[56]

Not deferential, but boastful, was Jonathan. His boasts were not as elaborate or long-winded as those of the frontiersman, but they bore the same touch of bluster and defiance. "I've lived in the back parts something," he states mildly. "I'm half horse, half alligator, and a little of the Ingen, I guess."[57] Wishing for refreshment, he says, "I'm as hungry as a juvenile hippopotamus, and as dry as a squash bed in April."[58] In a fighting mood he claims to be "jist about as savage as a cross-cut saw, and a leetle bit sharper;"[59] wrathful, he exclaims:

I'll whip the hull boodle of you at once. Make me mad, and I'll lick a thunder-storm! . . . Want to use fire weapons, I'll fight you with rifles loaded to the muzzles with three cornered slugs and rammed into each other. Get my Ebenezer riz, and you'd think somebody was a blowin' rocks! I've the almightiest notion to pick up this awful nigger and knock out somebody's brains with his shin!"[60]

In jaunty mood the Yankee boasts of other accomplishments: "I'm a team by myself, twenty oxen and a stallion; I come down to New York to see the place, and tell the folks a thing or two; I can play on the jews-harp, fiddle, fife, drum and bugle horn, the sweetest; I can dance anything from the college hornpipe to Jim Crow." "I'm the boy for a race, for an apple-paring or quilting frolic—fight a cock, hunt an opossum, or snare a partridge with any one.—Then I'm a squire, and a county judge, and a brevet ossifer in the militia besides, and a devil of a fellow at an election to boot."[61]

No trait is more deeply ingrained in the general conception of the Yankee than that of inquisitiveness.[62] The Yankee of the stage accordingly has moments in which he follows the customary formula of question after impertinent question. When the nosy one in turn is questioned about his name or birthplace, he has recourse to a conventional evasion. An illustration of both devices is afforded in a conversation in *Jonathan in England* between the Squire's testy guest, Oldskirt, and his overcurious valet, Solomon Swap:

Oldskirt. Show me to the housekeeper's room at once.
Swap. Jest stop a minute, will ye? You're a funny-looking critter; I'm darned if you haint? Say, now, what in thunder could have

brought you down here? You hain't a relation to the Squire, be you?

Oldskirt. (gruffly) No.

Swap. I reckoned as much. But you did come from London, now, didn't you?

Oldskirt. Well, suppose I did?

Swap. Well, I guess it must of been some special business to bring you so far. You didn't come for nothing, did you?

Oldskirt. What's that to you?

Swap. Cause I like to know. I guess you didn't bring any of your family along—but maybe you ain't got any.

Oldskirt. How's that your business?

Swap. O, nothing; only I'm zealous to larn; but be you going to stay long at our house?—if I may be so bold?

Oldskirt. (angrily) No, boldness! Ask again.

Swap. Yes, I say you're as crank as a cider-mill. I guess you didn't get up right end foremost this morning?

Oldskirt. Will you show me the way to the housekeeper's room, you confounded, guessing, inquisitive nondescript!

Swap. (aside) I'll coax him a speck. *(aloud)* Did you ever hear about the sea-sarpent, in these parts?

Oldskirt. (crabbedly) No; nor don't wish to. *(in a sarcastic manner)* Pray, my friend, where were you bred and born?

Swap. O, you want to know, as they say in Virginia, where I was raised. Well, may be you know where Boston, New England, is?

Oldskirt. (sharply) Yes.

Swap. Well, it warn't there.[63]

Jedidiah Homebred, in *The Green Mountain Boy,* when asked, "Well, what may I call your name?" replies, "You may call it the Great Mogul or the King of the Cannibal Islands if you're a mind tu, but it ain't."[64]

The insolence of the Yankee in the question-and-answer formula was matched by his impudence in sustained dialogue. This convention was a favorite one since its humor did not depend on situation but could be evoked in any ordinary conversation by the obtuseness of a rural Yankee. When, in one play, a plausible situation was contrived to heighten the dialogue of inanity, the effect was classic. In *Blanche of Brandywine* the Yankee, Seth Hope, is captured by the British and taken before a council of officers, among whom are Howe and Cornwallis, for questioning. In the resulting scene a number of familiar humorous devices, both of speech and of situation, are employed:

Howe. (angrily) I want you to step here, sir!

Seth. Well, there's no use a getting riled about it. I'm jest as meek and gentle as 16 lambs' tails, if you use me right—but if you don't, I can be jest as kantankerous as Aunt Patience's old brindle cow, and from *horns to her tail,* she is the crookedest varmint on this universal hemisphere.

Capt. Howard. Silence! fellow! Such remarks are in dem'd bad taste! The general doesn't wish to know anything of your relative's cow.

Seth. Well, I didn't know. I thought he mought, seein' as heow he'd got a *pet calf* in his paster! *(turns to Howe)* That was into him, captain, about a feet, wan't it? *(laughs loudly).*

Cornwallis. (rapping on table) Silence, fellow! Do you know that you are in the presence of General Howe, commander-in-chief of his majesty's forces?

Seth. Want tew know? *Be* you Howe? *(shaking hands).* Wal, *how* be you?

Howe. (indignant) No trifling, simpleton! but answer truly such questions as I shall put to you.

Seth. Jest so! A mighty slick coat you've got on, major; must a cost suthin' tew get that up. *(Goes up, feels the cloth).*

Howe. Stand off, fellow! Now Sir, your name? *(An officer at table takes down the replies).*

Seth. Seth.

Howe. Seth what?

Seth. Seth nothing.

Howe. No other name?

Seth. No, Major; my dad was an all-fired mean cuss, and he couldn't afford to give me but one name, and *that* was the meanest he could think on.

Howe. Where do you reside?

Seth. Which?

Howe. Where do you live?

Seth. Oh, I thought you wanted to know where I resided! Tew hum!

Howe. Where might that be?

Seth. Wal, it *might* be in Tophit, but it ain't. *(Turns and slaps Howard on shoulder).* I had him there, skeezicks—by gravy!

Howe. Your equivocation, sir, but confirms Captain Howard's suspicions that you are a spy!

Seth. (to Howard) Did you say that! you darned no-such-a-thing? I've a great mind tew pin your long ears back and swaller you hull! I hev, by gravy.

Howe. Come, come sir; if you are not less obstreperous you shall receive a taste of the cat.

Seth. Oh! talking of cats, I want to tell you about the time I bit a

piece off our he Thomas-cat's tail.

Howe. (angrily) This fellow's an idiot!

Seth. An idiot, Major? I'm a hull Lunatic Asylum!

Howe. Conduct him behind the lines, and dismiss him with a sound drubbing.

Seth. Don't you want tew ax me no more questions?

Howe. Begone, fellow!

Seth. (to Cornwallis) Mebbe *you* would like tew ax me suthin?

Cornwallis. Be off with you!

Seth. (to the others) Is there any gentleman here that wants to know nothin'?

Howe. (angrily) Captain Howard! Remove this fellow at once!

Seth. Now, Kurnel, don't be so crankey! I'm a goin'! Goodbye! *(seizing his hand).* . . .[65]

The situation that afforded the easiest and surest comic possibilities—and was consequently done to death—was the courting scene. This required little inventive contribution; Jonathan's impetuosity and his immediate rebuff were always sure of a laugh. So strained a plot-twist as the disguised kiss or marriage, in which the Yankee busses his veiled sweetheart only to discover a concealed black woman, is to be found in at least five plays. Occasionally some ingenuity is exercised within the courting formula: Curtis Chunk, in *The Stage-Struck Yankee,* falls instantly in love with the heroine of the play he attends, and throws over his own Jedidah on the spot. The love poem he sends her is indicative of the level of burlesque on which the Yankee played the role of romantic lover:

I write, dear Fanny, for to tell,
How in love with you I fell.
Except Jedidah, you're the fust
That ever made my heart to bust.

Jedidah, I have quit and
     cussed her,
All for you, you little buster!
Your eyes like lightning bugs,
     do glitter,
You most consummate
     beautiful critter.
And I shall be in tarnal torture
Till you let me come and
     court you.
I guess you'll find a lad of spunk
Is Curtis, called for short
     Cur-Chunk.[66]

In plays where the courting episode is minor, the impassioned Yankee is placed on view with a coveted or hastily snatched buss. Thus Jefferson S. Batkins, apologizing after the deed, in *The Silver Spoon:* "I couldn't help it, Hannah; the fact is, natur made a move, and I seconded the motion"; Welcome Sobersides in *Montgomery:* "I swar I'd swop my rifle for a buss of that pretty little squaw—My stars, what real

115

"Yankee" Hill as Nathan Tucker in *Wife for a Day*

"Well, I swow, if I had such a wife, I'd stand for Congress right off."

genuine rifle-bullets her eyes would be"; Hiram Dodge in *Yankee Peddler:* "Say, if you'll let me kiss you right straight in the meouth, I'll give you a hull string of sassingers for nuthin'."[67]

Yet at home, so Jonathan averred, a stout Yankee lass was pining for him. "I reckon Sal Snubbins will kind a wish she'd had me, arter all." "What would my sweetheart, Patience [Beanpole], say if she only knew I was dancing with these gals, with such short gowns on?" Rebuffed, he consoled himself with her memory. "Wall, yer needn't if yer don't want to. It don't make no odds to me. There's Melindy Jones down to Skow-

hegan—*she'll* have me, I reckon."[68]

Calvin Cartwheel in *The Brazen Drum* described some of the charms of his girl back home, Katy Kornsilk: ". . . her hair's so long she can kiver herself up in it, feet and all—and her cheeks, by the forewheel of old Phoebus' cart, if they ain't jist like two big peaches stuck in a lump of fresh butter—oh! great Goligy, but wouldn't I like to have a buss at 'em now."[69]

So far we have been considering the more frivolous mannerisms of the composite Yankee. But the Yankee is much more than a stage jester; he possesses what Howard Mumford Jones calls "the heart of gold which the Americans associate with a shagbark exterior."[70] In his moral strength and physical bravery Jonathan takes on heroic qualities that elevate him from buffoon to folk hero. Jonathan's heroism comes to the fore in some of the more lurid melodramas, wherein he champions the cause of Polish freedom against the Russians, makes a thrilling rescue from an overhanging limb of a baby adrift in a canoe about to plunge over a waterfall, or jumps through the window of the unscrupulous Count Almonte's Cuban mansion and forestalls his wicked designs on the Señorita Miralda. Other examples show the Yankee as a craven and a coward in some of the numerous battles and wars he participates in, but where this is the case, his fear is avowed candidly and comically:

Horsebean Hemlock. Which is the easiest way to die, to be cut in two with a cannon ball or to be frightened to death? For it seems to me one of 'em I've got to take.
Turill. Easiest always to die bravely.
Hemlock. Did you ever try it?
Turill. No. We have no cowards on board of the *Silver Arrow.* I'll place you at my gun, and, if you show fear, I'll ram you into it, and send you on board the king's ship in a hurry.

Hemlock. I shouldn't like that, by Judas. I think I'll try the being frightened to death first and if that don't do I can be shot afterwards.[71]

The quality of morality is closely associated with that of bravery. It is noticeably present in the plays revolving around the villain's attempted abduction or seduction of the heroine; Jonathan is brought within the plot structure by being asked to assist, and either indignantly refuses or agrees only to foil the scheme. Uprightness is also displayed in the Yankee's naive code of old-fashioned honesty. "I notice one thing," he says sententiously,

"the most fashionable people borrow the most money. I hope they pay, 'cause, Colonel, it is our doctrine up to Cranberry Centre that it ain't honest to borrow money and not pay it back agin. Now I may be a leetle unwise or so, but if I thought I had a drop of rascally blood in my veins, I'd bleed it out if I killed the crittar doin' it."[72]

Even when he is exposed to a bribe that he cannot resist, his yielding is made a matter of farce and his conduct is partially atoned for by his having previously pitched the villain out of a window, so that at the play's end Jonathan is still admitted into the party of victory and virtue.

There are further consistencies in the portrait of Jonathan that emerge from his dramatic adventures. The name bestowed on him, if it does not follow the generic title, is always of homespun timbre appropriate to his linsey-woolsey character: Aminadab Slocum, Jedidiah Homebred, Deuteronomy Dutiful, Zachariah Dickerwell, Sy Saco, Elam W. Pancake, Ichabod Inkling, Moderation Easterbrook, Podijah B. Peazley, Zephaniah Makepeace, Jacob Jewsharp, Lot Sap Sago, and so on. He tends to speak in monologues, because, first, it is difficult for him to converse with the normal characters except through the humorous dialogue; and secondly, frontier humor depends on the loose, rambling, seemingly spontaneous delivery of the backwoods storyteller. Much of the humor of the stage Yankee actor is in keeping with this oral method, and in fact the Yankee actor often inserted a Yankee story within the play, or between the acts. Another commonplace of the type Yankee is his Down East dialect, rife with vernacularisms and homely similes. As the Yankee himself put it, "You might as well try to back a heavy load up a hill, as stop my thoughts coming right out in homely words."[73] His words, like his manners, smacked of the farm and the countryside. When Enos Crumlett observes, "Might have hitched a yoke of cattle to that sneeze," or Seth Swap muses, "Misery seems to be piled up here in Cuba, like haystacks in a mowin' field,"[74] the Yankee is speaking in the traditional tongue of his New England soil.

117

The question of the antecedents of the first Yankee cannot be satisfactorily answered, since the Yankee was essentially a folk creation. Marston Balch, in an article entitled "Jonathan the First," unearths an English play with a Jonathen [sic] prior to the Jonathan of *The Contrast* and with similar characteristics, but it had no circulation in America.[75] Perley I. Reed sees in a character, Simple, in the anonymous *The Blockheads* (ca. 1776), the first native country bumpkin, though only a feebly developed one.

A fixed folk character, the Yankee did not change. Royall Tyler's play *The Contrast* (1787), the first native play to be written and produced in America, displays all the major conventions of the Yankee role. Jonathan of *The Contrast* is vigorously independent:

Jonathan. Servant! Sir, do you take me for a neger, —I am Colonel Manly's waiter.

Jessamy. A true Yankee distinction, egad, without a difference. Why, Sir, do you not perform all the offices of a servant? do you not even blacken his boots?

Jonathan. Yes; I do grease them a bit for him sometimes; but I am a true blue son of liberty for all that. Father said I should come as Colonel Manly's waiter, to see the world, and all that; but no man shall master me. My father has as good a farm as the colonel.[76]

He is unused to the ways of the big city, and talks companionably with a harlot whom he takes to be "the deacon's daughter." His sense of honor is shown in his reluctance to break his promise not to see another woman while he is away: ". . . you wouldn't have me false to my true-love, would you?" Yet he is an ardent courter, and faithfully follows Jessamy's directions on wooing the desirable Jenny at first acquaintance, with the invariable comic flurry: "Burning rivers! cooling flames! red-hot roses! pig-nuts! hasty pudding and ambrosia!" he spouts as he kisses Jenny, and yet to his wonder fails to captivate her. The original Jonathan too has a cornfed lass back home, Tabitha Wymen, the deacon's daughter—"she and I have been courting a great while, and folks say as how we are to be married; and so I broke a piece of money with her when we parted, and she promised not to spark it with Solomon Dyer while I am gone."[77]

An indication of Jonathan's potential heroism is afforded when he sees his colonel attacked by Dimple and rushes to defend him, declaring "I feel chockfull of fight" and "I'd shew him Yankee boys play, pretty quick."[78] The speech conventions are less fully developed than those of manner, since the humor of dialect did not begin to burgeon till the 1830s, but the homely simile and the vernacularism inevitably creep into Jonathan's utterances. The main themes of the Yankee tradition—naiveté, oafishness, and the contrast (here between the polished Jessamy who apes his English master's graces and reverence for Chesterfield, and the bungling honesty of the Yankee servant)—are strongly present in America's first native play.

From this one might suppose that Tyler's stage Yankee was faithfully copied by later dramatists. Even so, it would be expected that a character so transcribed would change considerably over a period of years; hence I believe it is more probable that a permanent Yankee folktype existed apart from his dramatic incarnation and was adopted, and not created, by the playwrights. As it was, the Yankee did not immediately rise to a position of importance in the drama, for in those plays following *The Contrast* that made use of him, he is restricted to a thinly sketched, clownish servant, exhibiting few facets of his many-sided personality. After 1825, Jonathan's versatility grows apace; he takes on stature and becomes alternately peddler, soldier, and sailor; he wanders in and out of a variety of dramatic vogues, the social comedy, the one-act farce, the Revolutionary play, the Civil War play, the musical comedy, and the old-fashioned melodrama, and finally achieves his own unrestricted vehicle,

"Yankee" Hill as Hiram Dodge in *The Yankee Pedlar*

"Well, I'm kinder apt to conclude this letter is to get me a 'likin'."

helplessly called the "Yankee play"; he travels and finds trouble and scrapes in France, England, Cuba, Poland, Algiers, Spain, and China. As the itinerant peddler, he is well caricatured as Hiram Dodge, in *Yankee Peddler:* "Fancy Ware! Fancy Ware! It was 'bout these parts I made considerable money last Spring, on Jamakee rum, inions, wooden cheese, Leather Hams, Pepper Cannisters, Sossingers, Mustard, Pocketbooks, and Rat-Traps. Fancy Ware! Fancy ware!"[79] As Nutmeg, the title character in Alphonso Wetmore's *The Pedlar,* produced in St. Louis in 1821, he entices Westerners with his cart full of wooden nutmegs and other notions. Because of the number of war plays, the Yankee in uniform becomes a commonplace, whether as private Seth Hope in *Blanche of Brandywine,* Sergeant Sobersides in *Montgomery,* or Drum-Major Cartwheel in *The Brazen Drum.* He also sees service on the seas: Horsebean Hemlock sails with the redoubtable Kyd in *Captain Kyd,* and Jonathan Seabright is boatswain of the *Constitution* in *The Patriot.* Where he does not have a vocation, Jonathan is usually a Down East farmer on his travels. The Yankee yarn has taken on the fabulous and eccentric proportions of legend.

There is a reason why 1825 is a signal date in the history of the stage Yankee. It was in this year that Samuel Woodworth's *The Forest Rose* was produced, presenting in Jonathan Ploughboy the first Yankee type to be exploited by a Yankee actor. The Yankee actor was a comedian who became identified with the generic figure and played it in a succession of plays; skilled comedians there always were, from Thomas Wignell as Jonathan of *The Contrast* to William Warren seventy years later as Jefferson S. Batkins and Enos Crumlett, who numbered the Yankee impersonation among their repertoire of comic parts, but too-popular actors were fatally typed as Down Easters and had to seek variety by placing the Yankee in new situations and exotic climes. A more convincing argument for the existence of a Yankee folk hero could scarcely be adduced than this attempted reproduction of the mythical Yankee by flesh-and-blood representatives.

The repertoires of the Yankee actors show many duplications. Such popular parts as Jonathan Ploughboy in *The Forest Rose,* Jedidiah Homebred in *The Green Mountain Boy,* Deuteronomy Dutiful in *Vermont Wool Dealer,* Lot Sap Sago in *Yankee Land,* Hiram Dodge in *Yankee Peddler,* Solomon Swap in *Jonathan in England* (changed to *Solomon Gundy,* the title of the character in the original play, when Hackett instituted proceedings against Hill for

Dan Marble as Jacob Jewsharp

MR. D. MARBLE AS JACOB JEWSHARP

Yankee in Time.

stealing the play he had previously stolen), and Solon Shingle in *The People's Lawyer* were played by virtually every comedian. Each star had in addition favorite characters and comedies with which he was associated; the successful Yankee actors hired their own hacks and play-doctors to provide them with vehicles. Of the host of hastily improvised farces at one time produced with such fertility—adaptations, revisions, and borrowings hastily patched together for the need of the moment—many are now the veriest scratchings in the theatrical records, and even the more popular pieces are often known to us only by their repeated appearances in these sources. From the plays that reached print, we are able to surmise the nature of those that did not; certainly the titles and heroes of these lost and forgotten patchwork pieces have a familiar ring.

To the Yankee actors must be ascribed the enriching of the folk character, through adept and elaborate mimicry that widened the possibilities of the part, and through the introduction of new plays designedly written to parade the Yankee. When Yankee Hill, greatest of the Yankee simulators, took over the role of Jonathan Ploughboy, he enhanced it with Down East ruralisms that were missing from the rendition of its first interpreter, Aleck Simpson, who made of it simply a comic New Jersey youth.[80] Hill, with his shrewd, puckish face and loutish yet sly manner, realized most closely the folk picture of the mythical Yankee, to the eyes of those who beheld him.[81] Other jesters slipped into the Yankee role: the burly James H. Hackett, who portrayed the frontier roarer Nimrod Wildfire as well as the canny Down Easter, and was in addition reputed an excellent Falstaff—fortunately for him, for Hill soon displaced him in public favor; Dan Marble, whose extensive repertoire of Yankee parts nearly equaled Hill's, most famous of them being Sam Patch, the jumper from Pawtucket; John E. Owens, who adopted Solon Shingle as his own and made the old farmer's sayings the catchwords of New York in the season of 1865; and of lesser renown, Silsbee, Locke, McVicker, and still others whose names today are only shadows.[82]

It is not primarily important that the Yankee plays, actors, and playwrights belong to a past era that has left little information about them for the present. What is important is the persistence of the genre, the medium, that guided many different men; within the varying dimensions of the Yankee part a rigid formula prevailed, prescribed not by dramatist or comedian but by the folk in whose collective fancy the comic, homely figure had taken form.

The vogue of Yankee representations that had its distant origin in America's first significant play in 1787 and rose to full tide in the 1830s and 1840s with the swelling current of native humor, had fairly run its course by the Civil War. A more demanding theater would not tolerate the flimsy vehicles that had served the Yankee actors, and a more educated public could hardly be satisfied with the stock portraiture that had appealed to an older generation. A newer vogue reigned, and novelists, poets, and dramatists alike dipped their pens into the ink of local color. The local-color formula rested on certain invari-

James H. Hackett as Solomon Swap
"You won't, will you?"

ables: the husking-bee and quilting-party atmosphere of a rural setting, a sentiment of nostalgia for the bygone day, and a sustained implication of the open-hearted virtues of the simple country folk. By degrees a local-color Yankee evolved; he was no longer pictured as the original from Down East making a spectacle of himself in the big city or the foreign land, but was revealed at home on his New England farm. This is an older man, a sage, weather-worn but young-hearted, crackling with dry wisdom and a crusty humor, welling with reminiscences of the days way back. And within him beats proverbially a heart of gold. The folk image of the country Jonathan has given way to that of David Harum.

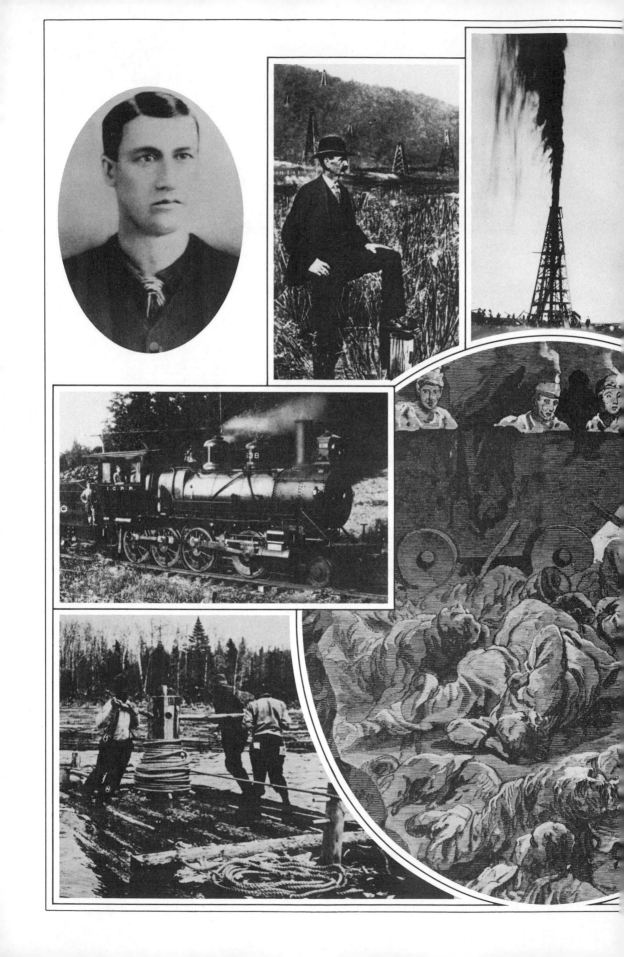

The Later National Period
The Economic Impulse

*T*he battlefields of the Civil War helped usher in the age of industrialism. Contracts let by the federal government to Northeastern factories for munitions and supplies contributed to the growth of mass production and technology that above all characterized the century from the 1860s to the 1960s. This is the period of the transportation revolution, marked first by the transcontinental railroads, then by the automobile, then by the airplane. It is the period introducing mass communications—the wireless, the telephone, radio, television. In this hundred years wizard businessmen created great industrial empires in oil, steel, coal, railroads, meat packing, agricultural machinery, automobiles. To man the factories the entrepreneurs beckoned the peasant population of Southern and Eastern Europe to America, and dozens of nationalities, led by the Italians and the Poles, emigrated in the hundreds of thousands. Negroes from the South streamed into Northern cities in an internal migration. Gary rose from the empty sand dunes of northwest Indiana in 1906 as a city of steel mills that supported more than a hundred thousand people by the 1970s. Over half the Gary steelworkers and their families were blacks from the South, who worked side by side with Southern whites, Serbs,

Croats, Greeks, Mexicans, Puerto Ricans, and half a hundred other peoples.

The overriding issues of the era were economic questions. They involved such matters as the balance of power between management and labor, a more equitable distribution of the nation's income, safeguards against unemployment and depression, the respective merits of capitalism and socialism, the degree of regulation government should exercise over industry. The political reform movements of Populism, Progressivism, the Fair Deal, the New Deal, and the New Frontier addressed themselves to these economic concerns. Meanwhile the United States grew to be the supreme industrial power in the world.

The largest bodies of mainstream American folklore collected in this period reflect the economic interests of men working in special occupations. These are the occupations of the extractive industries, out of doors and underground: herding cattle, cutting timber, mining for ore, drilling for oil. In the transportation industry legends grew around the railroader, and had the steamship succeeded the sailing vessel as a primary factor in the economy in the 1860s, the sailor would have been better remembered by the folk. Chanteys and ballads of the sea and the Great Lakes and nautical turns of speech linger on, but with the limited vitality of a preindustrial tradition. Folk legends have fastened onto the master workman, in his role as cowboy or lumberjack or railroad engineer, to the neglect of the captain of industry and the laborer on the assembly line. Something of the democratic, egalitarian spirit of the common-man folk heroes of the early national period has transferred to the occupational heroes, but these later swashbucklers command attention, not for their eccentricities of character, but for their prodigies of work. Occupational legends and ballads sound the heroic-tragic more often than the heroic-comic note. The dying cowboy laments on the lone prairie, the brave engineer perishes at the throttle, the intrepid river driver drowns in the log jam, the hard-working miner suffocates in the burning mine.

Notable lacks exist in the legendary lore of the later national period. For all its shattering impact on the American consciousness, the Civil War has left no coherent body of folk saga in its wake, for the same reason that the Revolution bequeathed few folk memories to later generations. Without a substantial military establishment in time of peace the folklore of war vanishes underground, to resurface mysteriously when a new conflict erupts. Scattered recollections of the Civil War have been assembled by Benjamin Botkin in one of his folklore treasuries, drawn mainly from printed sources, and traditions of the War Between the States undeniably endure in family circles. In his excellent collection of Kentucky lore as transmitted through the Couch family, *Up Cutshin and Down Greasy* (1959), Leonard Roberts has caught a round of Civil War tales dealing with hairbreadth escapes and haunted burial grounds. Residents of the Cumberland region of northern Tennessee and southern Kentucky sing verses and relate legends about Beanie Short, a guerrilla-hero or a rebel-villain, depending upon one's Confederate or Union sympathies. These are the seedbeds—the extended family, the regional locality—in which American war legends thrive, not the loose organizations of army veterans who meet once a year for a romp.

The folklore of immigrant communities in America presents a different question. These ethnic subcultures possess the cohesive group identity that nour-

124

ishes folk traditions. Yet surprisingly little ethnic folklore has been unearthed in the United States. The large concentrations of foreign nationalities cluster in the cities, and only lately has the folklorist turned his sights from the country flats and the mountain hollers to metropolitan areas. Even when the collector explores the urban terrain, he has tended to elicit "memory culture," the remembered traditions of the Old Country retained by first-generation immigrants. From this perspective have been recorded ample volumes of Polish folksongs and Armenian folktales from Detroit and Lithuanian folklore from several Northern cities. But these collections, valuable as cultural artifacts, illustrate immigrant rather than ethnic, Old World rather than New World folk patterns.

The key word here is "ethnic." As distinct from immigrant memory culture, ethnic living culture represents the active traditions of nationality groups, of whatever generation, responsive to American life. Over the past fifteen years I have directed a number of doctoral dissertations at Indiana University dealing with immigrant folklore: of Greeks in Florida, Finns in Minnesota, Hasidim in Brooklyn, Danes in Nebraska, Italians in Pennsylvania, Jews in Toronto, Swedes in Maine, Ukrainians in western Canada. The results have proved curiously uneven, and in some cases thin and disappointing. The Old World peasant *Märchen* and *Sagen* and songs we had expected to find had vanished. It turned out we were looking through the wrong end of the telescope, gazing toward Europe instead of scrutinizing the situation in America, where the telling of fairy tales and fairy legends served no function, but ethnic identity was taking on a new dimension. When a Greek leaves Greece for the United States his Greekness stands out, in his cuisine, dialect, faith, dress, customs. In a Greek coffeehouse in Gary, surrounded by men—women were not allowed past the door—reading Greek newspapers, sipping Turkish coffee and eating *galaktoboureko,* under a mantel bearing tufted sponges and a ship's model from the island of Kalymnos, whence most of the coffee drinkers had come, I felt like a visitor to the Aegean. But the streets of Gary lay outside the coffeehouse, and the life of the city and the steel mills had washed over these and all other Old Country folk. In my pilot trip to Gary and East Chicago I detected a new urban lore fermenting. Into this lore had poured three basic elements of the metropolitan region: steelworking, crime, and the racial-ethnic mix. The human side of labor in the steel mills, the city dweller's apprehension of muggers, dope addicts, and Syndicate agents, and the daily encounters between whites and blacks, Latins and East Europeans, boiled up into personal-experience stories, anecdotes, legends, jokes, slurs, slanders, rumors, horror tales—in sum a burgeoning folklore of the city. Ethnics contributed to this new lore by their very presence, as witness the recent wave of Polack jokes.

The scheme of this book, based on folklore of the majority culture, does not encompass ethnic or black folk traditions, neither of which are susceptible, for lack of data, to a long-range historical treatment. Black folklore is much better recorded than ethnic folklore. In the later national period the vigorous oral expression of the blacks finally came into public view. Initially, white collectors of Negro songs and tales emphasized what they considered the primitive aspects of slave and ex-slave mentality, and revealed more about themselves than about their subjects. The first field collection of Negro oral literature, *Slave Songs of the United States,* assembled in 1867 by three Northerners, provided a large sheaf of authentic song texts with musical scores and discussed Negro folk music seriously, but its trove of spirituals and ring dances confirmed the stereotype of a gospeling, shuffling, ecstatically shouting black man giving vent to childlike emotions. Joel Chandler Harris reinforced this stereotype when he selected animal tales of Brer Rabbit and all the "creeturs" in 1880 for his first volume of Uncle Remus stories. Other white collectors who followed him continued to emphasize narratives of talking animals and birds, under the assumption that the superstitious black, harking back to the infancy of mankind, still enjoyed a primeval relationship with the creatures of the forest. Not until late in the twentieth century did the inner content and full repertoire of the blacks' oral expression gain some measure of recognition. The new scholarship recognizes the covert protest against and deception of the white masters in slave spirituals edged with double meanings (as unraveled in 1953 by the black theologian Miles Mark Fisher in *Negro Slave Songs in the United States*). It perceives the overt protest in the blues, in Jim Crow and civil rights jests, in grim memorats of beatings and lynchings, and in the tale-cycle of master-slave relations about Old Marster and John.

Still more recently, the 1964 volume of Roger Abrahams, *Deep Down in the Jungle,* has revealed the updated patterns of Northern urban Negro folk rhetoric, in the powerfully obscene imagery of "toasties" (long verse narratives), "the dozens" (ritualized exchanges of insults), bawdy blues ballads, and scatological jokes. In the modern Negro repertoire a strutting badman of the Northern ghetto has replaced the cozening rabbit of the Southern briar patch. Here is part of a tale told by a young black in south Philadelphia in 1958, in which Brother Rabbit has been barred at the door from a party given by Brother Fox and Brother Bear to spite him:

So the Rabbit turned away with his head turned down. He feeling sad, downhearted, tears in his eyes. Felt like he was alone in the world. But then he got mad. He said, "I know what I'll do."

He went home and shined his shoes, and got his shotgun and went back and kicked the door down. "Don't a motherfucker move." He walked over to the table, got all he wanted to eat. Walked over to the bar and got himself all he wanted to drink. He reached over and he grabbed the lion's wife and he dance with her. Grabbed the ape's wife and did it to her. Then he shit in the middle of the floor and walked out.[1]

This is a far cry from Uncle Remus. Instead of remaining downcast and defeated, in a subservient role, the Rabbit transforms himself into the hustler and the hard sport, a menacing, triumphant figure, modeled on the militant black culture heroes of a new day.

So black folklore, like white, undergoes

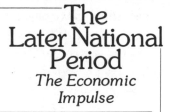

mutations reflective of changing historical contexts. How folk expression reflects the pageant of history can clearly

be seen in the legends arising from economic occupations.

Folklore of economic occupations

Folklore seizes on only those parts of
history that it finds magnetic, and in the
crammed century from the end of the
Civil War to the 1960s it showed strong
partialities and biases. Folksongs and
folktales celebrate the cowboy but not
the insurance salesman, the lumberjack
but not the factory worker, the railroad
engineer but not the chairman of the
board. Part of the explanation for the
bunchings and barren spaces in the
archives of folklore lies in the whims
and hunches of collectors in the field.
A few strike out on original paths, and
others follow, swelling the numbers of
examples of "Barbara Allen" or "The
Old Chisholm Trail." Still, we have to
consider what our existing resources tell
us, and they say plainly that the strength
of American folklore uncovered in this
hundred years, as it reflects American
historical conditions, falls to the great
outdoor and underground occupations:
cattle herding, lumbering, mining, oil
drilling, railroading. The folk heroes of
this lore are intrepid individualists with
special skills who work at dangerous
pursuits for a wage but who identify
with their employer, their industry, and
the free-enterprise system of their country. They see themselves as master workmen, proud of their expertise, loyal
to their bosses and their assignments,
unslacking in their enormous physical

efforts to perform their tasks.

Other folk-hero types did not emerge
in the period, and not for want of search.
Intellectuals sympathetic with the labor
movement sought diligently to unearth
traditions of the factory worker, picket
line, and labor union and found precious
little. Such compilations as John Greenway's *American Folksongs of Protest*
(1953) and Joyce Kornbluh's *Rebel
Voices: An I.W.W. Anthology* (1964)
disclose a high percentage of subliterary
compositions and a low incidence of
actual oral folkstuff. From the 1930s on,
a number of well-known "folk entrepreneurs," to use the phrase of Serge Denisoff, who has written their history in *Great
Day Coming: Folk Music and the American Left* (1971), attempted to woo labor
through simulated folksongs. Woody
Guthrie, Pete Seeger, Alan Lomax, Burl
Ives, and Paul Robeson all played a
part in this scenario. But although they
scored notable individual successes, they
failed to arouse a workers' movement
through "agit-prop" songs. No Okies or
Arkies sang the dust-bowl songs Woody
Guthrie wrote about their plight and
grievances.

Americans do not see themselves as
oppressed members of a working class,
and union members do not identify with
proletarian types in radical songs. Rather
they buy the American dream of the free

individual who, given a fair shake, may very well make it to the top. The worker on the assembly line has not inspired ballads or legends. Indeed, a factory does not generate heroic lore as did the cattle trail, lumber camp, mining camp, oil field, or enginehouse, for there is nothing potentially heroic in turning a wrench. Charlie Chaplin in *Modern Times* epitomized the degradation of the assembly-line robot. American folklore has chosen to celebrate the master workman in the pioneering days of the extractive and transportation industries, at the same time that the mass culture extolled Carnegie, Rockefeller, and Ford as self-made men, flinty individualists, creating industrial empires in a wide-open America through their initiative, dedication, and drive. The master workman and the empire builder stood on adjacent rungs of the American ladder of success.

Only in the case of the coal miners did the pride and joy of the master workman eventually turn sour. The colliers, family men who needed to provide for wives and children locked in the drab company towns, felt increasingly helpless before the giant forces of industrial technology; they did seek succor in their unions and some, in the secret organization of the Molly Maguires, struck back violently at the mine owners. But the verdict of folklore on the Mollies is mixed, and they never attained a clear-cut heroic stature.

Folklorists have drawn a blank too in probing for folk legends extolling the American businessman as a generic type. The landlord, the banker, the tycoon, the robber baron conjure up negative images in the American folk imagination, which has given its acclaim to red-blooded men hard at work in the open air with their hands, their brains, and their hearts.

Cowboys

The First Cowboy Folklorists

The cowboy as a stock figure on the American scene comes into prominence directly after and as a consequence of the Civil War. While Texas ranchers were off fighting for the Confederacy from 1861 to 1865, their wives and children looked after the cattle and branded the calves. Texas escaped largely unscathed from Union armies, and when the Texans returned home they found the ranges filled with cattle sleek from grazing on pastures where the buffalo no longer roamed, but no local market for all the beef. While a choice steer in Texas sold at home for six or seven dollars, in the Northern cities cattle sold at eight to eleven dollars per hundred pounds.[1] From this situation developed the long overland drive from assembly points in Texas to markets in Kansas and beyond, which reached its peak during the 1870s and 1880s and petered out by the mid-1890s. Various factors, such as the disastrous winter of 1886–1887 that dealt a blow to the ranching industry, the increasing number of settlers and barbed-wire fences along the trail routes, the growth of the railroads, and the stocking of cattle on the Northern plains, helped eliminate the drive along the Chisholm and other trails. Texas cowboys had tended cattle before the long drives and continued to ride the range after the drives ceased, but they achieved their greatest renown on these difficult and challenging forced migrations of livestock.

How the life of the cowboy on the open range and trail drive bred an occupational folklore is nowhere better illustrated than in Andy Adams's classic, *The Log of a Cowboy,* published in 1903. Although a work of literature rather than history, the *Log* sets forth in documentary fashion the drive of over three thousand head of longhorn cattle and four hundred saddle horses from south Texas on April 1, 1882, for delivery in early September to the government Indian agency for the Blackfeet in Montana. The enormous effort, skill, and ingenuity required to move the animals across the western tier of states and territories became clear in Adams's pages. There are difficult fords to cross where steers get bogged in quicksand, dry areas to test man and beast to their limits, blind stampedes that threaten to dissolve the herd, wearisome searches for missing horses, trouble from browbeating rustlers and Indians, working days and nights of eighteen hours in the saddle. A whole lore of the trail, with its technical glossary, takes shape. The sinful side of the Old West acquires sharper meaning too, as the trail-weary cowhands plunge into the excitement of the towns along the drive—Dodge, Ogallala, French Ford—with their monte games, saloons, clothing stores, dance parlors, and sudden shoot-outs. From the *Log* one appreciates the varied cast necessary to keep the drive going: the wealthy cowman and father-figure to the outfit who is selling the herd; the foreman, akin to a ship's captain; his *segundo,* the second-in-command, ready to move up from among the cowhands to assume the responsibility if the foreman is temporarily away or permanently disabled; the cook and the wrangler, who from the wagon tend the commissariat and the *remuda* of horses, which provide lifelines for the outfit; and the dozen cowhands, ready to take on various duties, as point men directing the herd from behind the lead cattle, or swing men, the outriders who keep the herd separated from range cattle, or as night guards for the bedded-down herd.

So realistic indeed did the *Log* seem to readers that a number of them accepted it as straight autobiography, even the celebrated cowboy illustrator and author Charles M. Russell. Actually Adams never did traverse the old Western trail, and prepared the geography of his novel by closely scrutinizing a map. He had driven horseherds to market many times between 1882 and 1890, but only herded cattle once. The authenticity of his fiction derived from his intimate acquaintance with the cow country and his alert ear for experiences and traditions of the trail. Andy inserted fictitious places into the *Log* among existing ones and brought historical persons, such as Bat Masterson, into his gallery of characters, to the further confusion of his captivated readers. When Andy's father picked up the book, he read the first sentence, which said that the writer's family had moved to Texas, and knowing it false, threw the book away and read no more.

Andy Adams was born in 1859 on a

farm in Thorncreek Township in Indiana, left home at fifteen, and reached Texas by 1882, where he stayed for eleven years as a ranch hand and trail driver. For the balance of his life, from 1894 until his death in 1935, he lived in Colorado Springs, Colorado, where he developed a new career as a writer of short stories, novels and plays. None of his other six books on the cattle industry equaled the fame of the *Log,* nor was he able to get any of his plays produced. His forte lay in writing fiction that read like fact, a genre he made his own, in an endeavor to counter the distorted picture of the cowboy offered in Western novels and dramas.[2] In the *Log* he did portray trail life in a convincing manner, and his verisimilitude included the folklore and traditions the cowboy was acquiring.

One element of tradition, never defined as such by Adams but increasingly apparent throughout the *Log,* might be called the cowboy code. The code called for hospitality and assistance on the trail between outfits, in the form of meals served from the chuck wagon to visitors from another herd, or information on trail conditions ahead, or the loan of men and horses to aid in fording a swollen river or to repair the effects of a stampede. As men of honor, the cowhands respected the brands of other herds and of the range cattle, and were prompt to "cut out" from their herd and return any strays. Faithful to their employer, they endured the trials of the trail, missing meals and sleep when the occasion demanded, swimming the rivers back and forth at the perilous fords, sitting in the saddle when their bones ached. In turn, their employer looked after them paternally, doled out their gold pieces along the trail but withheld enough to ensure them a stake, and blew them to a celebration at the trail's end. To his mounts the cowboy

tendered care and affection, for the horse was indeed part of the cowman, who was out of his element on foot. In town the genuine cowboy never laid hands on a lady or addressed her in any but the most seemly manner.

Storytelling around the campfire at night after the chuck-wagon dinner and singing along the trail during the day enlivened the cowboys' routine, and the *Log* records half a dozen yarn sessions and several snatches of songs. While the repertoire of cowboy songs has become familiar to the public through many compilations, no collectors have turned their attention primarily to oral narratives. The *Log* goes beyond mere mention of yarnfests to include full texts of the stories told, and is thus a prime source for this neglected part of the cowboy's folklore. Not all the stories are recognizable folktales, for just as ballad singers mingle Tin

"Storytelling Around the Chuck Wagon"
E. Boyd Smith, from Andy Adams, *The Log of a Cowboy*

Pan Alley songs with traditional ballads in their performances, so do raconteurs juggle personal experiences and more or less true anecdotes with twice-told tales. The baker's dozen of campfire recitals given in the *Log* all reveal traditional themes and attitudes, and some are variants of well-known fictions.

Tales, songs, sayings, beliefs, are all woven into the texture of cowboy life in the *Log*. The motivation of that life and the undercurrent theme of the lore is money, and the good things that money can buy. The image of the wealthy cowman or cattle baron Don Lovell, who contracted for beef cattle and paid off his men in gold coins, hovers before his Circle Dot outfit as the role-model of their particular trails. Promptly on receiving their pay, the cowpokes swarmed into town, to buy flashy cheap suits and seek to augment their stakes at the gaming tables. The cattle they so zealously guarded and nursed toward the trail's end, and sang to and yarned about, represented cash on the hoof. At the climactic moment when the herd was delivered to the purchasing agent and finally counted, he handed the money order to the contractor. This was the ritual termination of the great drive.

As Andy Adams's *Log of a Cowboy* is the first and classic narrative of the trail drive, so Jack Thorp's *Songs of the Cowboys* is the first and classic songbook of the range. Adams set his scene in 1882 and published his book in 1903; Thorp embarked on his song-collecting venture, covering fifteen hundred miles on horseback in Texas and New Mexico, in 1889, and printed his slender volume in Estancia, New Mexico, in 1908. To-

gether the *Log* and the *Songs* established the cultural myth of the cowboy, which would be expanded and reiterated in scads of cattle-country autobiographies and songbooks in the next half-century. The cowboy's code, the styles of dress, horsemanship, and manners associated with the cowpoke, the themes of his tales and verses, the backdrop of prairie, mesa, and canyon against which he was silhouetted, are all present in these two pioneer works.

Unlike the *Log,* Thorp's little collection of fifty pages does not stand by itself. It needs to be fleshed out with *Pardner of the Wind,* his own autobiography as told to Neil M. Clark and published in 1945, in which he recounts his Homeric experiences on the trail of cowboy oral poetry; with the much fuller reissue in 1921 of *Songs of the Cowboys,* marred by borrowings from John Lomax's 1910 collection, *Cowboy Songs and Other Frontier Ballads,* which had already fattened on Thorp's 1908 booklet; and with the splendid edition of the original booklet prepared by Austin and Alta Fife, the folklorists of Mormondom and the West, in 1966. The Fifes' edition recognizes this historical value of the twenty-three song texts printed by Thorp before the vogue of cowboy and Western songs swept the nation and permeated the media. The editors trace the subsequent dispersion of the songs in publications, recordings, and manuscript and field collections and analyze themes and images in the songs that illustrate the cowboy culture. This concordance, coming at the end of the Economic Life-Style period, surveys the whole era of the

cowboy that began on the open range in the 1880s and burgeoned into myth in the twentieth century in novels, films, and television dramas, as well as in histories, biographies, and folklore collections. Some of Thorp's little sheaf of songs, for instance "The Cowboy's Lament," "Sam Bass," and "Grand Round-up," were destined for fame, while others achieved little or no circulation, though all of them captured aspects of the cowboy's vision.

Although he spent half a century in cowboy boots, Jack Thorp grew up in the East. He was born in New York and went to Saint Paul's School, the ex-clusive preparatory school in Concord, New Hampshire, but when his father, a well-to-do lawyer, lost his wealth, Jack put his polo-playing experience to good use in buying Western ponies and training them for polo steeds. A strapping, hearty fellow over six feet whose home was in the saddle, he eventually came to New Mexico to pursue the life of cowboy and rancher, and died there in 1941.

Thorp has left us an engaging account of how he began his song hunt, in March 1889, at a cowhands' camp in south Texas that he had joined for the night while looking for stray horses from his own ranch:

I hobbled out my horses and rustled a plate and cup from the chuck box; coffee and a pot of stew were kept hot all night at such camps. Having eaten my fill, I inquired who had been singing just before I came in. Heads nodded at a colored boy known as 'Lasses. I asked if he would mind singing the song again. He did it for me. But he knew only two verses—that's all. And none of the other hands in camp knew more. That was one of the difficulties encountered in the earliest effort to assemble the unprinted verse on the range. None of the cowboys who could sing ever remembered an entire song. I would pick up a verse or two here, another verse or two there.

After 'Lasses finished, I sang a song and so did several others.

Somebody knew a couple of verses of "Sam Bass"—not the whole thing. The other songs he knew were about cotton patches, like one which celebrated a colored girl named Mamie—she picked her weight of cotton in the morning, 'twas said, then, with her feet under a bush and her head in the sun, went fast asleep. Cotton-picking songs were fine if you liked them, but they weren't what I was after. By the light of the fire I copied in my notebook the two verses of "Dodgin' Joe" which 'Lasses knew. Then I spread my tarp, wrapped my soogan* around me, and, with feet to the fire, fought off sleep for a while because a big idea was buzzing in my head. Here I was, I told myself, workin' for wages for the Bar W. Nothing on my mind. Not much in my pocket: three dollars or so, and no more comin'.

> The cowboy's life is a dreary life, though his mind it is no load
> And he always spends his money like he found it in the road. †

Nigger Add had told me the two horses I was looking for were safe in the L F D horse pasture; no need to worry more about them, I was handy with horses, and in cow country somebody was always wantin' horses broke; they paid wages for it. My saddle horse, Gray Dog, and my pack horse, Ample, were my own property. Right here on my own range I had ridden into Add's camp and heard part of a cowboy song brand new to me.

"If there's one here," I thought, "there must be plenty more off my own range that I never heard."

So I made up my mind to keep driftin'.[3]

So, long before the tape recorder or grants for field trips, Jack Thorp took it into his head to seek out cowboy singers and preserve their folksongs of the cattle range. The observations he made on this pioneer quest carry a good deal of truth about folk processes not generally understood by the public at large, accustomed to reading nicely rounded versions of pretty ballads and folktales. As Jack found out, ballads, like legends, do not come forth in full-bodied versions but in bits and pieces, which are continually being reshuffled. He recognized that the rounded texts in books and on records doubly falsified the oral tradition, by joining together stanzas and by bowdlerizing their salty language. A catchy ballad like "The

---

* *Tarp . . . soogan.* A bedroll was standard equipment for every cowhand. On trail herd or at roundup it was carried in the chuck wagon. When a puncher was "riding the chuck line," i.e., floating between jobs, it was tied behind the saddle. It was made up of a sheet of canvas, one or more soogans (i.e., blankets or homemade quilts), and sundry personal effects. [Fifes' note.]

† "The Cowboy's Life." Several cowboy songs carry this title. Thorp gives it as "The Pecos Stream," XVIII of this work. [Fifes' note.]

Old Chisholm Trail" had thousands of verses, Thorp noted, held together only by its *come ti yi youpy* refrain, and *every* cowboy knew a few and perhaps added some in his own rough idiom, which did not set well in print. The voices of the cowpokes were as rough as their lyrics, and historians of the trail drives argue whether the herders sang to quiet the cattle or to please themselves. In either case the cowboy song was less an art form than a cultural artifact.

Thorp's twenty-three songs project a self-image of the trail and range rider that forms the core of the cowboy myth. They show the qualities the cowboy admired and depict heroic figures embodying those qualities. Devotion to his work, whatever the hazard or tedium, characterizes the cowboy hero. He may be a tenderfoot, like "Little Joe, the Wrangler," who ran away from a stepmother who beat him and joined an outfit that in pity gave him the lowly position of wrangler to look after the extra horses on the drive. When the herd stampeded, Little Joe mounted his old brown pony to join the experienced hands in the mad chase to turn the leaders:

At last we got them milling and kinder quieted down
  And the extra guard back to the camp did go
But one of them was missin' and we all knew at a glance
  'Twas our little Texas stray—poor wrangler Joe.

Next morning just at sunup we found where Rocket fell
  Down in a washout twenty feet below
Beneath his horse mashed to a pulp his horse had wrung the knell
  For our little Texas stray—poor wrangler Joe.[4]

Thorp composed this song himself, writing beside the campfire on a paper bag, about an incident he had beheld on the trail. It caught on among the cowboys and the public, who bought over 375,000 records of "Little Joe, the Wrangler." Not one cent went to its creator, unknown at the time since he never signed his name to it in his 1908 booklet. Becoming a folksong, it went through the usual course of variations and even parodies. The subject was a natural; on the drive the stampede was the most feared and deadly disruption, and Little Joe, the aspiring cowboy, plunged into its midst in the effort to save the herd.

Another side of the cowboy-as-hero appears in "Bucking Broncho," a paean to the virility of the dashing horseman who broke in wild bronchos on the range and danced with comely lasses at the ball with equal abandon. The equation between subduing a bucking horse and a mistress is quickly made, whether in the chaste but rollicking lines of Thorp's first printed text, or in plainer rendition:

Lie still ye young bastard
  Don't bother me so
Your father's off bucking
  Another broncho.

This sour note from a jilted damsel is untypical of the admiration generally expressed in the song for the whirlwind lover:

"Riders Were Sent Through the Herd at Breakneck Pace"
R. Farrington Elwell, from Andy Adams, *The Log of a Cowboy*

He will rope you and throw you
   and when you're fast tied
Down on your bare belly,
   Lord God how he'll ride![5]

One outlaw-hero came to represent the generic qualities of courage, horsemanship, and independence prized by the cowboys. Sam Bass, Indiana-born, went to Texas at nineteen, raced horses, herded cattle on the trail, lost his money gambling, took to robbing trains with a gang of tough cowboys, outwitted the Texas Rangers, and in 1878, at twenty-seven, met his death through the treachery of a companion in the hire of the Rangers. The ballad that celebrated the life and death of Sam was sung in two thousand verses all over the Southwest, and it portrays him in the friendliest light. "A kinder hearted fellow, you'd scarcely ever see" than this "cow-boy bold."[6] His "four partners all daring, bold, and bad . . . whipped the Texas Rangers and dodged the boys in blue."[7] But, like Jesse James and Billy the Kid, Bass was betrayed to his death by a false friend who owed him money.

SAM BASS

Sam Bass was born in Indiana, it was his native home
And at the age of seventeen, young Sam began to roam.
He first went down to Texas, a cow-boy bold to be
A kinder hearted fellow, you'd scarcely ever see.

Sam used to deal in race stock, had one called the Denton mare
He watched her in scrub races, took her to the County Fair.
She always won the money, wherever she might be.
He always drank good liquor, and spent his money free.

Sam left the Collins ranch in the merry month of May
With a herd of Texas cattle the Black Hills to see
Sold out in Custer City and all got on a spree
A harder lot of cow-boys you'd scarcely ever see.

On the way back to Texas, they robbed the U. P. train
All split up in couples and started out again.
Joe Collins and his partner were overtaken soon
With all their hard earned money they had to meet their doom.

Sam made it back to Texas all right side up with care
Rode into the town of Denton his gold with friends to share.
Sam's life was short in Texas 'count of robberies he'd do
He'd rob the passengers coaches the mail and express too.

Sam had four bold companions, four bold and daring lads
Underwood and Joe Jackson, Bill Collins and Old Dad
They were four of the hardest cow-boys that Texas ever knew
They whipped the Texas Rangers and ran the boys in blue.

Jonis* borrowed of Sam's money and didn't want to pay
The only way he saw to win was to give poor Sam away
He turned traitor to his comrades they were caught one early
  morn
Oh what a scorching Jonis will get when Gabriel blows his horn.

Sam met his fate in Round Rock July the twenty-first
They pierced poor Sam with rifle balls and emptied out his purse.
So Sam is a corpse in Round Rock, Jonis is under the clay
And Joe Jackson in the bushes trying to get away.[8]

The cowboys who cherished the ballad about Sam Bass clearly identified with him. In his reminiscences of ballad collecting, John Lomax declared the song "was known by every cowboy from 1868 to 1892," and in his reminiscences of cowboy life, Charlie Siringo commented that Sam Bass was the hero of more young Texas cowboys than any other badman, and the song about him was the most popular.[9] Sam rode on one trail drive, in the fall of 1876, taking seven hundred steers he had bought in the ranch country of southwest Texas to sell in Kansas. With his partner, Joel Collins, he made a comfortable profit from the sale, but instead of returning to Texas the pair drifted off to the gambling halls of Deadwood in Dakota Territory, where they lost their stake to card sharps. Angered at being robbed, they decided to recoup by holding up stagecoaches. For the remaining two years of his life Sam lived outside the law as head of a band that robbed coaches and trains and, in his last abortive effort, tried to hold up a bank in Round Rock, Texas. Since he had

punched cattle for a time, and continued even in his desperado years to camp around his second home of Denton, Texas, plainly visible to his acquaintances, and furthermore, since he observed to the end the code of the cowboy—generosity, humor, courage, loyalty—Sam qualified well as a hero to cowboys.

Like the "Old Time Cowboy" limned in one of Thorp's ballads, Sam Bass had an open hand:

Did you ever go to any cowboy
  whenever hungry or dry
Asking for a dollar and
  have him you deny.[10]

Sam customarily returned a dollar to his stagecoach victims to allow them to buy breakfast. Seeing that a passenger on the Union Pacific from whom he had just taken twenty dollars had only one arm, Bass gave the money back to him. All along his trail he scattered the twenty-dollar gold pieces, minted in San Francisco in 1877, that remained from his most successful holdup, of the Union Pacific at Big Springs, Texas. For a

* Actually Jim Murphy.

137

breakfast or a night's lodging he left a gold memento, and for a fresh horse a whole handful of gold coins.

Sam had a sense of fun, a stock trait of cowboys, who relished practical jokes and windy brags. He hugely enjoyed hearing farmers talk about the notorious Sam Bass, and to draw them out would pretend that he was a Texas Ranger on Sam's trail. Speaking of a youth who had professed admiration for the bandit, Sam chuckled, "What do you reckon he would have said if I had told him I was Bass and had showed him a few twenties? I'll bet I could have broken his eyes off with a board."[11]

There was no doubting Sam's mettle. He did not rob a train and take off for parts unknown, but lingered in the vicinity, and when finally trailed by a posse, exchanged taunts across the woods with them or left messages for his pursuers with involuntary hosts. In his boldest escapade, Sam led his band back into Denton, his adopted home, while Texas Rangers and county sheriffs were hotly pursuing him, and in broad daylight relieved a livery stable of two saddle horses that a posse had taken from Bass a month earlier. On the way out of town he rode past the house of Sheriff "Dad" Egan, his former benefactor, who was sleeping upstairs, and yelled a friendly greeting to Egan's little boy. Sam laughed at death. "If a man could take me alive, he would make a thunder-mug full of money. But that's the point; I never expect to give up to any man alive, for I know it's death anyhow. So I'll die fighting."[12]

A hero of action must die valiantly, and Sam did. Mortally wounded in the shooting at Round Rock, he crawled underneath an oak tree, where the Rangers found him and brought him back to town. Dying, Sam answered their questions up to a point but refused to squeal on any of his companions.

"It is agin my profession to blow on my pals," he stated. "If a man knows anything, he ought to die with it in him."[13] Texans thought well of this loyalty, all the more in contrast to the turncoat, burly Jim Murphy, who met an appropriate fate:

But the man that plays the
 traitor will feel it by and by.
His death was so uncommon—
 'twas poison in the eye.[14]

Fearful and scorned, Murphy lived for less than a year after Sam's death, and came to his miserable end by inadvertently swallowing atropine meant to be dropped in his eye for an eye ailment.

Meanwhile the legend of Sam Bass flowered. He opposed bloodshed and had never killed a man, unless his shot was the one from three bandit guns that felled Deputy Sheriff A. W. Grimes in the store at Round Rock, a few minutes before Sam himself was mortally wounded. The farmers of west Texas felt sympathy for Sam in his battle with the railroads, their own enemy, which they sought to regulate through their granges. One farmer said to Sam he had heard the railroads had conned Bass out of a pile of money, and he was just getting his own back. Another said he didn't care how often Sam robbed the railroads, so long as he did not harm the citizens. A youth wanted to join Bass and his gang, since he could not make a living farming. These folk did not know they were communicating their sentiments directly to the outlaw himself![15]

Traditions told how the outlaw handed out twenty-dollar gold pieces for a dozen eggs or a pan of biscuits.[16] For an overnight's lodging he gave a poor widow fifty dollars and insisted that his men treat her with respect. His pursuers turned to jelly when they found themselves

in his presence. Treasure seekers have hunted all over Sam's stamping grounds for chests of gold he allegedly buried. In all ways Sam honored the cowboy code, even to his zest for gold. "Money will sweeten anything," he said.[17]

Aware of impending doom, Sam contrasted his fallen star to the life ahead for two boys who had chatted with him gaily. "What would I give to be in their place! I'd give all the gold I ever saw, and more too, if I had it. But it's too late now to think of that. I ought to have taken my father's advice when I was a little boy and shunned bad company; but, hell, there's no use thinking about it now. It all goes in a lifetime, anyhow."[18]

Sam's terse expression of regret and repentance sums up the theme of "the most famous of all cowboy songs":[19]

THE COWBOY'S LAMENT

'Twas once in my saddle I used to be happy
  'Twas once in my saddle I used to be gay
But I first took to drinking, then to gambling
  A shot from a six-shooter took my life away.

. . . . .

Send for my father, Oh send for mother
  Send for the surgeon to look at my wounds
But I fear it is useless I feel I am dying
  I'm a young cow-boy cut down in my bloom.

Farewell my friends, farewell my relations
  My earthly career has cost me sore.
The cow-boy ceased talking, they knew he was dying
  His trials on earth, forever were o'er.

Chorus:
Beat your drums lightly, play your fifes merrily
  Sing your death march as you bear me along
Take me to the grave yard, lay the sod o'er me
  I'm a young cow-boy and know I've done wrong.[20]

These stanzas from "The Cowboy's Lament" as printed by Jack Thorp in his 1908 collection closely fit Sam Bass's career and attitude, and they have served to sentimentalize the whole genus of the errant cowboy. As repentant Sam thought of his father, so the dying cowboy invokes, in various verses, his father, mother, sister, sweetheart. In one of the most popular quatrains, the lamenting cowboy asks that a number of "wild" or "jolly" cowboys—anywhere from four to sixteen—carry his coffin to his grave, as a symbol of his reunion with his kind. So did the cowboys on range and trail take back Sam Bass as they sang of his life and death.

"The Cowboy's Lament," also known as "Streets of Laredo," has been printed, recorded, parodied, and discussed more than any other song in the repertoire of American cowboys. Ballad scholars locate its antecedents in eighteenth-century drinking songs such as "The Unfortunate Rake." Collectors have found versions adapted to lumberjacks, miners, and skiers. Three professors of folklore have sung it on records. In one variation the cowboy sins not by gambling but by reading, deserts the cattle for novels of Zane Grey, and finally squanders all his money on books. A Swedish text from Minnesota ends:

En "cowboy," som dött för en mördares hand.
(A cowboy who died at the murderer's hand.)[21]

In their selection of revivalist songs in the cowboy idiom, *Heaven on Horseback,* the Fifes include texts of "The Cowboy's Lament" because of its hymnlike quality and religious overtones.[22]

While Jack Thorp's *Songs of the Cowboys* has received belated recognition as the pioneer cowboy-song collection, his *Tales of the Chuck Wagon,* which he published in Santa Fe in 1926, has gone practically unnoticed, because of the inattention to cowboy folktales. With his tales as with his songs, Thorp was strictly the amateur collector, unaware of the sensitivities of the contemporary folklorists who demand verbatim oral texts and full contextual and comparative data. But he had the sense to recognize that cowhands possessed their own store of traditional narratives which, as we shall see, contributed with the songs to the cowboy's image of himself.

Cowboy Folktales about Cowboys

As both a real and a mythic figure the American cowboy has attracted a host of biographers and interpreters. Long after his heyday during the great cattle drives of the 1870s and 1880s, the cowboy lives on in the fantasies of cinema and television. Latter-day cowboy film heroes, notably Tom Mix, Roy Rogers, and Gene Autry, have made familiar the image of the horseman in chaps and sombrero silhouetted against the plains, often as not singing one of the now famous cowboy ditties such as "The Old Chisholm Trail," "Git Along Little Dogies," and "Bury Me Not on the Lone Prairie." The historical cowboy did indeed sing—badly, according to his best friends—while herding cattle on the long drive—to calm them, it was said—and collections of cowboy songs have regularly appeared since Jack Thorp's *Songs of the Cowboys* in 1908. Austin and Alta Fife are at present engaged upon an exhaustive codification of cowboy balladry. Meanwhile the storytelling side of the cowboy has been all but ignored by folklorists.

That cowboys yarned is evident enough, for every book about the long drive and life on the range mentions as a favorite form of relaxation their swapping stories around the chuck-wagon campfire after the evening meal. Each cowpuncher was called on to sing a song, tell a tale, do a dance, or incur the penalty—namely, receive a taste of the leggins (the thick, heavy leg sheaths worn by the cowhands) across his bare backside. Range authors frequently reproduce the form of oral yarnspinning in their writings. Andy Adams introduced

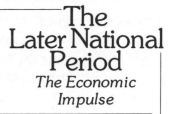
twenty-one campfire settings into his works of fiction, and his biographer, Wilson M. Hudson, brought together fifty tales from these sessions in an edition titled *Why the Chisholm Trail Forks,* unfortunately without folklore notes.[23] Jack Thorp's privately printed *Tales of the Chuck Wagon* seem on the whole closer to folk tradition than Adams's campfire tales.[24] The famed cowboy artist and raconteur, Charles M. Russell, published a series of orally delivered anecdotes and recollections, posthumously brought together in 1927 in *Trails Plowed Under,* and some can be recognized as traditional, particularly in the chapter "Some Liars of the Old West."

In the myth of the cowboy, toughness and callousness became conspicuous traits, exemplified by insensitivity toward death. There is a seeming ambivalence here, for in such ballads as "Little Joe, the Wrangler" the cowboy mourns in sentimental fashion his fellow killed in the line of duty. But the cowboy code accommodated loyalty to friends and courtesy to women on the one hand and steeliness under pressure on the other. Comic anecdotes play up the

"Cutting Out Cattle from the Herd"
Henry Worrall, from Joseph G. McCoy, *Historic Sketches of the Cattle Trade of the West and Southwest,* 1874

casualness with which the cowboy killed his man, as in the widely dispersed yarn of "Breaking the News." In one of its cowboy forms, ascribed to Teddy Roosevelt, a posse of cowboys discover they have hung an innocent man whom they took for a horse thief. One cowhand reputed to be a diplomat is entrusted with the task of telling the widow. Riding up to her home, he asks, "Are you the wife of Jack Smith?" "Yes, I am," she answers, a bit huffily. "No you ain't," he replies. "You're jest his widder. We got his body out there in the waggin, and it's dressed up mighty nice. We hung him for a horse thief, but please don't feel bad about that. He was plumb innocent. After we strung him up we found out he wasn't the guy we was looking for at all. We're all ready to swear he was innocent."

A version attributed to Mark Twain contains a more elaborate prologue, with a rancher on a spree riding his horse into Cheyenne and right through the swinging doors of "The Cowboy's Delight." To the dozing bartender he yells out, "I'm a-thirsting like the Prodigal Son. Pour me a straight and smell one yourself." The bartender raises up his head and his six-shooter and plugs the prodigal son through the head. A committee heads for the widow's house with the coffin, and the most tactful member accosts her, "Does Joe Toole live here?" "Yes," she responds. "Bet he don't," retaliates the spokesman, waving his hand toward the approaching wagon and coffin.[25]

A similar casualness toward the dead crops up in a memorable shooting incident in Dodge City reported in the reminiscences of Bill Jones of Paradise Valley in Oklahoma. The Dodge marshal, Mysterious Dave Mather, outdrew and plugged a tinhorn gambler in a dispute over cards in a saloon. The death of a tinhorn sport would have aroused

no interest, but the bullet that penetrated him went on to lodge in a sleeping hound that belonged to the saloon keeper, a fierce Irishman nicknamed "Dog Kelly" because of his ownership of a hundred canines. Kelly demanded an inquest into the dog's death; a jury was impaneled, and returned a verdict that the shooting had been done in justifiable self-defense since any dog should know better than to go to sleep in a Dodge City saloon. Several witnesses testified that they had never seen the animal take a drink, and that he therefore had no business in the saloon. The dog was buried with military honors at Boot Hill, where he was carried in a rigged-up hearse accompanied by the Dodge City Cowboy Band. A sermon was preached, the mourning cowpunchers sang "The Cowboy's Lament," and Dog Kelly wept. After the burial, Mysterious Dave ordered the undertaker to remove the gambler's carcass from the floor of the saloon and bury it without further ado.[26]

The cowboy's ability to consume whiskey and his compulsion to blow his wad in the saloons of cow towns became proverbial. Buck Winters blew fifty dollars in town one night, and next morning told his pals how it happened. He went into one saloon and set up drinks and eats for the crowd. That was ten dollars. He repeated this in another saloon for another ten and in a third for fifteen. A listener remarked that this only came to thirty-five dollars. Buck pondered. "I don't know, boys. By that time I uz gettin' pretty drunk. I'm afraid I must have spent that other fifteen dollars foolishly!" This is also told as a lumberjack story.[27]

The cowpoke's love of booze also generated its share of anecdotes. Charles Russell retells a sly story of a cowboy deriding the Indians' passion for liquor. "It's funny how crazy an Injun is for whiskey," the cowboy mused. "A few days ago I'm riding along—I got a quart of booze in my saddle pocket. I meet an Injun. He sees what I got, and offers me the hoss he's riding for the quart. To a man that wants a saddle hoss, this one is worth a hundred dollars. I paid six for this moonshine." "Did you make the trade?" "Hell no! It's all the booze I got."[28]

Kindred in theme is the tale of the Arizona breakfast, as related by a range humorist named Rip Van Winkle, "the drolliest man I ever saw," as one cowhand described him. Rip told how Arizona citizens feted a visitor representing a big New Mexican cattleman with a brass band, elegant hotel accommodations, and a splendid breakfast of a big bologna sausage, a bottle of whiskey, and a yellow dog. "What was the dog for?" asked a bystander. "To eat the bologna!" replied one of the Arizona boosters.[29]

A classic of the cow country concerns the rare steak. In one version the irate cowpoke yells to a waiter, "Take that steak back to th' kitchen and have 'em cook it some more. Why I've seen 'em git well that uz hurt worse'n that!"[30] A more elaborate form of this, "one of the oldest of all cowboy stories," in the words of the cattle-country historian Edward Everett Dale, has some fashionable customers in a Kansas City restaurant asking for successively rarer steaks. The last to order tells the waiter to make the steak extremely rare: "Just sear the outside a little." When the waiter comes to the cowboy seated at the next table, the cowpoke says, "Just cripple him and drive him in."[31]

The tale of the rare steak reached its climax in an account printed in 1885 of "A New Mexico Cowboy in London." A cowhand named Red Pugh, in London with a Wild West show, ordered a rare beefsteak from the waiter, who brought him one so rare that it jerked about on the plate. Thereupon Red drew out his gun and fired several shots into the flopping sirloin to kill it dead. A general pandemonium ensued, which led to the arrival of fifty London bobbies and the arrest of Red, by this time calmly eating his inert steak.[32]

Such was the *machismo* of the cowboy as illustrated in yarns about his he-man drinking and eating habits. But there was another side to the range rider reflected in the folktales. If he was a king on the prairie, he was a babe in the city. Individualistic, self-reliant, confident in his horse, his rope, and his six-shooter, the cowboy as trail driver and ranch hand held his head high. But on the occasions when he must go to town, he lost his *mana* and, like the Yankee in earlier yarns, stumbled and fumbled his way through an alien culture. Now he is the fool character, the noodle, the simpleton. In Chicago a cowhand, the aforementioned Rip Van Winkle, went to an eye doctor to get a pair of reading glasses. The oculist tested Rip on numbers on a board, then gave him a set of spectacles for ten dollars. "When I got back to my hotel," Rip recounted, "I bought a nickel newspaper and went upstairs and laid down on the bed and held the paper up in front of me. And fellows, I couldn't read a word." A buddy pointed out that Rip did not know how to read. "Well," countered Rip, "that's

1   BRANDING.

2   ON THE TRAIL.

3   HALTING-PLACE ON THE NINNESCAH RIVER.

4   SHIPPING FOR THE EASTERN MARKETS.

5   WICHITA.

6   HO. FOR TEXAS!

These six drawings represent various interesting features of the Texas cattle trade.

Sketch No. 1: The branding process, which takes place every spring and autumn. The cattle are driven along a narrow lane, just wide enough for two to pass abreast, and as they move slowly along, the hot iron brands the cattle owner's mark on the animal's flank.

No. 2: A drove of cattle on the march from Texas to Kansas, where they are transferred to the cattle cars and sent eastward by railroad. These droves vary from 500 to 8,000; during the long, four-to-five-month march the cattle feed on the luxurious grazing grounds of the Indian territory.

No. 3: The Ninnescah River Station, one of the chief halting places in Kansas, where the roads to the various grazing grounds branch off from the main trail.

No. 4: Cattle shipped from a station for the Eastern markets.

No. 5: Wichita, the grand central station for the cattle trade, is a driving business town in eastern Kansas.

No. 6: A party of cattle traders, or "cow boys" as they call themselves, who have sold their stock, going home to Texas. The camp outfit is loaded in the wagon, and a crowd of friends gather around to say goodbye and wish them a safe journey and return.

From *Harper's Weekly Supplement,* May 2, 1874

no reason for that doctor swindlin' me. He said plain as could be, he'd guarantee I could read with them ten-dollar glasses."[33]

Then there was the sad case of the cowpoke John Cox who took his bride of a few weeks, Eda May, into town to see the circus and enjoy a belated honeymoon. In their cabin in the lonely Arizona salt flats they had lived far away from cities, and knew nothing of them except a lurid description of an urban kidnapping gang they had read about in a Wild West magazine. They checked into a hotel, and John decided to get a haircut. Terrified of being left alone, Eda May asked John to lock her in and take the key with him. Once on the street John got shanghaied into a poker game by cowpuncher friends, and rode a lucky streak that lasted all night and into the following afternoon. Peering over a mountain of chips, John drew two queens to add to the pair in his hand. The four women on the cards brought to his mind a fifth he had forgotten. He jumped up and rushed out of the room, calling back to the boys, "I done left Eda May locked up in a room for twenty-four hours, *an' I ain't neither fed nor watered her!*" Poor John arrived too late to undo the damage. Eda May went back home to Utah and John reverted to bachelordom.[34]

Another yarn of a cowboy in difficul-

ties in a hotel presumably transpired in 1886 and found its way into print in 1894. A puncher from the Texas Panhandle wandered into a Denver hotel, resplendent in store-bought clothes and a red necktie. The clerk gave him a room with a folding bed, which the cowboy pretended to know about. He checked out in the morning without a word, and the chambermaid on entering his room discovered the bottom drawer pulled out as far as it would go, with all the rugs in the room piled in it and on the end a towel for a pillow. Pinned to the mirror he had left this note: "Gol dern yore folding beds. Why don't you make 'em longer and put more kivers onto um? Mebbe you expect a man to stand up and sleep in your durned old cubbert."[35] He had spent a rough night.

One theme of cowboy folk yarns dealt with the identity of the cowboy himself, as a type *sui generis* who could always be recognized, whatever his disguise, by anyone familiar with him on his home ground. The daughter of a Texas cattleman asserted that she could walk along the streets of any town or city and pick out the real cowboy, not by his clothes, but by his open countenance and clear eyes and mouth, stamped by the out-of-doors.[36] "Teddy Blue" Abbott, an old-time cowboy, once told Charlie Russell at a roundup in Calgary, Canada, that he had spotted a Texasman. "See that

"Drunken Cowboy on the Warpath"
Henry Worrall, from Joseph G. McCoy, *Historic Sketches of the Cattle Trade of the West and Southwest*, 1874

droop of his shoulders? He got that coming up the trail riding on three joints of his backbone." Teddy accosted the stranger, and sure enough, he was from Mobeetie, Texas, and a veteran of the long trail. "I believe I would know an old cowboy in hell with his hide burnt off," mused Teddy Blue. "It's the way they stand and walk and talk. There are lots of young fellows punching cows today [Teddy Blue wrote this in 1938] but they never can take our place, because cowpunching as we knew it is a thing of the past."[37]

Charlie Russell had his own story to tell about being recognized for a cowboy. Back in 1883 he made a killing at a gambling house in Cheyenne, went off to Chicago on a spree, and ended up sleeping off a jag in a strange rooming house with an unfamiliar bunkmate. "Neighbor, you're a long way from your range," comments the stranger. "You call the turn," says I, "but how did you read my iron?" The stranger explains. "It's your ways, while I'm layin' here, watchin' you get into your garments. Now, humans dress up an' punchers dress down. When you raised,

the first thing you put on is your hat. Another thing that shows you up is you don't shed your shirt when you bed down. So next comes your vest an' coat, keepin' your hindquarter covered till you slide into your pants, an' now you're lacin' your shoes. I notice you done all of it without quittin' the blankets, like the ground's cold. I don't know what state or territory you hail from, but you've smelt sagebrush an' drank alkali. I heap savvy you. You've slept a whole lot with nothin' but sky over your head, an' there's times when that old roof leaks, but judgin' from appearances, you wouldn't mind a little open air right now." And the stranger staked Charlie back to the cow country.[38]

The most original tall tale to issue from the cow camps involved a turtle herd. Thorp retold it in *Tales of the Chuck Wagon* and also in *Pardner of the Wind*. The yarn begins on the level of the soberest realism, as told by Peter Johnson, a foreman of the Bar W ranch in Texas, about two cowpunchers, Yost and Larrimore, who fell out over a girl. Larrimore won the girl, but Yost bit off a piece of his ear, and Larrimore nursed the insult.

Dining in a fancy San Antonio restaurant, Yost learned about the high price of turtle soup and conceived the idea of rounding up a herd of land terrapins to drive to market, like a herd of cattle. He and his Negro cowpunchers rounded up 14,986 turtles from the sand hills in gunny sacks, which at the expected price of $24 per turtle would bring a return of over $359,000. The herd could only make a few hundred yards a day, so that to cover the fourteen hundred miles to the Kansas market would take about fifteen years, but Yost plugged on, overcoming new difficulties as they arose. When the nights grew cold, he had his hands turn the turtles on their backs to keep them from stampeding, then found they kicked their legs all night and were too tired to travel the next day. So he decided to make camp for the winter and hired a ranchman to plow furrows in a sandy bottom. The turtles lay down in the furrows, the rancher dragged loose dirt over them, and the herd was safe for the winter.

Come spring, Yost started out again with his herd, now doubled by the birth of many small turtles, and reached Red River, where his former rival Larrimore had settled. Seeing his opportunity for revenge, Larrimore rode out to the center of the river and deposited a diving mud turtle on a stump between the banks. When the herd of land turtles entered the water in a long line, the lead turtle swam across the river until he encountered the log and the mud turtle, which dove into the stream, followed by every turtle in the herd. So Yost lost his whole herd, which, including the natural increase over the next fourteen years,

he figured would have brought him at market at least sixty million dollars.

This parody on the saga of the long cattle drive, narrated with realistic detail and deadpan solemnity, is a traveled tale. In Arkansas the turtle herder shod his tenderfooted turtles, whose iron shoes caused them to drown fording a stream, whereupon the herder dammed the stream, threw in heated rocks, boiled the water, and made turtle soup.[39]

A frog ranch forms the subject of a great whopper in Owen Wister's *The Virginian* (1902). The hero relates the story to exact revenge on the mutinous Trampas, who has gulled the Virginian with a tall tale about a train that ran so fast going downhill that when a man fired at the engine driver, his bullet broke every window and killed a passenger on the back platform. One of Trampas's followers had also just duped the Virginian's unsuspecting friend (the narrator in the novel) with a windy about a pregnant woman who, after being frightened by a rattlesnake, gives birth to a child with eight rattles. The friend laughed with the others, until he saw they were laughing at him. Biding his time, the Virginian launched into an elaborate recital of frog ranches. His exposition developed naturally enough following a meal of frogs' legs, from frogs he himself caught in the marsh near the train station at Billings, Montana, and served to hungry passengers stranded there. Actually the Virginian had only shortly before learned of the delicacy at an eating "palace" in Omaha. With the thought of frogs' legs on everybody's minds, and Trampas and his buddies all ears, the Virginian painted a glowing picture of

147

the vast markets for frogs, in big cities, on passenger trains, at Yellowstone Park, and of the high investment returns and the generous wages paid on the frog ranch he had seen at Tulare, California. Casually he dropped asides about the technology of frog ranching: ". . . it would give most anybody a shock to hear 'em speak about herdin' the bulls in a pasture by themselves. . . . Every pasture was a square swamp with a ditch around, and a wire net. . . . The big balance of the herd stampeded . . . they never struck any plan to brand their stock and prove ownership . . . same as cattle trains, yu'd see frawg trains tearing accrost Arizona—big glass tanks with wire over 'em—through to New York, an' the frawgs starin' out." As the rapt circle listened with mounting excitement and dismay, the Virginian capped his account with a feud between the great New York and Philadelphia chefs, each trying to capture the Tulare frog market and finally agreeing to a truce in which they eliminated frogs from their menus. "Frawgs are dead, Trampas, and so are you," concluded the Virginian, suddenly harpooning his victim. The admiring passengers, some stolid Indian chiefs standing by, and the crestfallen Trampas and his crew now all shook hands with and congratulated the Virginian on his outrageous fiction.[40]

A special point of folkloric interest Owen Wister makes manifest in his famous novel is the cowboy code governing the telling of tall tales. To seduce the unwary listener constitutes a triumph for the narrator, and to be trapped into swallowing the tale amounts to defeat for the dupe. Trampas drew first blood on the Virginian, but paid dear in consequence. In his repertoire of cowboy skills, the Virginian excelled also in drawing the long bow.

American raconteurs tell about other unusual herds taken to market. From Nevada comes a lumberjack's tale of driving a swarm of bees to market in California to pollinate fruit for California fruit growers.[41] In the Broadway comedy hit of 1918, *Lightnin'*, the title character, Lightnin' Bill Jones, known for shiftless ways and large stories, dryly remarks to a disdainful sheriff that he "drove a swarm of bees across the plains in the dead of winter once. And never lost a bee. Got stung twice."[42] In the Ozarks of Missouri and Arkansas, hillmen tell sober narratives of wild turkey herds driven to market in pioneer times. The turkey drivers corraled the herds in a narrow hollow near Hog Scald, Arkansas. Meanwhile a horseback rider in advance of the herd dropped shelled corn along the path, and a boy outpost cautioned farmers to tie up their dogs. At dusk the turkeys roosted in the trees until the following morning, and so proceeded until they reached the market at Springfield, Missouri. In one version the herd included five hundred tame geese along with three thousand wild turkeys, and the drivers ran into trouble when the geese refused to stop at nightfall with the roosting turkeys but spraddled on until they came to water.[43]

Although Owen Wister's hero has conjured up a frog ranch and Jack Thorp's narrator a turtle drive, both epics involve a parody on cattle raising. Together with the version from Arkansas, they point to a cherished Münchausen tradition among cowboys. This tale-cycle plainly displays the entrepreneurial imagination associated with American business enterprise and the American penchant for get-rich-quick schemes. The desire for instant wealth proved to be Trampas' undoing.

Supernatural legends rarely appear in the yarnfests, but there is evidence that the cowboy had his occult side. One autobiography of an old "waddy," as the cowboy was sometimes called, designates a haunted grove along the Pecos River. "Boy, in later year there were so many durned cow rustlers and hoss thieves hanged from the limbs of them cottonwood trees, the grove came to be plump ha'nted. Night horses staked out with a rope would get scared, break loose, and run off. And even old chuck wagon mules would hightail and *vamoose.* I've heard cowpunchers claim they could hear chains rattling at night, and sounds like someone gasping for breath with a rope around his neck."[44]

There is also the legend Andy Adams liked, about Stampede Mesa in Crosby County, Texas, where irate cowpunchers backed a nester (pioneer farmer) off the bluff on his horse to lie at the bottom with the mangled carcasses of the steers he had stampeded. Ever after, ghostly steers were seen on the mesa, and no herd could bed there without upset.[45] An old-time, gun-scarred Texan, Alvin Reed, told on tape about a hant he had seen in Black Canyon of a snow-white dog that would run twenty steps and disappear, and other cowpeople talked about La Loma de la Madre in Old Mexico, where one would hear "dogs a-barkin' and chickens a-crowin' . . . and big ol' Meskin [Mexican] spurs a-rattlin', ridin' and a-rattlin' . . . and you couldn't *see* nothin' or find nothin'."[46]

From the scattered, somewhat unsatisfactory sources, one can still establish the vitality of oral narration among the cowboys and reconstruct central themes in their repertoire of tales. Cowboy narratives run largely to humorous anecdotes and tall tales, but there are traces of somber legends of places haunted by the spirits of men hanged and gunned down. Besides general American whoppers of hunting, the weather, and the animal kingdom, cowboys yarn about themselves. These self-centered tales delineate a figure readily identifiable by his gait, posture, and personal habits as a master rider of the open range; a giant on horseback but a tenderfoot in town; a lover of whiskey and rare steaks; and a scorner of death. The sentimentality pervading cowboy lyrics and ballads yields in the tales to an almost sickly humor mocking lethal gunplay and violent killings. Cowboy folktales cemented the fraternal bonds among the herders of cattle,

"Cowboys Swimming a Herd Across the Platte River"
E. Boyd Smith, from Andy Adams, *The Log of a Cowboy*

who appeared curt and laconic to the outside world but turned garrulous among their own kind.

The Cowboy Code

One part of cowboy tradition that falls outside the usual genres of song, tale, and saying is the code of values that bound together the otherwise individualistic cowhands. Successive historians of the cattle range describe this code.[47] Among Michigan lumberjacks I discovered and wrote about a similar code of ethics and behavior. These codes are explicit although, like English constitutional law and American common law, they do not get formally written down, but can be communicated orally. Ramon Adams equates the "code of the West or the range code" with the notion of a gentleman's agreement in the absence of legal statutes on the Southwest frontier. By consensus of his biographers, the true cowboy was expected to possess courage, cheerfulness, love of his horse, loyalty to his outfit, respect for women, reticence, and the hospitality of the Westerner. Without such a code the society of cattlemen and cowboys would have dissolved into feudal wars and anarchy.

Pride in his special line of work came first in the cowboy's code. "There was no prouder soul on earth than the cowboy," wrote Ramon Adams. "He was proud of his occupation and held it to be a dignified calling." Only the skilled horseman could qualify as a cowboy, and workers on the ground—sheepherders, farmers, railroad laborers—belonged to lesser breeds. Adams tells of the cowboy who, asked by his boss to dig some postholes, swore that he "wouldn't be caught on the blister end of no damned shovel" and rode off to find more appropriate employment.[48] Old Westerners characterized the cowboy as "a man with guts and a horse."[49]

Confident in his abilities, the cowboy endured all the rigors of the trail drive without complaint and gave himself completely to the task of tending the cattle on the range and getting them to market. To complain about long hours, aches and pains, creature comforts, the food, was to violate the code. Indeed, whoever complained about the food must assist, or substitute for, the cook, according to a well-known tradition that gave rise to an oft-repeated tale of the cowboy who exclaimed, "This bread is all burned," and then suddenly catching himself, added, "but gosh! that's the way I like it!"[50]

Reticence or taciturnity as a part of the code derived from the frontier sentiment that a man's past was nobody's business but his own. His fellows judged him by how he lived up to the code of the present. For the complainer, the blowhard, the shirker, the liar, there was ostracism, or a ritual thrashing known as "putting the leggins" on a transgressing cowpoke. In his history of The Chisholm Trail, Sam Ridings recounts an instance of the custom applied to a young dude from the East nicknamed "Billings" because of his propensity for bragging about his valorous feats performed on his uncle's ranch near Billings, Montana. Starting a spring trip down the Chisholm Trail from Caldwell, Kansas, to pick up a herd of Texas cattle, a group of cowboys gathered around the chuck wagon to yarn. Billings led off with a vainglorious tale of how he, the terror of the Northwest, had separated a bully from his lady friend in a Billings dance hall and sent the ruffian skulking into the shadows. Texas Mike questioned the veracity of this brag, and Billings offered to take on any man who did not accept his story as truth. Tex replied in a little parable that no matter how bad a badman thought he was, there was always a badder a mile further up Bitter Creek.

Pecos followed this observation with a reminiscence of Billy the Kid, whom he recalled as a modest little tyke who wept over the bullet-riddled body of his dead boss and vowed revenge on his killers. Such a tenderhearted stripling was far more deadly, opined Pecos, than blusterers crowing about their own bloody deeds.

Next the talk shifted into hunting and trail experiences of a Münchausen flavor. Pecos had escaped from a buffalo by running up his gun barrel. Acey Wilde recalled the accidental shot from his gun that split a tree limb and caught nine turkeys by the toes, went on to kill a deer, and landed in a bee tree that yielded him a hundred pounds of honey. He loaded the game on a sled hitched to a horse with a rawhide harness and started off for camp, but a rain came up and stretched the tug a quarter of a mile behind him; Acey led the horse around a tree, fastened the tugs, set up his tent, and waited for the tugs to dry, when to his surprise they pulled the sled up to his tent. Gene Marsh told of a young fellow from the East, something of a track star at his school, who went to work for a sheepherder in New Mexico and rounded up jack rabbits under the impression they were lambs. Acey Wilde thought of the time he was trail driving in Kansas and stopped at a homesteader's to borrow a monkey wrench, and was told by the wife that there were sheep, horse, and cattle ranches in the vicinity, but no one had yet been foolish enough to start a monkey ranch.

At this point Texas Mike re-entered the forum with an allegedly true incident that happened when he was a lad. Dressed up in his best suit to go visiting, he had tried to feed a balky calf. Now he asked Billings to help him re-enact the scene, in which the calf got its nose in the bucket and shot a stream of milk all over Tex's ruffled white shirt:

The cry for vengeance went through my whole system, and (reaching out and grasping Billings firmly by the ears) I got that calf right square by the ears, so it couldn't bite away, and I yanked it up to the bucket just like this, and I stuck its nose down into the bucket this way, and while it kickt and cavorted around I held it there until it might near croaked, and pulled it over that barnyard and jerked it up and down just like this, and the longer I pulled the madder I got, until I threw that blasted calf away from me just this way, and went back to the house all soaked with milk and all tore up and ruint, and I have remained ruint to this very day.

While acting out this charade, Tex pulled and yanked at Billings, rubbed his nose in the dirt, and at length flung him away as if he were the calf. His audience split their sides at this traditional trick of the cow camps. But Billings failed to see the fun and reached for his Colt pistol. Tex ignored him and

Gene Marsh knocked the gun from Billings' hand, then proceeded to give him a verbal dressing down about the "well established rules and precedents of the trail." One rule was not to blow one's own horn but to let others find out a man's qualities for themselves. Another was to learn to take a joke in good spirit.

Continuing, Gene admonished the dumbfounded Billings, "It is through an act of kindness to you that we are about to administer unto you the old and established degree installing you into the body of cowboys who ride this trail, and we will do so with a painful but well meant and impressive ceremony." The cowboys wound a rope around Billings' legs, laid him across a log, and held down the terror of the Northwest, while Gene grasped a pair of heavy cowhide leggins in his hand and delivered another peroration beginning, "Young man from the Northern Country, before you can serve successfully as a cowboy on this trail, you must wear these leggins or chaparajos in a manner becoming to one of your proud profession." He then whaled the rear end of the would-be badman until he screamed for mercy, but, according to custom, Marsh administered six further blows to make sure the suppliant was in earnest. The victim released, Marsh made one concluding speech welcoming Billings to the fraternity of trail riders if he thenceforth ceased his bluster and threats, and assured him the cowboys stood ready to protect and defend him if he honored their unwritten laws. Billings shook hands with Tex, apologized to him, and thenceforth comported himself like a true cowboy.[51]

This whole chapter, "Tales of a Cow-Camp and Breaking in a Cowboy," possesses considerable interest for the student of cowboy tradition and custom. Its author, Sam Ridings, has endeavored to set down an unvarnished account of incidents and personalities in the great days of the cattle drive, as he recollected them from the early 1880s.

"Midnight Storm and Stampede"
Henry Worrall, from Joseph G. McCoy, *Historic Sketches of the Cattle Trade of the West and Southwest,* 1874

He has named names, given oral texts—in contrast to the bland paraphrases of cowboy tales too often found in the literature of the cattle range—and, in an appropriate context, delineated the custom of "putting the leggins on" an erring cowboy. The yarning rings true; several of the tales, such as the wonderful shot coupled with the stretching and contracting buckskin harness[52] and the sheepherder who rounded up jack rabbits,[53] are among the best-known American tall tales. Miraculous escapes from wild animals and absurd misunderstandings of words also provide a basis for well-liked humorous folktales.[54] The personal reminiscence of Billy the Kid, supplied by one cowboy, dovetails with comments about the Kid, covering the spectrum from eulogy to vilification, that strew the autobiographies and histories of the cattle country.[55] But Billings breaks with the convention of chuck-wagon yarnspinning, and in-stead of telling a tall tale or legend, blows off about himself. As an initial reprisal Tex then plays a practical joke on Billings, of a kind not as yet much collected by folklorists, in which the narrator of a tale tricks and discomfits his listener,[56] sometimes verbally, sometimes physically. (Mark Twain's story of "The Golden Arm," that builds up to a suspense-laden climax and then abruptly switches to a trick ending—"Who stole my golden arm?" "You!"—is an example.) Billings fails this test by displaying bad grace and ill temper and once again resorting to threats of gunplay. He has broken the code on several counts, in lack of reticence, of cheerfulness, and of loyalty to his fellow cowboys. Hence the ritual chastisement meted out to him of "putting the leggins on," a kind of initiation rite reserved for transgressors of the code to give them a chance to become members in good standing of the proud fraternity of cowhands.

Lumberjacks

In some ways the lumberjack echoes the cowboy as an American mythic figure. Both are sturdy individualists belonging to a golden age, roughly 1870–1900, when their skills and *machismo,* on range and trail for the one and in woods and on rivers for the other, contributed indispensably to the early success of the cattle and lumber industries. In his spring role as river driver, balancing on logs careening down swol-len streams and prying loose with his peavey the giant logs piled up into jams, the woodsman played a role as dangerous as the cowpuncher attempting to stem a stampede. The cowboys' outfit on the long drive and the lumberjacks' camp in the winter woods alike brought together groups of men in outdoors work who were isolated for many months from the rest of the world. A comparable hierarchy prevailed in these societies: the boss at the top, the chore-boy of the lumber camp and the horse wrangler of the trail outfit at the bottom, the cook occupying a special prestigious position in both instances, and the cow-punchers and woodsmen on the firing line. Some observers consciously link the two types. One comments that log marks resemble cattle brands.[1] Another proposes that a statue to the lumberjack be erected on the state capitol grounds at Minneapolis to match one of the cowboy at Austin, for the "cowboy is no more typical of the cattle industry of Texas and the western plains than is the lumberjack of the lumber industry of Minnesota and the Northwest."[2]

There is also the same variability in the generic name for the lumberjack as for the cowboy. Originally in the New England colonies, men who worked in the woods cutting trees and in the sawmills in the midst of the forests all went by the name of lumberers; but as the woods receded and the occupations became divided, the axe wielder was called woodsman, logger, lumberman, and shantyboy. Lumberjack was a relatively late term, coming from the Old Northwest and flowing back to the Northeast around the time of World War I. The Maine poet Holman Day adopted "lumberjack" from the Michigan novels of Stewart Edward White.

"Lumbering in Maine and New Brunswick — Drawing the Logs to the Creek"
From *Harper's Weekly,* September 25, 1858

In the Pacific Northwest a "logger" cut trees. But by whatever name, the "timber beast" stood as a breed apart. A newspaper story reporting a steamboat accident noted that "three men and a logger were drowned."[3]

Although the lumber industry is as old as the colonization of America, and masts for the king's navy were in demand from the start, the industry did not reach its climax until after the Civil War. By then the Maine woods were stripped of white pine and the mill owners had moved their operations to the Great Lakes states of Michigan, Wisconsin, and Minnesota, prior to the last big jump to Washington, Oregon, and California. So long as the white pine and hardwood remained, wood for construction outdistanced other building materials, and the lumber barons maintained their relentless assault on the timberlands. The end of the white pine and the modernization of the industry spelled the demise of the lumberjack. As one woods historian put it, "Today's lumberjack is a suitcase-carrying, pomade-using, Coca-Cola-drinking gent . . . a grease-monkey who works for an Organization. How can he feel about a chain-saw and an Organization as the old woodsman did about his axe and boss?" By contrast, the "old-fashioned, two-fisted, red-shirted woodsman . . . would work himself to a frazzle and cheerfully risk life and limb for a boss who gave him a fair shake."[4]

Lumberjack Songs

Recognition that woodsmen possessed their own store of folklore was given initially, as with the cowboy, to their songs. In 1924 Roland Palmer Gray brought out *Songs and Ballads of the Maine Lumberjacks,* and in the following years Maine and Michigan yielded additional harvests of lumberjack minstrelsy. From such scattered collections Malcolm Laws, in his index of native American balladry, identified twenty-eight ballads of the woods sung by lumberjacks.[5] Of course they sang many pieces that had nothing to do with cutting timber, and some of their woodsy songs, like "The Lumberman's Alphabet," do not contain sufficient narrative thread—as is true of "The Old Chisholm Trail"—to qualify as ballads. Still these twenty-eight testify to the existence of a sturdy indigenous songlore of the lumber camps.

These were never work songs, for the bite of the axe and the whir of the crosscut saw did not invite musical accompaniment, but strictly songs for pleasure sung in the bunkshanty at the day's end, or on Sundays, the only time, according to the anecdote, that the shantyboys saw the camp in daylight. After the evening meal, eaten in silence according to the code, the loggers repaired to the bunkhouse, hung out their wet socks on the drying racks, and amidst their malodorous scent regaled themselves around the deacon seat with songs, anecdotes, music on the mouth organ and jew's-harp, rough games of tomfoolery, and, on Saturday nights, stag dances. What the chuck-wagon campfire circle was to the cowboy, the bunkshanty after-dinner gathering was to the lumberjack.

The hazards and somber tragedies of work in the forests and on the river

"Dinner-hour in a Michigan Lumber Camp"
A Michigan lumber-camp scene drawn by Dan Beard for *Scribner's Magazine,* June 1893

drives provide the themes for a number of the woods ballads. In eleven the hero drowns, usually in the attempt to break a log jam, as in the most famous of all lumberjack folksongs, "The Jam on Gerry's Rock." Twice the central character is crushed to death by falling logs and twice he is mangled in a sawmill. Other, less mournful pieces deal with rigors in camp and on the drive and lusty fights and sprees. One favorite, "The Little Brown Bulls," supposedly composed in a northern Wisconsin lumber camp in the early 1870s, describes a betting contest in skidding logs on the tote road between McCluskey's big spotted steers and Bull Gordon's little brown bulls, a contest sharpened by ethnic rivalry between McCluskey the Scotchman and Gordon the Yankee. The Yankee wins, and McCluskey gives him the twenty-five dollars and a belt from his best mackinaw to use on the bulls, since it has not worked on his steers. Whether they are striking a tragic or a humorous note, the ballads lay emphasis on getting the work done as

a matter of personal pride, either in untangling the piled-up logs on the river or hauling a giant load of logs on the tote road.

Although I have done little folksong collecting, on a one-day foray deep into the Maine woods in the summer of 1956, I captured several of the most

"The Kitchen"

A Michigan lumber-camp scene drawn by Dan Beard for *Scribner's Magazine,* June 1893

celebrated loggers' songs. My field trip had actually taken me to the Maine coast in search of lobstermen's lore, but I turned inland for twenty-four hours to pursue the lead of a lumberwoods songstress hidden deep in the forest in a hamlet called Saponac. Only a dozen families lived in these backwoods and the township was on the verge of losing its incorporation. Saponac lay on a dirt road in a clearing, all three buildings of it, with its name scratched on a shingle by Huckleberry Finn, or so it looked. An old chap sleeping in a hammock roused up and directed me to the next patch of daylight, where I would locate the tarpaper dwelling of Martha Benson, my hoped-for singer. Martha's name had been given me by a student in my American folklore class at Michigan State University. In that course I required the students to turn in a collection of songs, tales, beliefs, or other kinds of tradition they had obtained themselves and documented by listing on the cover sheet the name, age, residence, and occupation of the tradition bearer, usually designated the "informant." This particular collection contained a sheaf of splendid texts of Maine lumberjack folksongs, with the name of Martha Benson, also a student at Michigan State but not in my class and not known to me, as the informant. A preliminary sketch offered precise details on Martha's habitat in the Saponac forest north of Bangor, where her family lived without benefit of running water or electricity. The fullness of the informant data and the excellence of the song texts so excited me that I interrupted my coastal collecting to make the

"Sunday in Camp"
A Michigan lumber-camp scene drawn by Dan Beard for *Scribner's Magazine,* June 1893

circuitous drive inland to Saponac.

While driving, and reflecting, I realized that the texts were far too good to be true. No such woods repertoire would turn up on the lips of a college girl. Martha at once confirmed my suspicions. She knew only a couple of songs, and those from college. A shy, sincere young woman with a strong Maine accent, she did indeed live as her friend had described, and obviously this false friend had designated Martha as her informant and then copied song texts from one of the standard book collections. Yet the day ended happily, for Martha's father, a bluff hearty woodsman, offered to take me to the nearest

157

town, Lowell, to interview some of his older buddies from the logging camps and river drives. The first lead proved abortive; the old woodsman said flatly he had forgotten all the songs he once knew, and waved us goodbye. Before reaching the second house, I suggested that we enter, sit down, and start talking before taking no for an answer. Our prospect, John Porter, in his late sixties, was watching a ball game on television. After some polite exchange he finally yielded to our persistence, switched off the game, and switched his mind onto old times in the lumber camp and the woods songs of yore. Fragments of a few came to his mind, but he suggested we see his son Don who lived a mile down the road. This seemed like a put-off, but we perforce drove away and found Don at home, a shocking sight, with one gaping eye socket, the result of an auto accident some years before, and ragged attire and heavy beard that accentuated his disfigurement. But he greeted us cordially and began singing in full, rich tones. Forty years old and basically a good-looking, sturdy fellow, Don had become morose since his accident and had turned recluse. Later I was told he had not sung in years, until the occasion of our surprise visit.

We all ended up back at John Porter's house, with father and son singing harmoniously, and their family gathered around appreciatively. By a curious irony, the day that had begun so disappointingly ended with a splendid recording on my Ampex of some of the well-known lumberjack ditties that the errant student had copied from Gray or other standard collections and turned in to my class as having been sung by Martha Benson.

The following is the text and tune of "The Jam on Gerry's Rock" as sung by Don Porter, who had heard it since he was ten years old:

THE JAM ON GERRY'S ROCK

Transcribed by Georg List

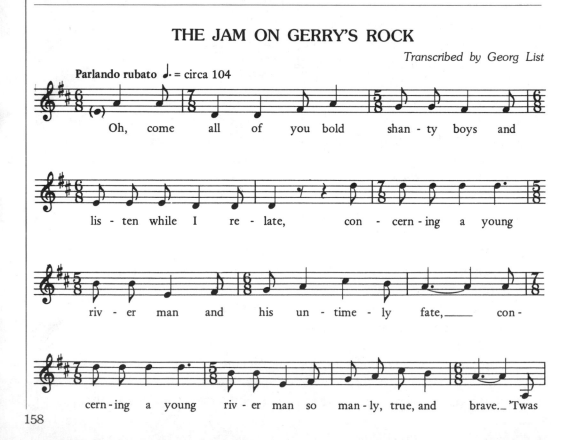

158

on the jam at Ger-ry's Rock he met a wat-er-y grave.—

'Twas on a Sun-day morn-ing as you will quick-ly

hear.— The logs were piled up moun-tain high, we could not keep them

clear.___ Our fore-man said, "Turn out, brave boys, with

hearts de-void of fear.___ We'll break the jam on

Ger-ry's Rock and for Ing-ham's town we'll steer."___

Now some of them were willing,
  While others they were not,
For to work on jams on Sunday
  They did not think they ought.
But six of our Canadian boys
  Did volunteer to go
And break the jam on Gerry's Rock
  With a foreman named Monroe.

They had not rolled off many a log
  When they heard his clear voice say,
"I'd have you on your guard, boys,

The jam will soon give way."
These words were scarcely spoken
  When an ash did break and go.
It carried off those six brave youths
  And the foreman Jack Monroe.

When the rest of our brave shanty-boys
  The sad news came to hear,
In search of their dead comrades
  To the river they did steer.
Some of the mangled bodies
  A-floating down did go,
While crushed and bleeding near the banks
  Was that of young Monroe.

They took him from his watery grave,
  Brushed back his raven hair.
There was one fair form among them
  Whose sad cries rent the air.
There was one fair girl among them,
  A maid from Saginaw town,
Whose moans and cries rose to the skies
  For a true lover who'd gone down.

Now Clara was a noble girl,
  A riverman's true friend.
She with her widowed mother dear
  Lived at the river's bend.
The wages of her own true love
  The boss to her did pay,
The shanty-boys for her made out
  A generous purse next day.

They buried him with sorrow deep,
  'Twas on the first of May.
Come all of you bold shanty-boys
  And for your comrade pray.
Engraved upon our hemlock tree
  That by the grave did grow
Was the name and date of the sad fate
  Of the shanty-boy, Monroe.

Fair Clara did not long survive,
  Her heart broke with her grief.
And scarcely two months afterwards
  Death came to her relief.
And when this time had passed away

And she was called to go,
Her last request was granted
  To be laid by young Monroe.

Come all you bold shanty-boys
  I'll have you call and see
Those two mounds by the riverside
  Where grows their hemlock tree.
The shanty-boys cleared off the woods
  For the lovers there laid low.
'Twas the handsome Clara Verner
  And her true love, Jack Monroe.[6]

This is the lumberman's classic. It falls into what Fanny Hardy Eckstorm and Mary Winslow Smyth, in their *Minstrelsy of Maine* (1927), call the middle period of Maine woods songs, the high point of ballad making, influenced by Scotch-Irish Canadian loggers coming down to Maine from the Provinces. This period, from about 1880 to the end of the century, was preceded by cheerful songs of the lumberman's life, lacking a narrative, and followed by song-poems of a didactic or descriptive turn, meant as much to be read as sung. "The Jam on Gerry's Rock" epitomizes the mournful strain and balladic formulas cherished by shantyboys in the golden age of logging. It has the death in action on the treacherous river drive, the subject of so many woods songs; the foreboding felt by the rivermen against working on Sundays; the traditional generosity of the shantyboys in taking up a collection for Clara; and the ballad romance, uncharacteristic of the woodsmen but so true to "Barbara Allen," of the lovers symbolically united after death. Fanny Hardy Eckstorm conducted an intensive detective hunt for the ballad's origins, and found the drowning of young Monroe located at six different places on the Penobscot River in Maine alone. Michigan too made its claims, supported by the reference to "Saginaw town." But every clue eventually led to another fatality, or to a folk etymology of a place name based on the ballad itself. In the end Eckstorm developed an hypothesis of two forms of the song, the older one based on an incident that had occurred on the Seboosis River in Maine around 1880, and the later one grafted onto this in Michigan and then drifting both eastward and westward. In the early form the head of young Monroe is severed, and his ladylove is not Clara Verner but just Miss Clark. By these tokens, Don Porter's text belongs to the later form, with its "crushed and bleeding" body of Jack Monroe and reference to the "handsome Clara Verner." But I did get another text of "The Jam on Gerry's Rock" from eighty-two-year-old Pompey Grant, who had spent all his life in the woods, although he lived only ten miles from the coast, in Columbia Falls, and Pompey in his somewhat garbled verses did allude to the severed head:

When the sad news at the camp
  The comrades came to hear
To search for their dead bodies
  Through sorrow, grief, and
    woe,
Lay bruised and mangled on
    the beach
  Was the head of John Monroe.

But he could not recall the final verses and so did not name the "girl from Saginaw town." Like so many woods singers of this piece, Pompey claimed that the drowning took place on the Penobscot or Androscoggin River, "them big rivers in the northern part of the state of Maine . . . in 'round Grand Stone . . . an awful piece of falls, rough water on the river there. But was right in that vicinity somewhere that happened."[6]

Another song I collected that night, this time from John Porter, "The Lumberman's Alphabet," is a standard piece in every collection and an occupational folksong *par excellence,* found also among sailors, and addressed to the artifacts and personalities of the occupation in question. It is not a ballad, as it pursues no narrative line, but a rollicking ditty enumerating major reference points in the life of the logger (or other occupational worker) according to words beginning with the letters of the alphabet in sequence. How closely the song is tied to work —and work was pretty much the whole of life for lumberjack as for cowboy, except when they went on their seasonal sprees—is seen in the preliminary remarks of John Porter before singing the song:

THE LUMBERMAN'S ALPHABET

Dorson. Now earlier you were telling us, Mr. John Porter, about conditions in the woods in the old days, and the hardships of the men on the drive. I wonder if you just would say a word about that, how hard and how long you worked.

John Porter. Well, we used to work from twelve to seventeen hours a day. We got two dollars and a half a day. We was fed four times a day. We had what we call breakfast, and first lunch at 9 o'clock. At 2 o'clock we had second lunch, and for supper around 9 or 10 o'clock at night, we called that supper. We broke ice water and at night we slept in tents. We cooked outdoors in bakers and open fire.

And when it came bed-time, we slept under spreads twenty feet long and seven feet the other way to cover us up. And you couldn't get up in the night. If you did, you'd have to set by the fire the rest of the night, because the men was so close and piled in like sardines. There was no way that you could get back into bed. We slept with our shoes under our head to keep them from freezing, and then, when we got up in the morning, we'd have to thaw 'em out by the open fire and kick 'em on. I would say that that was hardship.

Dorson. Now this song, "The Lumberman's Alphabet," describes something of the conditions there, doesn't it? "A" is for such-and-such.

John Porter:

Transcribed by George List

♩. = 63

"A" is for ax - es we ver - y well know, and

"B" is for boys that could use them al - so.

"C" is for chop - pers so read - y to be - gin, and

"D" is the dan - ger we al - ways stand in.

Oh, "E" is for ech - o that through the woods rang, and

"F" is for fore - man that head - ed our gang.

"G" is for grind - stone so mer - ry - go - round,___ and

"H" is for han - dle so smooth - ly was borne.

163

"I" is for iron we knock us a pine,
And "J" is for [unintelligible name] that's always behind.
"K" is for keen as our axes did keep,
And "L" is for lice that over us creep.
"M" is for moss we keep in our camp,
And "N" is for needles we mend with our pants.
"O" is for owl that hooteth by night,
And "P" is for pine we always fall right.

What's the other . . .
Don Porter. "Q."
John Porter. "U" is for uses we put our teams in.
Don Porter. "Q," I said!
Dorson. "Q" you left out.
John Porter. Oh, "Q."
Dorson. Yes.
John Porter. "Q" is for quarrels we never allow.
Don Porter. Go ahead.
Dorson. "Q" is for quarrels. Can you sing it?
John Porter. If I could think of the letters I can.
Don Porter. "Q."
Dorson. Yes, "Q" is for quarrels.
John Porter. . . . we never allow,
And "V" is . . .
Don Porter. "U."
John Porter. "U" . . .
Dorson. "P," "Q" . . . well, how does it end up?
What's the last rhyme on it?
John Porter. There's three more letters I cannot . . .
Dorson. Yes. "U," "V," "W," "X," "Y," "Z."
John Porter. . . . I cannot bring in rhyme,

But if you want any more of this song
You may . . .
I forget how that ends.[7]

John Porter had difficulty remembering the song because he omitted the chorus, always a stabilizing mnemonic factor for the bard. The text of this song included by Franz Rickaby in his *Ballads and Songs of the Shanty-Boy* (1926) concludes with the following three stanzas, and the chorus celebrates the contentment of the woodsman:

Q is for quarrels we never allow,
And R is for river our logs they do plow.
S is for sleigh, so stout and so strong,

And T is for teams that will haul them along.

U is for use we put our teams to,
And V is for valley we haul our logs through.
W's for woods we leave in the spring,
[And now I have sung all that I'm going to sing.]

There's three more letters I ain't put in rhyme,
And if any of you know them, please tell me in time.
The train has arrived at the station below,
So fare you well, true love, it's I must be gone.

Chorus:
And so merry and so merry are we.
No mortals on earth are so happy as we.
Hi derry hi, and a hi derry down.
Give the shanty-boys grub and there's nothing goes wrong.[8]

1. Surveying for a logging railway

Three scenes (here and on the following pages) of lumberjacks preparing a logging railway in the white-pine forests of Thunder Bay, Lake Huron, Michigan, from *Frank Leslie's Illustrated Newspaper,* March 3, 1888

Not all the items, of course, are equal in the lumberjack's cosmology. Moss was not a subject of concern to him, but lice certainly were, and entered into his jokes and games.

While the verse "Q is for quarrels we never allow" is true with respect to on-the-job hours, when not at work the woodsmen fought memorably. The savage fights of the lumberjacks became primarily the subject of prose rather than verse traditions, although once in a while a song describes fisticuffs. One verse account of a typical pitched battle between lumberjack brawlers pitted "Silver Jack" Driscoll, a semilegendary woodsman who cut pine in Michigan in the 1880s and 1890s, against a blasphemer in the camp, silk-tongued Bobby Waite. A strapping, six-foot-four Canadian-born logger, renowned for his mauling of camp bullies, "Silver Jack" was unjustly framed when he was drunk and sentenced to the penitentiary. While not churchgoers, lumberjacks, like cowboys, reverenced the Lord in a kind of natural religion. The fight between two good, tough men contains the slugging and chewing characteristic of shantyboy melees, and ends appropriately with "Silver Jack" and his victim drinking amiably to God.

SILVER JACK

I was on the drive in '80,
On the drive with Silver Jack,
He's in the penitentiary now.
But he's soon expected back.

There was a chap among us
By the name of Bobby Waite;
He was smooth, slick and
　　cunning
As a college graduate.

He could talk on any subject
From the Bible to Hoyle.

His words flew out as easy
As ever a man poured oil.

He was what you call a skeptic.
And he loved to set and weave
His tales of fancy wonders
And things we couldn't believe.

One day, while waiting for a
　　flood,
We all were sitting round,
Smoking Niggerhead tobacco
And hearing Bob expound.

He said Hell was all a humbug.
And he showed as plain as day
That the Bible was a fable,
And how much it looked that way.

2.

166

"You're a liar!" someone
  shouted.
"And you've got to take it back!"
And everybody started,
'Twas the voice of Silver Jack.

"Maybe I've not used the Lord
Always exactly white;
But when a chump abuses Him
He must eat his words or fight.

"It was in that old religion
That my mother lived and died;
Her memory's ever dear to me,
And I say that Bob has lied."

Now Bob he was no coward.
 And he spoke up brave and free;
"Put up your dukes and fight,
   my lad,
You'll find no flies on me."

2. Building a railway

They fought for forty minutes
While the boys would whoop
    and cheer:
And Jack spit up a tooth or two
And Bobby lost an ear.

At last Jack got him underneath
And slugged with all his might;
So Bobby finally agreed
That Silver Jack was right.

And when they got through
    fighting
And rose up from the ground
A friend fished out a bottle
And it went quietly round.

They drank to Jack's religion
In a solemn sort of way;
And just to clinch the argument
They worked no more that day.[9]

Pride of Michigan lumberjacks, "Silver Jack" fought bare-fisted and and drank himself sodden according to their code. But he believed in God, in his way, and in the gospel of work, as did every self-respecting wielder of axe and broad-saw—and rider of the range, for the ballad of Silver Jack also made its way into the cow camps.

Lumberjack Hero Tales

By contrast with the collections of lumberjack folksongs, the shelf of lumberjack folktales is empty, unless one places the Paul Bunyan books there, which he should not if he is concerned with oral traditional folklore. The numerous volumes on Paul Bunyan, mostly aimed at juvenile readers, belong not to a folk but to a literary and commercial impulse growing out of the booklets of William B. Laughead, advertising agent for the Red River Lumber Company

of Minnesota and California, issued from 1914 to 1930. Lumberjacks did yarn around the deacon seat, but their folk anecdotes are far removed from the syrupy confections about old Paul and Babe the Blue Ox.

The mass culture refuses to acknowledge the nontraditional nature of Bunyan, and it gets the books it wants. In the Upper Peninsula of Michigan in 1946, scores of veteran white-pine lumberjacks had little or nothing to say of Paul Bunyan, although I asked each one about the behemoth. Yet that year Stan Newton, from Sault Sainte Marie in the Upper Peninsula, put together a syn-

3.

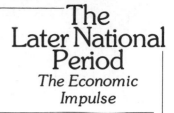

thetic batch of tales in *Paul Bunyan of the Great Lakes*, ignoring the living lore of the woods all about him and extracting copy from a Paul Bunyan column he ran in the *Upper Peninsula Development Bureau News*, to which contributors sent bits of whimsy. When a retired lumberjack, John E. Nelligan, brought the manuscript of his life as a woodsman to Charles M. Sheridan, a college graduate with writing experience, to prepare it for publication, his collaborator looked in vain through the work for Bunyan references. The editor of the historical journal that published Nelligan's manuscript commented on this lack:

3. Loading up

Apparently Nelligan, despite his diversified experience in the woods of New Brunswick, Maine, Pennsylvania, Michigan, and Wisconsin, had hardly so much as heard of the redoubtable Paul or of his blue ox, Babe . . . and at the good last Sheridan was forced to take a few items out of a book; for Bunyan stories belong in the chapter on camp recreation.[10]

At the same time, the editor decided to omit a chapter of unsavory anecdotes about a character given the pseudonym of Ferguson. One tale did get left in, telling how after the great Peshtigo fire Ferguson tried to abstract bloodstained dollar bills from a corpse on the pretext of helping remove the body, but was detected.[11] A story-cycle about such a knave did not sit well with the editor, concerned about his author's image, so he suppressed it in favor of Paul Bunyan fabrications. This is the process I have called fakelore.

A trickle of Bunyania does exist in oral tradition, but it does not run very deep. In the taped reminiscences, occupying eighty-eight book pages, of Louis Blanchard, a French Canadian lumberjack from Wisconsin, two sentences allude to Paul's daughter: "Well, I never heard of Paul Bunyan much, but I knowed his daughter. One time she carried a feather tick full of buckshot down the main street of Chippenay Falls and went through the board sidewalk up to her knees every step she took."[12] This has the characteristic ring of the few oral stories we can authenticate: brief, sidelong tall-tale capsules.

If lumberjacks never did make Paul Bunyan a folk hero, but at best a minor figure of tall-tale jokes with little vitality, whom and what did they yarn about? In American folklore the typical hero of spoken legend is a local character, a wag, an eccentric, talked about in close-knit circles for feats of strength or of eating and drinking, or for knavish tricks and clever sayings. The lumber-woods bred their share of such purely local folk heroes.

One is a Finnish strong man of northeastern Minnesota, Otto Walta. Like many of his fellow Finns emigrating to the north country of the Great Lakes states, Otto sought to homestead a farm from the stump-littered land cut over by the timber companies, but on occasion he worked as a lumberjack to make a stake. Photographs of 1920 show him in the company of other loggers in a lumber camp in St. Louis County. Otto was born in 1875 in Pomarkku, Finland, sailed for America in 1898, perhaps to escape the law, and died in 1959 after spending his last seventeen years in a Minnesota state hospital. He never learned English, and it is mainly, though not entirely, the Finns of St. Louis County north of Duluth who celebrate his deeds. Walta's biographer, Michael G. Karni, interviewed around one hundred people who knew tales of the husky Finn nearly a decade after his death and a quarter of a century after he was institutionalized.

Above all, the fabled Otto was herculean in his strength and capacity for work. His admirers conjectured him as six feet four inches and 240 pounds of bone and sinew, although hospital records list his height as five feet nine inches. A photograph shows a thick-shouldered, nearly square-faced man with a slight mustache and intense eyes. People claimed he could rip trees out of the ground, carry boulders, and bend a three-inch steel pry-bar into the

Otto Walta (second from right) and four fellow lumberjacks, probably taken about 1920, one of the rare occasions when he hired himself out
From *Minnesota History,* 1967

shape of a fishhook to pry up a pine stump—and this when he was an old man. Once he walked three miles across the swamp behind his homestead to the railroad tracks, ripped up an eight-hundred-pound rail with his bare hands, lifted it to his shoulder, walked back to his land, and went to prying up stumps by ramming one end of the rail in a hole he dug under the stump, setting the rail on a rock for a fulcrum, and leaning on the other end until the stump popped out of the ground like a potato.

A few days later six men from the Duluth, Winnipeg, and Pacific Railroad called on Otto. The rail was tilting against his bachelor's shack, built into a sandy ridge and topped by a rocking chair and lookout platform. They asked Otto who had helped him tote the rail across the swamp. When Otto replied that he had done it alone, they sniggered. Calmly he reached down, took a hold, swung the rail onto his shoulder, and strode around his clearing. Dumbfounded, the railroaders beat a hasty retreat. It would have taken a crew of eight to clear a road through the swamp and haul the rail back.

Stories of big eaters permeated the lumber country, for lumberjacks ate prodigiously and well as part of their rightful due in camp, and Otto Walta joined the ranks of these gustatory champions. He was said to have filled a twelve-quart galvanized pail with fresh cow's milk and drained it down in a gulp, then refilled it for another gulp. Once on his way to town, he stopped off at two

Finnish families several miles apart and ate their entire dinners. When his closest neighbor six miles away asked Otto to help him drag out of the bush a big bear he had just shot, Otto readily acceded, and on reaching the carcass, dug into it with a yell and gorged himself on four pounds of raw meat. His hunger appeased, he grabbed the bear's forepaws, slung the carcass over his back, and began tramping home through the brush. When his companion could not keep up with him, Otto suggested he climb on the bear's back.

Despite his physique, Otto was not much given to brawling. But once when ten French Canadian lumberjacks baited him in a boxcar in which they were all traveling, Otto grabbed one, twirled him over his head like a matchstick, and flung him at his fellows, who collapsed like a row of ninepins. Another time when he was whooping it up with his brother Antti in Superior, Wisconsin, a cop berated Antti for loud singing, called him a stupid Finlander, and lifted his club to strike him. Otto seized the cop by the coat collar and hung him on a spike protruding from a light pole eight feet high. In court next morning, Otto pleaded guilty to hanging a coat on the light pole but claimed he was unaware a man was inside the coat. The judge told Otto to go back to the brush and dismissed the case.

For all his might, Otto had a heart so tender he would not even squash the bedbugs in his mattress, so when they became too bothersome he moved down to his cellar, in the hope they would starve or leave, only to have the bugs downstairs force him to return. To save his horse he hitched himself to the plow and had his brother drive it, saying he could work harder than a horse anyway. He made special boots for his plowing, with plate-iron spikes. The quality that Otto Walta repre-

sented to his circle of admirers is *sisu,* the Finnish term signifying stamina, tenacity, and endurance. *Sisu* embodies folk values, like the Mexican *machismo,* and both traits have entered the American scene with immigrants and in-migrants.[13]

Parallel in some respects but quite different in others is the Swedish character Ola Värmlänning, whom Minnesota lumberjacks from Sweden talk about. Ola, like Otto, emigrated from the Old Country for reasons that are shrouded in legend. Some say that he was disappointed in love, others that he was the rejected black sheep of a wealthy family, still others that he was the errant son of a parson. Their heydays overlapped, the 1880s and 1890s being Ola's period. Ola too was both strong and gentle, and he likewise was the subject of droll anecdotes largely confined to an ethnic group. But where Otto dedicated himself to work, Ola succumbed to the bottle and spent his remembered years hanging around bars in Minneapolis and St. Paul, cadging drinks. A fine singer, an accordion player, and a confirmed prankster, Ola entertained for his whiskey. Although he was usually the petty trickster, his best-known exploit involved a trick on a grand scale. Ola blew into Minneapolis fresh from the lumberwoods north of Duluth, stopped at a railroad office, ordered a special train from Minneapolis to St. Paul at the earliest possible moment, and casually tossed on the counter the full amount in cash. The news spread rapidly to St. Paul via telegraph that a chartered train bearing an unknown dignitary was on its way. Excitement mounted and rumors flew that some high-ranking official, perhaps even the president of the United States, was on the train. A large, expectant crowd waited at the St. Paul Union Depot, to see dismount from the coach a lumberjack, none other than Ola, clad in high snowpacks

Sawyers of the Cutler and Savidge Lumber Company at Douglass, Montcalm County, Michigan, cutting a giant felled pine tree into lengths for hauling by the team seen in the background, February 1888

and a mackinaw, who gaily doffed his cap to the hoodwinked throng.

This adventure placed first in the memories of Minnesota Swedes and in the cheap paperback *Ola Värmlänning,* issued by a Swedish-language publisher in the Twin Cities around 1910. Doubtless Ola's fans rejoiced at an ordinary, anonymous lumberjack so discomfiting the city swells. The booklet sets forth a number of stories associated with Ola and in nine rough drawings pictures him as a youthful blond Viking with a jaunty cap atop curly hair. In these stories and in still-recollected oral tales, Ola out-

wits relatives, acquaintances, strangers, and policemen. Once while standing in a butcher's shop, Ola saw a policeman he knew pass by just as the butcher slipped out for a glass of beer, so he told the cop he was moving the butcher's stock for him, and would the patrolman kindly help him by carrying a pig's carcass to another shop. The officer of the law obliged and started off in the direction of the supposed shop with the pig that Ola had loaded on his shoulder. When the butcher returned to the shop and spied the empty hook, Ola pointed down the street to the policeman lurching under the weight of the porker. Butcher chased bluecoat, and Ola laughed heartily.

On rare occasions Ola displayed his strength. In one of the booklet tales he picked up a rookie Irish policeman and carried him under his arm to the police callbox, where he locked him in. Then he marched to the police station and handed over the rookie's badge, club, and revolver, and himself, with the request that thenceforth he be arrested more courteously. Old-timers recall Ola once throwing four St. Paul policemen into the Mississippi, at the foot of Jackson Street, and holding at bay a like number by swinging a pig's carcass in their direction. He had an obsession against cigar-store Indians and when sodden with booze would roar up the street crying, *"Inga tragubbar!"* ("No wooden men!"), wrench the figures from their bases, and hurl them into the gutter.

Ola's antics gave rise to sayings as well as tales. "'Correct,' said Ola Värmlänning, [when] sentenced to ninety days!" This Wellerism carried more punch for Minnesotan Swedes than simply saying "Correct." They also indulged in a word-play jest. One would say, "Ola, there is a louse on your shirt." The other would reply, "The poor wretch has gone astray," and picking it up, place it under his shirt, observing, "'Tis best thee come in where it's warm, otherwise thee'll catch a cold." This little comedy has the true lumberjack recognition of the louse, which the players dignify with elaborate rhetoric. Ola's biographer, Roy Swanson, has heard few, and tells none, of the off-color stories that the unknown author of *Ola Värmlänning* declared once were legion.[14]

The French Canadian lumberjacks had their own hero, Joe Mouffreau or Mouffron, who as yet has not found his biographer. In the Upper Peninsula I heard snatches about Joe: how in lumberjack fights he kicked lethally with his long legs, and once left his footprint on the ceiling. In his taped reminiscences, Louis Blanchard, the French Canadian woodsman of Wisconsin, recalled that the "big man we heard most about was Joe Mouffreau, a big Frenchman who was supposed to have come over from Canady." He was seven feet tall and wore size seventeen shoes. Joe would pull crooked logging

roads straight with his yoke of oxen, hitching them, with a great chain it took ten men to carry, to a hole the men dug around the start of the road, then giving a few yanks, whereupon the road straightened right out. He let his men sell the leftover road to peddlers. "Old Joe was an awful fighting man," Louie

A load of logs estimated at 100,000 pounds, ready to be hauled over the iced tote roads by a four-horse team to Hermansville, Michigan, to the mill of the Wisconsin Land and Lumber Company, spring of 1892

stated, and went on to ascribe to Joe the much-traveled anecdote about a fight with a braggart. In a saloon crowded with lumberjacks fresh off the drive, one logger filled with "Chippeway lightning" walked up to Joe and bellowed, "I can lick any man in the house." Joe looked down at the fellow, opined as to how that was pretty big talk, and started to move away. The whiskey-soaked jack followed him boasting, "Whenever I go up and down the Chippeway, by God, I always clean out the house." At this Joe's temper finally rose and he countered, "By God, if you're going to start cleaning out the house it's about time to start. I guess I'll begin before you get too much start on me." And with one punch Mouffreau knocked the loudmouth through the window.[15]

The fullest and richest folk-hero tradition that has been recaptured from the lumbering industry belongs to Maine, where the industry originated, and where woods traditions still persist. Indeed, the legends of George Knox, a lum-

berjack credited with supernatural and magical powers, only reached print in 1970. Their collector, Roger E. Mitchell, who had worked in the woods in Knox's area before committing himself to academic studies and earning a Ph.D. in folklore, discovered them in 1962, from students he was teaching in Bridgewater, Maine. In the end he recorded tales about George Knox from an even fifty tellers, and supplemented them with other tales in the archives of the Northeast Folklore Society. His monograph, *George Knox, From Man to Legend,* provides oral texts and pertinent information about the woods hero according to the best scholarly folklore procedures, so lacking in the case of Paul Bunyan.[16]

About all that history records of George Knox is his death from tuberculosis in 1892 at the age of thirty in the town of Blaine in Aroostook County, the northernmost and largest Maine county. Yet in the 1960s George is well remembered, as a man who sold his soul to the Devil and in return acquired diabolical

Teamsters on a sled load of logs, near Grindstone, Maine, early 1900s

powers: his axe could chop timber by itself. At George's bidding, great logs moved into the lumber yard from outside or onto the teamsters' load from the ground or into the river from the landing, although no one saw him at work. The other lumberjacks frequently heard the sound of chains, the thud of peaveys, and the voices of men during the night—and rarely, one or another sighted little men but George himself remained solitary, secretive, nocturnal.

Some described him, but in conflicting terms. One faction pictured him as larger than life, seven feet tall, with a set of double teeth that could snap a two-by-four-inch plank in half. Another, larger group described him as fairly ordinary-looking, about six feet, slim, black-haired, long-faced, with a dark mustache curled at both ends. One veteran lumberjack of ninety-four, who had known George, tersely noted that he looked tubercular.

So here is no strapping titan, in the majority view, but a slender, undernourished fellow who nevertheless performed gargantuan feats in every aspect of lumbering: as axeman, teamster, yardman, river driver. A covenant with the Devil, not awesome stature and brawn, enabled George to accomplish his wonders. Certain themes keep recurring in the anecdotes about Knox's powers. Besides lifting big logs, he also raised huge rocks that blocked the tote road or the mill landing or the planting ground, always with the same stealth, at night or alone, making good his vaunt that he would get the rock out of there. But on one occasion an eyewitness did observe George's wizardry. This was the grandfather of Kenneth Estabrook, a lumberjack and pulp contractor, who repeats his grandfather's tale in these words:

He said they [George and his father] were standing there talking and there was a big rock laying there in the barn door. They had to go around the rock to go into the barn. I don't know why they built the barn in front of a big rock, but anyway, it bothered them getting in and out of the barn.

George said to his father, he says, "Father, that rock has bothered you all your life." He said, "You tried to move it and you couldn't move it."

His father said, "That's right." Said he tried to blow it; guess it was too handy [to] the buildings for to put [a] big enough charge under it to move it.

Said George started walking towards the rock, and every step he took, the rock got a little smaller; and when he got up to the rock he reached down, picked it up and put it in his mouth and walked over across the road and spit it out.[17]

In all the stories of George Knox moving great logs and rocks and cookstoves, a suspicion lurked that he did so through the Devil's agency, and one series of legends emphasizes his infernal trickery. He cut off his own hand, or his sister's arm, and fastened them on again; he turned a black-and-white horse into an all-white one and back again to two colors; he charmed a schoolmarm into taking off her shoes and stockings, and a liquor dealer into thinking a one-dollar bill was a ten-spot. He turned silver dollars with which he paid a bill into dirt, and conjured up money from his pockets at will. Eyewitnesses swore he spelled whiskey out of trees and threw his voice into cows and horses and potatoes. When he whistled, deer ran out of the woods; he could turn fish into deer steak; set an empty table with fruit, bread, cake, cookies, and doughnuts when there was nothing to eat in camp; walk out of a locked jail; burn a rail fence to ashes by walking atop it; and empty a frozen water barrel overnight. Whether George learned his necromancy from the Devil's book on black art or from readily available books of magic exposing black art and teaching sleight of hand and ventriloquism was a matter that divided the rationalist and the supernaturalist wings of the Knox legend carriers. But many plainly avowed their belief in George's affiliation with the Devil:

They claim he sold himself to the Devil for twenty years for twenty dollars. (Clarence MacPherson)

He studied books and went to a crossroad, took a black cat and sold himself to the Devil. (Mrs. Clarence Foster)

. . . George bought a Black Panther book. Now when you broke the seal of that book you made your bargain with the Devil. That's what George did. When George bought the Black Book and sold his soul to the Devil, that meant he had to live like a devil, no good house, not even a good suit of clothes, and like I said the other day, not even a tombstone when he died. (Harold Farrar)

George had to learn the Black Art book. After that he went out in the woods at midnight. That is how he made contact with the Devil to sell his soul for twenty years for twenty dollars. (Hazel Harsey)

. . . everybody was afraid of him. Nobody wanted to work with him because something always happened to the person. He was jinxed and possessed by the Devil. (Boyd Bradbury)

They claimed he sold his soul to the Devil, had a league with him. He could throw his voice and you'd hear voices coming from everywhere. The men were scared of him and finally told him if he didn't cut that stuff out they'd kill him. (Jim Good)[18]

Legends of his death bore out the allegations of George's league with Satan.

He foretold the time of his death, putting a candle in his window and saying

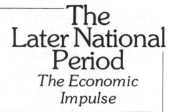
that when it burned out he would have died; watchers came over and found his corpse. Some aver he fought and flailed when the Devil came to take him and that his room smelled of fire and brimstone, chains rattled, and a big black dog lapped at his face. In one tale, Knox put up no resistance but meekly greeted the Devil when he came into his living room to claim him; in another he confounded Satan by exchanging the Black Book for the Bible and turning into a preacher. At his funeral the pallbearers complained of the weight of the casket and of a substance that oozed out and stank up their clothes.

George Knox is a genuine lumberjack folk hero, according to the canons of folklorists, and his legend runs counter to a number of stereotypic notions. His biographer Mitchell points out that while the Knox tradition is tenacious and pervasive in the area of its circulation, only lumberjacks and their families in that one area, the towns within the watershed of the Meduxnekeag River, carry the tradition. Even the woodsmen working in the nearby zone of the

River drivers on Wassataquoic River, Maine, early 1900s

Mattawamkeag River system knew none of the Knox stories. The folklore from the major Penobscot River network to the south flowed back into Knox country, rather than the reverse. So while Knox is truly a legendary lumberjack hero, he is not known to the entire fraternity of lumberjacks across the country, but just to those in his watershed.

Again, the term "hero" is somewhat misleading, for George Knox was feared rather than admired. From one viewpoint he exemplifies the skills and fulfills the dreams of the lumberjacks, for he is the master logger who can fell, stack, and load giant trees, build a lumber camp singlehanded, and summon forth the tasty food, whiskey, and cash money that are the woodsmen's strongest desires. In this role he does qualify as a folk hero. "He'd take a big log and roll it right with his hands more than an ordinary man could roll with a cant dog," declared Alec Muir. "Him was the best man I think I ever loaded a load of logs with," recalled James Votur.[19] But this note is drowned out in the allegations of devilment, secret doings in the night, and unnatural antics that made George Knox a bogeyman and a threat to ill-behaved children in the town of Houlton and its environs, who were cautioned, "I'll send George Knox to get you." Grown men too feared him, and when George reputedly promised Charley Friels that he would never want for anything the rest of his life if he bunked with him for one night, Charley dared not take the chance. George Knox was too much a Faust-figure to emerge as a local Paul Bunyan.

Whence, then, the Faustian strain? In the Knox legend the supernatural hero of the seventeenth century blends with the occupational lore of the nineteenth and twentieth centuries. The devil and witch traditions never completely died, but retreated from the center to the peripheries of American life. In his study of George Knox collector Mitchell mentions several other woods personalities reputed to have covenanted with the Devil. The legend of Knox recalls that of George Burroughs, who at the time of the Salem witchcraft trials aroused suspicions of diabolical dealings in the minds of his neighbors because he could carry molasses and cider barrels and hold a seven-foot-barrel gun at arm's length as if it were a pistol.[20] Settlers in Massachusetts who ascribed extraordinary deeds of strength to satanic compacts carried such ideas to Maine and injected them into the lumbering industry.

In the lumber camps the tough, wily, and idiosyncratic boss became the favorite subject of little cycles of anecdotes. In my *Bloodstoppers and Bearwalkers* I presented some of these bosses and the legends I heard about them in Michigan's Upper Peninsula. For some reason, probably because they are too localized to have very general interest, the camp bosses have not otherwise received their due as lumberjack folk heroes, but here is one story John Nelligan tells on himself when he was boss on a river drive in Wisconsin:

I always drove my men pretty hard, for I knew that men had more respect and worked better for a boss who was not easygoing. But it seems that, as is usually the case, I had a reputation for being much harder than I really was. One of my rivermen fell in the stream once and was under just about long enough to repeat the Lord's Prayer—

which he probably did. When he was pulled out and restored to an interest in life, the first thing he gasped out to the man who had saved him was: "For God's sake, don't say anything to anybody about how long I was absent from work! If Nelligan heard about it, he'd dock me sure for the time I was under water!"[21]

This is the tough boss living up to his own stereotype. In a lumber camp outside Newberry in the Upper Peninsula I heard "Moonlight Harry" Schmidt, the boss there, tell on himself the folk anecdote of the choreboy who asked him what time he should wake the teamsters. "Any damn time you find them asleep," Moonlight Harry says he said, but other tough bosses are supposed to have expressed the same sentiment.

Camp bosses had to be tough because the ordinary lumberjack to whom they served as father-figures reveled in toughness and fighting. "They were whiskey-fighting men," one old jack told me in Michigan, and I set down several well-remembered battles in *Bloodstoppers and Bearwalkers.* Every commentator on lumberjack folkways alludes to fighting. Peaceable enough in camp, the shantyboys unleashed their animal passions in their spring orgies, much like the cowboys after the long drive, and when sodden with drink they lunged at each other. But where the cowboys shot it out, the lumberjacks spurned guns or knives and hammered at each other with bare fists until one or another lay senseless, then jumped on the prostrate foe with caulked boots. This savage pummeling was all part of the logger's *machismo;* as he gave full measure of his energies to his work, never asking respite for fatigue or illness or damp,

so in his brawling he fought to the last ounce of his endurance.

Told on the level of realism, fight stories soared toward the incredible. In his poetic account of his life as a Maine woodsman, Gerald Averill tells of two loggers flailing at each other without a pause for an hour and ten minutes, until they could only paw wildly at one another as they lay spent on the ground.[22] This kind of report is echoed several times over in the Michigan reminiscences of Dorothy Dill, titled "Lumberjack Stories." Recalling the heyday of the white-pine lumber camps in the 1880s, the author speaks of a fight challenge given lumberjacks of Traverse City by lumberjacks of Manistee that produced "one of the greatest unwritten battles of Michigan history," lasting two solid hours before the Manistee invaders yielded and left town. Dill describes another fight at a camp in Boyne Falls between two lumberjacks who speared each other with their cork boots, then for variety chewed each other's nose and ears, before the gaze of a raw recruit, sixteen-year-old Art Laddie. Although he had just entered the camp a few minutes before, Laddie turned tail and ran home. In addition Dill presents "one of the greatest unrecorded fistic encounters in history," lasting three days, when Billy Taylor and Jimmy Fitzgibbons met on successive noons on the street in front of the Eagle Hotel in East Jordan and pummeled each other with bare knuckles, abetted by molars and river spikes, until the end of the third afternoon, when they suddenly broke off and helped each other limp to the bar to drink in amity. These battles royal end with a folktale, told as true, of John Kildee, a lumberjack in Traverse City, who after a few drinks waved his arms and shouted, "I kin lick anyone in the counties of Gran' Traverse, Leelenau, and Benzie." Thereupon a bystander gave him a rap that laid him low. John picked himself up, grinned, and said, "Wal, I guess I took in too much territory."[23] This recalls the earlier anecdote fastened onto Joe Mouffron.

John Nelligan in "The Life of a Lumberman" observed, "Fights of all kinds were common, but some of them became traditional,"[24] and proceeded to reconstruct several. Hailed as "the greatest 'jack' battle of the ages," a fight that took place in the notorious lumber town of Seney, Michigan, is one such traditional combat. Tim Kaine, a well-known lumberjack fighter and protector of weaker men against bullies, once asked his boss John Dugan, a notorious slavedriver, for a few days sick leave. "I'll make you a whole lot sicker," thundered the boss and struck Kaine with his heavy hardwood cant hook, knocking him unconscious. When Kaine came to, he packed his clothes and left camp, vowing revenge. He had to wait four years, until the day he saw Dugan alight from a train pulling into Seney. Kaine promptly challenged him and they set to it in the street, pounding each other for the best part of an hour without letup, two mighty men putting every ounce of muscle into their blows. When one fell to the ground he staggered up again promptly, aided by the shoving crowd, to avoid receiving the hobnailed

boots. At length Kaine smashed Dugan off his feet, bloodying his nose and mouth, and although Dugan managed to regain his feet he could no longer defend himself, and Kaine walked away the victor. This fight, unlike most in lumberjack annals, did result from a grievance. In many cases the shantyboys fought just for fun. While told by an eyewitness, John I. Bellaire, himself an ex-lumberjack, this fight tale portrays two stereotypic characters: the tough, ruthless camp boss and the heroic lumberjack.[25] One story that reached the newspapers told of a pugnacious liquored-up lumberjack in Minocqua, Wisconsin, who bet five dollars he could lick a pit bulldog that had vanquished all its fellow canines and even overcome a wolf. This "fightingest jack" got down on hands and knees and growled, but failed to impress the bulldog, who chewed off one side of his face clear to the cheekbone.[26] A Michigan lumberjack calling himself "the man-eater from Peterborough" also fought bulldogs for free drinks.[27] Certain lumberjack battlers attained a fame bordering on legend. In bars in upper Michigan's Newberry and Grand Marais, roaring Jimmy Gleason lured victims into frays by dragging his mackinaw behind him by one sleeve and daring another lumberjack to step on it. When one did, Jimmy began to roar, charged his opponent like a mad bull, and put many a good man to sleep with his sledgehammer fists.[28]

The best-known lumberjack fighter in Michigan was "Silver Jack" Driscoll, who came down from Peterborough, Ontario, to cut timber in the Saginaw Valley, and later logged in the Upper Peninsula and northern Wisconsin and Minnesota. Muscular John Driscoll received his nickname from his prematurely white hair, although some said it derived from his habit of carrying pure

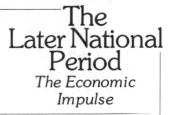
silver nuggets on his person. In 1882 he was sent to Jackson prison for a five-year term, on what appears to have been a frame-up; enemies put a revolver and $2.50 in his pocket when he was drunk and claimed he had robbed them. "Silver Jack" exemplifies the lumberjack code, in spite of the blemishes of the prison record and his continuous fighting, for the tales depict him as a thrasher of bullies and defender of the weak. In the fight memorialized in the ballad printed on pages 66–68, Silver Jack, a nominal Catholic, tangled with an atheist. In his cups Silver Jack threw out his barrel chest, clenched his fists, and bellowed, "I am still king of the woods."

Accounts of his death describe him as drowning in the Tahquamenon River, being shot in an Upper Peninsula train, dying in state prison or a Ewen saloon, or simply wandering off to the Washing-

The beginning of a spring log drive on the Muskegon River, Michigan, in the 1890s, with lumberjacks now doubling as river drivers

ton pineries. The most credible version makes him the victim of his own April-fool joke. In bed with pneumonia on March 31, 1895, in the Ottawa Hotel in L'Anse in the Upper Peninsula, he arranged to have the woman who brought his breakfast next morning shout that he was dead. Then when the hotel caretaker, a credulous Frenchman named Oliver Durocher, came running into the room, Silver Jack would rise up and shout, "April Fool." Only next morning, he was really dead.[29]

In his most famous fight Silver Jack tangled with another bruiser, Frenchman Joe Fournier, also a subject of legends. Possessed of a double row of teeth, Fournier would bite chunks out of counters in saloons. Matching this, in various Michigan towns Silver Jack was reputed to have knocked down an ox with a blow of his fist (as Barney Beal the lobsterman was said to have laid low a horse with one punch in Portland, Maine) and to bend horseshoes with his hands. "The tales about him, even in 1938, are wondrous and apparently without end," wrote Stewart Holbrook in his informal history of the American lumberjack. Observers reported that Fournier grasped Silver Jack by the throat for nearly an hour, butting him with his thick skull every so often, as they writhed on the floor of the Red Keg saloon in Averill, Michigan. Driscoll freed himself from the stranglehold by jabbing a caulked boot into Fournier's foot, causing Joe to relax his grip in pain, whereupon the two giants sprang to their feet and began slugging and butting until Silver Jack sidestepped one of Fournier's charges and let him crash his head into the oak bar. The fight over, they drank in friendship, according to the lumberjack code.

In his drinking, fighting, and working habits, the lumberjack strove for superhuman achievement. He needed no Paul Bunyan to overstate his already hard-to-believe actualities.

Three Maine river drivers working on headworks (a capstan on a raft) in order to haul a boom of logs down a lake, ca. 1900

Miners

Coal-Mining Songs

One day in 1924 a newspaper reporter for the *Pottsville Republican,* charged with developing a newsbeat in the heart of Pennsylvania's anthracite-coal fields, stopped at the public library and asked for a book of miners' songs. The librarian told him she had no such book. Surprised and disappointed, George Korson turned away mulling over why he always heard Tin Pan Alley music on his rounds but never indigenous songs of mining life. Cowboys, lumberjacks, and sailors had songs; why not miners? Subsequently he repeated his request at other libraries in Schuylkill County, with always the same negative answer. Anyone who made the same inquiry today would promptly be informed about four books on coal miners' ballads and folklore written by George Korson. For when he approached the miners directly, he discovered that they did indeed know, sing, and compose ballads and lyrics about their lives.

Korson enlisted the aid of the United Mine Workers union, and with their cooperation published three volumes on the anthracite colliers of northeastern Pennsylvania: *Songs and Ballads of the Anthracite Miners* (1927), serialized in the *United Mine Workers Journal* the year before; *Minstrels of the Mine Patch* (1938), subtitled "Songs and Stories of the Anthracite Industry," a reworking of the earlier collection; and *Black Rock: Mining Folklore of the Pennyslvania Dutch* (1960), which took a long historical look at the hard-coal country and then concentrated on the Pennsylvania German farmers who, along with British colliers, followed by Slavs and Austrians, mined for "black diamonds." In between these books Korson traveled around the country, following the trail of the bituminous or soft-coal miners, and issued the results in *Coal Dust on the Fiddle: Songs and Stories of the Bituminous Industry* (1943). Some of his song recordings he also made available through an album in the record series of the Library of Congress folksong archive.

Ballad scholars in university English departments steeped in the genealogies of Francis James Child's English and Scottish folksongs did not evince immediate enthusiasm at the new revelation of American balladry. Just as the Chaucer specialist at the University of Texas had told John Lomax to peddle his cowboy songs elsewhere, so did John Spargo, a Virgil scholar, reviewing *Coal Dust on the Fiddle* in the *Journal of American Folklore* (which never reviewed *Minstrels of the Mine Patch*), brush it off in these words:

T̶o some it will seem noteworthy that miners should write ballads at all; but after reading a few of these carelessly-written versicles, some readers will take an attitude like the one Dr. Johnson expressed about a dog's ability to walk on its hind legs.

To which deprecation Benjamin Botkin, who had just brought forth *A Treasury of American Folklore,* responded:

It is hard to believe that . . . we find a reviewer in the pages of this Journal writing about the coal miners of the United States as if they were performing animals. . . . But it is not only because coal miners' songs are new that folklorists write like this. It is also because folklore is old and tired. There is dust on our fiddles, and it smells not of the colliers but of the libraries. It is time that folksong scholars stopped thinking of folksong in terms of the English and Scottish ballads. It is time that they did a little more digging in the rock.[1]

Anthracite coal miner working a seam, in northeast Pennsylvania, ca. World War I

The tide turned, and in the 1960s both *Minstrels* and *Coal Dust* were reissued with appreciative forewords by folklorists.

As the anthropologist and folklorist are wont to do, Korson identified closely with the people whom he was portraying—a trait that anthropologist Melville Herskovits called secondary ethnocentrism—and wrote his books from the miners' point of view. They set forth a litany of hardship, deprivation, suffering, and despair, punctuated by mine disasters and strikes. From his first work as a slate picker in the breaker at eight and door tender underground at ten, until his arthritic and tubercular old age, the collier lived, so it seemed, a mean and hopeless existence, strangled by the operators, and the pawn of a fluctuating market. Only the union salvaged some dignity and hope for the coal worker. Yet the songs that Korson collected do not confirm so joyless a picture or self-image. Unlike the collectors of cowboy and lumberjack minstrelsy, Korson set a stage for his ballad sheaves with vignettes of the miners' workaday world from which the bards drew their themes. He divided up his books into subtopics with subheadings, much like newspaper features. Then he grouped together songs dealing with accidents and cave-ins, boy colliers, the Molly Maguire terrorists, long strikes and the conditions that caused them, miners on the job and carousing, and ethnic rivalries among the mine workers. The miner —the coal miner, anyway—had come into his own as a sentient being with his special ways and emotions.

Excited by Korson's discoveries, other folklorists set after the songs and traditions of Western metal miners, but none struck a rich vein. They hunted in the silver mines of Utah and the copper mines of Montana, but such pieces as came their way proved to be mostly popular songs or parodies of older folksongs.

Throughout the repertory of coal-mining ballads and lyrics echoes the theme of the miner's pride in his work and his skills, of his fearlessness and his heroism in the midst of underground dangers. The title of his best-known folksong is, appropriately, "The Hard-Working Miner," and its verses reinforce the caption:

To the hard-working miner whose dangers are great,
So many while mining have met their sad fate,
While doing their duty as miners all do,
Shut out from daylight, and their loving ones, too.[2]

But work is not necessarily drudgery and discomfort. Some songs sing in rollicking tones of the satisfactions with pick and hammer and dynamite cap, and joyously announce, "A Miner's Life for Me." The paean commences, "A miner leads a jolly life," and breaks into this merry chorus:

A miner's life for me
With the boys that's light and
    free,
So join with me and give a
    hearty cheer.
For frolic, fun and mirth,
You may search all o'er the
    earth,
A miner's life is happy all
    the year.[3]

And out West, "The Miner Boy" expresses similar sentiments.

Drink to the health of the
    miner boy
That works down in the ground.
When his work is over,

He comes whistling home with
    joy,
Happy is the girl
That marries the miner boy.[4]

Joy arose in good part from the sense of satisfaction the old-time miner derived from his expertise in swinging and aiming his pick with proper force and accuracy. The pick miner "was as much the master workman as the locomotive engineer with his hand on the throttle," Korson declared. "The straight-shorn pillars sometimes found in old abandoned mines stand as a monument to the sheer artistry of those early picksmen."[5] When the pick gave way to the automatic drill, the miner lost much of his *élan*. Coupled with his authority as a workman under cramped, dark, and dangerous conditions was his heroism when the dreaded cave-in, explosion, or fire, with the release of poisonous gases, spread death throughout the shafts and tunnels. True stories of the self-sacrifice and bravery of miners who could have saved themselves but rushed

Coal miners prepare to descend slope into Thomaston Mine, Schuylkill County, Pennsylvania, 1897

to the aid of their stricken fellows seemed to follow each new tragedy. "Some of the noblest deeds of man have been performed by workers in the anthracite industry," marveled Korson.[6] Among many instances he cites what a participant priest described as "one of the greatest acts of heroism I have ever heard or read of."[7] The scene was the St. Paul Mine at Cherry, Illinois, November 13, 1909, which was sealed off by the mine officials with two hundred workers still in the seams when hay bales caught on fire and the flames rapidly spread to the timbering. After several days the shafts were opened and mine inspectors descended to search for corpses. But one group had survived for eight days, at the end without food, water, or light. As they were being led to safety, one of the entrapped miners, Walter Waite, heard that other miners still needed rescue elsewhere in the mine. He threw off the blanket shielding his eyes from the light and cried, "Well, then, by God, I am not going out of this

188

mine until I get the others." The rescue party had to force him into the cage and up to the surface.

Disaster ballads dwelt on these heroics, and the term "hero" becomes affixed to the miner as a matter of course.

And ten heroes lost their lives
Trying to save their comrades.

And think of the true-hearted
    heroes that's toiling
In the midst of great danger
    their comrades to find.

Oh, how little did those heroes
    dream
As they went to work that morn
That soon they would be carried
Back all shattered and torn.[8]

And for what does the miner toil at the risk of limb and life? Certainly for no base ends, but for the greater comfort of his fellow man.

The miner pants for no
  glory goal;
In vain to him may the
  battle roll;
Yet his manly heart and his
  fearless soul
Sing—"Ho! success to the
  gleaming coal."[9]

His one self-interested motivation—and here the miner differs conspicuously from lumberjack and cowboy—is that of caring for his wife and children. The miner is no lone rider of the range or monk in the lumberwoods but a family man returning each night to a company-owned home to wash off the soot and dust from the day's work. His boys would follow in his steps soon enough as slate pickers and mule tenders.

His wife is his queen
  and his home is his palace
His children his glory,
  to maintain them he tries,
He'll work like a hero;

he faces all danger,
He'll deprive his own self
  their bare feet to hide.[10]

This strain sounds frequently throughout the miner's verses. He works to feed and shelter his dear ones.

Says good-bye to wife and baby,
  Stops to kiss them at the door;
He doesn't know if he'll see them
  In this life any more.[11]

With the rise of the unions, such as the Workingmen's Benevolent Association, the Knights of Labor, and the United Mine Workers, and the growing militancy of industrial strife, the miner-hero found a new cause. He now fought with his union against the mine bosses. New deeds of heroism emanated from pitched battles waged between the hired hooligans of the mine companies and the striking miners. Terence V. Powderly, head of the Knights of Labor, equated the valor of the picketing miner with that of the working miner.

In strikes, coal miners have always shown the most sublime fortitude and greatest endurance . . . it requires the most heroic type of manhood to seek a living in the mine, and he who has the courage to make that step in the dark each day, which every miner does, must be made of good stuff. . . .[12]

So the miner as hero appears in ballads and verses, asserting his independence and fearlessness not by working but by striking. A poem of the 1870s, "What Makes Us Strike?" sets forth the miner's view:

A miner? Yes, sir, I work in the coal.
    . . . . .
And think myself as good, sir, any day

As any man that walks upon this earth.
No matter what his name or place of birth.
I wouldn't bow my knee to General Grant,
Never did—nor could—and what is more I shan't.

. . . . .

A pretty independent lot we are likewise,
And will allow no boss to tyrannize,

. . . . .

And consequently we good wages like,
And when we can't get that, why, sir, we strike.[13]

The ambivalence that runs deep through the Economic Life-style expressed itself earlier with the coal miners than with other occupational groups. Their onerous conditions of work, helplessness before the corporate employer, and family obligations all heightened the discontents and frustrations of the colliers. In place of the individualistic pride of the master workman arises the collective sullenness of the union, with eruptions into strikes and pitched battles. Is the miner an occupational hero fighting bravely for his economic rights, or is he a lawbreaker and anarchist destroying life and property? In the case of the Molly Maguires, both history and folklore respond to these questions.

The Molly Maguires

In the history of the anthracite coal industry the most lurid chapter concerns the secret organization known as the Molly Maguires. Associated with violent crimes and sensational murder trials, toppled by a Pinkerton detective who revealed their secret passwords and plots, enmeshed in capital-labor, Protestant-Catholic and English-Irish enmities, it is no surprise that the Mollies have inspired books, movies, and folklore. The folklore has taken the form of ballads and folk laments, curses, and anecdotal legends. One historian of the Mollies, Arthur H. Lewis, asserts that still today "discussion of the Molly Ma-

guires is taboo among a fair portion of the population of Schuylkill, Carbon, Northumberland, Columbia, and Luzerne counties," where live the descendants of Mollies hanged on scaffolds by executioners for the commonwealth of Pennsylvania."[14] Yet some Pennsylvanians talk freely, and Lewis drew from the memory banks of his father's friends in reconstructing his chronicle, while in the 1950s George Korson recorded stories still rife about the dreaded Molly Maguires.

Secretive and mystery-laden as were the operations of the Mollies, a great shaft of light has illuminated their actions and lives, in consequence of the trials with their detailed testimonies and newspaper coverage, the daily report sent to his superiors by detective James McParlan, and the confessions and revelations of some defendants who turned state's witnesses. These sources provide what is unusual in American history, a view of the hidden folk, in this case illiterate Irish Catholic miners and their English, Welsh, and Pennsylvania German peers who lived in mine patches of northeastern Pennsylvania in the 1860s and 1870s.

Two opposing myths—and here I mean historical myths compounded of the values and biases of a given period—have enveloped the Molly Maguires. Accounts written at the time of their trials, between 1876 and 1880, and re-

190

Miners setting up timber supports underground, Schuylkill County, Pennsylvania, 1907

flecting the groundswell of indignation and fear of the Mollies over the preceding twenty years, cast them in the role of lawless and violent agitators and sadistic murderers, loathed by the majority of God-fearing Irish mining families as well as the rest of their communities. In this scenario, the Irish hatchet men killed enemies in cold blood, often for trivial or fancied grievances, even in broad daylight before eyewitnesses who dared not testify and knew in any case they stood no chance of gaining a conviction by frightened jurors facing cocky defendants with ready-made alibis. The Molly Maguires, so ran the script, were an arm of the miners' labor union, engaged in sabotage and destruction of the mine owners' property and attempt-

ing to subvert the industrial progress of America. Courageously battling them through the constitutional procedures of the courts stood the hero, Franklin B. Gowen, himself the son of an Irish immigrant, youthful district attorney of Schuylkill County and president of the Philadelphia and Reading Railroad, an enlightened and progressive mine owner and eloquent pleader at the bar.

In the twentieth century a new version emerged, indebted to left-wing sympathizers with the labor movement. Now the conspiratorial plots of the Mollies all stem from the minds of the mine operators, bent on creating a false monster as a means of vilifying the union and subjugating the miners. Working from dawn to dark for a pittance, robbed

Mollies kidnap a miner who has refused to go on strike with them, pin his feet to a log with nails, drive spikes through his coat sleeves, bend his arms backward, gag him, and abandon him in the wilderness, Luzerne County, Pennsylvania, November 1874.
From Allan Pinkerton, *The Molly Maguires and the Detectives*

The Pinkerton detective James McParlan, posing as James McKenna, is initiated into the Molly Maguires in "Muff" Lawler's house, 1874.
From Allan Pinkerton, *The Molly Maguires and the Detectives*

of their earnings through the check-weighman who underweighed their coal and the company store that overcharged them, condemned to ill health from the underground gases and dust, in continuous danger of their lives from cave-ins and fires, the miners lay helpless under the heel of the operators. Gowen

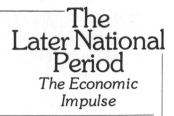
in particular sought, through a monopoly of the coal beds and railroad lines of the anthracite country, to throttle all opposition. His wild expansionist schemes compelled him to reduce labor costs without regard to human needs and human dignity. It was only fitting that, after plunging his company deeply in debt, he died by his own hand in 1889. Against Gowen's power and wealth only the Molly Maguires, martyred heroes to the cause of labor justice, dared strike a blow.[15]

Recent chroniclers see the truth as lying somewhere in between. Gowen's own biographer considers that the industrialist appeared in his least favorable light in the Molly Maguire trials.[16] Some of the twenty executed Mollies were convicted on insufficient or unreliable evidence in the heat of the moment. Contrary to Gowen's charge, the union, known as the Workingmen's Benevolent Association, did not sponsor the Mollies or sanction violence.

The origin of the name Molly Maguire is shrouded in legend. By the mid-nineteenth century it had become a byword in Ireland, used to threaten landlords. One popular version presented Molly as a hapless old widow evicted from her little farm in County Antrim by ruthless bailiffs and constabulary, who threw her possessions into the road, knocked down the house, and left Molly amidst her weeping daughter and grandchildren. A wholly different account makes Molly into a strapping, heavily armed Irishwoman leading gangs of young transvestites on nocturnal sorties.[17] A song about Molly Maguire portraying her as an organizer of bold Irish lads against tyrants and the police qualifies as a folksong, for it turns up in variants on both sides of the Atlantic. Apparently it originated from an actual incident in County Cavan in 1845, in which a secret band shot to death a justice of the peace, an Orangeman named Andrew Bell.[18] In the song Bell's ghost returns to torment his murderer, Pat Dolan, for whom the ballad is named.

One night as I lay upon me bed,
  I heard a terrible rattle;
Who wor it but Bell, come back from h— —l,
  To fight another battle!
Then at his brain I took me aim—
  He vanished off in fire—
An' as he went the air he rent
  Sayin', I'm conquered by Mollie Maguire.

> In the rendition given by Allan Pinkerton, founder of the famous Pinkerton detective agency that employed Mc-Parlan, the song's hero, Pat Dolan, makes his way to the United States.

> Now I'm in America,
>   An' that's a free nation!
> I generally sit an' take my sip
>   Far from a police station!
> Four dollars a day—it's not bad pay—
>   An' the boss he likes me well, sir!
> But little he knows that I'm the man
>   That shot that fien' o' h— —l, sir![19]

In Pinkerton's book about the Molly Maguires the ballad is sung by McParlan in 1873 in a saloon in Pottsville, where he is trying to ingratiate himself with Irish miners. The audience joins in vociferously on the chorus, and the detective realizes at its completion that he has indeed struck a responsive chord and is on his way to being accepted by the Mollies. Here is an illustration of a process always intriguing to the folklorist, the transatlantic crossing of ballads and tales, which can be readily surmised but rarely pinpointed. In this instance we have both Irish and American texts, the latter with an obvious American addition; we have their likely carriers, such as McParlan himself, an emigrant from the Ould Sod; and we have receptive conditions in the new land for the migrant song. Not merely the ballad text but the methods and the spirit of the Molly Maguires are conveyed in "Pat Dolan," which portrays the audacious resistance of young bloods against tyranny in the name of a "free nation," the selection by lot of the death dealers, and the devil-may-care gusto with which Pat shot even a ghost. Throughout the ballad the name of Molly Maguire echoes as a symbol of the fearless, fighting miner. His hatred of Orangemen and the Establishment carried over to Pennsylvania, where the Pat Dolans nursed grudges against English and Welsh foremen and supervisors in the mines. "Pat Dolan" is the only extant ballad that portrays the Mollies as reckless, triumphant heroes.

The most famous of all American mining ballads, "The Mines of Avondale," while it has nothing to say about the Mollies, commemorates a tragic event in which the Molly Maguires did become involved. As the lumberjacks sang about "The Jam on Gerry's Rock" and other drownings on the river drive, so did the miners compose and sing ballads about disasters far greater, in terms of loss of life and protracted suffering: fires, explosions, cave-ins, and suffocation from gases underground. The first large-scale tragedy in the Pennsylvania hard-coal fields to shock the world took place on September 6, 1869, in the Avondale mine situated between Wilkes-Barre and Scranton, and cost the lives of 111 miners and boy helpers. A fire that started in the shaft at about ten in the morning swept rapidly throughout the chambers of the mine extending to a thousand feet beneath the earth. The shaft afforded the miners their only entrance and exit, and the flimsy breaker atop it soon burst into flames. Only the enginehouse, containing a fan that ventilated the mine, was fireproof, and since in the confusion no one turned it off, the fan for ten hours kept circulating the noxious gases and fumes released by the conflagration. Finally at midnight, rescue attempts commenced. Two Welsh miners, Thomas W. Williams and David Jones, volunteered to descend, but both suffocated to death. Eventually other rescuers discovered the heaped-up, bloated corpses lying behind a hastily

194

1. Tamping a charge
2. The miner's chest
3. Mining and loading coal

Coal miners of Pennsylvania in the Honey Brook Mines at the intersection of Carbon, Luzerne, and Schuylkill Counties, sketched by Theo. R. Davis for *Harper's Weekly*, September 11, 1869. Sequence of nine drawings of miners at work below and above ground (continued on following pages).

thrown-up barricade. The newspapers broadcast the piteous details of the entombment and the shock of the bereaved families, but a ballad—written, some said, by a Jewish peddler from Scranton—best caught the grief and terror of the miners and their families. For decades it was sung in barrooms, down in the mines, and in miners' cottages. A text has been recovered in Newfoundland, and a field recording was issued by the Archive of American Folk Song in the Library of Congress (Record 76).

4. Stable in the mine
5. Bottom of the slope
6. Honey Brook breaker no. 2

7. Dumping mine cars
8. Separating the different sizes of coal
9. Slate pickers

9

THE AVONDALE MINE DISASTER

Transcribed by Melvin LeMon

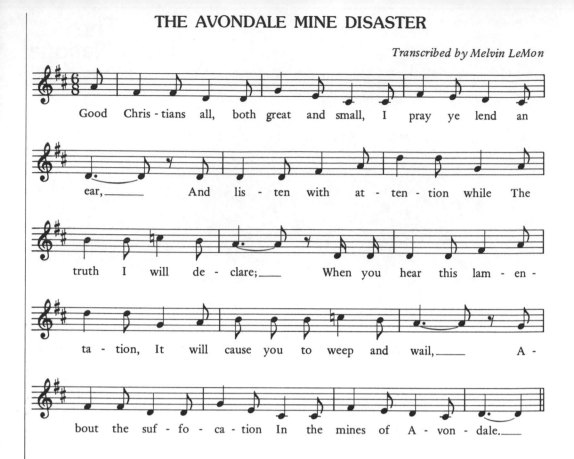

Good Chris-tians all, both great and small, I pray ye lend an ear,___ And lis-ten with at-ten-tion while The truth I will de-clare;___ When you hear this lam-en-ta-tion, It will cause you to weep and wail,___ A-bout the suf-fo-ca-tion In the mines of A-von-dale.___

On the sixth day of September,
  Eighteen hundred and
    sixty-nine,
Those miners all then got a call
  To go work in the mine;
But little did they think that day
  That death would gloom
    the vale
Before they would return again
  from
The mines of Avondale.

The women and the children,
  Their hearts were filled
    with joy,
To see the men go work again,
  And likewise every boy;
But a dismal sight in broad
    daylight,
  Soon made them turn pale,

When they saw the breaker
    burning
  O'er the mines of Avondale.

From here and there, and
    everywhere,
  They gathered in a crowd,
Some tearing off their clothes
    and hair,
  And crying out aloud—
Get out our husbands and
    our sons,
  Death he's going to steal
Their lives away without delay
  In the mines of Avondale.

But all in vain, there was
    no hope
  One single soul to save,
For there is no second outlet

From the subterranean cave.
No pen can write the awful
  fright
And horror that did prevail,
Among those dying victims,
  In the mines of Avondale.

A consultation then was held,
  'Twas asked who'd volunteer
For to go down this dismal
  shaft,
  To seek their comrades dear;
Two Welshmen brave, without
  dismay,
  And courage without fail,
Went down the shaft, without
  delay,
  In the mines of Avondale.

When at the bottom they
  arrived,
  And thought to make their
  way,
One of them died for want
  of air,
  While the other in great
  dismay,
He gave a sign to hoist him up,
  To tell the dreadful tale,
That all were lost forever
  In the mines of Avondale.

Every effort then took place
  To send down some fresh air;
The men that next went down
  again
  They took of them good care;
They traversed through the
  chambers,

And this time did not fail
In finding those dead bodies
  In the mines of Avondale.

Sixty-seven was the number
  That in a heap were found,
It seemed they were bewailing
  Their fate in underground;
They found the father with
  his son
  Clasped in his arms so pale.
It was a heart-rending scene
  In the mines of Avondale.

Now to conclude, and make
  an end,
  Their number I'll pen down—
One hundred and ten of brave
  stout men
  Were smothered underground;
They're in their graves till the
  last day,
  Their widows may bewail,
And the orphans' cries they
  rend the skies
  All round through Avondale![20]

This ballad sets the mode for the verse laments of American miners that would follow. It begins with a note of joy in work on the part of the men and their families, shifts to despair and terror at sight of the fire, accentuates the heroism of the would-be rescuers, and ends with a morbid summary of the casualties. A second Avondale ballad, similar but distinct, accuses the company of neglecting proper precautions for the miners' safety, a charge echoed by press and public.

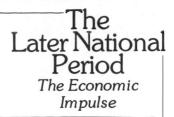

1. The coal-mine calamity, September 6, 1869. Miners volunteering to descend the shaft and search the mine. 2. Reservers discovering corpses at the scene of the disaster. 3. Removing the bodies of the victims from the mine. 4. Hoisting the dead through the shaft of the mine.

Wood engravings in *Frank Leslie's Illustrated Newspaper,* September 25, 1869, depicting the Avondale mine disaster, which gave rise to America's most famous coal-mining ballad

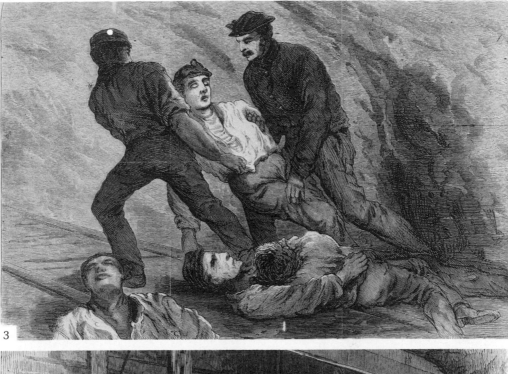

3

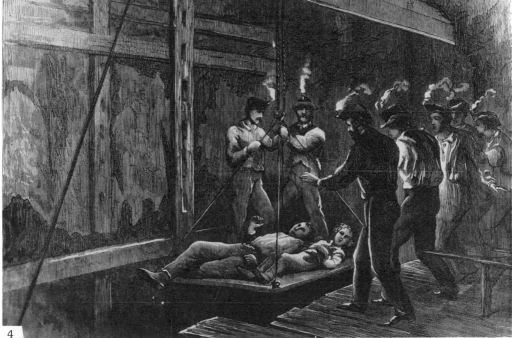

4

I never shall forget the sight as through the shaft they came
And weeping friends stood waiting by, their cold remains to claim,
While their souls may have ascended up to God who gave them
  breath,
To plead against the Company whose greed has caused their
  death.[21]

The shock of the Avondale catastrophe solidified the coal workers, English, Welsh, and Irish, who paraded through the mining towns bearing placards asking for support of the Avondale victims, protection in the mines, and better wages. A united labor movement seemed ready to rise from the ashes of Avondale. Then a rumor sped through the anthracite country that Irish Molly Maguires had ignited the fatal conflagration, as one of their acts of sabotage against the mine owners, heedless of consequences to their fellow miners. A wave of revulsion rose against the Irish miners and split wide the ranks of the coal workers. Instead of becoming a cohesive force, the Avondale disaster turned into a divisive one. And how did the rumor start? The *Philadelphia Evening Bulletin* of September 11, 1869, conjectured that mine owners had propelled the rumor, and writers of the period did not hesitate to credit Franklin B. Gowen with its contrivance. Stung, the Molly Maguires then did launch upon a series of destructive acts, culminating in the burning of the Franklin B. Gowen Colliery in Shamokin, Pennsylvania, on February 13, 1872. Gowen swore retaliation but was unable to secure a conviction.[22]

Avondale became a haunted ground. Living miners saw ghosts of their dead fellow workers in the underground chambers and fled in dismay. A reminiscent witness of the disaster recalled that one miner, striking a lucifer match across his damp clothes shortly after the fire, caused light flashes that led another to cry "Ghost!" and run for his life.[23]

The train of events associated with Avondale finds a striking parallel in the Italian Hall fire that appalled the copper-mining town of Calumet in Michigan's Upper Peninsula in 1913. Who set the fire that started the crowd of festive miners and their families stampeding toward a door that swung inward and cost the lives of eighty-four children in the melee never was determined, but the mine operators and the miners' union flung bitter charges at each other, management even claiming that the union ignited the fire in order to cast blame on the owners. The fire occurred during a protracted and ugly strike when tempers were raw and edgy. Woody Guthrie wrote a ballad about the Italian Hall fire, highly sympathetic to the miners, and a body of folklore grew around the catastrophe, such as the lucky escape of the Finnish miner who heard his teakettle whistling as he went out the door to Italian Hall and turned back at the ill omen. In the lore of the copper country, the fire signalized the treachery of the mine owners in the year of the strike, a bitter year from which the economy of the region never recovered.[24]

Convicted Mollies in jail wrote songs in the folk tradition that preserve their sentiments and point of view—by no means uniform, for two turned state's evidence and were tagged as squealers. Jimmy "Powderkeg" Kerrigan, a bodymaster (local officer) of Tamaqua and a finger man who pointed out the human target to Mollies from another district, according to the Molly practice, threw in the sponge during the first trial of a series that led to the downfall of the secret society. A cocky, shifty-eyed bantam enjoying the spotlight, Kerrigan jauntily faced the prosecuting attorney in the Mauch Chunk courtroom, where he and two youths, Michael Doyle and Edward Kelly, were to stand consecutive trials for the assassination of a mine boss, John P. Jones. But as the evidence mounted against Doyle, Kerrigan lost his nerve and started to "sing." On January 28, 1876, he wrote out a voluntary confession casting light on several of the murders committed by the Mollies. Doyle and Kelly were sentenced to death and hanged on Black Thursday, June 21, 1877, while Kerrigan escaped the noose and lived until 1903. After writing his prose confession, Kerrigan composed a confessional ballad of fifteen stanzas, subsequently printed in the Mauch Chunk *Coal Gazette.*

"Jimmy Kerrigan's Confession" follows the traditional mode of the lament by the turncoat seeking to redeem himself in the world's eyes. Powderkeg needed good will, for if the Molly haters did not take him in, the Mollies would certainly do him in.

Two Molly Maguires murder a mine superintendent, John P. Jones, near the railroad station at Lansford, Pennsylvania, September 3, 1875.

From Allan Pinkerton, *The Molly Maguires and the Detectives*

You know I am that squealer they talk so much about,
And sure you know the reason, of which I have no doubt.
If not, I will tell you as nearly as I can,
So please in kindness listen to Jimmy Kerrigan.

He then recounts how he fought for his country on the Union side in the Civil War, and how, at its conclusion, he had settled down in Tamaqua as a peaceful family man when certain Mollies led him astray. Kerrigan gives close details on the Mollies' plans for the killing of John P. Jones:

On the first day of September in eighteen seventy-five,
Returning from my work, at Carroll's I did arrive
To take my beer, as usual, but did not get a fill,
When Carroll said, "Kerrigan, here are men for Summit Hill."

Jimmy Carroll was secretary of the Tamaqua chapter of the Mollies, officially known as the Ancient Order of Hibernians, and like many of the Molly hierarchy ran a tavern where amid the whiskey drinking and jig dancing the members of the order discussed bloody business. Summit Hill was a borough in the area of Lansford, and John P. Jones the mine foreman was to be shot there for blacklisting a Molly named Hugh McGehan, himself a murderer.

Powderkeg protests that he wants no part of the affair, but allows himself nonetheless to be coerced into leading the young Molly conspirators.

Says I, "Why, Carroll, I have got to work, with them I cannot go."
"Kerrigan, you know better, and what you say is not so."
So lastly I consented and fixed myself in style
To lead, as he requested, young Kelly and Michael Doyle.

Another conspirator now enters the scene, a tavern keeper in Storm Hill and treasurer of the Molly Maguires' chapter there, Alexander Campbell, who would hang for Kerrigan's accusation— unjustly, some thought.

We arrived at Alex Campbell's at half past nine or ten.
When Campbell did accomp'ny us from there to Summit Hill
Saying, "Hugh, these are chaps we've talked about, and who have
  left their homes
To satisfy the rest of us—to kill the hated Jones."

Campbell here explains to Hugh McGehan that Mollies from another district have come to "return the favor" (as the exchange of killers between bodymasters in different communities was called) and avenge the insult to Hugh. The trio proceed to their task, with Kerrigan pointing out the person

of Superintendent Jones to Doyle and Kelly, and arranging to meet them after the murder. In the ballad Powderkeg continues to play the role of reluctant and remorseful confederate.

On Thursday we had a glance at Jones but failed the deed to do.
The command "Thou shalt not kill" once more appeared in view.
But Campbell he insisted and the following day we went
And did the bloody deed over which we now repent.

Kerrigan's better feelings finally prevail and he reveals the "whole story," not only for his own sake but for that of his country.

When Doyle was tried and I saw it was no use
For me to hold my tongue, I resolved to let it loose;
I told the whole story from beginning to end
And think that since I have told it the country's on the mend.

Now the ballad author firmly allies himself with the Pinkerton detective McParlan, who had suddenly become a romantic and daredevil hero throughout the nation. If McParlan could play the double role of Molly and informer, then perhaps some of his luster would rub off on Kerrigan, who, he would like his listeners to believe, is making a similar contribution to law and order. Actually, he suggests, he had seen through McParlan's disguise all along, and the detective and fellow Irish Catholic was in effect aiding Kerrigan.

I had one to assist me who was both good and true
To religion and to country, nor less to me and you:
His name was James McParlan; he's a credit to his race.
A clever chap, still young in years, and honesty's in his face.

Kerrigan has to make his peace also with the Irish-American community at large and the Ancient Order of Hibernians. He draws a distinction, historically valid, between the chapters in the anthracite counties run by the Mollie Maguires and those outside the coal country. He has realized that the priests, at first divided in their views, have increasingly turned against the Mollies.

That this society was a shame to Irishmen you know,
Though outside the coal region I learn it is not so.

For there they do their duty and churches they supply
To teach the way of holiness and fit all men to die.

But not so in the coal fields where by church they are accursed,
And excommunicated, which still made matters worse . . .

The ballad concludes with a didactic
verse:

MORAL

And before I do lay down my pen, I'll address these words to ye,
Abstain from drinking liquor, and from all bad company;
For if you don't, you will it rue unto the day you die,
And with this I shall leave you, and bid you all good-bye.[25]

The quondam Molly has turned his back on his former buddies and their whole organization as drunkards, murderers, and corrupters of young Irish miners. He puts in a good word for one of the convicted killers, young Kelly, who was "I think, a little past nineteen/Led astray, as it was thought, by a chap named Jerry Kane," referring to a bodymaster of Mount Laffee. The Kehoes and the Kanes were the culprits, McParlan and Kerrigan himself were on the side of the angels. Of the rollicking, bravado spirit of "Pat Dolan" celebrating the Robin Hood deeds of the Molly Maguires, not an echo sounds in this whining plaint.

Among his fellow Hibernians, Kerrigan had talked in a different vein, bragging about his part in the murder of the policeman Benjamin Yost. To McParlan, in his role of James McKenna, Powderkeg crowed, "You'll allow that I know somethin' of a job that I planned meself, and wor there on hand, when it wor all done."[26]

Another informer, Michael "Muff" Lawler, one time bodymaster at Shenandoah, generated a Molly ballad, but as subject rather than author, and the point of view differs noticeably. The anonymous composer of this piece, which was actively sung in the mining towns, derides Lawler, who talks in Irish brogue to the prosecution lawyers and judge and plays the part of a simpleton, the stage Irishman. George Korson first recorded it in 1925 from an ex-Molly living in Philadelphia and marveled at the "mocking tone and the trembling voice with which that man sang it for me."[27]

Detective McParlan had wormed his way into Lawler's confidence and gained entrance into the Molly Maguires through his sponsorship.[28] Muff bred gamecocks known as "mufflers," hence his nickname, and also contracted with miners seeking jobs. A heavy-set, black-haired, black-whiskered, fairly imposing man in his forties, Lawler fell from grace in his lodge for slowness to arrange a murder. He lost his title, was expelled, and ironically had to plead with McParlan to regain membership, in vain.[29] The Mollies turned viciously on Muff, gave him a beating, and after his arrest with other members, when the society had been exposed, refused him funds for legal aid. Being already suspected of informing, he had reason to follow the path of Kerrigan, and by squealing did escape the noose, although not the derision of his former associates. The whole episode, encapsulated in the ballad, illustrates the fragile structure, overt suspicions, and shifting relationships that led to the collapse of the Molly Maguires.

MUFF LAWLER, THE SQUEALER

When Muff Lawler was in jail right bad did he feel
He thought divil the rooster would he ever heal,
"Be jabers," says Lawler, "I think I will squeal."
"Yes, do," says the Judge to Muff Lawler.

It was down in the office those lawyers did meet,
"Come in, Mr. Lawler"; they gave him a seat.
"Give us your whole history and don't us deceive."
"Be jabers, I will," says Muff Lawler.

"There are some o' thim near," he says, "and more o' thim far;
There are some o' thim you'll never catch I do fear."
"If they are on this earth," he says, "we'll have them I'm sure."
"Yes, but be jabers they're dead," says Muff Lawler.

. . . . .

"Now I'll commence," he says, "me whole story to tell,
When I go back to Shenandoah, I'll be shot sure as hell."
"We'll send you to a country where you're not known so well."
"Be jabers, that's good," says Muff Lawler.[30]

In spite of their declarations of innocence, ten Mollies did hang on Black Thursday, and the ballad makers now sought to convey to doubters the bravery of the condemned men on the scaffold, as final proof of their guiltlessness. Quoting noble sentiments from a swarthily handsome, close-lipped Tamaqua miner convicted of murdering Yost the policeman, the ballad of "Thomas Duffy" makes its subject into a stouthearted Irish hero. The piece begins with the same two lines as does "Hugh McGehan," in typical Irish "come-all-ye" folksong style:

Come all ye true-born Irishmen wherever you may be
I hope you will pay attention and listen unto me.

Duffy is being murdered on the gallows
by "false perjurers," but he does not
flinch.

Thomas Duffy on the brink of death did neither shake or fear,
But he smiled upon his murderers although his end was near.

. . . . .

He scorned his prosecutors although he stood alone,
As did many a gallant Irishman before England's king and throne.

. . . . .

He mounted on the scaffold with a firm and steady tread,
Resembling a young nobleman a-going up to bed.

Now he makes his final speech to the crowd, taking his brother's hand, denying complicity with Kerrigan, asserting he bears no malice toward anyone, and so dies strong in faith and light in conscience.

The rope was dropped around his neck and the warrant
    to him read,
And in twenty minutes after, brave Duffy he was dead.
God rest his soul; he perished there to friends and country true,
And he kept his secrets to the last as Irishmen should do.[31]

There were people in Pottsville who believed in Duffy's innocence. True, he had a reputation for drinking and brawling, and had once called policeman Yost a "Dutch son of a bitch," cause enough for Yost to clap him in jail.[32] Hence Duffy presumably had a motive for Yost's murder. But Father Daniel McDermott, an outspoken critic of the Mollies, declared, "I know beyond all reasonable doubt, that Duffy was not a party to the murder of Policeman Yost. . . ."[33]

Two songs about Thomas Duffy have survived. George Korson obtained the one just quoted from a manuscript version written down in 1881, in the possession of a miner bard. Another, different piece written as if delivered by Duffy but supposedly the composition of a literate jailbird, Manus Coll, known as Kelly the Bum, appeared in the *Shenandoah Herald* of September 9, 1876.[34]

In writing these personal ballads exonerating themselves or their friends, the Molly Maguires merely followed a tradition to which they had been exposed all their lives. Throughout the eighteenth and nineteenth centuries, ballads circulated in Ireland with the currency of newspapers today and fulfilled much the same function. With the decline of the Gaelic tongue, ballads in English became a vehicle of communication as well as entertainment, sung by itinerant minstrels at fairs and gatherings and by jolly pub crowds. Some dealt with star-crossed lovers, some with comic characters in the stage-Irish manner, others with local incidents and personal tragedies. The Irish martyr-hero emerges as a recurrent figure in small episodes forgotten in history but faithfully preserved, with due accounting of dates, names, and places, in these street songs. So too, in jail and in the taverns, Mollies responded to their crisis and downfall in the way that unlucky Irish soldiers, freebooters, and outlaws had regularly faced the gallows, by writing laments. The Mollies' best defense came, not through the pleas of their lawyers, but from their own verse.

The curse of man and judgment of God entered into the folk legends that swirled around the Molly Maguires. As in the rest of the folklore, which reflects the ambivalent attitude of public, press, and church toward the secret order, the curses worked both for and against the Mollies. The malediction of a priest, Father Daniel J. McDermott, has passed into the traditional lore of the coal fields. While it was he who asserted the innocence of Thomas Duffy and took the part of the miners

against the greedy operators, Father McDermott nevertheless regarded the Mollies as a dangerous and godless organization. Coming to Centralia in 1896 as a young cleric of twenty-six, he learned from a parishioner that older men had gotten her boy drunk and then administered to him the oath of the Mollies. Under questioning the youth admitted the facts. The Sunday following, Father McDermott spoke from his pulpit and threatened to reveal the names of the two Molly Maguires who were luring unknowing lads into their "foul and wicked society." The parishioners gasped, and feared for the life of their priest, who throughout the week received veiled threats. On the ensuing Sunday he did announce the names of the two, who thrice brazenly denied

A Molly Maguire shoots Gomer James, a Welsh miner tending bar at a picnic in Shenandoah, Pennsylvania, August 14, 1875.
From Allan Pinkerton, *The Molly Maguires and the Detectives*

their membership in the death-dealing group. Thereupon he snuffed out the altar candles and cursed the pair, while miners and their wives wept in the pews. Shortly afterwards, the one was crushed to death in the mines, while the other went to prison for fighting and killing a man in a tavern. So runs the tradition.[35]

Yet some Mollies swore their innocence persuasively, and when words failed to convince, called for a supernatural sign. Strapping Alex Campbell, charged with killing mine superintendent John P. Jones, declared in court, "God knows that I am innocent of any crime, and the people know it, and the Commonwealth knows it." On the day of his death, Black Thursday, he reiterated his in-

Mollies murder Thomas Sanger, a colliery boss, and William Uren, a miner, at Raven Run, Pennsylvania, September 1, 1875. Sanger calls to Robert Heaton, a proprietor of the colliery, to fire on the retreating assassins.
From Allan Pinkerton, *The Molly Maguires and the Detectives*

nocence and, as the Mauch Chunk sheriff approached to lead him to the gallows, bent to the ground, gathered dust in his hand, and dragging the iron ball and chain to the cell wall, clapped his hand high on the wall, crying, "There

is the proof of my words. That mark will never be wiped out." And thereafter the handprint on the wall has fascinated onlookers, despite efforts of sheriffs to remove the blemish.

Another version has Tom Fisher, who was executed in Mauch Chunk on March 28, 1878, for the murder of mine superintendent Morgan Powell seven years before, making the mark. Fisher claimed right up to the scaffold that he had been inside a saloon when the fatal shots were fired outside, and on the night before his hanging, the informer Kelly the Bum admitted to a jailer that he had lied about Fisher's involvement in the murder of Powell. As the sobbing youth was led to the scaffold, he placed his right hand on the wall of cell number 8 and proclaimed, "My mark will stay here as long as this prison remains."[36] Though Fisher's mother was Irish, his father was Pennsylvania German and so was Sheriff Jacob Raudenbush, and the lore of powawing and *Hexerei* now blends with Irish Catholic belief in the miraculous. The *Philadelphia Evening Bulletin*, in a story from Mauch Chunk on November 16, 1931, stated that Tom Fisher's handprint, after fifty-four years, had disappeared from the cell wall. "For more than a half-century the imprint has been there and reappearing under each fresh coat of whitewash and paint. Thousands of Philadelphians have traveled from all parts of the state to see it."[37] The story went on to say that Sheriff Robert L. Bowman, weary of the sightseers, had scraped away the plaster with a knife, filled the hole with cement, and painted it over, thus, according to the newspaper, effectively removing the handprint. In the view of one skeptic, a long-time native of Carbon County who as a boy had seen Alex Campbell, a plumber fitting pipes in the cell had steadied himself by placing a hand against the wall when the plaster was fresh. After Campbell's execution the story arose connecting Campbell with the print.[38] But Arthur H. Lewis, writing in 1964, quotes the then sheriff of Jim Thorpe (as Mauch Chunk was renamed) to the effect that the plainly visible mark of Fisher's hand continued to attract hordes of the curious.[39]

A graduate student writing on the legend in a folklore journal in 1971 notes current attention to the handprint, which she illustrates in a photograph of the cell wall. For the Now Generation she offers her interpretation, that the mark serves as a reminder that murder, even when sanctioned by the state, is still murder.[40]

Besides the handprint on the cell wall, other signs supported the legend of the Mollies' innocence. The vengeance of the Lord could be read into the series of sudden deaths that overtook those who brought Molly Maguires to trial and the scaffold. On Friday the thirteenth— an ominous day indeed—in 1889, Franklin B. Gowen, in good health and vigorous at fifty-three, put a bullet through his head in a hotel room in Washington, D.C. No reason was ever forthcoming for the sudden suicide, but some speculated that he had brooded over his part in the hangings of Black Thursday. Five other members of the prosecution were reported murdered within two weeks after Black Thursday, and two witnesses supposedly met violent deaths on the night of the hangings,

A savage battle between the Molly Maguires and the Sheet Irons, at Number Three Hill, Mahanoy City, Pennsylvania, March 17, 1875, during a strike in the coal mines.
From Allan Pinkerton, *The Molly Maguires and the Detectives*

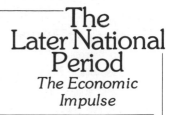
a legend printed as fact by Julia Johnsen in *Capital Punishment* and Harry Elmer Barnes and Negley K. Teeters in *New Horizons in Criminology*.[41] The Mollies were reputed to have exacted retaliation by such murders.

Memories, hostilities, and narrations kindled by the era of the Molly Maguires still arouse families in the anthracite country. In 1958 George Korson interviewed an eighty-seven-year-old woman, Mrs. Howard Kahler, Sr., who was eight when three Mollies were hung in Bloomsburg and remembered Thomas Kelly squealing on several Mollies. "Kelly the Bum we called him. They locked him up for his own protection. If they [the Mollies] would have got hold of him, it would have been no Kelly. There wouldn't have been [anything] left of him to be showed." One still-current anecdote tells of a Pennsylvania Dutch miner, who had lost a leg in a mine accident, clubbing Molly Maguires with his peg leg when they broke into a saloon where he was fiddling and started a ruckus. In another an Irishman, openly critical of the Mollies, found himself one day in a Molly-infested saloon and had to pay drinks for the house every time he ordered a drink for himself.[42] Small in themselves, these tales loom large to the people who live in the anthracite counties and relive the turbulent history and folklore of the Molly Maguires.

Returning to our original question, Does folklore present the coal miner as a master-workman hero of the Economic Life-style or as a labor radical?

The earlier ballads definitely affirm the heroic qualities of the miner as skilled workman, happy and optimistic in his pursuit, courageous in time of danger, devoted to his family. With the rise of the labor movement, accelerated by the panic of 1873 and producing the Knights of Labor in the early 1870s, the American Federation of Labor in 1886, and the United Mine Workers of America in 1890, the status of the collier shifts. No longer the independent craftsman, he has become the union laborer, still a hero, but now fighting against the owners and their hired strikebreakers rather than against the forces of nature. In the special case of the Molly Maguires, who resorted to violence against bosses and foremen, the folk cast their verdict for the condemned Irish colliers and denounce the informers who squealed on them and the tycoon, Franklin B. Gowen, who persecuted them. All is not clear-cut; mention of the Mollies still arouses distrust and foreboding, but not to the same extent as mention of the squealers Kerrigan, Muff Lawler, and McParlan. In the American tradition, no squealer has ever received folk approbation. Benedict Arnold is beyond redemption. The verdict of history has arrived at a more moderate judgment than that of folklore, dividing the blame between the Mollies and the operators. But in the handprint legend of the condemned Molly and the divine providence that struck down Gowen, folklore has recognized the Mollies as valiant fighters for economic justice to the exploited workingman.

Oil drillers

The cowboy had his horse, the lumberjack his axe, and the miner his pick, but beside them in the turbulent Gilded Age appears a new occupational hero, not previously seen on history's stage, and with no familiar identifying symbol: the driller for oil. He responds to a new industry, oil, greater than cattle, lumber, or coal. Technically known as petroleum, oil was popularly dubbed "liquid gold" or "black gold." Now indeed has the industrial age come upon America.

Drilling teams with their strange-looking tools and rigs, dwarfed by the man-made forest of derricks stretching into the sky, would seem too mechanized to be good carriers of folklore. One folklorist thought otherwise. As George Korson interrogated the coal miners for folksongs, so Mody Boatright, a University of Texas professor, interviewed the roughnecks and wildcatters of the oil fields and found them, while lacking in minstrelsy, profuse in other kinds of folklore. Field collectors had not assembled a single volume of tales for cowboys, lumberjacks, or miners, in the course of producing a shelfful of ballad books. But oil workers rarely sang. For one thing, their frenzied boom towns failed to generate the kind of enduring community spirit that knit together men on the long drive, or in the lumber camp, or within the mine patch. Rather the oilmen lived in a supercharged atmosphere of strike-it-rich overnight millionaires, roaring geysers and flaming lakes of oil, electrifying rumors, disappointing dry holes, quiet towns swelled tenfold in a twinkling at the news of a flowing well. Confidence men, gamblers, speculators, loony prospectors, penurious farmers, stolid Indians, drifters, deadbeats, and bigtimers were all caught up in the madness. The substantial ethnic groups of Irish, Welsh, and Cornish who had singing traditions did not join *en masse* the rush to the oil fields. But if the oil drillers did not sing about their work, they strung out anecdotes, legends, sells, tall tales, and hair-raising experiences in great gushers of oral narrative. Also they observed prescriptive beliefs, taboos, and customs in the detecting of the black gold.

In 1945 Boatright brought out the first of three unusual books on oil drillers' folklore, *Gib Morgan, Minstrel of the Oil Fields,* a slender collection of biographical facts and tales about a storytelling character well known to oilmen. The title is a catchy misnomer, since Gib was strictly a narrator of fabulous tales, not a composer or singer of ballads. Born in 1842 in Callensburg in western Pennsylvania, close to the scene of the first oil well at Titusville in 1859, he died in 1909, the year the oil boom reached its height, after a lifetime of work and fun in the oil fields. In *The Folklore of the Oil Industry,* which he published in 1963, Boatright established the patterns of folk tradition that had formed over the past century as Americans probed and drilled for oil wells. One large class of folk beliefs and behavior dealt with the discovery of oil, which took on the proportions of a giant treasure hunt. Dreams, ghosts, doodlebugs, crackpot inventors, seers, and second-sighters all helped guide or misguide prospectors to the underground pools. A second class covered all the legendary tales, heartwarming and heartbreaking, of locating gushers by chance, luck, intuition, and hunch, and conversely, missing them through ironic twists of fate. In a third category of folklore, Boatright identified among the oil workers a number of folk stereotypes resembling earlier American folk figures.

A posthumous work, in which Boatright collaborated with William A. Owens, a quondam collector of Texas folksongs and Columbia University professor of literature, came out in 1970 under the title *Tales from the Derrick Floor: A People's History of the Oil Industry*. This was a book of oral history, a new branch of historical research based upon tape-recorded interviews with active participants in the drama of oil, but leavened by the folklorists' approach. The man on the job rather than the president of the company intrigues the student of folklore, and Boatright and Owens present the tape transcripts of oil-field reminiscences from a hundred persons connected in one way or another with oil drilling. Their musings include the already-known folk legends of doodlebug users and lucky strikes, but they disclose another vein of folklore just now gaining attention, what might be called traditional attitudes and folkways. The cowboy and the lumberjack codes belong to this vein, and the oil driller too developed his folk philosophy.

So still another major American occupation resting on use and abuse of the land's bounty generated its body of folklore. More technological, more directly industrialized than the other occupations—the early pick miner relied on simple tools and the strength of his back—oil prospecting and oil drilling made real the nation's dream of wealth. The resulting folklore appears in one sense incongruous, to the extent that the old tales, legends, and superstitions always tied to pastoral life are now adapted to machinery. But in another sense the folklore logically reflects the industry that, in its initial stages, depended more on the turn of fortune's wheel than on scientific prediction. And the chief protagonist, the driller, "went through a stage similar to one that the trapper, the miner, and the cowboy went through, one in which a chief satisfaction was a pride in his manliness."[1] While he sought riches, the oil driller did not necessarily aspire to be an oil magnate, any more than the cowboy or lumberjack hoped to become cattle or lumber barons. He found his stimulus and reward in the ethic of work and the aristocracy of skill.

The oil driller as a folktype shared characteristics of the cowboy, lumberjack, and miner. Like them all he liquored up and fought viciously in saloons when off the job, stuck to his post in spite of danger and discomfort when on duty, and exuded the mystique surrounding such an independent daredevil. An anecdote about a Wyoming oil boom illustrates popular attitudes toward the driller. After the wildcatter struck oil, the usual turmoil ensued of promoters and drilling crews frantically seeking leases and building derricks. Nearby farmers gazed in wonderment at the new breed of roughnecks invading their fields. One farmwife and her sixteen-year-old daughter working in a field beheld a team of drillers approaching. The girl had never seen men other than farmers and sheepherders, and asked her mother, "Look, Mama, what kind of men are they?" "Hush, child!" warned the mother. "You had better go to the house. These are oil men and you are

Portrait of Gib Morgan in the uniform of a Civil War veteran

From Mody C. Boatright, *Gib Morgan, Minstrel of the Oil Fields*

too young to know anything about them."[2]

Such was the image the oil driller projected and in which he gloried. As with Gib Morgan, the driller wandered from one field to another, when old ones were drilled out and new ones opened, from Pennsylvania, West Virginia, and Ohio through Illinois and Arkansas to Kansas, Oklahoma, and Texas. Often he had grown up on a farm, used farm tools, worked in cotton mills and sawmills, so when agricultural technology reduced the need for farm labor, these country lads, familiar with machines and accustomed to long hours, flocked to the oil fields. There they worked on cable-tool crews as tool dressers, on rotary crews as roughnecks, and hoped to reach the head position of the operating crew, the driller.[3] It was the driller who supervised his personnel and equipment in the operation that ran twenty-four hours a day, and guided the boring

of the well from the first few hundred yards of spudding through to the grand climax of reaching the oil sand or to the dismal moment when the well was plugged up as a duster. Experienced drillers were always in short supply and need tolerate no interference from their bosses, for they could always pack up and go. Ever-present danger from escaping gas, explosions, fires, and falling or breaking machinery added to the aura of the driller. In his behavior and ethics, he observed a code. He worked unstintingly, displayed courage and confidence, took pride in his expertise, spoke little, drank heavily, and wore distinctive apparel.

Tales of Gib Morgan

The driller's emphasis on technical skill and personal achievement can be seen in the cycle of tales that Gib Morgan spun about himself and that others repeated. Gib spoke for the cable-tool driller against the new system of rotary drilling, introduced in 1901 at Spindletop, Texas, and championed, curiously enough, in the name of Paul Bunyan. The cable-tool system depended on an up-and-down churning motion of a blunt bit at the end of a cable, while in the hydraulic rotary system a steel pipe with its cutting edge was rotated to force its way through rock and earth. When shifting sands and shales defeated efforts of cable-tool drillers to reach the ocean of oil buried at Spindletop, engineers devised the rotary system, which successfully brought in the greatest gusher in oil history up to that time. Since the two systems required different kinds of machinery and different crews, the cable-tool and rotary drillers squared off against each other. Cable-tool drillers doubted the practicality of the rotary principle and referred to its adherents as "boll weevils" (from Texas), "cajuns" (from Louisiana or Texas), "prune pickers" (from California), and "sheepherders" (from Wyoming). They prided themselves on their superior finesse and sensitivity. Meanwhile the rotary drillers vaunted the greater speed, depth, and power of their system and disparaged the cable-tool operators, many of whom had drilled in the East, as "horse thieves" (from Clarion County, Pennsylvania),

"hardheads" (from Tennessee), "yellowhammers" (from Ohio), or just generally "jarheads" and "yo-yo's."[4] In their competition, the rival crews turned to champion drillers who performed extraordinary feats with one or the other type of rig. Gib Morgan, growing up in Pennsylvania and working in Eastern oil fields, represented the cable-tool drillers, and Paul Bunyan, imported from Northwest-

Drake Well, Pennsylvania, the first oil well drilled in the United States, 1859

ern lumber camps, the rotary drillers. In 1932 a collector of California oil workers' idiom, Frederick R. Pond, reported whoppers ascribed to each. He had heard of Gib using a blacksnake in West Virginia, where such snakes grew to great lengths, for a drilling cable, and of striking white sand in his drilling operation through which flowed pure buttermilk.[5]

Gib Morgan resembles other American folk narrators in some respects, but he is the first industrial Münchausen to appear in the United States. The spinner of "large" and "tough" yarns who makes himself the hero of his fictions is familiar enough in both Europe and America. Davy Crockett belongs to this mode, and so do Abraham "Oregon" Smith, who related wonders of the Oregon country to his cronies in the Midwest; Jim Bridger, the mountain man who beheld a petrified forest; John Darling, the raftsman and woodcutter of the Catskills; and other local storytelling characters. During their lifetimes they fas-

The first oil wells pumping in the United States, at Titusville, Pennsylvania, 1860

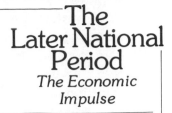

tened traditional tales onto themselves, and their contemporaries and later generations repeated the tales as cycles attached to the narrator-heroes. Thus, as in the Crockett almanacs, the point of view alternates between first and third person. So with Gib Morgan, whose adventures are presented by Boatright in the third person, although Morgan told them as personal sagas. Gib departed from the traditional stock of American tall tales about remarkable hunting and shooting, rich and poor soil, extremes of weather, and feats of strength—a few of which did enter his repertoire—to concentrate on the esoteric mechanics of his industry. He is first and foremost the oil driller and oil promoter, from Pennsylvania and West Virginia to Texas and Louisiana, and around the globe wherever oil was sought in his day: the Fiji Islands, South America, India, Russia, Italy. To understand his successes and failures, his ingenious surmounting of obstacles,

the pals and pets he acquired, and the point of his jokes and sells, the listener (or reader) must possess familiarity with the technology of oil drilling. Gib Morgan is regaling an audience, not of eighteenth-century farmers or trappers or woodsmen, but of late-nineteenth-century technicians. As one old oilman who knew Gib recalled, "Most of his stories were more or less technical [in] nature and it would hardly be interesting to those that did not understand the terms and the conditions that we worked under in the oil fields."[6]

Consider, for instance, the tale of "Gib's Biggest Rig." At first glance this appears to be another American extravaganza of the biggest and the best. We are told that the "Standard rockhounds" (which the *Petroleum Dictionary* of Lalia Boone explains as meaning geologists for the Standard Oil Company) had run into difficulties while drilling in Texas in what seemed a likely spot.

They had sent their crack drilling crews and production men down, but the formation above the oil sand was so cavy that they hadn't been able to make a hole. They would start with a twenty-four-inch bit and case with a twenty-two-inch casing. Then they would make a few more feet of hole and would have to set a twenty-inch casing. They would cut a little more ditch and then they would have to case again. And it would go on like that until the casing became too small for the tools to go through, and after all that expense they would have to abandon the hole.[7]

In lay language, the ground being drilled was so soft and porous that it kept falling into the well. The drillers employed a bit, or cutting tool, twenty-four inches in diameter to penetrate the earth and

then lowered lengths of pipe twenty-two inches in diameter into the hole to shore it up against cave-ins. But because of the constant caving of the sides, they had to keep reducing the width of the hole and of the pipe until finally they could no longer lower the cable and the bit—the so-called string of tools—into the hole. This was actually the situation at Spindletop in south Texas that led to the invention of the rotary rig. But Gib preferred to solve the problem with his own cable-tool method. When John D. Rockefeller called him in as consultant, Gib pondered the matter, then ordered special tools, both big and little, from the Oil Well Supply Company at Pittsburgh, and proceeded to Texas to erect his rig.

The derrick covered an acre of ground, and since Gib expected to be there for some time he fixed it up nice. He weatherboarded it on the outside and plastered it on the inside. It was so high that he had it hinged in two places so that he could fold it back to let the moon get by. It took a tool dresser fourteen days to climb to the top to grease the crown pulleys. That is the reason Gib had to hire thirty tool dressers. At any time there would be fourteen going up, fourteen coming down, one on the top and one on the ground. A day's climbing apart he built bunk houses for the men to sleep in. These bunk houses had hot and cold showers and all the modern conveniences.

By the time the derrick was up, the tools began to arrive from Pittsburgh. The biggest string of tools reached to within ten feet of the crown block. The drill stem was twelve feet in diameter. At the first indication of caving Gib cased the well with thousand-barrel oil tanks riveted together. This reduced the hole to twenty feet. He put on an eighteen-foot bit and made about fifty feet of hole before he had to case again. Down about five hundred feet he had to go to a smaller bit, one about six feet in diameter. At a thousand feet he was using standard tools. At two thousand feet he was using his specially made small tools and casing with one-inch tubing. But he hadn't figured it quite fine enough, for he hadn't got the oil sand when the smallest drill he had wouldn't go through the tubing. But that didn't stump Gib. He brought in the well with a needle and thread.[8]

Some familiar tall-tale exaggeration, both of the very large and the very small, can be found here. The great derrick calls to mind Paul Bunyan's great lumber camp, and the hinged derrick suggests the hinged mast on Old Stormalong's great sailing ship, also contrived to let the moon pass by (motifs never properly reported in oral tradition). The size of the tools and the hole are at first absurdly overstated and then absurdly understated, with success finally crowning Gib's efforts, not through Paul Bun-yanesque superpower, but by means of Yankee ingenuity. But none of the extravagance arouses much merriment without comprehension of oil-field operations.

The derrick is the structure, directly above the hole being bored for the well, that supports the ropes and pulleys used in lowering and raising the drilling tools. Atop the derrick is the crown pulley, the wooden block holding the pulley wheels over which the drilling cable must pass on its way up and down

An oil boom town, Seminole, Oklahoma, in 1927. Wagons carried equipment to well sites when automobiles mired in the deep mud.

into the borehole. Tool dressers assist the driller in handling and servicing the rig and keeping the various tools in good working order. The drill stem, in the cable-tool system, is a heavy steel shaft onto which the bit jars and connections are screwed to form the so-called "string of tools." Jars are two connecting steel links between the four iron sinker bars, intended to keep steady and weight down the drilling tools, and the poles or cables supporting the drilling tools. The links slide on each other to a distance of from six to thirty-six inches and allow the tools to fall on the downstroke with increased force, but jar or jerk them on the upstroke so they will not get lodged in crevices or cavings on the sides of the well hole. The purpose of all this apparatus is "to bring the well in," that is, to keep the hole open until the drilling has reached the oil pool or oil sand, with the result that the oil will flow or gush from gas pressure up the hole to the surface.[9] Using a needle and thread in the minuscule borehole to replace the bit and cable is the ultimate in Lilliputian burlesque of cable-tool drilling.

Most of Gib's tales require similar explication for the uninitiated, with one fortunate consequence, that he has never been catapulted into the limelight as have other more readily comprehended occupational heroes with much shakier credentials, such as Paul Bunyan and Pecos Bill. Two associates who

221

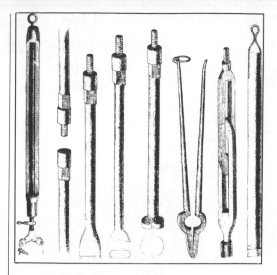

"Implements Used in Boring"
From *Harper's New Monthly Magazine* April 1865

figure in several yarns, Big Toolie and Strickie the boa constrictor, also reflect Gib's synthesis of the tall-tale tradition with oil technology. When a giant tool dresser—twenty-eight inches between the eyes and as tall as a derrick, who could grease the crown pulleys without lifting his feet off the ground—showed up for work, Gib dubbed him Big Toolie. A good-natured fellow, Big Toolie enjoyed a joke, and while Gib sat on the driller's stool overseeing operations, his oversized helper sneaked around the side of the derrick and put his foot on the walking beam to stall the engine or throw the belt off the pulleys. To teach him a lesson, Gib suddenly pulled the engine lever to muster a full head of steam just as Big Toolie was about to tread the walking beam. Up rose the beam, hurling Big Toolie over the derrick and head first into the slush pit. Picking himself up, he walked over to Gib, thrust out his hand, and said, "Mr. Morgan, I'm your man from now on."

Translated, this means that Big Toolie applied his weight to one end of the large beam rising from the derrick floor. The seesaw motion communicated by the engine to this "walking beam" acted to raise and lower the drilling tools.

Big Toolie intended to throw this whole drilling operation out of kilter. In reprisal Gib turned on the power so sharply that the beam upended with tremendous force instead of with its regular oscillating rhythm. The slush pit into which Big Toolie tumbled contains the mud and cuttings emptied from the hole during the drilling.[10] Robin Hood might have perpetrated such a trick on Little John, but with fewer Rube Goldberg trimmings.

As for Strickie, Gib came upon him in a South American jungle, in a swollen stupor after absorbing a gang of monkeys. Gib had just exhausted ten thousand feet of cable drilling a deep well and had wired the States for more steel cable. Seeing Strickie, who was about twenty blocks long, gave him an idea. He had his crew drag the boa back to the rig, spike his head to a spoke in the bull wheel, wind him around the shaft, and splice his tail to the cable. Then he started up the engine and recommenced the drilling, with Strickie effectively extending the cable length and providing more give than a steel cable. That was the beginning of a beautiful friendship. Gib fed the boa two hundred monkeys every three weeks and slaked his thirst every night, after unwinding him from the bull shaft, with a barrel of whiskey. Grateful Strickie slept in front of Gib's bunkhouse door and guarded him faithfully.

Soon Gib came to appreciate Strickie's value in a variety of drilling operations. He found he could use him in place of the bailer fastened to the sand line to

The spring-pole method of drilling, also known as "stomping down a well." Most of the first prospectors used this cheap though strenuous process. Manpower exerted on stirrups and handle could drive the drilling tools suspended from the center rope to a depth of several hundred feet.

clean out cuttings at the bottom of the borehole. When he was lowered, the big snake simply sucked in all the pumpings—mud, sand, and water—and on being raised to the top, slithered over to the slush pit and disgorged them. Once when Gib lost his tools in the well, after the cable bootjacked off (divided in a way resembling a bootjack) and the latch broke in the horn socket (the implement used to extricate lost and broken tools in the well, consisting of a conical socket to slide over the broken part and a spring latch to grip the part), Strickie signaled Gib to tie him to the cable and lower him into the well. Down in the well Strickie acted as a fishing tool (any one of specially designed tools used to recover broken and lost drilling tools in the borehole) by swallowing the rope socket, the sinker, the jars, and half the drilling stem and carrying them up in his belly. Another time when the well had begun to show oil but Gib was running out of cable,

even with Strickie tied on, the boa fortuitously shed his skin and provided Gib with the needed extra cable-skin to bring in the well.

Here, as the equivalent to the fiery steed or steadfast hound or other comparable animal friend of the warrior and hunter hero, is a tool-beast rendering service to the occupational hero. "It was not long until Strickie was the most valuable piece of equipment Gib had."[11] Just to fathom Strickie's services, as fishing tool, bailer, and cable extension, requires a detailed knowledge of oil drilling. Again, both exaggeration and ingenuity characterize the boa. He is a mile long, and he knows enough to unwind the sand reel (a drum used to raise and lower the bailer) before Gib can tie on the bailer, so that his master will realize the snake intends to substitute himself for the bailer (also known as the sand pump).

Some frequently told American windies gravitate to Gib's repertoire, such

A "borer," as the first drillers were called, at work inside an early cable-tool rig

as the tall tales of the reversible dog, of shingling the thick fog, and of the mules who think popping corn is snow and freeze to death. Yet even here the folktale may be adapted to the oil fields, as with the giant mosquitoes whose bills are bradded by men hiding from them within a large structure—in Gib's case a great oil drum—which the mosquitoes then carry off. Such stories tie Gib to the enveloping network of American Münchausens, but by contrast they indi-

William A. (Uncle Billy) Smith, driller of the world's first producing oil well, the Drake Well, at Titusville, Pennsylvania, 1859. Uncle Billy is seated on a wheelbarrow in the foreground. The well, with derrick and drilling machinery housed in wooden buildings, appears in the background.

cate how distinctive and esoteric are the majority of his oil-field narratives. These narratives derive from the technological processes of the oil industry, and they confirm the ethic that man's work plus machine power applied to the land's bounty yields wealth. Gib strikes not only oil but buttermilk (one formation of sandstone is actually known as buttermilk sand), bay rum, champagne, rubber, and horse-piss. At Beaumont, Texas, after the Spindletop gusher came in he built a hotel forty stories high, complete with a narrow-gauge railroad train to take guests from the elevators to their rooms, bathroom taps from which flowed bourbon, rye, Scotch, Tom Collinses, and other drinks, and south and east exposures in every room, made possible because the hotel was mounted on a turntable.

Paul Bunyan presented a challenge to Gib, and the oil-field whoppers attached to Paul's name seem closer to oral sources than the vast majority of his exploits as a lumberjack.[12] Some of the same lies are attributed to both, such as the giant hinged derrick and the well that was drilled into rubber, and there is the same close concern with technology. John Lee Brooks, a Texas professor from Southern Methodist University, who first heard of the oil-field Paul Bunyan in 1920 and set out earnestly on his trail several years later, to his disappointment encountered only scattered and fragmentary incidents and not the coherent tale-cycle he had antici-

A rotary rig in the Sour Lake oilfield, Texas, about 1905

226

pated. But of course oral hero tales are anecdotal and allusive, and the Paul Bunyan references reported by Brooks sound the more authentic for being slight and episodic.

In the oil fields Paul assumed various guises, not only as a driller but also as a pipeliner and a builder of rigs, tanks, and telegraph lines. He was the inventor of tools and deviser of methods to facilitate the drilling and processing of oil, and his great size and strength abetted his technological skills. Oilworker Paul is Gib Morgan and Big Toolie in one. As a rig builder (the carpenter of the oil fields) he sighted with perfect accuracy without a plumbline, built a pair of the great wooden bull wheels (on which the drilling cable was wound) in half a day unaided, hung the walking beam, and skidded a rig (moved a derrick on rollers) several yards by himself. In the face of the unexpected he displayed presence of mind and resourcefulness. On the California coast he was "shooting" a well by planting at the bottom of the hole five hundred quarts of nitroglycerine, known as "soup," to break up the sand and start the oil flowing. But the soup exploded on the way down, and the oil spouted forth in a torrent before the crew could prepare the storage tanks. In a twinkling Paul jumped toward the well and sat upon the pipe, effectively damming the flow of oil. But the resulting pressure from oil and gas drove the casing in the well clear out of the ground and toward the heavens, where Paul hung for three days until his crew could build a derrick and reach him. Meanwhile they capped the well and saved the oil.[13]

Here a roughneck tells how Paul lost his temper and resorted to brute strength to bring in a well:

"I worked for Paul on one of them deep wells once," said Fat. "It was out in Arkansas. Jimmy Blue was running the rig and we was drilling with standard tools. We got down thirty thousand feet and struck a rock formation that a bit wouldn't touch. And we was using a pretty good sized bit too, drilling a fifty-inch hole.

"Well, we worked on this formation for three weeks without doing any good and then we called up Paul. Paul he come out there and took charge of the rig himself and worked for three more weeks, day and night, without doing anything except ruin a lot of bits. And finally he got so mad that he jumped down on the derrick floor and pulled up the bit with his hands. Then he threw it down into the hole as hard as he could throw it. Well, we busted the rock that time. The bit just kept on going and when the line run out it pulled derrick, rig, and all into the hole after it.

"We got a gusher that time. But when Paul seen that the rig had pulled Jimmy into the hole with it he was just about to plug off the

Drillers with drilling tools used in the early oil fields of western Pennsylvania, primitive by today's standards but effective in launching a new industry

hole and abandon it. But in a few days we got a telegram from Jimmy in China saying that he had a 100,000 barrel gusher and was spudding in on another location.[14]

Oil-Money Legends

The oil-field tall tales by Gib Morgan and about Paul Bunyan seem less far-fetched when placed alongside the true tales, the credited legends, and the gargantuan hoaxes and swindles that eddied through the oil towns. When truth is so fabulous, fables appear plausible. In the wake of every oil boom, from Titusville, Pennsylvania, in 1859 to Spindletop in 1901 and the other Texas gushers —Burkburnett, Hogtown, Desdemona, Mexia, Ranger—followed pandemonium and stories of sudden fortunes, not simply from oil but from selling and leasing land, renting rooms, building hotels and restaurants, even peddling water on the streets. Then there were

misfortunes to match. Each chapter in the saga—from the first hunches as to the oil site, the efforts of the optimist to attract capital, the dry or blocked holes, the renewed attempts, the crushing technical obstacles to overcome, the red-letter day or night when the well comes in, the ensuing frenzy to obtain leases and capital to dig rival wells, the millions made and missed, to the recriminations and lawsuits after the big strike—generated its rumors, marvels, and protolegends.

Consider, alongside the yarn of Paul Bunyan sitting on the spouting well to dam it, the actual account of how a drilling crew capped the great Lucas gusher that opened the Spindletop oil field. When the oil finally soared up from

1,020 feet in the ground to tower more than a hundred feet above the top of the derrick in a continuous six-inch stream, flowing—or rather losing— 100,000 barrels a day, the successful drillers, Jim, Curt, and Al Hamill, then faced the task of controlling the precious fountain.

The Hamills built a carriage inside the derrick. This was composed of two light railroad irons attached to the first girt above the floor. Then they bolted two-by-eight-inch plank supports to six-by-four-inch boards to constitute a frame. Off to the side of the well the gate valve was assembled with an eight-inch collar and an eight-by-six-inch swedge nipple with a six-inch tee. There was another nipple for the upright gate to be used for release. When everything was in readiness, the apparatus was to be launched against the column of oil. This was the critical part of the operation.

A gate valve was placed over the casing to increase the diameter of the flow, leaving an area of "play" around the six-inch pipe. The carriage was then successfully drawn over the well by block and tackle in spite of the violent impact of the oil column. The assembly was drawn down by turning long screw bolts until the short nipple with an eight-inch tee could be attached. This done, and the oil freely flowing through the vertical pipe, the gate was gradually closed, diverting the stream into the horizontal pipe. This gave the crew a chance to work around the well, within the derrick, and place foundations for anchorage to hold down both the apparatus and the casings. Old rope was calked into the larger pipe around the six-inch and secured with heavy wrought-iron clamps, tightened with set screws to prevent the six-inch pipe from moving upward. Finally, the gate valve on the horizontal pipe was gradually closed and the flow of oil was completely shut off. It was a masterful operation and a demonstration of intelligence and ingenuity.[15]

There is little the layman can make of this, other than to recognize that somehow the driller has assembled irons and boards, pipes and valves—in what came to be called a "Christmas tree"—to stifle the geyser. In a sense Paul Bunyan sits on the well, with the uneasy presentiment that the oil might burst its casing and blow him sky-high.

As for the turntable hotel with running bourbon that Gib built, it seems not all that fanciful in the face of the real-life "Aladdin" stories of instant multimillionaires. After the Lucas gusher came in, a commissary clerk who had invested his $60 savings in four acres of land to keep from spending it sold his acreage for $100,000. A Negro farmer returning to Beaumont, where he owned a little farm he had been trying in vain to sell for $150, met a stranger who offered him $20,000 for his tract. He signed the deal, only to find a second stranger ready to pay $50,000. The new landowner made over the deed of sale to the new purchaser and cleared $30,000 within fifteen minutes. But the third owner shortly disposed of the farm for $100,000.[16] A pattern binding these word-of-mouth and newspaper stories arouses the suspicions of the folklorist. In a comparable episode, a reporter from the *St. Louis Post-Dispatch* getting off the train at Beaumont met a townsman who offered him a lease in the Bullock survey for $1,000. Not knowing the land, the reporter declined. Next day he met the landowner, who remarked that two hours after meeting the reporter he had sold the lease for $5,000, but within a few hours it was resold for $20,000.[17] Rags to riches was the leitmotif of these narratives. Oil spelled money, possessions, luxuries, heaped at one's feet by Dame Fortune. The oil fields not only created money but attracted money, to finance the purchase of land and equipment and storage and transportation and stock in corporations that sprouted like derricks on the flats. In the oil towns banks proliferated, silver dollars lay stacked like cordwood on their floors, waiting to be shoveled and counted, oilmen threw away five-dollar bills that got mixed in with their hundred-dollar, thousand-dollar, and five-thousand-dollar notes.

Accompanying sudden wealth in the boom towns came instant sin, available in the gambling houses, dance halls, saloons, and brothels that transformed quiet, churchgoing Beaumont into a Sodom with "the most notorious red-light district in the western hemisphere, if not the world."[18] One of the town's leading citizens often said that he would far rather have forsworn his gains from oil than see Beaumont reduced to a city of iniquity, and his thought permeates the oil-money legends: great wealth acquired through speculation, undeserved luck, or deception leads only to profligacy, dissolution, and ruin. "Coal Oil Johnny" became the prototype of the wastrel. Conversely, in the rags-to-riches formula the hard-working and thrifty American soul, conscious of the Puritan work ethic, keeps on the job even after acquiring a fortune in oil. A related pattern emphasizes the ludicrous gratification of simple wishes by the new oil millionaire. In a fourth category fall the unlucky who miss the oil strike seemingly by a sleight of fate but actually because they lack the persistence and determination that, in the American ethos, bring rewards. These cautionary tales point up one consistent moral: Money obtained without work is tainted money, and leads its owner to ruin.

Hence the fables of Coal Oil Johnnies. As defined by Mody Boatright, "A Coal-Oil Johnny is anyone who squanders an oil fortune, large or small."[19] The original of this character type was John Washington Steele, who in 1864 inherited a large sum of money in cash from his aunt and a farm on Oil Creek in Pennsylvania that yielded fat royalties on leases to oil drillers who kept bringing in lucrative wells. From three wells alone, struck in May 1864, Johnny received a thousand dollars a day. Just turning twenty-one, he proceeded to go on perhaps the biggest spending spree in American history and folklore. Within six months the unsophisticated farm boy had rid himself of a cool million. A contemporary newspaper article stated, "perhaps no man in the United States ever squandered as much money in the same space of time.[20] Teaming up with a suave sharper bearing the apposite name of Seth Slocum, who was going to show him big-city living, Steele moved into the fashionable Girard House in Philadelphia and went berserk. Paying all the bills, he outfitted himself, Slocum, and sundry hangers-on with the finest boots, hats, tailor-made suits, watches, and rings, and drove around Philadelphia in a flaming red carriage with brass knobs on whose sides were painted derricks, oil tanks, and wells spouting streams of oil in the shape of dollar signs. A coachman in red livery spanked a team of black horses in red finery while Johnny and his parasites reclined on silk cushions. "That's Coal Oil Johnny and his gang," a newsboy was supposed to have said when the careening coach splashed a mud puddle over an irate citizen, and the name stuck.

Johnny stayed in his cups while his money lasted, and dreamed up stratagems to dispose of his wealth. He would walk down the streets of Philadelphia with dollar bills stuck in his hatband and through his buttonholes and let urchins grab for them, or he would simply throw them out of his carriage. In the bars he paid for everyone's drinks, including the street loungers trailing him, and left a hundred-dollar bill on the counter as a memento. He smashed silk hats with his cane for fun, up to a hundred a day, and gave a ten-spot to their owners, who often had purchased old hats for a pittance anticipating Johnny's game. But in his autobiography Johnny denied some of the most glorious larks attributed to him. He never, so he said, left the Girard House in a huff when other guests complained of his cornet playing and moved into its rival, the Con-

"Coal Oil Johnny" standing at the site of the famous Hammond Well
From John Washington Steele, *Coal Oil Johnny: The Story of His Career as Told by Himself*

tinental Hotel—which, the story went, he rented for a day at eight thousand dollars plus salaries, expenses, and damages. Legend says he promptly fired the insolent clerk who had rebuffed him at the Continental and flung open the hostelry free of charge to all Philadelphia in a mad orgy. This tale of the wealthy guest, often a Jewish businessman, turned away by the hotel clerk, who then buys the hotel to fire the clerk, recurs in American folklore. Johnny also denied the anecdote that he had given a hack driver $3,500 to buy his own rig.

And how did it all end? In his brief heyday Coal Oil Johnny found himself the most talked-about and the most reviled character in the news. Editorials and sermons blasted his spendthrift ways. He became the subject of a popular song and lent his name to cigar and soap brands. But his bubble collapsed as suddenly as it had inflated. When the day came that the strongbox in the Girard House held no more of his banknotes, Johnny ran up bills against the million dollars he shortly expected William H. Wickham, future mayor of New York, to pay him for his farm. But Wickham withdrew the offer, claiming the wells had failed to produce sufficient oil, and instead brought suit against young Steele. Creditors and lawyers descended upon him, and in 1866 Johnny gave up and left the Pennsylvania oil country destitute and looking for a job. His conniving friend Seth Slocum died within two years. The remainder of his long life, till 1920, Johnny spent in penance and obscurity, as a sober teamster and baggage agent.[21]

No moral could be plainer, and it was brought home repeatedly in the folklore of undeserved oil fortunes. A pioneer oilman, Chris Schmoker, made the point succinctly: "People went crazy. They didn't have a lick of sense. They were left worse off than ever after it was over. All their horse sense was gone, and they were unwilling to work hard like a man ought to in order to earn his living."[22]

In the boom town of Ranger in west Texas, the famous McCleskey well of 1917 brought sudden opulence, together with a string of comic stories about the newly rich known as "McCleskeys" and their tragic counterparts, the "Coal Oil Johnnies." A farmer who had never seen more than a few hundred dollars at a time signed a lease on his land to an oil company for $30,000. He and his equally hard-working wife went on a spree. They bought a bright red touring car—somehow in these tales the vehicle must be red—and drove to New York to indulge in theater, champagne parties, furs, and jewelry. On returning to Ranger they found their bank account overdrawn but drove on home, confidently expecting royalties from the well the company was drilling close to a gusher. In a few days the farmer saw workmen sealing off the well. "We're plugging it; it's a dry hole," he was told. Sorrowfully he gazed at his weed-grown fields and drab dwelling.[23]

In a variation, another farm couple decided to continue their simple ways after oil was found on their land, and to give presents to their relatives. But their next of kin took to quarreling over the size of their gifts and thanked Zeke and his wife only with sour looks and sharp words. Zeke took to wandering in the woods, and then his mind wandered. Bringing home three thousand silver dollars, he sorted them in piles on the floor, counted one heap, saying, "This is for Sallie," then waved her away, counted another, "This is for Herman," then waved him away. With a gleaming eye, he repeated the little game for all his relatives, then scattered the piles, then began counting again, "This is for Sallie, this is for Herman."[24]

Behind the Coal Oil Johnny stories lay practical considerations. Owning land on which drillers had found oil did not guarantee limitless wealth. The wells could produce little, or they could run dry after a high production, or the price of petroleum could drop. At one point oil sold at Spindletop for three cents a barrel and water for six dollars a barrel. So the lucky landowner needed to keep his business wits about him. Accordingly, as Boatright points out, the rags-to-riches sagas, which exaggerate the farmer's poverty before the oil strike and his wealth after it, applaud the industrious who maintain their sanity and balance and will to work. An early settler of Desdemona, south of Ranger in central Texas, sold his farm outright for a quarter of a million dollars when the oil companies came in, and then took

The famous Lucas well at Spindletop, Texas, which came in on January 10, 1901. Captain Anthony Lucas thereby proved the feasibility of drilling on salt domes in flat country, and opened up Texas as a major oil-producing area.

a job as a roughneck at five dollars a day helping around the well on his former land. "I can save the principal and live on the five-spot," he told his cronies.[25] Or again there was "Mrs. Slop," as the newspapers dubbed her, folk heroine for a day during the Spindletop madness. She was actually a garbage collector in Beaumont named Mrs. Sullivan, who sold a lease on her little pig farm to an oilman for $35,000. Next morning she was driving around Beaumont in her old wagon making her garbage rounds.[26]

Then there were the "McCleskeys" — actually antedating the McCleskey gusher and circulating from the very first oil boom at Titusville, Pennsylvania, in 1859 — the heartwarming anecdotes of farmer folk who in their moment of ecstasy satisfied simple wants. When her well came in, one Oil Creek woman ordered a bottle of olives from Pittsburgh, saying that all rich people ate olives. A farmer with thirteen hounds announced that he would use his oil income first to buy them meat and second to buy himself a red automobile (red again!) in which his friends could ride if there was room after the dogs had jumped in. An east Texas farmer cashed his first oil check and then hastened to the store to buy a forty-dollar Stetson and a five-dollar bunch of bananas. The hat was a status symbol and the bananas a special luxury. One chap, overnight worth nearly a million, said, "I'm going to build a house on the Stephenville road so I can see what's going on." Some farmwives, on learning the good news, took dire vengeance on the objects they had been slave to over the years. One, bent

"A farm family of colored people made wealthy by the oil well in the background. The ancient buggy was succeeded by a modern limousine."
From Boyce House, *Oil Boom*

over a dishpan, deliberately upset it on the kitchen floor, went to the wood-shed to fetch a stone hammer, and then smashed every dish in the house. Another burned, and a third tore into tatters, the family's homespun clothing.[27]

But of all the McCleskey legends, one concerning a new axe showed the most vitality. Back in the Oil Creek days, a farmwife chopping wood asked her husband, after he rushed in to tell her oil had been found on their land, if they could buy a new axe, as the old one was full of nicks.[28] An old nester of Desdemona who struck it rich set out to buy the finest axe he could find, and then announced his intention to run a grindstone with a gasoline engine, saying, "I'm going to cut some post oaks just to see how a sharp axe feels."[29] As it happened, the author who reported this last instance, Boyce House, earlier in his book *Were You in Ranger?* had attached a similar saying to the wife of John Mc-Cleskey, the thrifty farmer on whose property the first oil well in the great Ranger field blew in. John asked his wife what she would like him to purchase for her with their new means. She responded, "Well, the blade of the old axe has a nick and I would like to have a new one to chop kindling with."[30] This was a woman who had worked hard all her life and taken in washing for a little extra cash.

The late Mody Boatright became interested in the veracity of the tale and ran down variants from Beaumont and Vann. A neighbor of the McCleskeys, in a taped interview, doubted that "Aunt Cordie" had ever uttered the remark. An oilman from the Ranger area also questioned the incident, but recalled "an old West Virginia story" of three sons of a hard-working widow who went to town to celebrate after oil was located on her farm. During the spree they tried to think what to get their mother, and one suggested a new axe.[31] Clearly this is a legendary episode, traveling across the oil fields from Pennsylvania to Texas, and in its course sanctifying the industrious, frugal American farmer and his wife who will employ their new fortune first of all to acquire a basic farm implement. In other "McCleskeys," the farmer refuses to allow the oil company to commence drilling operations until he has harvested his fall crop.

Legends of wealth from oil wells harmonize with legends of the driller in stressing rewards for the hard-working and deserving, not for the idle profligate.

Railroaders

A Brave Engineer

The rise of the railroads as a major transportation industry in the decades following the Civil War called into being an army of men to run and service the trains that moved passengers and freight across the nation. Engineers, firemen, brakemen, Pullman porters, conductors, switchmen, mechanics in the round-house, stationmasters, dispatchers, all shared in the fraternity of the rails, as did the hoboes who rode the rails. But no folklorist appeared to do for rail-roaders what George Korson did for coal miners and Mody Boatright for oil drillers. In *A Treasury of Railroad Folklore* (1953) Benjamin A. Botkin and Alvin F. Harlow put together a gener-ous sampling of anecdotes and reminis-cences about the days of steam, but these belong largely in the realm of personal history, the context of lore rather than the lore itself.

Better collected are the songs by and about railroaders, some written by Tin Pan Alley songsmiths and based on tra-ditional verses, some composed by en-gine wipers and boomers and elevated to sheet-music status. These songs in-clude ballads of train wrecks and other railroad scenes; work songs accompany-ing the beat of laborers—often Irish and Negro—as they tamp ties and line track; lyrics of hoboes grabbing rides on the rails; symbolical and allegorical songs comparing life to a train ride or em-ploying snatches of train imagery; and blues and instrumental pieces inspired by the sight and sound of trains. These folk, hillbilly, and commercial songs pre-sented several viewpoints, sometimes of the engineer or other crew member, sometimes of the passengers or riders on the rails, sometimes of workers on the track, and sometimes of observers watching the train speed on its journey.[1]

One figure emerged from this amor-phous train lore to symbolize the Amer-ican railroadman in the folk and popu-lar imagination: John Luther "Casey" Jones. Although he was fairly well known and talked about in railroad circles, Casey did not inspire legendary tales, nor was he, like Gib Morgan, a story-teller. His folk fame depends on a bal-lad written upon the circumstances of his death by Wallis Saunders, a Negro roundhouse engine wiper for the Illinois Central. The manner of meeting death is always a key episode in the forma-tion of heroic legend, and secondary incidents can readily be adjusted to sup-port the capstone. Casey Jones died at 3:52 A.M. on April 30, 1900, at the throttle of his engine, Number 382 on the renowned Cannonball Express of the Illinois Central running from Chicago to New Orleans. Seeing the red lights of a caboose loom up in the darkness ahead of him at Vaughan, Mississippi, Casey barely had time to warn his Negro fireman, Sim Webb, to jump from the cab, while he grabbed for the brakes. When the wreckage was cleared, Casey was found dead with one hand on the air-brake lever and the other on the throttle (or the broken end of the whistle cord). No heroic-age champion could have died more fittingly, in the heat of action, spurning the chance to save his own life so that he could protect his crew and passengers. And none else were hurt, so Casey preserved his record of never having caused a fatality during his career as engineer. There were the further facts that Casey had taken on a run immediately after finishing his regular run, to substitute for a sick fellow engineer on the Memphis-to-Canton leg, and that he had made up all but two of the ninety-five minutes the new train was running behind "the advertised." Given the glamour and swagger of the railroad engineer running his pet engine on a crack express at the turn of the century, before railroad practices and procedures had become routine, the ingredients for ballad success are all present.

In terms of folklore, Casey Jones exemplifies the unwritten code of the railroad engineer, and he is the hero of a folk ballad that achieved a sensational popularity when adapted into a Tin Pan Alley song. The code called for devotion to duty in the face of hazards and obstacles and personal risk; protection of the train and the lives aboard, as a ship captain looked after his ship and its people; adherence to the advertised schedule as a point of honor; pride in his engine and skill in its handling, as a cowboy knew and cherished his horse; faith in railroading, and consequently, in the industrial future of the nation.

All these attributes John Luther Jones possessed and displayed to the full. Born March 14, 1863, somewhere in the back country of southwest Missouri, at thirteen he moved with his family to western Kentucky, where his father taught school in the hamlet of Cayce, pronounced like his own nickname, Casey, which derived from the village. Three years later he journeyed to Columbus, Kentucky, a

Casey Jones
Frontispiece in Fred J. Lee, *Casey Jones, Epic of the American Railroad*

terminus on the Mobile and Ohio line, and there worked his way into railroading, as telegraph operator, brakeman, and fireman. Finally in 1890, when he had entered the employ of the Illinois Central, he graduated to the right-hand side of the cab as engineer. All Casey's three brothers too became strapping six-foot engineers. Himself six foot four, sturdy of build, with a long head, firm jaw, clean handsome features, and shiny black hair, Casey in his photographs exudes a youthful strength and determination.

A biographical legend took shape following Casey's death at the throttle that filled in the outlines of heroic saga. There was his love affair with his engine, Number 638, which he first beheld in Chicago at the World's Columbian Exposition of 1893, in the exhibit of the

Illinois Central Railroad in the Transportation Building. (Casey had to part from 638 when he assumed the Cannonball run.) Number 638 belonged to the Rogers consolidation, 2-8-0 class, the figures standing for two pilot wheels, eight drivers, and no trailers. A gleaming black monster designed for heavy freight, it captured Casey's heart at first sight, and he wangled permission to drive it from the fair with right of way, except for first-class trains, across five divisions to Water Valley, Mississippi, the terminal from which he was operating. In those days of railroading, engines and their equipment possessed their own individuality, for instance in the engine whistle, personalized by each hogger. Casey's whistle was made of six thin tubes bound together, the shortest half the length of the longest. When, in the art known as "quilling," he sounded six chimes on his whistle, its piercing calliopelike tones ringing across the countryside informed all hearers that Casey Jones and Number 638 were hurtling down the tracks. With his own hog, his loyal fireman, his pet whistle, Casey did resemble the knight of old on his charger, carrying his prized weapon, attended by his man. Wives and sweethearts bridled at the affection, endearments, and feminine names engineers bestowed on their hogs.[2] On at least one occasion Casey talked to 638 as if it were animate: "Good old gal! You know you can make it. Don't fail me now!" slapping the cab with his palm as if he were caressing a spirited filly. According to his biographer, Fred J. Lee, Casey was exhorting 638 to breast Bolivar Hill, the steepest grade between Jackson and Water Valley, without doubling engines, that is, hooking on a second locomotive to help drag an extra-heavy load of freight up the incline.[3] But to fulfill this boast to the yard crew, Casey resorted to a daredevil stratagem: he screwed down the pop valve, so that his hog was actually carrying 195 pounds of steam when the gauge registered 175, the maximum permitted on that class of engine by strict company regulation.

This daredevil trait becomes a factor to consider in the still-open question as to Casey's responsibility for the fatal wreck. An official report laid the blame on Jones for failing to observe the flagman placed a thousand feet ahead of the caboose, or to hear the torpedo exploded on the track thirty telegraph poles before the stationary freight cars, two devices required by safety regulations of the company. The Illinois Central attributed Casey's negligence to the fatigue of the double run and the engineer's craze for speed—he must have gone a hundred miles an hour on some stretches and was probably hitting seventy-five when he saw the caboose and slowed to thirty-five before the impact. But Sim Webb the fireman saw no flag and was unsure of hearing torpedoes. In terms of legend making, the posthumous debate enhanced Casey's status as the self-sacrificing hero maligned by the blackguarding corporation. Biographer Lee supplied other folklore touches in the dreams and premonitions of Casey's death by his sister Emma, the ballad writer Wallis Saunders, and fellow engineer Colie Chandler. After Casey's death, Negro firemen on the

The Famous No. 638
This photograph, taken shortly after Casey Jones was assigned to the engine, attests his pride in his new acquisition. Casey is shown seated with hand on throttle. The man standing in the gangway is J. W. (Bull) McKinnie, who fired for Casey for two years.
From Fred J. Lee, *Casey Jones, Epic of the American Railroad*

Mississippi division of the Illinois Central kept hearing his warning whistle when their trains passed over the site of the collision. A stand of corn grew alongside the death-spot every summer, self-seeded from the kernels scattered over the ground when engine 382 plowed into the rear of the freight cars.

Americans bought more than a million records of the ballad of "Casey Jones" in the years before World War I, and they have kept on listening to recordings and singing the piece, as a popular song, as a folksong, and in parodies, up until the present day. In consequence, Americans know the name and fate of Casey Jones very well and link him with such well-known pseudo-folk figures as Paul Bunyan, Johnny Appleseed, and Buffalo Bill. Yet apart from the ballad the man was but a shadow, and in 1924 *Adventure* magazine posed the question, "Did Casey Jones ever exist?" Fred J. Lee's full-length biography interweaves imaginary situations and conversations with a close knowledge of railroading life, and

contributes to the blur of fact and fancies surrounding Casey.

In folkloric terms, he is primarily the ballad hero, and the history of the ballad has shaped the image of the fearless engineer. This history falls into four parts: first, a tradition of Negro railroad songs about a loose-living, fast-driving engineer; second, a composition drawing from this tradition but specifically applied to the wreck at Vaughan by Wallis Saunders, the Negro engine wiper who knew Casey, which launched a string of folk variants; third, a vaudeville version with a rollicking chorus, published in 1903 by T. Lawrence Siebert who wrote the words and Eddie Newton who furnished the music, and popularized by a vaudevillian brother act of Bert and Frank Leighton, whose other brother Bill was an engineer on the Illinois Central; and fourth, many parodies, some highly ribald, of the popular hit. On a collateral line can be mentioned other railroad ballads about train wrecks which have won folk audiences and display general similarities.

The Casey Jones ballad begins as a Negro folksong and ends as a white sheet-music song. With the advent of the railroad, blacks quickly developed familiarity with the iron horse and filled jobs on the train and roundhouse crews. They became "fascinated by the train-song," according to Howard W. Odum and Guy B. Johnson, the sociologist collectors of *The Negro and His Songs,* and talked much about holding responsible positions on trains as engineers or brakemen and dealing with emergencies.[4] Railroad incidents and images entered the floating balladry of the Negro repertoire and provided a reservoir of song elements from which Wallis Saunders could have drawn in composing "Casey Jones." John and Alan Lomax have identified some of these ballads and ballad snatches: "The Wreck of the Six-Wheel Driver," about engineer Joseph Mickel who bumped head on into another locomotive, with its mournful refrain, "For I've been on the Charley [or Chollo] so long" (been on the bum); "Ol' John Brown," about a fireman whose "back's most broke/But he must shovel coal to make the engine smoke"; and "Charley Snyder," about another "good engineer" who told his fireman "All he needed was water and coal."[5] When the Lomaxes visited Canton in 1933 to interview Wallis Saunders, they learned that he had died, but were able to talk with a friend who had worked with him in the roundhouse, seventy-year-old Cornelius Steen, and recorded from Steen a railroad song from Kansas City about "Jimmie Jones":

On a Sunday mornin' it begins to rain,
'Round de curve spied a passenger train,
On the pilot lay po' Jimmie Jones,
He's a good ol' porter, but he's dead an' gone,
Dead an' gone, dead an' gone,
Kase he's been on de cholly so long.[6]

According to Steen, this song so appealed to Saunders that he tacked on other verses, and after Casey's death changed Jimmie Jones to Casey Jones and the porter to an engineer. A song text about Casey that the Lomaxes recorded in Texas, which they title "Nachul-born Easman," reveals the darker undercurrents of the "been on de cholly" theme. "Easman" is a Negro folk term for a wandering hustler who scrounges off women, and the chorus sets down his brag:

Oh, my honey, who tol' you so?
Nachul-born easman, ev'ywhere I go.[7]

The song describes Casey's wreck, but in a manner quite unlike the well-known ballad. Casey ignores the flags being waved by trainmen trying to stop him as he races to make up lost time, and he tells his fireman they are running on a double track and will not hit the locomotive speeding toward them. The singer explained that Casey in his cups saw two tracks where only one existed. No details of the crash are given, and the ballad ends with bite and irony:

When Casey's wife heard dat Casey was dead,
She was in de kitchen, makin' up bread,
She says, "Go bed, chilluns, an' hol' yo' breath,
You'll all get a pension at yo' daddy's death.

Casey called up his wife and son,
Willed them an engine, had never been run.
When Casey's son did come of age,
Says, "Daddy's done willed me a narrow gauge."[8]

In a later collection of folksongs, the Lomaxes printed further mocking verses about the reactions to Casey's death as chanted by Negro blues singers:

When the women all heard that Casey was dead,
They went home and re-ragged in red,
Come a-slippin' an' slidin' up and down the street,
In their loose mother-hubbards and their stockin' feet.

Here come the biggest boy, comin' right from school,
Hollerin' and cryin' like a doggone fool,
She say "Quit cryin' boy, an' don't do that,
You got another papa on the same damn track."[9]

A five-stanza text collected by Odum and Johnson, published in 1925, also displays a casual structure and interpolates sexual innuendoes. Only three verses deal with the wreck. The last again suggests Casey's promiscuity:

Womens in Kansas, all dressed in red,
Got de news dat Casey was dead.
De womens in Jackson, all dressed in black,
Said, in fact, he was a cracker-jack.[10]

If Wallis Saunders drew upon the black tradition of ironic train songs in his composition about Casey, so too the white ragtime music-makers Siebert and Newton in their sheet-music version dipped into this folk stream. Lawrence Siebert apparently had heard "Been on the Cholly So Long," and with his partner, the piano player Eddie Newton, placed Casey on a Western railroad and added the notorious verse in which the not-so-mournful widow tells her children to hush their crying because they have another daddy on the Salt Lake line.[11]

Since the vaudeville version incorporated folk elements, it attracted folksingers and parodists and encouraged folk variants, in a recycling process. Casey the popular ballad hero turns out differently from the moral strait-laced teetotaler of Fred Lee's biography. He is the easman and railroad boomer who has women all along the line, and his wife plays the same two-timing game. Whenever the song hit was played, Casey's widow reportedly left the room in high dudgeon, and eventually threatened suit against the music publishers.

Casey's legend somehow ran off the hero track. After his death the legend of the brave engineer seemed well under way. His successor as hog on the Cannonball, Henry A. Norton, recalled that Casey had three passions: "devotion to his engine, a desire to maintain schedules, and a distinctive type of locomotive whistle."[12] Another engineer lauded Casey's ability to get more mileage from a tankful of water than any other hogger on the track, and cracked that "when Jones ran for water he took his train right with him."[13] But there were innuendoes about Casey's private life that began to surface. In the text ascribed to Saunders and printed by Lee, the opening stanza applies to Casey what could be considered a derogatory epithet:

Come all you rounders if you want to hear
The story told of a brave engineer;
Casey Jones was the rounder's name,
A high right-wheeler of mighty fame.[14]

"Rounder" or "boomer" refers to the itinerant railroader moving from one railroad line to another, as the oil boomer migrated from one oil-field boom town to another. A short step leads from the rounder to the hustler or easman, who is on the prowl looking for women, liquor, and gambling joints. In a note Fred Lee is quick to remove any suggested taint upon his hero. "Rounder," he conceives, is intended affectionately. Casey worked for only two railroad companies in his life, whereas his younger brother Frank, sometimes also called Casey, did hog out West, and could accurately be called a rounder. Perhaps, Lee opines, this was the Casey of whom Siebert and Newton were thinking when they retained the term "rounder" and gave the ballad a Far West setting.[15] When the two traveling vaudevillians heard the tune and some of the words hummed by Negro youths in New Orleans, Siebert wrote out comic lyrics and Newton set the melody to ragtime. The partners presented their piece at the Ship Café in Venice, California, outside Los Angeles, where the Three Leightons, another vaudeville team with a railroad background, heard it and performed it successfully at the Orpheum Theater in Los Angeles in 1909.[16] From then on there was no stopping "Casey Jones."[17]

Other Brave Engineers

While Casey Jones represents the devotion and heroism of the railroad engineer, he is not *sui generis*. Only his name has reached the public, but other brave engineers whose qualities and fates are much like Casey's are memorialized in balladry. The trainsong second only to "Casey Jones" in popularity, "The Wreck of Old 97," also deals with the death in the cab of a hogger bent on making up for lost time, in this case on a run on September 27, 1903, from Monroe to Spencer, Virginia. The engineer, Joe Broady, hit a curve on a downhill trestle at full speed:

He was found in a wreck with his hand on the throttle
And was scalded to death by the steam.

The message came in on a telegram wire,
And this is what it said,
"There's a brave engineer lying over Danville.
But he's lying over Danville dead."[18]

Outside Hinton, West Virginia, only five miles from the Big Bend Tunnel where John Henry swung his hammer against the steam drill, a landslide covered the track of the Chesapeake and Ohio Railroad on October 23, 1890, and caused the engine of the Fast Flying Vestibule to turn over. The ballad of "The Wreck on the C & O" also celebrates an heroic engineer who bid his fireman jump and stayed to meet his fate:

I want to die on the engine I love, 143.

Or in a variant:

His head upon the firebox door, the burning flames rolled o'er:
"I'm glad I was born an engineer to die on the C & O Road."

Another text pronounces the people's judgment on the brave engineer:

There never was a braver man than Georgia Alley born
To die upon the C & O Road, one reckless July morn.[19]

And yet another ballad, "The C & O Wreck" (or "The Seno Wreck"), based on a tragedy caused by a bridge collapsing under a train at Guyandotte, West Virginia, on January 1, 1913, echoes the lament:

Ed Webber was the engineer,
A brave and faithful man;
He went down on his engine
With the throttle in his hand.[20]

The master workman versus the businessman

Certain common attitudes linked the early cowboy, lumberjack, miner, oil driller, and railroad engineer. Each displayed pride in his work skills and fearlessness in the face of danger, and expressed these traits in songs and tales. Further evidence of their common outlooks can be seen in the interchange of ballads between one occupation and another. A similar case could, I am sure, be made for tales, were they more substantially collected. Miners, cowboys, and railroaders have variously appropriated the mournful ditty recounting the trials of a particular occupation: "Only a Miner," "Only a Cowboy," "Only a Brakeman," or "Only a Hogger." While the pieces as a whole may differ, they contain free-floating stanzas that match up.

Lumberjacks, cowboys, and railroaders all relished song narratives describing miserable work conditions experienced in lumber camps, or on buffalo hunts, or along the trail, or with railroad outfits. Deluded by flattering promises, they journey to distant points—to French Canada in the original Maine-woods song, which in its turn derived from an English sea song that built upon an English love song—and find the food, bedding, and facilities intolerable. The lumberjacks complain of "jabbering Frenchmen"; the buffalo-hunting cowboys of mosquitoes, fleas, and lice; the railroader of the heavy work striking a ten-pound hammer upon a drill. These songs carry the titles "Canady-I-O,"

"Michigan-I-O," and "The Jolly Lumberman" for the lumberjacks; "The Buffalo Skinners" and "The Buffalo Range" for the cowboys; and "Way Out in Idaho" and "In the State of Arkansas" for the railroaders. "The Cowboy's Lament," or "The Streets of Laredo," the classic cowboy folksong, has in the course of its innumerable variations penetrated other occupations and professions, including those of the lumberjack and the miner. Since lumberjack and cowboy shared the same kind of transcendental religious sentiment, they could share a ballad expressing that viewpoint. So rarely reported a lumberjack song as "Silver Jack," known in only two texts, one from a clipping (see pp. 166–68), has surfaced in the cowboy repertoire in the Fifes' collection *Ballads of the Great West.*

My thesis up to now has followed a fairly straightforward line. The period of unprecedented economic and industrial growth following the Civil War bred an occupational folklore that reflected the values of work and wealth. But this period is characterized by a deep ambivalence in its economic loyalties. Work to be sure remained honorable, but as the economy shifted from an agricultural to an industrial base, from handcrafts to machine-made goods, from personal buyer-seller relationships to the vast impersonal network of mass distribution, the onlooker and even the participant grew puzzled as to who was doing the work. The owner-manager on the telephone? The human automaton on the assembly line? Or was it the machine that was actually doing the work? Nor was wealth so simply defined as in the past; it had become a complicated matter of securities and stock shares in vast invisible corporations. When the cowboy received his pay in gold coins at the end of the trail, he knew just where he stood in respect to work skills and monetary compensation, and one day he might buy cattle and land with his gold and become a rancher. But the industrial age gradually swallowed up the master workman and replaced him with two combative and unequal figures, the capitalist-banker-businessman-tycoon and the workingman. Corporation and labor union locked horns in combat. A series of bloody strikes, such as the Homestead strike in the steel industry in 1892 and the Pullman strike in the railroad industry in 1894, poisoned the atmosphere. Both the capitalist and the worker acquired unfavorable images: the capitalist as exploiter and the worker as radical.

Folklore reflects the ambivalence issuing from the tensions in the Economic Life-style that were clearly apparent by the turn of the century, as well as the homogeneity of the master-workman traditions dating from the 1870s, 80s, and 90s. In the twentieth century the occupational hero fell somewhere between capital and labor and could go either way. To the Wobblies, Casey Jones turned out to be a scab. Qualities that endeared Casey to capital besmirched him with labor, who marked him as a company man. With the rise of the radical labor movement, climaxed in the years before World War I by the formation of the Wobblies—the Industrial Workers of the World—Casey's star descended. In the words of Carl Sandburg, "Casey Jones" invited parody by "lumberjacks, college girls, aviators, and doughboys."[1] The Wobblies elevated their own martyr-hero, Joe Hill, inveterate foe of exploitative capitalism and himself a ballad writer. One of his songs, "Casey Jones, the Union Scab," written in 1911 and printed in one edition after another of the IWW song book, portrays Casey as a scab operating his engines during a strike and landing in hell. Sometimes he scabbed on the Southern Pacific Railroad, but once he turned up on the Duluth, Mesabi, and Northern Railroad, which continued to carry iron ore when the IWW struck it in 1916.[2] A version collected from tradition in Nevada in 1940, by way of California, has reduced the original eight stanzas to six by omitting two verses in which Casey scabs on the angels in heaven and is fired down the Golden Stair by the angels' union. One intriguing verbal corruption changes Hill's "They said it wasn't fair/ For Casey Jones to go around a-scabbing everywhere" to "go round in his cabin everywhere."[3] In altering "scabbing" to "cabin" the folk clearly deviated from the ideology of radical labor.

Here is Joe Hill's anti-Casey piece:

CASEY JONES—THE UNION SCAB

The workers on the S.P. line to strike sent out a call;
But Casey Jones, the engineer, he wouldn't strike at all;
His boiler it was leaking, and its drivers on the bum,
And his engine and its bearings, they were all out of plumb.

Chorus:
Casey Jones kept his junk pile running;
Casey Jones was working double time;
Casey Jones got a wooden medal,
For being good and faithful on the S.P. line.

The workers said to Casey: "Won't you help us win this strike?"
But Casey said: "Let me alone, you'd better take a hike."
Then Casey's wheezy engine ran right off the worn-out track,
And Casey hit the river with an awful crack.

Chorus:
Casey Jones hit the river bottom;
Casey Jones broke his blooming spine,
Casey Jones was an Angeleno,
He took a trip to heaven on the S.P. line.

When Casey Jones got up to heaven to the Pearly Gate,
He said: "I'm Casey Jones, the guy that pulled the S.P. freight."
"You're just the man," said Peter; "our musicians went on strike;
You can get a job a-scabbing any time you like."

Chorus:
Casey Jones got a job in heaven;
Casey Jones was doing mighty fine;
Casey Jones went scabbing on the angels,
Just like he did to workers on the S.P. line.

The angels got together, and they said it wasn't fair,
For Casey Jones to go around a-scabbing everywhere.
The angel Union No. 23, they sure were there,
And they promptly fired Casey down the Golden Stair.

Chorus:
Casey Jones went to Hell a-flying.
"Casey Jones," the Devil said, "Oh fine;
Casey Jones, get busy shoveling sulphur—
That's what you get for scabbing on the S.P. line."[4]

There was yet another side to Casey, the sporting man, already implicit in the early Negro railroad stanzas about the "easman" and being "on de cholly." This development, traceable in the off-color ballads and tales of genuine folk currency that rarely see print, wins Casey and some other folktypes admiration for their sexual prowess, as an extension of their *machismo*. In myriad obscene parodies and couplets sung at drinking parties by college students, servicemen, and hardhats, Casey emerges as a phallic hero. An extra stanza left out of printed variants of the train-wreck ballad suggested this dimension of Casey:

Casey said before he died,
"There's two more women I'd like to try."
"Tell me what they can be?"
"A cross-eyed nigger and a Japanee."[5]

From this suggestion developed an independent bawdy ballad celebrating Casey's phallic prowess:

Casey Jones was a son of a bitch,
Parked his train at the whorehouse switch,
Walked up the steps with his cock in his hand,
Said, "I'm gonna screw a hundred whores or I ain't a man."

He lined a hundred whores up against the wall,
Said, "Before I'm done I'm gonna screw them all."
He screwed ninety-eight until his cock turned blue,
Then he backed off and jacked off and screwed the other two.[6]

A chorus for one of the variants goes:

Freight train boogie, movin' down the line,
Freight train boogie, a-w-w-w-w-l the time.[7]

The supervirile railroad engineer is by no means unique among occupational folktypes. We have already seen the sexual imagery manifest in the song of the cowboy riding his bucking broncho. Sexual symbolism can be applied to each occupation: the railroader with his hand on the throttle, the cowboy shooting his gun or mounting his horse, the lumberjack swinging his axe and the miner his pick, the oil driller paying out his string of tools into the borehole from which surges forth the precious liquid. Gib Morgan lowered his enormous pet snake into the hole and named his giant assistant Big Toolie! In each case the master workman assumes the role of the mighty lover. Instead of representing the solid economic virtues of sobriety, piety, thrift, love of family, and support of church and community, he becomes the gay deceiver, the libertine and profligate. In this second role he does indeed represent the underside of the Gilded Age, the public and private immorality of the era that Vernon Louis Parrington called "the Great Barbecue." And of course the occupational workers in their after-work stretches did relax in the brothels, bars, and gambling houses of Sin City.

Another folkloric mirroring of the ambivalence of the period can be seen in the manufacture of giantesque folk heroes dramatizing the achievements of

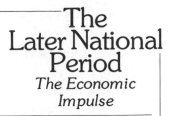

a particular occupation. How fitting that the age of manufacturing should produce synthetic demigods! Paul Bunyan, the oversized lumberjack, was the first and the archetypal comic demigod, rising from the merest trickle of oral anecdote to the position of nationally celebrated colossus, mainly through the efforts of an advertising manager for the Red River Lumber Company, William B. Laughead, who mixed little stories about Bunyan with sales pitches for lumber in promotional booklets. After first seeing print in a Detroit newspaper column in 1910, Paul spread his wings in the Laughead booklets, which commenced in 1914, and made his indelible mark in full-sized volumes in the 1920s. Paul inspired a gallery of imitators with even fewer folk credentials than he himself possessed: Pecos Bill, the giant cowboy, riding a mountain lion and swinging a rattlesnake for a lariat; Febold Feboldson, the giant Kansas farmer, twisting cyclones into knots; Joe Magarac, the giant Pittsburgh steelworker, squeezing molten iron through his fists to form steel rails; and others of the same ilk, who in the 1930s all found eager readers for their puerile adventures. These figures were created out of whole cloth by writers and promoters, in the process I have called fakelore, since they never entered into oral traditions, either before or after the publication of their deeds. Still, they do constitute a conscious imitation of folklore patterns, maladroit as they may appear to a later, better-informed generation, and they do respond to the values of the later decades of the Economic Life-style. As the Red River Lumber Company sponsored Paul Bun-

yan, so did the United States Steel Corporation underwrite Joe Magarac. The title of one Paul Bunyan volume designated him as a "Work Giant," and this was the theme the corporations stressed in the promotion of their heroes: productivity, ingenuity, monumental output, veneered with a happy glow of on-the-job fun and frolic. The mass media and the mass culture, in the forms of widely sold books—often written and illustrated for children—Walt Disney cartoon films, newspaper and magazine features, and Paul Bunyan statues and carnivals, brought those jolly work giants to the attention of the public.

Paul Bunyan made by far the broadest penetration into the American consciousness. From 1939 to 1941 I subscribed to a news-clipping bureau for references in the nation's press to Old Paul and was deluged with a flood of clipsheets about the mountainous logger.[8] The journalistic copy revealed the symbolic, if not the folkloric, role of Paul Bunyan in American life, and the multiple, sometimes conflicting and ambivalent purposes that he served. He emerges as the pseudo-folk hero of twentieth-century mass culture, pressed into service to exemplify "the American spirit." To different vested interests he offered different meanings. The *Daily Worker* and author Ida Virginia Turney, whose *Paul Bunyan, the Work Giant* was published in Oregon in 1941, perceived in Bunyan the spirit of the American workingman. The *Daily Worker* ran a longish piece on "Paul Bunyan, Child of Rebellion" in its issues for April 9, 1939, and April 20, 1941, the first slanted toward children, which announced, "This legendary hero of the American worker lives forever in the stories of the tall-timber country of the West." An introductory paragraph hailed him as the "sinew and brain, courage and soul of America's frontier folk," while a tantalizing reference to "richly obscene" tales intrigues the folklorist, for the published narratives about Paul are sugary pap. The *Worker*'s feature writer also alluded to tales that "roundly ridicule the swivel-headed boss," sidestepping the fact that Paul is a boss-workman himself.

On the other hand, the lumber companies and some artists admired Paul as symbolizing the efficiency of American capitalism and the happiness of the workingman-as-potential-capitalist. The *New York Times Magazine* commented on March 23, 1941, discussing new logging techniques under the caption "Modern Paul Bunyans":

There is more machinery in the woods now than there was in the days of Paul Bunyan, but the machinery has not changed the men. Lumberjacks are still cut to Bunyan's measure—strong men who love their jobs because the work is dangerous.

A story in the Tacoma, Washington, *News-Tribune* for September 9, 1941, associated Paul Bunyan with the logging industry's successful endeavors to meet the demands of national defense:

Paul Bunyan, mythical giant doer of big jobs, and symbol of the West Coast lumber industry, is enjoying a great revival in 1941. Never since the year he worked so hard he sweat out the Great Salt Lake, according to the loggers, has he done more big things all at once. Typical of Paul's productions for national defense are Douglas fir keel timbers for the navy's new fleet of minesweepers, of which a few are pictured on a truck-haul. Each stick is 110 feet long, 16½ inches wide and 10½ inches thick. "Just two axhandles short of being as long as Paul Bunyan's backbone," says the oldtime timberman.

The graphic and visual arts, from sculpture to woodcarving, music, drama, choral operetta, ballet, radio, and films, all explored the Paul Bunyan theme and produced their interpretations. An heroic sculpture of Paul representing Efficiency attracted considerable attention at the World's Fair of 1939 in New York. Under headings such as "Myth Enlivens New York Fair," a number of newspapers carried an illustration of Paul and Babe with these explanatory lines: "Portraying vigor and efficiency, Paul Bunyan, genial and legendary titan of the north-woods, is the subject of this sculpture by Edmond Amateis. As one of an American folk-lore group, it will adorn the façade of the Health Building of the New York World's Fair 1939." With him is shown his ox, Blue Babe, and Shanty John, a woodsman friend perched on the giant's arm.

Thus the proletarian and capitalistic readings of the meaning of Bunyan. Other artists, journalists, and promoters saw in Old Paul the invincible brute strength of America, a performer of enormous tasks, a braggart and a blowhard, a fantasy, a deified woodsman, and a gargantuan comic dummy useful to

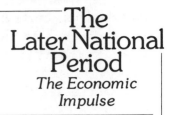

resort owners in attracting tourists. No clear image emerges from the written and artistic commentary. Paul the master workman serves both capital and labor.

The folklore of the extractive occupations that burgeoned in the 1870s, 80s, and 90s celebrated the master workman rather than the businessman or the laborer. What did folklore think of the businessman?

Through much of American history the businessman has suffered from a poor press among the folk. In popular and folk symbolism he has suggested the special interests, the robber barons, the stock manipulators, the exploiters of consumers and laborers, the builders of monopolies. Jefferson attacked Hamilton and the Federalists in the election of 1800 as the money interests, because of Hamilton's funding schemes that wedded government and business. Jackson successfully toppled the Whigs in the election of 1832 when he vetoed the bill for the recharter of the Bank of the United States as unconstitutional, un-American, and undemocratic, and if his facts were faulty, his sense of the public pulse was uncannily accurate. In *Progress and Poverty* in 1879, Henry George singled out land speculators as the particular bogey businessmen who caused depressions. In the crucial election of 1896, William Jennings Bryan came within a hairsbreadth of toppling McKinley and the Republican party on the issue of free silver as the poor man's currency versus gold as the businessman's money. The terms Wall Street, banker, capitalist, conjure the Devil in the rhetoric of American symbolism, as opposed to the saintly virtues residing in Main Street, farmer, workingman. The folklore of ballads, tales, and proverbs says little about the businessman, and nothing that is good. In the one article on the businessman in American folklore, written in 1944, Kenneth W. Porter makes the point that the farther from primary economic processes of growing, making, and trading the American man of business grew, the less he was understood and appreciated by the folk.[9] Porter found only one example of a businessman acclaimed in a folk ballad, "Jubilee Jim" Fisk, who nearly wrecked the national economy in the years immediately following the Civil War with his stock swindles and money market chicanery. But the ballad compliments Jim's grand style and good heart:

I'll sing of a man who's now dead in his grave,
  A good man as ever was born.
Jim Fisk was his name, and his money he gave
  To the outcast, the poor, and forlorn.
We all know that he loved both women and wine,
  But his heart it was right, I am sure:
Though he lived like a prince in his palace so fine,
  Yet he never went back on the poor.[10]

Nothing here about business practices; Jubilee Jim is a rakish Robin Hood, whose flamboyant ways dazzled the populace. He sat in a chair studded with gold nails and washed in a bowl encircled by a frieze on the wall of nude nymphs dancing on a rose and gold background. "Diamond Jim" Brady, who lived till 1917, exceeded Fisk in his opulent and extravagant life style, and is remembered not in ballad or legend but as a proverbial figure of allusion for his spendthrift habits and giant appetite.

The occupational folklore of the great extractive industries reflects the values, not of the businessman, but of the individualistic workingman. He is, however, no unskilled laborer or assembly-line drudge. Although he is paid a wage, he possesses expertise that his employers value and he himself vaunts. Potentially he could climb the ladder of American business success to a top rung as a lumber, coal, or cattle baron, an oil or railroad tycoon—although few did, and we are given sad pictures of destitute Maine ex-lumberjacks, their strength and energies dissipated, winding up their lives in Bangor flophouses. Within reach did lie the status positions of lumber-camp boss, foreman of the mines, trail boss, oil-field driller, and railroad engineer, each commanding a crew of workers from whose ranks he himself had risen. If the lumberjack, cowboy, and driller were nomadic, the miner and engineer enjoyed family life, and the others too might eventually settle down.

All the occupational folktypes accepted the American economic creed: the gospel of work, the abundance for all, the reward for industry, the merit of free enterprise. When they protested, and resorted in desperation to unionism, as did the miners and railroaders, they did so not to subvert capitalism, as would the socialists, Marxists, and anarchists of the period, but to ensure their equal opportunity for the good things of the land. This is the point that Henry George contended for so persuasively in *Progress and Poverty,* that the agrarian workingman was the future capitalist, deprived of his rights only by swindling land monopolists. The occupational heroes took pride in possessions, as did the cowboy in his horse, his saddle, his costume, his rope, his guns, or in the sense of secondary ownership, the engineer with his hog and the driller with his rig. They identified with their companies, their industries, and their capital-minded country.

Wealth for wealth's sake was never their goal, nor the goal of the Economic Life-style. Andrew Carnegie defined the matter very neatly in *The Gospel of Wealth* when he laid upon the millionaire the obligation of redistributing his wealth for the benefit of the community, not as a dole but as an enrichment of the public satisfactions available to all. As early as 1820 Daniel Raymond had enunciated the principle that no man should acquire more than he can innocently consume. Great wealth, with its suspected taint of great power and chicanery, has never attracted a favorable symbolism in America's folklore.

The Contemporary Period
The Humane Impulse

*U*nlike earlier periods, heralded by revolution and civil war, the new historical era of the present has burst upon the nation without a definite marker. My own choice for a beginning date is 1964, when the Berkeley Free Speech Movement dramatized the emergence of the counterculture. Social critics today accept the fact of a cultural revolution that commenced in the 1960s. Among a thousand possible quotations, one from the *New York Review of Books*, refers to "a conflict between 'two cultures,' a conflict that has riven the country more deeply than perhaps any division since the Civil War."[1] Already historical landmarks identify institutions and symbols of the counterculture: Woodstock (1969), the open-air rock festival in upstate New York attended by half a million youths; *Hair* (1968), the spirited rock-musical comedy that captured on stage the street culture of the hippies; *Rolling Stone* (1967) the biweekly news magazine devoted originally to rock music but expanding to cover related activities of the youth culture. At their inception, these and other manifestations of the new culture aroused violent controversy, but now the mammoth outdoor rock festivals take place regularly in different parts of the country, *Hair* has become a stand-by in the theater, and *Rolling Stone* is accepted as the *New York Times* of the counterculture. When *Hair* was first

253

performed in Indianapolis the letter columns of the *Indianapolis Star* were filled with torrid communications condemning the production as bestial, degrading, and treasonable, or praising it as wholesome, lighthearted American fun. Four years later, in 1972, when it played in the Indiana University auditorium in Bloomington, the audience of adults and students responded as if they were watching *Peter Pan,* politely appreciative at the repeat of a sweet old favorite.

Has the counterculture produced a folklore in less than a decade? I would not have been prepared to accept the possibility had not sheaves of counterculture folklore been literally thrust into my hands when I taught at the University of California at Berkeley in the

Woodstock

spring of 1968. The folklore of the counterculture proves to be largely a druglore. Cycles of legends have grown around potheads and acid heads, narcs

and busts. The illegal consumption of narcotic drugs presents one of the main crisis points in contemporary society. Dissident youth have identified their use of mind-expanding drugs with their battle for freedom from the repressions of a soul-shriveling System. This fermenting druglore reflects the prominence of marijuana and LSD in the hip subculture. A teacher of folklore at Berkeley in the late 1960s enjoyed an unparalleled opportunity to train participant-observers who could knowledgeably record the traditions of their peers. Three excellent younger folklore professors, Alan Dundes, Roger Abrahams, and Barbara Kirshenblatt-Gimblett, have generously made available to me their own student collections of druglore to supplement mine.

Although one of the chief legend-cycles among undergraduates revolves around cheating in courses, in the case of druglore the anecdotes and beliefs are so readily available to the student collectors (while so inaccessible to their seniors) as to remove the temptation to fabricate, which is a far more difficult process anyway than to record. Since no previous druglore collections had reached print, there was no opportunity to plagiarize, although with motorcycle-gang lore, two yeasty collections turned in to me had been lifted straight from Hunter Thompson's book on the Hell's Angels. But very few of the students had direct access to the Hell's Angels, while all had easy access to bust-avoiding and draft-dodging legends.

Besides the hip drug subculture whose folklore is presented here, other constituencies of the counterculture may

Demonstrator and troops at the Pentagon demonstration march, 1967

well be developing their own traditional lore. A cohesive, close-knit group with shared esoteric interests and practices, be they cowboys or college students, keelboatmen or hippies, will develop their own idioms and ways. Whether the gay and women's liberation movements have reached this point remains to be demonstrated. Some student collectors have compiled lexicons of the folk terminology of homosexuals; "glory hole," for instance, refers to the hole drilled in the partition between toilets in a men's john through which pederasty can be performed. With all highly visible in-groups there coexist an esoteric and an exoteric tradition: that within the group and that about the group. The exoteric or outsiders' gags and jokes usually strike a hostile and derisive note, while the esoteric or insiders' lore projects the values of the group.

The druglore in the following pages comes almost wholly from within the "head" community and reflects its perspectives. Cops and other figures from the straight world are the enemy, dopers are the trickster-heroes. In working through and systematizing hundreds of student collections, I gradually came to perceive the recurrent patterns and formulas, stock characters and repetitive

Allen Ginsberg

256

situations that are characteristic of folk traditions everywhere.

That druglore strongly represents the folklore of the counterculture or the new culture is perfectly fitting, for the drug question has increasingly absorbed America's attention. A symposium in *Playboy* for September 1972 on "The Drug Explosion" announces that "it is no longer a question of American society's coping with the drug culture—they are now one and the same." In his introduction to the group of articles, Dr. Joel Fort stresses that drugs are a problem for all ages, not simply for youth, but that some—alcohol, tobacco, caffeine, sleeping pills, tranquilizers—enjoy social acceptability while others—marijuana, LSD—do not. And a lengthy extract in *Psychology Today* for October 1972 from a forthcoming book by Dr. Andrew Weil, *The Natural Mind,* proposes an unemotional look at drugs to see how they may contribute to a higher consciousness. "The issues raised by drugs touch closely upon our profoundest hopes and fears," he states, and contrasts the better, altered states of consciousness, which he calls "stoned," with the ordinary ways, which he calls "straight," following the terminology of the youth culture.

Folklore of the youth culture

Four years after the Free Speech Movement in Berkeley I had the opportunity to teach at the University of California and experience the Berkeley scene at first hand. This was the spring of 1968, and I taught American folklore to a large class, some 250 students. As part of their work for the course, each student turned in a field collection he or she had made personally, on a project that I approved as feasible and folkloric. The students, eager to discuss their ideas, were unlike any students I had previously encountered at Ivy League or Big Ten schools. Bright, in a special way—defiant, aggressive, insistent, persistent, scornful of the norms and taboos of the Establishment, disdainful of middle-class dress, they seemed continually high, perhaps on LSD and marijuana but rather, I suspected, on the electric currents of the times, charged up with their battles and successes against the university administration, the trustees, the governor, the System. Along Telegraph Avenue the street culture flourished, and emptied across Bancroft Way into Sproul Plaza, the incandescent square between the administration and the student-union buildings opening into the campus, where folksingers performed, speakers harangued, hippies lolled, dogs cavorted, and all the young had their day in the sun. The street culture blended into the student culture, and one could not readily draw a line between them.

In my huge, auditorium-sized classroom, students walked continually in and out of the lecture as if it were a motion-picture show, one of the prerogatives they had won from the turmoil of the Free Speech Movement. Also up and down the aisles raced panting dogs, sometimes pausing to rest on the platform where I faced my clientele. Although I could never be sure whether I would get out alive each day, the Berkeley semester was by far my most exhilarating teaching experience. There was always a long line of students waiting during my office hours, or after class, to discuss their collecting projects, and at the end of the last class, after a semester of hissing, glaring, talking up, and walking out, they delivered a thunder of applause while I stood and blushed. These students were alive and reacting every moment.

So we talked about their ideas for fieldwork, and some began suggesting, or raising questions about, unconventional pursuits that gave me pause. Are these matters folklore? they asked. One afternoon three young women sat in my office to discuss their term projects. The first wanted to know whether a collection based on recurrent images experienced on LSD trips would be considered folkloric. The second presented the same request. When the third finally moved up to the consulting chair, she apologized, "I am afraid I don't have anything quite so dramatic."

Whether or not a given student participated actively in the youth culture, none could be impervious to it, for it flowed all around, in conversation, on the plaza, in the ubiquitous underground press, in the Establishment press reporting freaky doings as a daily happening. During my stay in the spring and summer months of 1968, I recall the *San Francisco Chronicle* carrying

A late afternoon swim in Connecticut

illustrated stories of a nude man walking a dozen blocks down a main thoroughfare at high noon to the amused stares of passers-by; of Sergeant "Sunshine" of the police force smoking grass on the steps of the police station, surrounded by admiring street people, a moment before his arrest; of gays parading before the city courthouse with placards, "Hire a Homosexual"; of a lone dissenter smashing utility poles with a bulldozer, literally trying to bring down the power structure. This was a topsy-turvy world, filled with racks of obscene comic books, icon posters of anti-heroes, the sound of rock, the garb of monks, the whiff of grass, the ambiance of flowers, incense, beads, organic foods.

Before long I decided that the spawning traditions of the student culture did fall within the province of the folklorist, and encouraged the students to collect them. They turned in fascinating collections of the esoteric lore of marijuana smokers, LSD trippers, motorcycle gangs, hippies, homosexuals, former drug addicts, divided according to the folklore genres of trickster tales, jokes, tall tales, sayings, folk speech, games, beliefs, riddles, folk art, legends. There was no question of the oral circulation and variation of those items that had not yet reached print; the only question was whether they had endured sufficiently in time to merit the label "folklore." To this I had two answers. First, in spite of the novelty of the materials, their themes and motifs followed time-honored formulas of the folk. If the drug culture among youths was a new phenomenon, the drug user outwitting the

Girl in Haight-Ashbury

narcs (narcotic agents) and the fuzz (police) presented a familiar trickster pattern. Second, in modern mobile America with its electronic communications systems, the spatial element dominated the temporal element in the folklore-making process. The lore of hippiedom spread rapidly across the nation and over the world in a few short years. The youth culture was not going to wait to grow old to generate its traditions.

From the folklore archives of the University of California at Berkeley, the University of Texas at Austin, and Indiana University at Bloomington and Indianapolis, where students have deposited collections and reports, I have obtained, categorized, and selected the examples of youth-culture folklore that

259

follow. Sometimes these student folklorists will offer explanations of codes and values implicit in their materials that the older reader would most likely not perceive.

Two worlds collide in the folklore of the youth culture. The System, or the straight world, stands in opposition to the world of the heads, freaks, gays, motorcycle gangs, street people, and communes. Characteristics of the counterculture reflected in its nascent traditions are, first, knowledge of and experience with drugs; second, knowledge of although not necessarily participation in "the Movement," an umbrella label for draft resistance, peace marches, and student-power and minority-power action; and third, knowledge and analysis of pop and rock music and musicians.[2] The only youth group opposed to the System whose folklore falls outside these rubrics are the Hell's Angels and their emulators, who stress liquor rather than drugs and *machismo* rather than love and peace. At the unhappy Altamonte festival of 1970, stained by a death, the flower people invited the Hell's Angels to serve as the festival police, in a rare juncture of the two extremes of youthful dissent. The endeavor to shock straight society, whether through deviant behavior, attire, speech, or music, unifies these lores. Tom Wolfe's chapter in *The Electric Kool-Aid Acid Test* relating the visit of the Angels to Ken Kesey and the Merry Pranksters in their Redlands retreat documents in his zingy manner the rapport and camaraderie the two unlike bands of dissenters found in each other's uninhibited company.

Druglore

Cops and Dopers, Narcs and Heads

In getting high on pot (marijuana), acid (LSD), and speed (amphetamines) the smoker, swallower, or shooter of the drug seeks liberation from "the System" by, on the one hand, defying its punitive legal restraints and shocking its adult members, and on the other, by opening the mind to perceptions and sensations not available in ordinary humdrum life. The ideal of travel and mobility, on both the physical and the mental plane, occupies a central place in the social thought of the drug culture—thus the film *Easy Rider*—and drug stimulation contributes to this ideal. Pried loose from its anchorage in the lackluster, deadening rat race of the competitive society, the mind soars to new visions, associations, sensory experiences. "Trip" is the key term for the desire of the drug user, who journeys literally on the road and metaphysically in his hallucinatory flights. Tom Wolfe's incandescent reporting of the cross-country journey of the Merry Pranksters in *The Electric Kool-Aid Acid Test* illustrates a now classic trip.

Some familiarity with the main classes of drugs and social attitudes toward them within the head culture is needed to comprehend druglore. A "head" is an habitual drug user. (My comments are all secondhand, based on student observations.) On the lowest level of danger, judicial and physiological, although still possibly hazardous on both counts, is marijuana. Smoking grass gives a relaxing, euphoric sense accompanied by the thrill of taboo breaking and lawbreaking, so that some defenders of the weed argue against its legalization for fear smokers will then gravitate to hard drugs. A deeper stage of penetration into the hip drug subculture comes with the taking of acid, best known in the form of LSD (lysergic acid diethylamide) and other hallucinogenic drugs, in capsule, powder, or liquid form. Acid expands the mind—hence the term "head"—and breaks the customary train of associations. Stories of acid trips emphasize the psychedelic effects, the lights and colors and flickering waves that flash before one's eyes, and these effects are simulated in drug parlor games. Such trips may endanger and derange insecure personalities, and trippers are advised to undertake their voyages in company with trusted and knowledgeable friends. The third group, the speed drugs, are, unlike grass and acid, addictive; the speed freak tends to become antisocial and hostile after descending from his orgasmic high. Hence the street people who emphasize doing one's thing and sharing universal love draw a line between acid and speed. They disavow the purpose of the amphetamines, barbiturates, and opiates, which is to provide an immediate kick for their user. In the counterculture and its folklore, marijuana and LSD receive the plaudits.

Another distinction that needs to be spelled out in counterculture folklore is that between the hippie and the head. Berkeley students speak matter-of-factly of the "hip drug culture." According to one student observer, most hippies use drugs and all condone their usage. But some drug users are pseudohippies who affect the long hair, beads, and monkish costume of the true hippie, but do not share his values—the essential brotherhood of man, the sacredness of the individual, and the identification of the good by the simple sensation of feeling good. True hippies live in families, communes, and cooperatives.[3]

The basic headlore story pits cops against dopers, in the idiom of Austin, or narcs against heads, in the parlance of Berkeley. "Narc" stands for "a narcotics agent who disguises himself as a hippie and associates with hippies on a personal level; after he has gathered sufficient evidence he turns them all in. A narc is considered more abominable than a uniformed or plain-clothes policeman because of the hypocritical disguise."[4] Since heads continually fear arrest, or "getting busted," to the point of paranoia, they view cops and narcs with extreme hostility as their direct enemy and as tools of the Establishment. In the stories constantly retold by heads, they manage to outwit or outluck the police looking for their stash (cache of drugs). "There are as many of these stories as there are recording tapes to take them down," observes one student collector.[5] Loosely anecdotal in form, headlore narratives are recounted as true, and the assertion of veracity—as in almost all druglore—indeed forms part of the recital.[6] No single episode is unbelievable, but the recurrence of similar situations and the stereotyping of the main actors point to familiar folklore patterns. Cops and narcs replace the stupid ogres, the witless devils, and the numskulls of medieval tales, and the dopers and heads assume the traditional role of underdog trickster-heroes. Told for true, cops-and-dopers stories indulge in fantasy, for, as a participant-observer notes, in real life the cops usually win. The psychological function of druglore is explained by one analytical folklore student, who asserts, "Esoteric-exoteric lore of the drug culture serves as a reaffirmation of the values of the drug culture and as a buffer against the hostility of outgroups."[7] Jokes and slurs from Middle America about hippies constitute exoteric lore. What hippies tell among themselves grows into esoteric lore, employing idioms and interior references incomprehensible to the straight members of the mainstream culture. Rejected and condemned by the dominant culture, which considers them deviants and lawbreakers, the dropouts proclaim their virtues. In the same way the ring-tailed roarers of the early frontier exaggerated their Western speech and costume that so astounded Establishment Easterners. Legends and beliefs extol the liberating qualities of marijuana and LSD. Heroes arise who manufacture and distribute drugs of therapeutic and magical potency. There is feedback between the outside and the inside images of the deviant. In the exhilarating rock musical *Hair* the patronizing straight couple who visit the street people become the subject of ridicule in their clumsy attempts to identify with hippies.

The exoteric image may be construed very seriously indeed. A headlore student collector in Texas established rapport with a commune group known as the Motherfuckers, who originated in New York's Lower East Side and followed the pop festivals from Woodstock, New York, to Lewisville, Texas. In Austin, Texas, a police officer told the student, "Yeah, we had a special briefing on those Motherfuckers right after they hit town. They're some kind of secret society that you have to kill a police officer to belong to. So we're not harassing them—it's them or us and it's damn sure going to be them."[8] On hearing this statement repeated by the student, the Motherfuckers laughed loudly until the sobering thought dawned on them that the cops might shoot them down in the street at sight. In this instance the members of the esoteric group did not attempt to live up to the exoteric conception of their behavior.

Behind these stories lies a deep paranoia—readily admitted to by the potheads, acid heads, and speed freaks—of being busted by the police. A release from the paranoia comes through the tales exchanged at marijuana parties about lucky or clever escapes from busts. In the following memorat a twenty-three-year-old drug seller, Frank, finds himself in the situation every head, and particularly every dealer, most dreads:

It seems that one of the favorite pastimes of long time drug users is the recollection of funny or very unusual experiences (which is only likely since most takers do it for its unusuality). As with Frank, most of these involve a confrontation with the user's natural enemy, the policeman.

"I was driving on the Nimitz Freeway at around two o'clock in the afternoon one day, completely stoned on acid when a cop pulled me over to the side. I was really freaked out and was sure I was going to get busted, so I rolled up all the windows of my car and refused to even let the cop speak to me. This made the cop so mad that he started screaming for me to roll down the window, he cursed and yelled for about three minutes when all of a sudden I rolled down the window and said in a very cool voice, 'I'll have two hamburgers and an order of fries.' This remark, instead of infuriating him, actually made him laugh and he told me he was at first going to give me a speeding ticket but decided to let me off with a warning instead."[9]

Alongside the embroidered folktale of yesteryear, this anecdote seems pretty thin. But it faithfully represents the crisis point of the drug culture and provides a fairy-tale ending. No situation terrifies the head more than to be caught by a cop while high—here, to make it worse, at the wheel of a car. The head reacts with the characteristic absurdity of the trickster figure, which would seem to invite swift and awful punishment but instead pays off with a sudden reprieve from the unsuspecting cop.

A similar situation is described by the twenty-four-year-old wife of a drug dealer:

These people were being watched by narcs and they were out driving one night, really stoned, and they had this new guy who had just been "turned on" with them, and they were passing this joint around when the cops stopped them. Well, the narcs pulled up in front and the cops were in back and they [the heads] had all the windows rolled up and the doors locked and the new guy was just hysterical. He was yelling, "What are you doing? Cops!" and waving the smoke around and trying to blow it out the air vents. And by then the cops were banging on the doors, and this guy [the new fellow] was just going crazy.

The guy next to him took a last puff on the joint and put it out on his tongue and [swallowing gesture] rolled down the window and said, "May I help you?"[10]

The student collector explained that the triumph of a head who beats the police is seen as a victory for all users. She added, "The story serves as a release of tension and also as a lesson in evading police, that you can only be busted if they actually find grass." It also in- cludes the motifs of initiation of a new member into the hazards of the cult and the head's means of self-protection.

Hiding the evidence occurs in other tales as a way of outsmarting cops at the perilous moment when the stoned driver faces authority:

263

I've heard a story about a head who was in a car that got stopped and he was holding 60 tabs of acid—it was in a plastic bag—and before the cop came up to the car, he swallowed the bag. So the cop searched the car and didn't find anything. When the cop left, the guy tickled his throat with his finger and barfed the plastic bag back up. The acid was still okay.[11]

Some stoned hippies were buzzing around in Port Arthur [Texas] in a station wagon and the driver had a lid setting in his lap—you know—the windows all clouded with grass smoke—the whole bit—and a cop stopped 'em. So when they rolled a window down this cloud of smoke started pouring out. The cop ran over and said, "What's going on in there?"

The driver suddenly realized he had a lid of grass on his lap. He grabbed it up and threw it in the cop's face and screamed, "WE'RE BUSTED!"

Janis Joplin

Well, it was a real windy day and the cop had to let them go—all the evidence blew away.

[The student collector adds this note:]

Informant, a twenty-one year old college student at the University of Texas, said he has heard this story several times from different people in Port Arthur, but no one seems to remember exactly who was involved. Indications that the story stems from an actual happening include the fact that it is widely known, especially among high school students, with little or no variance in substance or detail (the car involved is always a station wagon). One indication that it isn't true is that there aren't enough hippies in Port Arthur to fill a station wagon.

A Dallas "head" was coming back from California and got stopped by a cop somewhere in Arizona. The cop looked around in the car and then said, "Whaddya got in the trunk?"

"Oh, I got a pound of grass and a bunch of hot motorcycle parts."

The cop absorbed that for a minute and then said, "Awright, get outta here, wise guy."

You know what was in the trunk? A pound of grass and a bunch of hot motorcycle parts![12]

The known truth behind these tales, according to their tellers, is the likelihood of a hippie-looking driver being stopped, interrogated, and searched by the police purely on suspicion. Not all cops are considered numskulls, a classification the dopers particularly reserve for police in the hinterland, as in this tale from an eighteen-year-old street person, Ginny Motherfucker:

A friend of mine knew these heads who were driving through New Mexico and got stopped in this dipshit little town and one of them was holding eight grams of hash [hashish, a derivative of marijuana resin]. The city cop decides to hold them to see if they are wanted, so when he searches them at the jail, he finds the hash and wants to know what it is. The cat he took the stuff from says that it's just eight little brown rocks and goes into this big rap about what *groovy* little brown rocks they are. The sheriff didn't sniff them, I guess. Anyway, he got tired of listening to the cat rap, so he went ahead and locked them up and when he had checked them for charges, he let them go and the cat got his "little brown rocks" back.

On the street in Haight-Ashbury

[The student collector appends this commentary:]
This is one of many "small-town cops and dopers" stories that have been circulated since Taos, New Mexico became a Mecca for hip communes. The focus of this type of story is the ignorance of drugs and drug people often displayed by small town police. Strangely enough, such stories are often combined with tributes to the ability of big-city cops ("Now if that had been an Oakland pig . . ." or "A lower East Side narc would have . . ."), who are the butt of many other stories.[13]

Other tales portray deliberate deceptions of the narcs by sharp-witted heads. Here a twenty-three-year-old student at San Francisco State University relates such an account; he heard the tale at a pot party in 1964 and subsequently told it to the student collector at another pot party:

I heard about some narkies who planted themselves in the Hot Dog Palace [a notorious hangout for drug users] in SF. They went up to this guy who was a contact and said they wanted some shit [any kind of drug, originally heroin or a "mainliner" drug but now often used for pot].

He said, "Okay, bring a hundred dollars here tomorrow night and I'll fix you up."

The pusher's girl had a vision or something that this was a narkie and so the guy bought a sack of flour and put it in a paper bag. He went to the café and traded the sack for a hundred dollars and all kinds of cops jumped out. He kept saying he didn't know what it was all about and when they got to the station, he said he had merely sold a sack of flour for a hundred dollars. They looked inside the sack and had to let him go. He got to keep the hundred dollars.[14]

Again this sounds like an idealized situation in which the enemy—"the man"—for all his careful planning and infiltration ends up discomfited. The dealer (contact, pusher) wins, and even if the head in this case gets nothing but flour, he avoids a bust. Realistic as the story appears to be, it contains a well-known supernatural motif, "Prophecy through dreams." The warning dream of the pusher's girl averts the bust.

In a cops-and-dopers story from Texas, the dealer tricks the police with a play on words. The University of Texas student who reported this incident insisted it was a true story:

Hitchhikers

A guy thought his phone was tapped, so he called up a friend and told him: "I have a suitcase of keys ["Ki" (short for *kilo*), in head slang denotes two pounds of marijuana] and I'll meet you tomorrow at six at the corner of——street."

The next day they went to the assigned street corner, and the narcs walk up to bust them. And they open the suitcase, and out fall assorted keys (door keys and skeleton keys).[15]

This stratagem recalls one of the devices used to outwit the Devil by unfortunate mortals who had contracted to sell him their souls for gold. A cobbler gave Satan the sole of a shoe when the Devil showed up to claim his due.[16]

One last automobile-and-cops story, told by a nineteen-year-old "anonymous speed freak, a street person, a pusher," portrays the head as a quick-thinking, resourceful hero figure:

This guy wanted to shoot up some coke [cocaine] or something, so he goes into a drug store and says he wants to score some points [buy some needles for intravenous injections] 'cause his roommate is a diabetic. So the cat behind the counter gives him the big, suspicious eye and asks how many. He says how many does he have to buy to get a reduced price.

Anyways, he scores 100 points. He sells 25 of them right away and stashes 40 dex [Dexedrine] in the bottom of the box. He gets about a block from the place where he scored the dex and there's the old red light and siren. The cop has just stopped him for a tail-light, but he sees the box of points on the seat. So the cop says, "What's that?" The head says it's some needles for his roommate and his roommate's a diabetic. The cop says, "Lemme see." So he [the head] reaches back and pours the points *and* dex out all over the seat. He grabs up a handful of points and gives them to the cop. The cop says, "You sure you can get these without a prescription?"

He said, "Yes sir," and the cop let him go. The cop never even saw the dex.

[The student collector adds this comment:]

This is a "cops and dopers" story that extends the general attitude about police to include other straight people. It is performed with vocal characterizations and expansive gestures, but the most apparent thing about the performance, among the listeners and from the informant, was the pride and wonder at the "balls" and "cool" of the head and obvious relish at the stupidity of the druggist and policeman.[17]

While cops detain the head driving an automobile for some traffic violation

or because of his appearance, narcs with foreknowledge of stashes enter homes of drug users intending to make an arrest. Invading one's home is, under the American Constitution, a violation of sacred privacy—one's home is one's castle—and especially resented by pot-heads and acid heads. As one student folklorist writes, "To the member of the drug subculture one force remains a constant enemy, a group of men that seem dedicated to destroying the user's way of life. This is the police force."[18] So the "bust-trick" story celebrates the sly and clever head who fools the cops when they seek to cross his threshold.

A glorious bust, in which the dopers defeat and discredit the cops, is described in the classic documentary of headlore, Tom Wolfe's *The Electric Kool-Aid Acid Test.* Mystified by the goings-on in Ken Kesey and the Merry Pranksters' woodsy retreat at La Honda,

California, a swarm of sheriffs, deputies, federal agents, police dogs—"the whole freaking raid scene"—descended on them, on April 23, 1965, looking for hard drugs. But the Pranksters had anticipated the bust, and the frustrated raiders had to content themselves with accusing Kesey of trying to flush marijuana down the john, while he claimed he was merely painting flowers on the toilet bowl. When one of the posse reached into a Prankster's pocket and drew out a vial of clear liquid, the Pranksters in unison chanted, "Hey! Play fair! Play fair! Be fair, cops! Play hard but play fair." They gleefully recognized the ritual game in which they were participating.[19]

There are still other ways of putting down narcs:

Narcotics officers came to a high school classroom to give a lecture on the dangers of drug use. At the end of the lecture one cop passed around ten joints [marijuana cigarettes] saying, "I'm passing out ten of these and I better get ten back. If I don't, nobody leaves the room and we have a complete search."

When he collected them again he counted. There were eleven.[20]

This anecdote includes a folk trick but also reflects the social reality of drug use in the high schools.

A number of anecdotes tell about

heads buying oregano thinking it is grass. In the following tale a cop makes the blunder:

Dave told me about this chick who was almost busted. Two cops entered her house with a warrant. They were looking for grass. While one of them was searching the place, the other whispered to her, "Don't worry, I've dumped it."

They couldn't find anything so they left. Then she checked her stash and it was still there in the closet. She couldn't figure out what

269

the cop meant. A couple of days later she noticed that a can of oregano in the kitchen was empty.[21]

The friendliness displayed by the one cop to the girl pothead in this narrative comes to the fore in other tales in which the law enforcers cooperate and conspire with the lawbreakers. Paradoxical as it seems, a whole cycle of druglore tales deals with cops taking dope.

Cops as Heads

Why would "the enemy" join forces, surreptitiously, with the youthful drug users they so vigorously persecute? The widespread beliefs and legends among heads that a large number of cops and narcs regularly get stoned support the defense mechanisms of dopers. Such legends reveal the hypocrisy of the police officers in denouncing the heads whose life-style they secretly wish to emulate. Some tales display the naiveté of cops who cannot distinguish one drug from another, with serious consequences to themselves. The newspaper stories and pictures in the *San Francisco Chronicle* in the spring of 1968 about Sergeant "Sunshine," dressed in his police uniform,

Plastic marijuana plants, invented by two Californians named Jerry McGregor and Warren Ziebarth. The plants, ranging in size from 20 inches to 5 feet, were manufactured early in 1970 and sold under the registered name of Cannabis Sativa. Shown here: McGregor and Ziebarth, with plants, at the Hall of Justice in San Francisco.

smoking a joint in the midst of laughing street people just prior to his arrest, lend color to the legends. A picture somewhat later showed him not so happy. Berkeley heads declare that the narcs and the fuzz smoke the marijuana which they confiscate at busts, and even participate in pot parties, as the following headlore stories from the Bay Area bear witness:

A friend of mine says he was picked up once when he was hitching by a well-known area newscaster, and after rapping for a while they went to the newscaster's home and smoked grass. And the newsman explained that when they heard about busts of different drugs they'd go to the police department to check out stories and obtained free samples of drugs to test and see what they were like.

My friend heard this in 1967 in Berkeley. He says it's true and that it just shows how law-abiding the police are. (Told by a college dropout, 21.)

I met this guy in a fraternity. We had a few beers together and he told us that his entire house turned on with grass. They have parties all the time. Last weekend a couple of Berkeley cops dropped in. They asked if they could have some grass; got stoned; and then left.
He says most of the cops are heads anyway. It really blew my mind. He was a really cool guy. (Told by a baker's helper, 24.)

Two San Francisco policemen visited an apartment whose residents were notorious drug users. At the time the residents were smoking hashish. The police said they were cool and merely wanted to get stoned, so the heads let them in and turned them on.

Five minutes after the high officers left the apartment it was busted by two different policemen. (Told by a male student, 21.)

This guy I know in San Francisco told me this; it happened to a friend of his.

One day a couple of guys were turning on with LSD using sugar cubes and a couple of cops knocked at the door asking for his roommate. The guys panicked but coolly asked the cops in. They asked for coffee and proceeded to put a couple of sugar cubes in the cup! Everyone played it real cool and the cops swung way out and stayed there all day, saying, "Wow, I never felt like this before." After about six hours they came down and left.

The guys were scared but never heard anything about it. (Told by a male social worker, 26.)

A girl with a lid [one ounce] of marijuana was hitchhiking when two officers pulled over and searched her. They found the pot and admonished her for breaking the law. After warning her of the consequences of possessing marijuana, they took the lid and drove off, presumably to smoke the stuff themselves. (Told by a female artist, 21, Huntington Beach. The collector also heard two close variants in Los Angeles and Santa Barbara.)

Old Fred told me about these two cops in LA, they were narcs. They both finally dropped acid and the next day they threw their badges on the chief's desk and said, "We're not with you any more."[22]

One explanation from a collector that reduces the implausibility of these allegedly true accounts—always told at second or third hand—states that Berkeley police are required to have two years of college, and that therefore they identify with college students more than do the usual run of police officers. By reputation the Berkeley cops appear more easygoing on hippies and more lax in enforcing the narcotics laws. In curious contrast with the cop-confrontation tale is the narrative of the policeman who deliberately looks the other way to avoid making the bust. The inference is that law officers as heads themselves do not wish to arrest fellow drug users.

Alan and his friends used to have a house across from a junior high in Marin. They were drug freaks, and always had grass or speed or something around there. Word got around and teenybops started to stop by. And the narcs found out about it and came to see them.

And while they were talking there was a bag of acid and some speed lying around, and all the narcs did was to tell them to keep cool about the whole thing and they didn't want teenybops around and wouldn't do anything about it if they [the heads] kept them away.

They were never busted afterwards. (Told by a male college dropout, 21)

Midway between the cop-outwitted and the cop-as-head stereotypes comes the cop accidentally freaking out. This tale-type combines elements from both the other cycles, by showing the policeman as an unsophisticated drug taster who "trips" himself while trying to make a bust:

There was a carload of freaks driving in the country with a jar of untabbed acid. They got stopped by the highway patrol for speeding and had their car searched. The cop found the jar and asked what it was. "Oh, that's just a jar of sugar."

So he sticks his finger in and tasted it. "That's not sugar, you better follow me back to town."

About thirty minutes later the cop's car swerved off the road and ended up in a ditch. He was blowing his mind, and the heads just drove away. (Told by a male student, 20.)

Supposedly, a narc was on a bust. After successfully confiscating a large amount of sundry narcotics, the narc came across a small pill box containing a gram of a strange white substance. "Ah," said the narc, "pure uncut heroin."

In order to confirm his hypothesis, he licked the substance to check for the characteristic heroin taste. "Hm," said the narc, "this is taste-less, it must be—Y E O W, E I E E E!" He then slumped to the floor in a catatonic position.

He is now in a state institution still in his catatonic coma. For what he thought was pure heroin was actually pure acid. (Told by a male student, 21.)[23]

The teller of the last variant had himself heard three variations of what is clearly a well-known and satisfying legend in headlore circles. One collector noted that his version "was told in a cheerful manner, with a lot of laughter mixed in with the narration. The teller and the listeners took great pleasure in the idea of a policeman on a drug trip, especially LSD."[24] Although printed texts, even when literally collected, fail to convey the stylistics of delivery, such as gesture, intonation, and histrionics, some collectors allude to these elements of the taletelling, and any experienced folklorist can visualize them, especially in the last, dramatically structured narrative. One readily conceives the narrator, in the role of the narc, expressing his delight at discovering the supposed heroin, cautiously tonguing the drug, then screaming and jumping six feet in the air as the acid hits him, and finally collapsing in a heap as he twitches and goes rigid in his catatonic state. Meanwhile the circle of appreciative heads double over with glee at the enactment of the enemy's fall. Behind the amusement lurks the somber thought that a tragedy did overtake "the man" and that some hospital hides his secret, so the playlet conveys pathos as well as comedy. These stories are told for true.

Other persons in the straight world also turn on unwittingly, and thereby hangs another theme:

A head that a friend of mine knows was over at his girl's house and he hid his stash of grass in her old man's tobacco can. So her old man came back unexpectedly and found this long-haired cat there. He figured anyone with long hair is a hippie, so he started preaching about the dangers of grass. And while he was doing it he picked up his tobacco can and filled his pipe.

So he sat there and got stoned out of his gourd while he was preaching against weed. (Told by a male student, 21.)[25]

According to the collector the motif of this tale emphasizes a very real social situation: that of "masses of people having rigid prejudices about a life-style they know nothing about," when their own life-style leaves much to be desired. This point of view comes out strongly in a father-son confrontation:

This man was having a cocktail party for all his friends, and he went out to the guest house where his son and his friends were having a party. And they were smoking grass and the father just blew his top. He was really drunk and he called his son out and told him all this stuff about how he was ruining his health, and conforming to his friends, and so on.

And then the kid said, "Look at you, Dad," and said almost the same things to him. And the father just stood there and the kid said, "Aren't you going to say anything?"

And the kid said, "Yes, we do think alike, we just don't think about the same things." (Told by the wife of a drug dealer, 24.)[26]

The policeman, the father, the professor, the employer, all are authority figures cut from the same Establishment cloth. In the sad cautionary tale above, the old and the young generations and life-styles speak past each other. The son sees liquor as a means of deadening the senses already numbed by physical gratifications, and drugs as a means of expanding senses to enjoy a world freed from the incubus of materialistic strivings.

Paranoia

In druglore the head is an anti-Establishment hero defying the rules of the System and continually skirmishing with the arms of the law. He is cool, but he lives under constant tension, anxiety, and fear of getting busted, like any outlaw. The drug culture honestly recognizes and even takes a perverse pleasure in describing this mood. Believing in the sincere expression of their emotions, members of the hip drug society candid-ly reveal their paranoia. A favorite term in their lexicon, "paranoia" is a useful word summing up their state of distrust of the straight world, ever ready to bust its critics and defiers, whether student potheads on the local level or the Chicago Seven, the Berrigan brothers, and Angela Davis on the national level. "Paranoia is in the air of every hip community these days," notes one student folklorist.[27]

Some beliefs, memorats, and legends obtain their momentum from the paranoid outlook. A subterranean lore permeating the hip drug subculture conveys hints, tips, and recommendations on how to escape the narcs, the bust, and the jail. Do not deal in drugs, is one solemn caution. "Have you ever dealt?" asked a female student collector of a Berkeley undergraduate. "I've mediated," he answered. "I don't dig dealing, you know, because sometimes people get busted and then say, 'Hey, let me out and I'll tell you who I got it from.'"[28]

The collector added that LSD guilt-by-association was a common fear among acid heads. In her high school in 1966, students believed that the narcs would release a youth caught with drugs if he or she divulged the names of three other possessors of illegal drugs. When a dealer was busted, his clients immediately became paranoid about the police finding an address book, letters, or pieces of paper listing names of his customers. Cops might let a user go but never a pusher.

Folk beliefs gather around what constitutes evidence in court. One such belief holds that a head can attempt to identify a narc by simply asking the suspected infiltrator, "Are you a narc?" If he is, he must say so, for should he deny his identity and then make an arrest, his testimony will become inadmissible evidence—according to "folk law." (This erroneous notion arises from misreading the law concerning entrapment.) A related idea maintains that when the police enter a house to make a bust, they will find the drug evidence they seek no matter where it is hidden, even if they have to tear apart walls and floors and slice up bars of soap. Since every house in Berkeley contains dope in one form or another, says folklore, the narcs will surely find their evidence. But if they are not looking for drugs, they won't see them even when they are in plain sight. A nineteen-year-old female student at Berkeley related how the cops came to her house one night when a joint was lying on the floor, cigarette papers were scattered on the table, and a hookah lay nearby. They ignored all this and instead pointed to a street sign the heads had stolen. This incident confirmed their conviction that only dealers and the paranoid were ever arrested by the narcs.[29] A joke tells of one dope dealer who was so paranoid that he could look over both shoulders at the same time.[30]

In paranoia tales the dopers are the losers. While not so common as the triumphant stories, these stress the point that a careless or rattled doper betrays his cause and himself.

You know, in Harlem slang "The Man" means two things: a pusher and a cop. This head walked into a bar wanting some joints, and asked the bartender, "Hey, you know where the man is?"

The bartender nodded and pointed to a cop in the corner. The guy went over and asked him for some pot. He got busted. (Heard at Yale by a Berkeley graduate student, male, 24.)[31]

In the following automobile-confrontation story the heads lose their cool and are penalized, a lesson underlined by a Berkeley student of twenty-two.

We were driving through Los Gatos on our way to a drive-in movie. We were all smoking a little grass, with Pete and I having about half a lid [ounce] each on us. I guess I must have been driving a little erratically 'cause a cop stopped us. He must have suspected that we were smoking grass 'cause he immediately asked if he could search the car.

I was getting really freaked out but thought that if he searched the car and found nothing he would let us go, so I said "Okay." What I didn't know was that Pete had really freaked out when he saw the cop and stashed his stuff beneath the front seat. That was the first place the cop looked, and so we got fucked.

I shoulda never let him search the car 'cause I don't think he had enough evidence to get a search warrant. As it turned out we both got two years' probation, which isn't bad except that it's still a felony on our records.[32]

> Somehow the loser stories have more the ring of truth than the winner stories, an observation the collectors sometimes make. But loser stories too may verge upon fable.

A man was trying to cross the Mexican border with some heroin in a plastic bag up his ass. The bag broke and when he collapsed at the customs station, they took him to a hospital and found he had died of overdose.
[The student collector adds this note:]
I heard this story twice, once in El Paso, Texas and again in Portland, Oregon. This is one of the few stories I've run across where the dopers lose. Perhaps it's significant that the doper is a smack freak [heroin user], because being strung out on any drug is considered very uncool and most heads could not identify with one very strongly. (Told by a male student, a drug counselor, 22.)[33]

Paranoia often finds expression in cautionary tips and painful remembrances. "It's been my experience," notes a participant observer, "that the 'pig rap' or the discussion of police harassment of heads always arises when heads get together. This practical practice is in response to the paranoia of potheads afraid of being arrested. To calm the tension of this fear, heads employ precautionary measures for their physical and mental welfare."[34] So they exchange descriptions of close calls and pass along the lore of the streets. At a drug rap in Lubbock High School in Texas, paranoid students claimed that when the cops stopped a suspected head on the road, they not only searched the car but scraped under the suspect's fingernails and checked the findings under a microscope to see if he had been smoking. "Cops can pick you out as a doper from the blister on your lip," is another apprehension.[35] "If you're in a city like San Diego, don't travel main streets, because a cop might

An arrest in Berkeley

see you and flash bad and he'd stop and hassle you," counseled a twenty-one-year-old drug dealer from Oakland, in whose world-view "pigs are an institution which interferes in one's life situations if one is a head."[36] Youthful heads regard San Diego and all southern California as an area notorious for police harassment of suspected drug users. The constant fear of being watched and suspected sometimes leads to unnecessary evasive action.

About two years ago at Oxford [a Berkeley College co-operative dormitory] somebody had a radio stolen from their room, and so he called the cops in. As soon as the Oxfordians got word of this, the house began resounding with the noise of toilets being flushed as everybody got paranoid and started ditching their stashes.

The guy whose radio was stolen was fined twenty-five dollars and had to pay back all those who had lost their dope.[37]

And so the stories go, one triggering another in the universal manner of tale-swapping circles. "I usually tell this incident when everyone else is reciting their most paranoid-inducing incidents about freakouts and busts," remarked an eighteen-year-old Berkeley student after telling of a "greasy bust" at Oxford when a cop chasing a purse snatcher into the dorm smelled grass and arrested two students in whose room he found an open lid. At the station one of the students discovered that he had five joints in the lining of his coat, and hastily stashed them in the crannies of the waiting room, only to have the cop return to say he was dropping charges because the search had been conducted illegally. The students were released with nothing more than a severe case of hypertension and a new paranoia experience to relate.[38]

Owsley: King of Acid

In the warfare between narcs and acid heads that followed the passing of state and federal legislation between 1966 and 1968 rendering illegal the possession of hallucinogenic drugs, a mysterious and potent figure emerged in newspaper stories as "Mr. LSD," "the Henry Ford of Acid," and "the LSD King." Anecdotal legends about Owsley, as he was usually called, proliferated throughout the youth drug subculture. They celebrated him as a hip-hero manufacturer of the best LSD tablets available, invulnerable to the narcs, the patron of the rock band the Grateful Dead, and a self-made millionaire although a dropout from the System. Oral legendary traditions about him circulated among street people and college students.

Augustus Stanley Owsley III is the primary folk hero of Bay Area heads. This character has such a mystical quality about him that any particular story concerning his activities is bound to be both fantastic and quite possibly true.

Owsley is the son of a wealthy family. In a few years before the illegalization of LSD in California, Owsley made over a million dollars through the sale of that drug. He was recently arrested for possession of over ten million dollars' worth of LSD. Owsley's name lent to any particular variety of LSD, such as Owsley purples or Owsley 1000's, is an almost certain way of promoting a sale because this man, according to folk belief, deals only in the finest quality of acid.

Owsley was a part of this group of Kesey and the Merry Pranksters and he made millions of dollars selling his acid, and he made just the best acid anybody's ever had. And so his reputation has grown since the days that LSD was legal. He's a legend, but he's a real person, and he had a really good reputation among the early acid heads.

Everybody related to LSD at all is acquainted with this aspect of Owsley, that he became a millionaire by synthesizing LSD and selling his product before it became illegal.

The Merry Pranksters played a big part in the early acid tests held in San Francisco when LSD was still legal and which turned San Francisco on to acid.

Owsley—before he was busted in Orinda there were rumors he was in the City [San Francisco], on the East Coast, up in the mountains, but wherever he was, he was sitting up there making good acid and it's gonna get to us. The only way that anyone can sell acid is to say that it's Owsley's.

She said Owsley had kind of an electric glow around him. I heard he never talks.

Owsley was at Golden Gate Park one day giving away acid. Thousands of caps. Well, the cops found out and went to bust him but when they found him all the acid was gone. Somebody said he dropped about ten caps he had left when he saw them coming. (A superhuman feat.) I heard he's taken so much that that's a normal trip for him. (LSD does not build a physical tolerance, however.)

The police wanted to question him but he put them down so bad they just let him go.

There was this congressman in Kentucky who had a son who was really flipped out. He had a secret laboratory where he made acid. It was supposed to be the best acid around until he got busted.

It was purple and had hardly, if at all, any speed in it.

Osley [sic] was his name. There still might be some around because he made a lot of it.

Osley [sic]—the perfect LSD for street use. It is the purest, safest acid. He was the original underground chemist, forty years old, very careful; he even changed his molds often so nobody would forge! He wanted to get the best mind trip possible, understood Eastern philosophy.

In 1965 [when LSD was still legal] prominent people took acid. Doctors and lawyers would applaud when Osley walked into a restaurant.

I heard Owsley and a friend were cooking some acid. [The chemical process used in making LSD involves the use of heat.] They had all the ingredients going and were waiting for it to finish. The cops learned about it and came over to bust him.

It turns out that they came too soon and the acid wasn't formed yet. They couldn't bust him.

I heard Owsley is an asshole. Really on a strong ego trip. I know a guy who talked to him. He thinks he's God.

I don't know why he's never been busted. Maybe he's a narc creating more prospective busts.

There was an ex-professor in California who decided to go into the acid business full time. His name was Owsley. He made dynamite acid "Amerika" will never forget. He was a genius and had his own special formula. You could tell Owsley acid from others because it was blue until others started coming out to pass as Owsley.

He was finally busted.

I have a friend who used to live with Owsley, and he said that Owsley had a thing about strychnine. And he thought strychnine was a really good thing to take, of course not in lethal doses but in doses that wouldn't murder you. Strychnine was supposed to get you really high. And this person said he used to shoot strychnine with Owsley and he also said that Owsley put strychnine in his acid to make it more intense.

And I've heard this from a couple other people. And also I've heard that Owsley puts Methedrine in his acid to make it more intense.

Stanley Owsley was the manufacturer of LSD. His acid is supposed to be ace. You don't get burned with it. He is the legendary chemist who got it all together. He was a millionaire, devoted his whole life to manufacturing acid.

Owsley's the guy who kind of made acid. There were rumors going around that he was a doctor, that he was a European exiled Swede. He was arrested a couple of months ago, and it turned out he was only a kid. Twentyish.

You mean Stanley Augustus Owsley III? He's a millionaire's son and also a millionaire himself. He made it on LSD 25. He just got out of jail. He bought the lysergic acid from the army four to six years ago. He purchased four fifty-five-gallon drums full of lysergic acid.

Up until recently acid was legal—then it was made illegal and everyone started using it. But just before it was made illegal, Owsley, a chemist, built a lab and made acid. During this time he made up to ten million caps, which means, at a low estimate, he could have made up to ten million dollars making acid legally.

He lives in the Berkeley hills and is a millionaire hippie.

As everyone knows, the best acid made in this country is made by Augustus Stanley Owlsley [sic] III. To my knowledge he started producing *circa* 1964, in great quantities. His stuff was so good, and there was so much of it around, that for a while acid was called "Owlsley" acid. Almost makes you think of Kleenex. His first stuff was in small transparent capsules, and the stuff was in purple powder.

Nowadays, when somebody says, "I dropped some real good acid the other night," the obvious question is, "Wow man, was it Owlsley?"

Owsley is a real mystic. He has a certain aura about him. He's immune from the narcs. He just shows up somewhere like the Fillmore or in the Park [Golden Gate] and hands out thousands of caps of free acid. Then he disappears. The cops can never bust him.

He once gave some acid to a narc who would have busted him but didn't when he found out who he was.

I heard that Owsley gave something like $20,000 to the "Grateful Dead" [the first psychedelic rock band] to go out and buy some equipment.

On one Saturday afternoon when they were having those things on Mount Tamalpais—like mass meetings on the mountain—Owsley flew in in a helicopter. He got out and just distributed like Jesus,

and then pulled out — a real classic type of thing.
A friend of mine was there and he got some of the acid.

Owsley's into sound. He's taking Fender Princeton Amps and taking out the speakers and doing something which makes the speakers distort, which sounds really great. He's done a couple of amps. I think he did one for one of the guys in the Quicksilver Messenger Service. (Told by a student band player, 19, who had seen Owsley in a music equipment store.)[39]

The greatest Owsley story tells of his visiting a group of Free Speech Movement activists in jail. Owsley astonished the Berkeley radicals by appearing dressed in a purple velvet suit and carrying a Bible. He opened it solemnly and with a grave countenance proceeded to read passages aloud. When the suspicions of any possible passers-by had been allayed, he revealed that the Good Book had been dipped in acid so that the jailmates could "groove" on its pages. Owsley passed it around, each tore out a page from his favorite section — one from Jeremiah, most from Job — and sucked on the sheets until all were wiped out.[40]

So the legends fanned out and multiplied. One report had Owsley allied with the cops against the Mafia, and another leagued him with the Mafia, who paid off the cops to let the acid flow freely.

From the folklorist's point of view, the stories about Owsley told throughout the hip drug culture meet all the specifications of heroic legend except that of duration over time. In form the Owsley cycle resembles closely the traditions of the powerful lobsterman Barney Beal on the Maine coast. Both sagas found their expression in small, independent anecdotes that reiterated certain key themes — Barney's size and strength, Owsley's skill at making and selling LSD — and wandered off the main track. Barney exemplifies the strong hero, who can fell a horse with a blow of his fist, lift up a two-hundred-pound water barrel, and stave in the chest of an opponent with his bare hand. Owsley represents the magician-trickster, who can always escape the narcs, and whose mind-expanding pills give *mana* to their takers. Both have assumed the role of father-figures protecting their people, in the one case united by blood — many of the Maine coastal fishermen belong to the Beal clan, and an island is named for them — and in the other by acid. With the might of his flailing arms Barney protects the Maine fishermen against revenue men and Gloucester poachers, and lifts an anchor that two of his fellows cannot budge. Even so does Owsley bring solace to acid heads in jail, sponsor rock musicians, and, like Jesus distributing loaves and fishes, spread his tablets among the flower people. Both are strictly in-group heroes; lumberjacks ten miles inland from the Maine coast had not heard of Barney Beal and the straight world knows not the name of Augustus Owsley Stanley III. And as with all mortal heroes, no matter how potent, they too met their fate. Barney strained his heart one summer hauling a dory that it took four ordinary men to lift; and the day came when the narcs busted Owsley through the treachery of an informer.[41]

Who is the real Owsley? The *San Francisco Chronicle* and *Examiner* and *Los Angeles Times* have given him full coverage since 1966, established his biography, and peered at his legend. His baptismal name is Augustus Owsley Stanley III, and he was born in 1935 in Arlington, Virginia, son of a well-to-do government official and grandson of a United States senator from Kentucky who said prophetically in 1922, "You cannot milk a cow in America without a federal inspector at your heels." In time his grandson would be able to substitute "make a tab" for "milk a cow." Young Stanley went to Washington and Lee High School in Arlington and attended the University of Virginia, but he broke with his family at eighteen and headed for California. In 1956 he entered the air force and served a year and a half at Edwards Air Force Base, where he acquired electronic skills that led him to short-lived broadcasting and engineering jobs. He himself never took a chemistry course, but at the University of California in Berkeley in 1963 he met a chemistry major, Melissa Dianne Cargill, who accompanied him when he dropped out after one semester. They rented space behind a vacant store in Berkeley, and Owsley — the name he took for himself — devised a makeshift laboratory in the bathroom. Moving his operations to Los Angeles in 1965, close by Los Angeles City College, he purchased eight hundred grams of lysergic acid from two chemical companies and began manufacturing and selling his blue, aspirin-sized tablets, which sold on the street for about five dollars a dose. The Los Angeles police department narcotics chief, Captain Alfred W. Trembly, testified to a Senate investigating committee that Owsley paid $20,000 in new hundred-dollar bills for five hundred grams of lysergic acid bought from Cyclo Chemical Corporation. Owsley's production was estimated at ten million tablets. These purchases were then legal, and lysergic acid did not become hallucinogenic until blended with the diethylamide radical. By thirty-one Owsley was a millionaire.

The police kept surveillance of his activities and made attempts to charge him. Acting on a tip that he was manufacturing methamphetamine (trademarked as Methedrine and called meth by drug addicts), a dangerous stimulant, they raided his Berkeley laboratory, but found no illegal drugs. Owsley obtained a court order and compelled the police to return his laboratory equipment. But his string ran out on December 21, 1967, when agents of the Federal Bureau of Drug Abuse, Berkeley police, sheriff's deputies of Contra Costa County, and California state narcotics agents descended on the house in Orinda, a town in the hills east of Berkeley where he had set up a sophisticated chemical laboratory. "Raiders Find Drug Factory; LSD King Held"; "'King of Acid' Under Arrest"; "LSD Tycoon Held After Orinda Raid" headlined the newspapers next day, and the *San Francisco Chronicle* carried a picture captioned "King of Acid" showing a profile view of Owsley as a studious and youthful-appearing fellow with a large cap pulled down over his spectacles. On November 7, 1969, he was sentenced in federal court to three years in prison and fined $3,000 for manufacturing and possessing LSD. Out on bail, he was rearrested January 31, 1970, in a hotel in the New Orleans French Quarter with eighteen others charged with possessing marijuana and LSD, and in Oakland on July 13 he was once more arrested on similar charges. On July 21, 1970, Federal Judge William T. Sweigert revoked Owsley's $35,000 bail, saying that his continued freedom would endanger the community. Owsley was then transferred from the Oakland county jail to the federal prison at Terminal Island in Los Angeles Harbor. On August 5, 1971, the Ninth United States Circuit Court of Appeals upheld the three-year prison sentence for the third time. Owsley's lawyers appealed on the grounds that the federal agents had failed to discover LSD tablets, only powder, in the Orinda laboratory, and the question then hinged on the salability of LSD in powder form. An associate of Owsley had betrayed him and informed the Feds that Owsley was about to begin tabbing. Shades of Sam Bass and Jim Murphy!

The newspaper reports give hints of Owsley's legendary status. By 1966 he had acquired the reputation on the West Coast as "Mr. LSD." The *San Francisco Chronicle* reported October 5, 1966: "Any time he appeared at a public gathering of the acid set he could count on a round of applause. In the San Francisco area, where he was more widely known, it often would be a standing ovation." His generosity overcame the suspicion of heads about anyone as old as thirty-one (as he was in 1966). He furnished the LSD to spike the Kool-Aid at the City's first Trips Festival in Longshoremen's Hall on January 21, 1966, a scene immortalized in Tom Wolfe's *The Electric Kool-Aid Acid Test*. A straight psychiatrist, aghast at seeing a thousand heads turned on simultaneously, asked a policeman if he feared trouble, and the law officer replied, "No, sir! These folks is filled with LOVE, man." In good part Owsley helped bring LSD from a small intellectual coterie in 1963 to the youth culture three years later, when its use was still legal. He allowed a rock-and-roll group to practice behind his dilapidated Berkeley cottage, until the neighbors complained, and he is publicly identified on a 1966 Capitol Records documentary LP entitled "LSD" as the sponsor of the Grateful Dead, who supplied the background music. On the record the narrator tells of a chemist who made a million dollars on LSD, and users at an acid party are then heard talking about their supplier: "Owsley makes great acid"—"Owsley really knows how to make acid"—"So that all the impurities are taken out"—"Owsley really has dynamite, righteous acid." On Haight-Ashbury, the "King of Psycho-pharmacology" gave away five thousand STP pills (a stronger drug than LSD) in one grand gesture. His professed goal was "to turn the whole world on."

Although labeled "Hippieland's Court Chemist," in his personal appearance Owsley resembles the motorcycle gangs more than the hippies. Once he showed up at a bank in boots, black leather jacket, jeans, and a white crash helmet. One reporter placed him in the stereotype of the playboy who likes to "drive fast cars, live in cool pads, and squire groovy chicks."[42]

The esteem for Owsley's tablets extended to medical circles. A young physician, Dr. Richard Rappolt, who worked part-time for the San Francisco public health department, administered Owsley's LSD to a pregnant woman who had tried to induce an abortion through an overdose of the drug ergotamine. The large overdose had caused the patient's uterus to "churn horribly" for hours, while her fingertips turned icy cold, a sign (according to the paper) that they might drop off.

"She happened to have purple Owsleys in the house," reported the doctor. "She said she had had a couple of good trips with it. It looked like it might be a fatality. I felt her condition, anyway, couldn't get worse. It struck me that LSD might be used as an antagonist [to the overdose].

"I had her drop two of the Owsley capsules. Originally these were alleged to contain between eighty and one hundred milligrams of LSD. I waited for fifteen minutes. She seemed to be better. I had her drop another. After forty-five minutes she really calmed down. Her uterus stopped churning. I said for her to drop one every hour."

Bleeding continued for two days, but then the woman, a registered nurse, returned to normalcy, and went to a gynecologist to have her uterus scraped. The abortion attempt had succeeded. When asked why his patient did not hallucinate, Dr. Rappolt explained that the severe pain prevented any illusory experiences. "When someone has a clamp on your testicle, you don't hallucinate," he suggested. Subsequently he tried the same remedy with success in a similar case and gave credit to "Owsley's acid—the product of Augustus Owsley Stanley III, a bigtime dealer in LSD who has a reputation in the drug underground for not polluting his product with speed [amphetamines] or other agents."

A close look at Owsley through the eyes of one of the Grateful Dead, Jerry Garcia, and his "old lady," Mountain Girl, one of the Merry Pranksters, is afforded in a long *Rolling Stone* interview printed in the issue of January 20, 1972. The interviewers were Charles Reich, of *The Greening of America* fame, and Jann Wenner, editor of *Rolling Stone*. In the course of the taped interview sessions, which touched on many aspects of the youth rock culture in the Bay Area, Owsley's name came up several times. Recounting several memorable acid scenes, Mountain Girl remembered one at Muir Beach where Owsley was present:

That was a particularly nice one. One of the highlights of that one was—dare I say, shall I breathe his name?—Owsley pushing a chair along this wooden floor, this old wooden chair, running it along the floor making this noise, the most horrible screeching and scraping. It went on for hours, I'm not exaggerating, it just drove everybody completely up the wall. That was really an incredible exhibition of making yourself . . . uncomfortable . . . making other people uncomfortable.

Jerry. No, man, it was just the guy completely freaked out with his body running around . . . that's what that was, I mean he was completely freaked out.

Mountain Girl. He was scraping that chair and listening to the noise

and lovin' it, I guess that was what was happening.
Jerry. How do you know?
Mountain Girl. Oh . . . I watched him for a really long time.
Jerry. That wasn't it. I talked to him about that a lot and he just—his mind was completely shot, he thought they'd come and taken it from him.

> Interviewer Reich then asked if Owsley
> was part of the Berkeley psychedelic
> scene. Garcia agreed.

Right. He didn't get along too good with our more wilder version, because . . . well, the big straight psychedelic scene always called our scene too high-energy, you see. . . . "Too high-energy, you can freak out in there, you know." That was what they always used to say.
Mountain Girl. Hardly anybody did.
Jerry. Owsley did.

The conversation between Mountain Girl and Jerry developed into a dialogue over the differing points of view of the Merry Pranksters and the Grateful Dead. Mountain Girl asserted the Pranksters had limited themselves to acid, taken only on Acid Test night, while the Dead had gone really weird. Jerry conceded that the band had lived off Owsley's good graces and his money, in a house that Owsley rented. "Owsley's trip was he wanted to design equipment for us and we were going to have to be in sort of a lab situation for him to do it." This situation lasted for about a year, but the musicians wearied of the experiment and finally took to screaming at Owsley and parted company with him.

Owsley sold his fancy equipment and replaced it with "regular standard simple-minded plain old equipment so we could go out and work."

Later in the interview Jerry was asked if he still saw Owsley. Yes, Jerry had worked on a play with the inmates at the Terminal Island federal prison and visited with him. "Owsley is a hero." Jerry was very much looking forward to having him out and working again, as he was such a tremendous asset.

Jann asked, "Owsley had a really weird role in the whole thing. You think he's mellowed quite a bit?"

Jerry responded with an extended eulogy that captures elements of the Owsley legend:

Right. I think that he still has the capacity to be what he is. But I think that there's an important lesson involved which took us a long time to snap to, which is this: Owsley is the guy who brought a really solid consciousness of what *quality* was, to our whole scene. And that's been the basis of our operations since then: being able to have our equipment in really good shape, our P.A. really good, stuff like that. We try to display as much quality as possible in the hopes of being able to refine pieces of what we do. And that's the thing that Owsley does like no other human being that I know can do or devote his attention to, and that is that thing of purification. It's a real thing with him. He's really really good at it. Owsley's a fine guy. He's just got an *amazing* mind.

He's got enough of *every* kind of experience, man! There's almost nothing the guy hasn't done. You know he's a licensed blacksmith? Not only that, but he's got a first class broadcaster's license, too. He worked for years in TV. He's also an *excellent* auto mechanic; he's obviously a chemist. There's almost nothing that he doesn't do, or at least have a good grasp of. He understands just about every level of organization. He's just incredible, he's got some incredible capacity for retaining information.

Freakouts

Druglore abounds with horror tales and thrill experiences. In his rejection of the mind-numbing and spirit-withering effects of the System and his acceptance of pot, hash, acid, and speed as a means of enlarging his vision, the head knowingly embarks on a hazardous course. He can be busted by the narcs. And he can damage himself through overdoses, wrong doses, or repeated doses that send him on bad trips and wreak havoc on his body and mind. To compensate, there are the moments of ecstasy, eu-phoria, and transcendence. Narrators of drug experiences stress these two themes and, like folk performers everywhere, attempt to shock and awe their audiences with ever more hair-raising scenes.

One group of horror tales emphasize the ill effects of drugs upon a particular user, although, as so often in folklore stories, the report comes at second or third hand. These alarming accounts show an affinity with the sick-joke cycle ("Otherwise how did you enjoy the play, Mrs. Lincoln?"), as in the legend of the mushy acid head.

As the legend goes, there was a head in the Haight-Ashbury who was dropping acid three and four times a week. After a while he began to complain of acute headaches. He went to see a doctor and although the doctor couldn't find anything wrong he placed the guy in the hospital. Less than a week later the guy was dead.

When an autopsy was performed the guy's brain, which was about the consistency of oatmeal, had to be spooned out of his head.[43]

Many such sick legends—for these are not jokes, but declarations of alleged facts—circulate about cases of acid droppers who end up in mental hospitals. There was a guy who took acid every day until he couldn't talk, and his friends carried him to the hospital. ("There was a guy" or "There was a head" corresponds to "One time there was" as a formula opening used in southern Appalachian and Ozark folktales.)

A player in Shiva's Head Band rode down the drag nude on a bicycle one day in 1967. The cops took him to a hospital and gave him three shock treatments, which wiped him out. He was in a haze for months.

A prominent professor at the University of Texas, who taught both German and chemistry (surely a folklore vagary!), kept dropping more and more acid. He became violent, lost his mind, and took to sitting in the Chuckwagon day after day, wearing the same gray Mao suit and staring at people, never talking. One day in a paranoid spell he hit a person who he thought was after him. The police arrested the prof and took him to the state hospital for shock treatment. He is still there.

There was a guy who took LSD to the point that he thought he had a hole in his body. He kept the imaginary hole plugged up with his finger to prevent the air from escaping and his body from deflating. They sent him to a mental hospital.[44]

The mental hospital itself is a scene prominent in headlore and characterized in Ken Kesey's novel and play, *One Flew Over the Cuckoo's Nest*. In this scene straights and freaks coexist in uneasy tension, and the onlooker is hard put to it to tell whose behavior is antic and whose is sane. In some dope stories the heads engage in grotesque stunts and perform taboo actions for limited spans without penalty. Their humor turns on the erratic perceptions and responses of dopers to the outside world, a world taken solemnly and regarded as solid by the straights. Incongruities and absurdities highlight these drug tales, which can be read as put-ons and put-downs of straight society as well as caricatures of roles the straights ascribe to freaks. Here, as the collector says, a speed freak gives vent to his paranoid aggression:

An old meth freak had been shooting up a whole lot of speed one night up on Sabine Street. He ran out of the house and into the front yard in his undershorts and started tackling the shrubs, screaming, "I've got you now, you sonuvabitch."[45]

In a comparable performance, the head hallucinates and then turns aggressive:

I heard about a guy who took peyote and kept waiting for the effects. We went to the john and when he was standing in front of the urinal he saw a blue flight of stairs going right up the urinal, outside and way up in the air. He just stared at it for a long time, zipped up his pants and went out.

He started thinking about it, decided what he really wanted to do was go up those stairs and went back. But they were gone. He started hammering at the urinal screaming for his blue stairs.

A buddy finally came in and took him out before someone called the cops.[46]

One can read here a put-on of the consumer community in the head's heedless, obsessive desire for a fancied object.

Because of the high priority assigned bathroom installations in the plastic culture, freaks seem to take particular satisfaction in putting on their scene in lavatory settings. Here is another example, related by a twenty-two-year-old coed majoring in English at Berkeley:

A friend of mine told me this story about some friends of his.

A guy took a leaf his roommate had around the apartment. He chewed it for about half an hour and began to notice he had no concept of space—he kept knocking into things yet felt no pain. He threw off all of his clothes and ran into the bathroom to take a shower. He started screaming and screaming about a barracuda in the toilet.

His roommate was frightened since he couldn't control him and called Cal [University of California] hospital. Two campus cops came to get him—and he was standing in the bathroom talking to the barracuda, stark naked. One of the cops looked around and said, "Well, where is this crazy guy?"

Dumb cops! But wow, can you imagine taking some leaf somebody gave you without checking up on it? It scares me![47]

Two common drug-story elements meet in this put-on, the cops as numskulls and the freak as prankster. The teller accepts the narrative as a cautionary true tale warning against the indiscriminate use of narcotics or opiates.

A nice synthesis blends the following freakout-aggression tale with the heads-tricking-the-cops formula:

Listen, a friend of mine told me this, so I think it's pretty straight.

These two guys decided to take belladonna. I think it comes in a leaf form. Anyway they chewed some and waited for a while and nothing happened, so they chewed some more and then went into a room to listen to some records.

All of a sudden, mad chaotic noises started coming out of the room, screams and tearing, ripping sounds, things crashing all around. The neighbors called the cops who found the two guys stripped naked, pulling the plaster off the walls, the light sockets and wires out, trying to pry up the floors, breaking the door down. They were put in the can.

The next day some friends in the same apartment house came down to get them out. The cops said they were holding them on narcotic charges. Someone said, "But they were just using belladonna." The cop said, "Oh is that all? There's no law against that!"

So they let them free! The friends asked the guy why he was tearing up the room like that and he said, "Man, I was taking on the whole South Vietnamese army."[48]

According to the collector, the auditors savored the put-down of the police even more than the put-on of the heads. Freakout experiences run the gamut from the terrifying to the titillating, and one can never be too sure whether they are meant to shock, amuse, deceive, or inveigle the listener. He cannot readily draw the line between the genuine alarm and the mocking playlet that ensue from an LSD trip.

Druglore Local Legends

Most of the legendary narratives in the hip drug culture concern freaks and heads, and are classified by the folklorist as anecdotal or personal legends. The parallel category of local or place legends, attached to the land or to a landmark, cannot prove so bountiful in a mobile and primarily urban subculture—although the communes, if they last, will certainly generate geographical traditions. Yet some legends of locality have taken root in the soil of druglore. They show an affinity with the myriad legends of buried treasure, lost mines, and lucky finds that kindle the human imagination, except that in this case the treasure is no pot of gold, just pot.

The best-known tradition of buried pot concerns a particularly potent strain of marijuana called "New York White," news of which excited the underground pot culture of Berkeley in the spring of 1965.

Rumor had it that when New York heads were suspecting a police raid, they would flush their marijuana down the toilet. Thus before long the weed was flourishing in the rich organic environment of the sewer system. Since the plants received no light, part of the photosynthetic process was impaired and the plants were virtually white, hence the name "New York White."[49]

Well, if so enticing an object throve in a known, albeit uninviting locale, why would not some adventurous freaks undertake the quest? Because, according to a newspaper story, full-grown alligators prowled the sewers of New York. It seems that Miami vacationers returning to New York in the winter brought back baby alligators as pets for their children. The more the alligators grew

291

the less ideal they appeared as playmates, and their owners, too tenderhearted to skin them for their hides, mercifully flushed them down the toilet. Some survived in their new environment and confronted sewer maintenance workers, who publicly protested at this unnecessary additional hazard to their occupation. The newspapers published the matter, and tales began to circulate. Some alleged that snakes were slithering along the pipes of New York's water system, oozing out of spigots in washbasins and coiling happily in toilet bowls. A giant python was supposed to inhabit the plumbing of a large New York tenement.

A drama student in Los Angeles, a young woman of twenty-one, synthesized the two reports in this fashion:

"I've a good story for you. Joel and Larry told it to me when I was in Berkeley. Have you heard about the alligators in New York? It's really a funny story. There are three alligators that were flushed down the toilets there, and alligators can live in sewers, of course. Now, what else often gets flushed down the toilet? Think."

"Shit?"

"Oh God! Grass. And the grass grows down there and it's supposed to be great. But nobody can get any of it because of the alligators. It's too dangerous and no one is willing to chance it. How would you like to come face to face with a giant alligator in the sewer?"[50]

Another student collector notes that the name "New York White" parodies other brand names, such as "Acapulco Gold" and "Panama Red," that potheads give marijuana according to color and presumed place of origin. Feces in the sewers, so ran the legend, provided a fertile medium for the growth of the illegal plants.[51] Some says that marijuana also grows in Berkeley sewers.

A persistent legend theme concerns the lost marijuana field or the lost stash, for which the hopeful freak searches in vain. As in American buried-treasure tales, the prize almost always eludes the seeker. A twenty-three-year-old female clerical worker in Berkeley recounted this version of the elusive field, which she heard about on six different occasions:

There is a legend in Marin County [California] that there is a lost marijuana field in the hills near Bolinas or between the Stinson Beach highway between Mount Tamalpais and the Muir Woods, which was planted by a group of people in 1943. Five or six persons have told me about this field, all of whom "knew" somebody who was in the original planting group. The date, 1943, has been consistent from all sources.

I have been on three expeditions to find this field and know of eight other attempts to find this field between 1960 and 1963. The group supposedly collected three quart jars of marijuana seeds and scattered them in a one hundred or two hundred square foot meadow in a circle of trees and brush. Nobody has ever found this field of course.[52]

Paradoxically, a field for which no freak looked, and where a narcotic plant not only grew but, with the aid of man, filled the air with heady fumes, has also entered tradition. This is the legend of the hemp farm, located in various places in Indiana. During the Civil War—or World War I in another variant—Hoosier farmers grew hemp as a stout fiber for ropes, bags, and other such products useful as military supplies. After the war the demand for hemp slackened and most of the crops were abandoned. But some plants continued to grow, and kids in the neighborhood came by to pick them, not for the tough fiber, but for the tender flowers and leaves from which hashish is obtained. Dismayed, the authorities had the picked-over fields burned. In no time the whole countryside turned on. Heads came from all around, just to breathe the air. The authorities burning the fields became stoned too. One of the more sympathetic officers reportedly said to some of the bystanders, as they inhaled deeply, "Don't say we've never given you anything!" These burning hemp farms are located in northern Indiana, but tradition places one in New Mexico, where at the time of the crop burning the winds changed and caused the whole population of a nearby town to get high.[53]

Because the drugs they desire are expensive and illegal, freaks respond eagerly to rumors and assertions of a cache of narcotics that eluded the police. In his column in the *San Francisco Chronicle* Ralph Gleason printed various such legends of the lost or hidden stash. One, previously unreported, is told by a young bohemian, artist, and part-time laborer in San Francisco:

Yes, stories like that come up usually after somebody gets busted. You know, when somebody goes to jail somebody else knows the guy had a big stash and the heat didn't find it.

Once a friend and I heard about a connection we knew getting busted, dig, and the guy that told us said the connection left a half a piece in the pad somewhere and why don't we score on it. So we cut on over there [Fell Street in San Francisco] that night and knocked like we just wanted to talk to this guy, you know, but if it was cool we were going to go in his pad and look for stash, dig.

Well, we were there about a minute and the heat walks up and wants to know what's happening. So we said the guy wasn't home and we were just going to split. So they shook us down and let us go and as far as I know there's still a half an ounce of shit in that pad some place.[54]

Freudians who see a symbolic correlation between gold and feces, both representing a precious substance, can point to the slang use of "shit" for marijuana as another link between the legends of buried treasure and of the hidden stash.

In one unusual memorat a traveling freak does find dope, when he is not specifically searching for a cache or a field. This "legendary dope tale," as the collector calls it, was told at a pot party where everyone was exchanging such stories, and is a personal rather than a place legend. The teller is a nineteen-year-old Indiana youth who gave his occupation as "traveling."

I was out in California during the summer just traveling around. I'd been doing a lot of dope, mostly grass, but was slowly running out of money. So finally I found myself without any money or any place to stay. It ended up with me sleeping on the beach for one night with plans on hitchhiking back home the next day. At the time I was totally out of grass, and despondent because I didn't have any money to buy some.

So I got up the next morning quite unstoned and started towards the road to begin hitching. No rides came along, so I started walking. Before long I glanced down and there was a baggie lying beside the road. I picked it up and my gosh, it was half full of grass. Naturally this gave me a little boost in spirit. I went into the woods beside the road and did a joint. It turned out to be some of the best I'd had in a long time. Feeling much better I started hitching again. Before long three freaks in a Volks bus stopped and picked me up. We got around to smoking some grass and I rolled quite a few out of my bag. But the strange thing is that it never seemed to go down in quantity. It looked like exactly as much as I started out with.

I rode on with them for about three hours until they had to turn off. Even though I had dope they laid another lid on me for free—it seems as though they had quite a bit. I thanked them and took off truckin', both bags of dope in my knapsack. About an hour later I stopped to roll a joint, but when I looked for that dope I'd found, it was gone. I *know* it was in my knapsack because I'd checked it before I started walking. And it was in the bottom, so it couldn't have just slipped out. Besides, the other dope was still there.

I finally decided that there must have been a mystic bag of dope—one that could only belong to people who didn't have any. Because I found it when I was out, it never seemed to get smaller, and it disappeared after I got some other dope. I just picture it appearing all over to the poor unfortunates who don't have any dope.[55]

Clearly present here is the magical motif familiar in Old World *Märchen* of the inexhaustible purse or bread basket that keeps filling up to succor its poor or hungry owner. A magic stump supplies whiskey for a witch in the Schoharie Hills of New York; a magic bottle furnishes drink in the Ozarks; magic sticks bring forth food in the piney-woods country of New Jersey.[56] The "mystic bag of dope" updates the motif of magic food and drink with grass, its equivalent for the hip drug subculture. As the proverb goes, "Grass will get you through times of no money, but money won't get you through times of no grass."[57] In the youth culture order of priorities drugs far outstrip dollars. The coda in the tale above expresses the sense of a supernatural benefactor, such as the Three Nephites in Mormon legend, or the Virgin Mary in East European peasant tales, or Catholic patron saints who bring help and sustenance to their flocks. Who may emerge as the guardian angel of dissenting youth has not yet been determined, although Owsley plays that role in some legends in which he freely dispenses his tabs.

Druglore Latrinalia

Graffiti, a new entry in the genres of folklore, consists of sayings scribbled, chalked, painted, or charcoaled on any kind of publicly visible surface from Grant's Tomb to the Atlantic City boardwalk. The Columbia University philologist Allen Walker Read once presented a learned paper to the American Folklore Society on graffiti he had studied on the walls of New York subways. One that stays in the mind is "Jackie Kennedy picks her nose." While graffiti are personal and written, they often embody or parody traditional sayings and beliefs, and they definitely express folk values and attitudes. The graffito about Mrs. Onassis rebukes the media for according her excessive adulation and publicity and reminds the world that she is an earthly goddess.

Latrinalia—inscriptions in public toilets —provide a wealth of graffiti with reverberations of the drug culture. Student folklorists have collected and reported such latrinalia, documented not by informant (who is usually not visible at the time of the inscribing) but by locations of the particular restroom. As with other items of counterculture folklore, glosses from the young collectors afford helpful insights into the texts.

Ronald Reagan mainlines Kool-aid.

(Men's room, Barrows Hall, University of California, Berkeley)[58]

This latrinalium, like the graffito about Mrs. Onassis, displays *lèse-majesté* toward a public personality. The relentless foe of the drug culture, Governor Reagan of California, a former movie star, is pictured shooting his veins full of a children's drink, the very drink Ken Kesey's Merry Pranksters spiked with LSD to turn on a whole sector of Los Angeles.

Timothy Leary drinks martinis.

(Men's room, Wheeler Hall, University of California, Berkeley)[59]

While Reagan is the ogre, Leary is the fallen idol. The father-figure and first martyr-hero of the LSD movement (dismissed from Harvard for advocating and experimenting on students with the drug) and the eloquent expositor in the pages of *Playboy* and elsewhere of the mind-expanding delights of LSD, Leary has ceased to turn on his constituency. As one Berkeley student in 1968 explained his decline: "Timothy Leary used to be a folk hero but he isn't any more. Most people seem to think he pushes his trip on other people, and that he's trying to get everyone else on his thing, and this is violating the number one rule, which is that everyone has their own trip."[60] This student and others resented the religious presentations, and the charges for admission, made by Leary in a cross-country tour in 1967. Acid heads don't want to incorporate LSD into a religion and pay Timothy Leary when they are high, added this student commentator.

Christ was a hippie.

(Women's restroom, Pizza Haven,
Bancroft Way, Berkeley)

Give me librium
or give me meth.

(Wall in Haight-Ashbury,
hence not technically a latrinalium,
unless the wall was used as a latrine.)

Candy is dandy,
But acid's faster.

(Women's restroom, Pizza Haven,
Bancroft Way, Berkeley)[61]

Originally the popular rhyme, used in a poem by Ogden Nash and repeated by every schoolboy, ran "Candy is dandy but liquor is quicker."

People who live in glass houses shouldn't get stoned.

(Restroom wall of Montgomery Ward's,
Monument Boulevard, Pleasant Hill, California)

People who live in grass houses must get stoned.

(Men's room, Land's End Pub, California
Street, San Francisco)

It is said that man who
sow grass in neighbor's yard
has no pot of his own.
— Confucius

(Bathroom wall of Griffiths Hall,
University of California, Berkeley)

A loaf of bread
A bottle of wine,
A bag of weed,
And you, you.

A friend with weed
Is a friend indeed.

(Both on bathroom wall at Panda Terminals,
2211 Wood Street, Oakland, California)[62]

The student collector saw a friend write the "loaf of bread" on the wall of the men's room, a rare instance of the folklorist being able to identify the inscriber of a graffito.

Where there's dope
there's hope,
Take tea and see.

(Men's room in Robbie's Cafeteria
on Telegraph Avenue, Berkeley)[63]

A media commercial attacking coffee is adopted without change: "Take tea and see," but since tea is another colloquialism for marijuana, the cliché and the commercial form a happy union.

Southern Pacific has
fewer Larks.
Northern Pacific has
fewer Narks.
Support your local
passenger trains.

(Men's room, Wheeler Hall, University
of California, Berkeley)[64]

This complex latrinalium refers in the first line to the crack train between Los Angeles and San Francisco, named the "Lark," that was taken off in 1970 with the reduction of train services. Since LA and the City are both centers of the drug culture, the "Lark" would be a natural run for narcotic agents to travel on, in distinction to the routes serviced by the Northern Pacific. The third line parodies the right-wing political slogan "Support your local police." The whole text mocks the use by police officers of the "Lark" for their surveillance and expresses satisfaction at the demise of Southern Pacific's most elegant train, yet another symbol of the materialistic power structure.

Druglore Jokes

As the latrinalia indicate, the lexicon of the hip drug subculture breeds a humor of word play. Among drug freaks there circulate a string of joking or riddling questions and punning jokes and sayings whose humor rests on the esoteric meanings of their folk speech, uncomprehended by the straight world:

The concerned father came home to find his daughter and her friends smoking marijuana. Grabbing the pot out of her mouth, he exclaimed, "What's a joint like this doing in a nice girl like you?"[65]

A variant elaborates on the situation:

Once upon a time there was a nude pot party which was raided by the police. Of course everyone panicked and their first thought was to hide their marijuana cigarettes. Since everyone was nude this presented a problem. However, one clever girl chose the only obvious place on her body to hid the cigarette. One of the arresting officers, upon making a thorough search and finding the cigarette, commented, "What's a joint like you doing in a girl like this.[66]

Here are some riddling questions.

What did one marijuana plant say to the other?
Let's get out of this joint.

What is the LSD set known as?
High Society.

What is better than LSD?
SEX, if you have the right pusher.[67]

In druglore humor a number of jokes center on hippies. These jokes percolate through the mass media and appear in comic books and cartoon strips, which stereotype the hippie as a hairy, unkempt, ragged fellow wearing beads and sandals. The following examples are limited to oral versions heard by student collectors. These youthful folklorists frequently observe that hippies do not tell jokes, though they also comment on the pot parties with their rounds of taletelling and joke telling. But they distinguish between a drug freak and a hippie. The hippie is an itinerant wholly immersed in the counterculture as a total way of life, and indulgence in pot or acid or other narcotics may or may not be part of this life-style, whereas the head regularly partakes of illegal drugs although he may not drop out from straight society in other ways. It seems unlikely that the true hippie would joke on himself, and his meditative, introspective nature seems little calculated for explosive laughter. Derisive hippie jokes are told by straights outside the hip culture. In his several roles the hippie is sometimes a hero overturning an Establishment figure, sometimes an existentialist clown, sometimes the stupid ogre of fairy tales.

Double meanings of words and phrases in the druglore lexicon furnish the seeds of some humorous anecdotes:

There were two hippies in a room and they were smoking pot and taking LSD. And one hippie turned to the other and said, "Hey man, go turn on the radio." So the hippie got up, walked over to the radio, and facing it he said, "I love you."

There's this guy who's really high, loaded, a knocked-out cat. Then this old lady walks up to him and says, "Do the cross-town buses run all night long?"
And he says, "Doo da, do daa."[68]

The happy-go-lucky pothead (not identified as a hippie in this joke) tunes in on the lady traveler's inquiry according to the rhythm of Stephen Foster's song: "The Camptown racetrack five miles long . . . doodah! doodah!"

Two stoned hippies were crawling along the railroad tracks. One looked back at the other and said, "This sure is a long ladder."
The other said, "Yea, but the handrail is out of sight."[69]

Again we see the clown whose perception of his environment in his drugged state turns the normal scheme of things topsy-turvy—a state that straights deem ludicrous and pathetic but that the hippie regards as desirable. At times, though, there appears to be a method in the hippie's madness.

A hippie was driving the wrong way down a one-way street, and a policeman pulled him over and said, "Look-it buddy, didn't you see the arrows?"
"No man, I didn't even see the Indians."
(The joke teller recalled having first heard this told on a beatnik.)[70]

In nineteenth-century anecdotes the Yankee retaliated on the city wiseacre with similar edged retorts. Looking over the orchard on his summer cottage in the hills in Vermont, the big-city magnate pokes a thumb at a fruit tree and announces importantly to the local yokel, "You'll never get a peck of apples from that tree." "You're right," says the Yankee. "It's ash."

The hippie as ogre is depicted in the joke about the cannibal restaurant:

A sign in a cannibal restaurant read:

```
MISSIONARY DINNER ........................ $3.00
OIL MAN DINNER .......................... $3.00
HIPPIE DINNER............................ $6.00
```

Reading this menu, a prospective client asked why the hippie dinner cost twice as much as the other two selections. The restaurant owner replied, "Have *you* ever tried to clean a hippie?"[71]

This hostile unpleasantry was told by a woman in her late forties with a Ph.D. in linguistics. Although Jews will tell jokes making fun of Jewish over-sensitivity to anti-Semitism and Polish-Americans will tell jokes caricaturing the dirty, stupid Pole—if they are far enough removed from their immigrant origins—the youth culture has not yet attained the distance necessary to see humor in self-parody. More to its taste is the tale of the hippie as trickster-hero, as in this story of "The Hippie and the Shopkeeper":

One late afternoon, this hippie walked into a grocery store and said, "I'd like to buy some dog food."

The storeowner looked at him and asked him, "You got a dog?" The hippie replied, "Yes." He said, "Well, prove it to me."

So the hippie goes out the door, half a hour later comes back, shows the owner the dog, the owner sells him the dog food, and the hippie goes about his way.

About half an hour later the same hippie came in, said, "I'd like some birdseed." The storeowner looked at him, said, "Do you have a bird?" The hippie replied, "Yes." Storeowner said, "Prove it to me."

So he goes out, comes back about half a hour later, has this bird in a bird cage, says, "Here." So the storeowner sold him the birdseed and he walks on.

About half a hour later he comes in with a shoebox under his arm, with a hole cut in the top. Storeowner looks at him and says, "What do you want?" He said, "Stick your hand in this box." Storeowner stuck his hand in the box, and was feeling around and said,

"What's in here?" The hippie replied, "What does that feel like to you?"

Said, "Feels like shit."

Said, "That's right. I want a roll of toilet paper."[72]

In stories such as this the hippie takes his place with Hodja Nasreddin, Tyl Eulenspiegel, Brer Rabbit, Anansi the Spider, and other trickster underdogs who turn the tables on the high and mighty.

Drug Games

Games learned by informal individual and group transmission, on the playground, in the park, in the parlor, exhibit all the variations characteristic of other forms of folklore. Specialists have classified folk games into such groupings as ball games, running games, courting games, play-party games, and the like, according to the central action involved. The hip drug culture too has developed its games and recreations.

Within the subculture these pastimes are designated "drug games," "stoned games," and "sensory-awareness games." They differ from other folk games in using the drug experience — pot or acid — as a point of departure to further the group revelry. Stoned games aim at heightening visual, aural, and physical sensations, and since they eschew competition in the spirit of communal pleasure sharing, are technically classed as recreations rather than games. Some involve daredevil stunts that defy the System. Others concentrate on the means of consuming the dope.

The sensory-awareness games, sometimes also called psychedelic games, intensify the mind-bending effects of the drugs through manipulation of readily available objects. A coat hanger and a piece of thread enable two heads to play a game called

COAT-HANGER CHIME

You take a wire coat hanger and untwist it, shaping it into a large curve. Tie a length of thread on both ends of the hanger. The person who you are going to have receive all the groovy sensations hangs the contraption on his head, thread side up, hanger hanging down in front. The person then sticks the thread in his ears with his fingers. Now you are ready to play the chime. Another person stands in front of the person who is wearing the chime, and proceeds to tap the metal sharply with metal, plastic and wood objects. The sound waves travel through the metal to the thread and directly into the ears.[73]

In another psychedelic game the accessories are cellophane, tin foil, and a match:

ZILCH

Zilch is the name of the game. It is played by taking a long piece of cellophane, generally the type that clothes are returned in from the cleaners [i.e. plastic bags], and rolling it up so that it is a long jelly roll. It is helpful to tie knots in it to keep it from unraveling. At the top a piece of scotch tape will affix it to the ceiling and allow it to hang. On the floor beneath it is placed tin foil or aluminum foil. Then the bottom of the cellophane is set aflame, the lights in the room are turned out and everyone watches it burn. It burns in an upward direction, slowly at first and more rapidly later, and flaming bits of cellophane drop to the covered floor at increasing speeds. It is quite beautiful to watch and the viewers are generally, but not necessarily, stoned on marijuana. Afterwards, the viewers share their thoughts on what they saw. Often the viewers realize that their thoughts were phallic and that the burning cellophane was a phallic symbol.

The game is not one in which there is a winner or loser. There is no competition at all. The game is played by females as well as by males and in mixed company as well as separately. It is called a "Zilch" because of the sound made by the dripping.[74]

A variant of "Zilch" is known as

FLAMING GROOVY

Mykel [a twenty-one-year-old male street person] first ran into this "stoned" game in 1968 at a party in Berkeley. Many, if not all, the people there were stoned on acid when someone shouted, "It's Flamin' Groovy time!"

You take a plastic cleaning bag and tie it in knots, thereby compressing it in space. Then hook the plastic to the ceiling or hang it on a hook and set a pan of water directly under it. Turn out all the lights, then light the end of the plastic on fire. The resultant light show of dripping, sizzling fire is a Flaming Groovy and a "stoned" game.[75]

Other sensory-perception games are even more slightly structured. In "Twirling Incense" the players create glowing points of light in a darkened room by lighting thin sticks of incense and twirling the tips around in fanciful patterns. Or lighted cigarettes can be used. The point is to draw visions in the air, simulating those in the mind's eye. "Tin-can Star Show" depends upon Christmas-tree lights (borrowed by two enterprising Berkeley students from a tree in Ida Sproul Hall) and a tin can or shoebox in which holes are punched and the lights inserted. In an otherwise dark room the apparatus produces a mini-heaven on the walls and ceiling. "Cosmos" requires only a television set and the hyperactive imagination of the stoned observer. Turn the set on to static, eliminating picture and sound, and watch happenings unfold among the prancing dots. "Strobe Lights" as played in college residence halls needs only electric-light switches that the stoned students flick on and off rapidly and erratically to give psychedelic effects. Players can move when the light is off and freeze when it is on, make strange faces in the intervals, and otherwise stimulate each other's awareness.

Some drug games call for physical exertion that increases the exhilaration of the players. "Dead Bird" takes its name from a cry that any member of the group may shout, and so compel the others to fall to the ground and stick their hands and feet in the air. There they remain until another player yells, "All right, you're exonerated," whereupon all rise again until the next command. A twenty-year-old Berkeley student, Jim Rosenfield, tells how in 1967 he was crossing Wilshire Boulevard in Los Angeles with two companions, all extremely stoned on mescaline. As the light turned green for them to cross, two police squad cars stopped on the red. In the middle of the intersection one of Jim's buddies yelled, "Dead bird!" All three dropped on their backs in the street and elevated their legs. The second friend quickly shouted, "All right, you're exonerated—let's get the hell out of here." Comments of the police are unreported.[76]

"Chinese Fire Alarm" deliberately takes place in the midst of traffic. When the car carrying the freaks stops at a red light, they all dash outside and run around the automobile as many times as possible before the light turns green. The more skilled the player, the more times he can lap the car.

Then there are games with competitive elements concentrating on dope consumption. In "Russian Roulette with Acid" a tab of acid is stirred into a cup of water and placed among a number of identical cups filled only with water. Each player drinks a cup, and the one who comes upon the LSD is declared the winner. Drawbacks of this game of chance are the difficulty heads encounter in locating enough identical glasses, and more importantly, the lack of acid for all but the one lucky fellow. Yet participants speak of getting "contact highs" just on the supposition that the tab is in their cup.[77] In reverse, everyone gets stoned in "Smoke to the Death," a pot party at which marijuana cigarettes are passed around until, one by one, the players become too high to smoke any more. But the last one smoking is the loser, because he has failed to get completely stoned, and all the others are winners. This contest, usually not too popular because of the expense, may be held to celebrate the purchase of a large amount of marijuana.[78]

Word games also titillate the stoned. In "Hah!" the players, all high, sit in a circle. One person starts off with a "Hah!" The player next to him utters a "Hah! Hah!" The third extends the iteration to "Hah! Hah! Hah!" and the game continues until one participant gives in to his risibilities and starts laughing, whereupon he is pronounced the loser. In a variation the players lie on the floor, each with his head on another player's stomach. Hence when the speaker utters his "Hah's," he bounces the head lying on his stomach and hastens the moment when one of the group breaks into gales of laughter.[79]

Verbal precision is demanded of the freaks who play "Tiger's Tooth and Panther's Paw." Sitting on the floor in a circle, one person starts the game by handing a match or similar slight object

302

to the player on his left, saying "This is a tiger's tooth," and then handing a comparative object to the player on his right, saying "And this is a panther's paw." The two recipients say "What?" and he repeats the phrases. They then turn to their respective neighbors, hand over the objects, and repeat, from the left, "This is a tiger's tooth," and from the right, "This is a panther's paw." These recipients then say "What?" and the original starter repeats the phrases which go on down the line to the third pair, who say "What?" And so on. When the items cross the middle of the circle, all semblance of sanity vanishes.[80]

Then there are mind games. In "Imagery Telepathy" one of the freaks sitting around meditatively thinks up a scene in his head. He may, for example, envision pine trees in the snow. Once the image is formed he cries, "I've got it." The others concentrate and try to pick up on the scene. Each person present then makes a guess in turn. The object is to see how well the players can tune in on each other's minds. A related pastime is "Drawing Pictures," in which close friends sit around and draw their conceptions of each other. "The pictures are not portraits, they don't look anything like the people, but they're identifiable just the same. Like I drew a picture of Sharon—just a chick with stars for eyes—but everyone knew it was Sharon."[81]

And one could go on with the list of imaginative games in which members of the hip drug culture heighten their perceptions, their awareness, and their sense of community, and reassert their defiance of a too-familiar System.

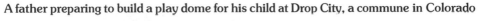

A father preparing to build a play dome for his child at Drop City, a commune in Colorado

Draft dodgers

As the pill peddler is admired in the youth culture for his risky defiance of a repressive system, so is the draft dodger lauded as an anti-hero outwitting a cruel Establishment. A churning body of lore about draft-dodging techniques and stratagems washes through the youth culture. While this draftlore is separate from druglore in theme, the two overlap to a large degree. The drug freaks become the draftees; the confrontation scene shifts from the narc at the bust to the sergeant at the induction center. This is the moment of truth, when the young man believes he must use all his wits against the minions of the System to avoid imprisonment, in jail or in the army. His peers applaud his cunning and enlarge upon it in their circles for the benefit of future inductees.

The draft dodger and malingerer as hero would seem to be a sharp break with American traditions glorifying the fighting man. Yet antecedents of the malingerer as clever trickster exist in folk anecdotes of earlier wars. Consider this narrative reported in 1968 by the collector, a schoolteacher who first heard it twenty-five years earlier at Camp Roberts, California:

War resister David Harris, just released after 20 months in federal prison, on arrival at the San Francisco airport with his wife, Joan Baez, their son, Gabriel, and dog, a Siberian husky named "Moon Dog"

One elaborate stratagem has the offender walking around the camp bent over picking up scraps of paper muttering all the time, "That's not it." He continues this on duty and off. Called in by the C.O. he shambles into his office and starts shuffling through the papers on his desk, again mutters as he picks up each paper, "That's not it."

The C.O. puts him in the hospital for observation, and the soldier continues his performance. At length the hospital psychiatrist decides that he must be "off the murky end" and fills out a section eight [insanity] discharge. Called in by the psychiatrist, he starts going through all the papers on the psychiatrist's desk again muttering "That's not it" until he comes to his section eight discharge. He grabs it and shouts, "That's it!"[82]

In another form of this story, the gold-bricker in World War II rides an imaginary motorcycle all around the army camp until committed for psychiatric observation to an army hospital and finally given a section eight discharge. Thereupon he mounts his phantom motorcycle, rides it to the hospital entrance, parks it by the gate, and starts to walk away. "Hey, don't you want your motorcycle?" an orderly yells after him. "No thanks, I don't need it any more," replies the ex-GI.[83]

But in the counterculture stories of the Vietnam war, the anti-hero never gets into uniform. The draft-opposition legends and formulas have happy endings, with the youth fooling the army officers and army psychiatrists into thinking him of unsound body or mind. Varied and prolific are the devices recommended to inductees to ensure that they flunk their physical examination at the induction center. Drink a bottle of soya sauce to raise your blood pressure. Eat glass so that you will urinate blood. Imbibe gallons of milkshakes before going in to raise your blood sugar. "I know about this kid who didn't sleep for three days before his physical and took speed and didn't wipe his ass. He got out."[84] "A fellow spent the night before the test in the shower which affected his asthma adversely."[85] The one-liners grow into paragraphs as the storyteller begins to spread his wings:

March on Washington, 1965

Here is another story about someone who beat the draft. They went down there and they were going to feign having tuberculosis, and what they did was, they put some iodine on the back of a cigarette and they smoked the cigarette. And what happens is these pieces of iodine got in their lungs. When they appeared on the X-ray which they gave to test for tuberculosis, it looked as if they had spots on their lungs.

And they got out for faking tuberculosis.[86]

Some of the hearsays take on fuller details and become freakout pranks. One series deals with the draftee who hides objects up his anal orifice. The first of the three to follow was told by a twenty-three-year-old "unemployed Buddhist," and was later published in the Berkeley *Barb*:

Oh, there was this guy who stuck a rat up his ass. Then when they were looking for hemorrhoids they saw this long tail hanging out. So they said, "What's that?" The guy said, "That's my pet rat."

"Well, take it out!"

"No, it's *my* pet rat."

There was a guy who was so desperate to beat the draft that he inserted an egg into his ass. When he was subsequently called in to the proctologist during the course of the inspection, the proctologist inspected his rectum and this egg fell out on the floor. And in front of everybody the egg cracked open and inside was a tiny paper American flag.

At which point this guy started to sing "The Star Spangled Banner" and he was promptly given a 4-F.

This is the best story I ever heard of getting out of the draft. This guy shoved crunchy peanut butter up his ass before going to his physical. When the time came to have asses examined, he pulled his pants down, and just as the captain was approaching him reached back and got some peanut butter from his ass and ate it.

It grossed the captain out so badly, he just let him out.[87]

The teller of the third story was himself a rather unwilling inductee, who had made no attempt to evade the draft but appreciated the ingenuity of the imaginative draft dodger. Since the inspection of the draftee's open buttocks by the army doctors represents the most demeaning position in the whole medical examination for the antiwar and anti-Vietnam youth, the trickster in these stories unexpectedly turns the situation to his own account. Instead of being humiliated and coerced, he shocks and deceives the army personnel into thinking he is nuts. Meanwhile he shows his disdain for the system and its false patriotic values.

Another way whereby the draftee could manifest his disdain for the military system and at the same time feign mental illness was by urinating in public.

A demonstrator at the Democratic Convention in Chicago, 1968

I heard this story about this guy who went down to the draft board, and when he went down there he didn't say anything. He said absolutely nothing all the time. And the only thing he did was, when they gave him the forms to fill out he just pissed all over them.

And anything they ever gave him he just pissed all over and they eventually threw him out.

One of my friends went down to the center. There was a guy there with long hair halfway down his back. He said he wanted to see a psychiatrist. They told him to wait, and after about twenty minutes the psychiatrist came in.

The guy said, "Can I go to the bathroom now?" The psychiatrist said, "Sure, go ahead." So the guy pissed all over the floor. The psychiatrist yelled at him to get out. He got 4-F.[88]

Encounters with the psychiatrist at the induction center form a favorite theme of draft-evasion tales. "Kiss the doctor" is one terse recommendation to the hopeful draft dodger.[89] One time it nearly backfired:

This guy was called in for his physical, and he told them he was a homosexual. And when he went to see the psychiatrist he convinced him, or thought he convinced him, that he was a homosexual by telling him stories about the experiences he [the inductee] had supposedly had. But actually he hadn't had any.

So the psychiatrist said, "O.K., I believe you, we won't be bothering you any more." Then the psychiatrist started coming on to him pretty strong, saying things like "Why don't you come to my house for dinner tonight?" And the guy said, "No, I would rather not." And the psychiatrist said, "I can show you a good time."

But the guy said "No" and finally he just left.[90]

Frequently at the physical examination the draft dodger stages a performance, much of the same order as a freakout. Indeed, freakout behavior in the past may have contributed to the ingenuity and expertise of the put-ons staged by the draftee endeavoring to convince straight observers—army officers, doctors, psychiatrists—that he was a weirdo totally unfit for military service. For example, he might feign a suicide attempt:

Oh yeah! A friend of mine got called back to Baltimore for his physical. He didn't know what to do. He snuck in a razor and slashed both wrists. (He had already figured out the safe places on his arm: and besides, how could you go wrong with all the doctors there!) I don't know if he got out.[91]

A student collector writes of another put-on: "An invariably amusing folktale of the drug culture is the story of an individual taking his pre-induction physical while high on LSD. Inevitably the prospective soldier is pronounced psychologically unfit for service by the psychiatrist."[92]

I knew a guy who went in and immediately curled up in a prenatal position. There he was, balled up in the corner and nobody could talk him into moving. Finally they carried him to the shrink and he uncurled, looked around and said, "Mother, where are you?"[93]

Some freaks enhance their dramas with props:

I've heard of a guy who dropped 500 mics [a lot] of acid and dressed up as a wizard. Took a goat with him and walked with a staff. He had a huge ruby ring that he kept whispering into.

He got out. It took him a few days to flip back in from being a wizard though.[94]

In its most elaborate form, the draft-
dodging freakout involves a whole cast
of characters and a procession:

I heard about this guy who had to go down for his physical one morning. So what he did is he came to Ludwig's Fountain on the Cal Campus at six in the morning dressed as Jesus Christ. And he had on these long flowing robes and he had a full-faced beard and the whole bit. And he started just sorta preaching at all the people as they walked by telling them to follow him down to his draft board as his disciples so he could go down and just prove how freaked out he was. And he gathered a very large crowd until about nine in the morning he had fifty followers.

At which time they proceeded to go down to the draft board, and he said, "I am Christ." And he looked like Christ, you know, and he convinced them that he had all these followers who were his disciples.

And he convinced them that he was so freaked out that they gave him a 1-Y.[95]

So in this spate of legendary tales the draft dodger takes his place with other admired anti-heroes of the youth culture bucking with their wits and guts a relentless, implacable, but dull-minded System.

What will be the future of the Humane Life-style and its associated druglore? Each of the three previous life-styles has lasted a century or more, and while the technology of the late twentieth century may accelerate the pace and change of American lives, any fundamental shift in national patterns should endure for a number of decades. Each new social, cultural, and political revolution has achieved a synthesis with its predecessor; there is a coming to terms, an adjust-

Camp set up in Dunn Meadow at Indiana University during a period of campus unrest in 1969

ment, a tempering of the values in the one period with those in the next. Religion hardened into orthodoxy, democracy into factionalism, capitalism into materialism. The counterculture will not erase the acquisitive culture but soften and humanize its materialistic edges. If McGovern fell far short of Nixon's vote in 1972, still the radical left did wrest control of the Democratic convention and nominate one of the two major candidates in the election. Historically, major political parties have absorbed and so defused the thrust of strong protest and third-party movements, and law and custom have already recognized the spirit of the new liberation, in matters ranging from hair styles to equal rights for women.

In every period bodies of folklore have reflected the currents of change, the new values, the new ethics, the new road to happiness. The saint, the backwoodsman, the cowboy, and now the hippie on first appearance alarmed a society that ultimately came to appreciate their strengths and American individualism. Folklore and legend will, I believe, prove as true an indicator in the twentieth century as they proved in three earlier centuries of the nation's shift to new and higher ground.

Notes

Identifying Folklore

1. Stephan Thernstrom, "Urbanization, Migration, and Social Mobility," in Barton J. Bernstein, ed., *Towards a New Past· Dissenting Essays in American History* (New York: Pantheon Books, 1968), p. 167.

American Life-styles and Legends

1. Samuel Eliot Morison, *Builders of the Bay Colony* (London: Oxford University Press, 1930), p. 60.
2. Henry Steele Commager, in his Introduction to Alexis de Tocqueville, *Democracy in America*, trans. Henry Reeve (New York and London: Oxford University Press, 1947), p. xi.
3. Nicholas Gargarin, in the *Harvard Alumni Bulletin* 71, no. 11 (April 28, 1969): 39.
4. Paul Goodman, *Growing Up Absurd* (New York: Vintage Books, 1960), p. ix.
5. Charles Reich, *The Greening of America* (New York: Bantam Books, 1971), pp. 362-63.
6. Michael Rossman, *The Wedding Within the War* (Garden City, N.Y.: Doubleday & Co., 1971), p. 267.

The Colonial Period:

The Religious Impulse

1. Katharine Briggs, *Pale Hecate's Team: An Examination of the Beliefs on Magic Among Shakespeare's Contemporaries and His Immediate Successors* (New York: Humanities Press, 1962), pp. 151-52.
2. Keith Thomas, *Religion and the Decline of Magic* (New York: Charles Scribner's Sons, 1971), p. 470.
3. *Ibid.*, p. 474.
4. Alan Macfarlane, *Witchcraft in Tudor and Stuart England* (New York: Harper & Row, Publishers, 1970), pp. 110-13.
5. Quoted in Macfarlane, *Witchcraft*, p. 115.
6. Cotton Mather, *Magnalia Christi Americana*, reprinted in Richard M. Dorson, ed., *America Begins: Early American Writing* (Bloomington: Indiana University Press, 1971; originally published 1950 by Pantheon Books), pp. 269-71.

7. Edward Johnson, quoted in Dorson, *America Begins*, p. 280.
8. John Winthrop, *Journal "Historie of New England 1630-1649,"* ed. J. K. Hosmer (New York, 1908), vol. 1, pp. 266-68, reprinted in Dorson, *America Begins*, pp. 121-22.
9. Increase Mather, *Remarkable Providences Illustrative of the Earlier Days of American Colonisation* [reprint of *An Essay for the Recording of Illustrious Providences*, 1684] (London: John Russell Smith, 1856), from "The Preface," unpaged.
10. Cotton Mather, *Magnalia Christi Americana: Or, the Ecclesiastical History of New-England* [1702], 2 vols. (New York: Russell & Russell, 1967), vol. 2, p. 342.
11. I. Mather, *Remarkable Providences*, pp. 23-24.
12. *Ibid.*, pp. 55, 60; C. Mather, *Magnalia*, vol. 2, p. 362.
13. I. Mather, *Remarkable Providences*, p. 61.
14. *Ibid.*, pp. 57-58.
15. C. Mather, *Magnalia*, vol. 2, p. 366.
16. George Lyman Kittredge, *Witchcraft in Old and New England* (Cambridge, Mass.: Harvard University Press, 1929), pp. 155-58.
17. C. Mather, *Magnalia*, vol. 2, p. 402.
18. Richard M. Dorson, *Jonathan Draws the Long Bow* [1946] (New York: Russell & Russell, 1969), p. 172.
19. *Ibid.*, pp. 172-73.
20. C. Mather, *Magnalia*, vol. 2, pp. 398, 405.
21. Francis James Child, *The English and Scottish Popular Ballads*, 5 vols. (Boston: Houghton Mifflin Co., 1882-98), vol. 2, p. 143.
22. *Ibid.*, p. 153. Cf. John Brand, *Observations on Popular Antiquities*, ed. Henry Ellis (London, 1813), vol. 2, pp. 513-14.
23. C. Mather, *Magnalia*, vol. 2, p. 468.
24. Cotton Mather, *The Wonders of the Invisible World* [1693] (London, 1862), p. 165.
25. *Ibid.*, p. 166.
26. Emelyn E. Gardner, *Folklore from the Schoharie Hills, New York* (Ann Arbor: University of

Michigan Press, 1937), p. 89, n. 20, gives references.

27. *Ibid.,* pp. 28-29.

28. Isabel Gordon Carter, "Mountain White Folk-Lore: Tales from the Southern Blue Ridge," *Journal of American Folklore* 38 (1925): 372-73.

29. Vance Randolph, *Ozark Superstitions* (New York: Columbia University Press, 1947), pp. 228-29.

30. C. Mather, *Magnalia,* vol. 2, pp. 450-52.

31. *Ibid.,* p. 453; I. Mather, *Remarkable Providences,* p. 133.

32. C. Mather, *Magnalia,* vol. 2, p. 388.

33. *Ibid.,* pp. 404-5, 498.

34. Winthrop, *Journal,* vol. 2, pp. 9-12, 82-83.

35. *New England Historical and Genealogical Record* 35 (1881): 242.

36. *Massachusetts Historical Society Collections,* 2nd series, 7 (2nd ed., 1826): 19-20.

37. John Smith, *Travels and Works* (Edinburgh: John Grant, 1910), vol. 2, pp. 658-59.

38. Jasper Danckaerts and Peter Sluyter, *Journal of a Voyage to New York* (Brooklyn, 1867), pp. 218-20.

39. Cotton Mather, *Late Memorable Providences Relating to Witchcrafts and Possessions* (London: printed for Thomas Parkhurst, 1691), p. 44.

40. The quotations are, in order, from *ibid.,* pp. 95, 96, 99, 11.

41. I. Mather, *Remarkable Providences,* p. 176.

42. *Ibid.,* p. 189.

43. C. Mather, *Magnalia,* vol. 2, p. 473.

44. *Ibid.,* p. 478.

45. C. Mather, *Wonders of the Invisible World,* pp. 80-84.

46. C. Mather, *Magnalia,* vol. 2, pp. 454-56.

47. *Ibid.,* p. 457. For Goody Glover, see George Lincoln Burr, ed., *Narratives of the Witchcraft Cases, 1648-1706* (New York: Barnes & Noble, 1959), p. 273, reprinting Robert Calef, *More Wonders of the Invisible World* (London, 1700), p. 9.

48. Kittredge, *Witchcraft,* p. 90, quoting C. Mather, *The Wonders of the Invisible World* (Boston, 1693), pp. 99, 113.

49. Kittredge, *Witchcraft,* p. 91.

50. Randolph, *Ozark Superstitions,* p. 287.

51. *Ibid.,* p. 70.

52. John Hale, *A Modest Enquiry into the Nature of Witchcraft* (1702).

53. Quoted in Kittredge, *Witchcraft,* p. 338.

54. C. Mather, *Magnalia,* vol. 2, p. 475.

55. Kittredge, *Witchcraft,* p. 9.

56. Gardner, *Schoharie Hills,* pp. 66-68.

57. Richard M. Dorson, *Buying the Wind: Regional Folklore in the United States* (Chicago: University of Chicago Press, 1964), pp. 55-56.

58. Kittredge, *Witchcraft,* pp. 9-10.

59. *Ibid.,* p. 218.

60. Gardner, *Schoharie Hills,* pp. 75, 78-79.

61. Kittredge, *Witchcraft,* pp. 243, 265-75.

62. C. Mather, *Wonders of the Invisible World,* pp. 80-84.

63. I. Mather, *Remarkable Providences,* pp. 153-55.

64. *Ibid.,* p. 98.

65. Cotton Mather, "A Brand Pluck'd Out of the Burning" [1692] in Burr, ed., *Narratives of the Witchcraft Cases,* p. 261.

66. Quotations from selections in Dorson, ed., *America Begins,* pp. 280-82.

67. Quoted in Robert Calef, "Another Brand Plucked Out of the Burning, or More Wonders of the Invisible World" [1700], in Burr, ed., *Narratives of the Witchcraft Cases,* p. 309.

68. Edward Johnson in *Massachusetts Historical Society Collections,* 2nd series, 8 (2nd ed., 1826): 28-29.

69. Fred W. Allsopp, *Folklore of Romantic Arkansas* (New York: Grolier Society, 1931), vol. 1, pp. 234-38, and Randolph, *Ozark Superstitions,* pp. 275-76.

70. Newbell N. Puckett, *Folk Beliefs of the Southern Negro* (Chapel Hill: University of North Carolina Press, 1926), pp. 550-51.

71. Harry M. Hyatt, *Folk-Lore from Adams County, Illinois,* 2nd ed. (n.p.: Memoirs of the Alma Egan Hyatt Foundation, 1965), pp. 748-50, nos. 15612-16.

72. George Bishop, *New England Judged: The Second Part* (London, 1667), p. 138.

73. George Keith, *The Presbyterian and Independent Visible Churches in New-England and Else-Where, Brought to the Test . . . With a call and warning from the Lord to the people of Boston and New-England to repent. . . .* (London: printed for T. Northcott, 1691), p. 225.

74. *Ibid.,* p. 226.

75. *Ibid.,* p. 225.

76. *Ibid.,* p. 223.

The Early National Period:

The Democratic Impulse

1. Richard M. Dorson, ed., *America Rebels: Narratives of the Patriots* (New York: Pantheon Books, 1953), pp. 34-59, 147-87.

2. Gerald Parsons, "Sam Patch Falls Again: Second Thoughts on a Folk Hero," *New York Folklore Quarterly* 25 (1969): 83-92.

3. Herbert A. Wisbey, Jr., "Reply to Gerald Parsons' Sam Patch," *New York Folklore Quarterly* 26 (1970): 78-80.

4. *Sketches and Eccentricities of Col. David Crockett of West Tennessee,* new ed. (New York: J. & J. Harper, 1833), pp. 79-80.

5. William H. Jansen, in *Hoosier Folklore* 7 (1948): 47-49. Professor Jansen noted the correspondence of the kleshmaker to the skowmaker story, which he saw in John S. C. Abbot's *David Crockett* (New York, 1874), but did not locate in the *Autobiography* of Crockett.

6. The texts of these stories are on file in the Indiana University Folklore Archives.

7. *Sketches and Eccentricities,* pp. 58-59.

8. *London and Westminster Review* 32 (1839): 136-41, signed H. W., quoted in *The Crockett Almanacs,* ed. Franklin J. Meine (Chicago: Caxton Club, 1955), p. xix.

9. *Sketches and Eccentricities,* pp. 65-66.

10. James A. Shackford, *David Crockett, The Man and the Legend,* ed. John B. Shackford (Chapel Hill: University of North Carolina Press, 1956), pp. 258-64.

11. *Sketches and Eccentricities,* pp. 77, 171.

12. Shackford, *David Crockett,* p. 62.

13. *Sketches and Eccentricities,* pp. 77-78, 108.

14. *Ibid.,* p. 75.

15. *The Life of David Crockett, the Original Humorist and Irrepressible Backwoodsman, An Autobiography* (New York: A. L. Burt Company, n.d.), p. 239.

16. *Ibid.,* pp. 243-44.

17. Kenneth W. Porter, "Davy Crockett and John Horse: a Possible Origin of the Coonskin Story," *American Literature* 15 (1943-44): 10-15.

18. Albert Bigelow Paine, *Mark Twain, A Biography,* 3 vols. (New York, 1912), vol. 1, pp. 59-60.

19. Vance Randolph, *Sticks in the Knapsack and Other Ozark Folk Tales* (New York: Columbia University Press, 1958), pp. 115-16.

20. Jesse W. Harris, "Myths and Legends from Southern Illinois," *Hoosier Folklore* 5, no. 1 (March 1946): 17-19, "Coon Skin Deception."

21. Jesse W. Harris, "The Catskin Legend in Southern Illinois," *Journal of American Folklore* 58 (1945): 301-2.

22. *Ibid.,* p. 302, and Motif K261.1, "The price of mink skins," in Ernest W. Baughman, *Type and Motif-Index of the Folktales of England and North America,* Indiana University Folklore Series no. 20 (The Hague: Mouton & Co., 1966).

23. Charles E. Brown, *Whisky Jack Tales* (Madison, Wis., State Historical Museum, 1940), p. 2.

24. Robert Gard, *Johnny Chinook* (New York: Longmans, Green & Co., 1945), p. 101. See all references in Baughman, *Type and Motif-Index,* under Motif K258, "Stolen Property Sold to Its Owner."

25. From James B. Davis, *Early History of Memphis,* 1873, sent by A. B. Armstrong to Texas Folklore Society Publication no. 18, *Backwoods to Border,* ed. Mody C. Boatright and Donald Day (Austin: Texas Folklore Society, and Dallas: Southern Methodist University Press, 1943), pp. 147-48. Cf. Shackford, *David Crockett,* pp. 203-4.

26. Crockett, *Autobiography,* pp. 272-73.

27. Captain R. G. A. Levinge, *Echoes from the Backwoods* (London, 1849), vol. 2, pp. 11-13, quoted by Franklin J. Meine in his "Introduction" to *The Crockett Almanacs,* p. v.

28. "Col. Crockett and the Bear and the Swallows," in *The Crockett Almanac 1840* (Nashville, Tenn.: published by Ben Harding, n.d.), pp. 25, 28. (The cacography has been corrected.) This story is type 1900 in Antti Aarne and Stith Thompson, *The Types of the Folktale* (Helsinki, 1951).

29. Randolph, *Ozark Superstitions,* p. 47.

30. Edward A. Armstrong, *The Folklore of Birds* (London: William Collins' Sons & Co., 1958), pp. 179-85.

31. Richard M. Dorson, ed., *Davy Crockett, American Comic Legend* (New York: Rockland Editions, 1939), pp. 97-98.

32. Sent in by A. B. Armstrong to Boatright and Day, eds., *Backwoods to Border,* p. 148.

33. From Thomas Bangs Thorpe, "The Disgraced Scalp-Lock" (1842) in Walter Blair and Franklin J. Meine, eds., *Half Horse, Half Alligator* (Chicago: University of Chicago Press, 1956), p. 78. This work contains nearly all the known sources of the Mike Fink tradition.

34. *Davy Crockett's Almanack 1838* (Nashville, Tenn., n.d.), p. 47.

35. Blair and Meine, *Half Horse*, pp. 68-69, 238-39.

36. *Ibid.*, p. 52, from Morgan Neville, "The Last of the Boatmen" (1828); p. 59, from anon., "Mike Fink: The Last of the Boatmen" (1829); p. 64, from the *Crockett Almanac* for 1837; pp. 69-70, from T. B. Thorpe, "The Disgraced Scalp-Lock" (1842); p. 95, from Joseph M. Field, "Mike Fink: 'The Last of the Boatmen'" (1847); p. 209, from the *Crockett Almanac* for 1850; p. 210, from the *Crockett Almanac* for 1851; p. 227, from Ben Cassedy, *The History of Louisville* (1852).

37. *Ibid.*, p. 21, from James Keyes, *Pioneers of Scioto County* (1880); pp. 83, 86, from the *Western General Advertiser* (1845).

38. *Ibid.*, p. 89, from John S. Robb, "Trimming a Darky's Heel" (1847); p. 59, from "Mike Fink: 'The Last of the Boatmen'"; p. 150, from Emerson Bennett, *Mike Fink: A Legend of the Ohio* (1848); p. 219, from *Autobiography of Rev. James B. Finley* (1854).

39. *Ibid.*, p. 91, from Robb, "Trimming a Darky's Heel."

40. *Ibid.*, p. 60, from "Mike Fink: The Last of the Boatmen" (1829), perhaps written by Timothy Flint, Cincinnati editor of the *Western Monthly Review*, in which the article appeared.

41. *Ibid.*, pp. 83-84. This tale belongs to type 901 in Aarne and Thompson, *The Types of the Folktale.*

42. Blair and Meine, *Half Horse*, pp. 228-29, from Ben Cassedy, *The History of Louisville* (1852).

43. *Ibid.*, pp. 85-86, from a letter by "K" to the *Western General Advertiser*, Cincinnati, February 11, 1845.

44. From Ben Cassedy, *The History of Louisville, From Its Earliest Settlement to the Year 1852* (Louisville, 1852), pp. 72-79. Reprinted in Blair and Meine, *Half Horse*, pp. 229-30.

45. Blair and Meine, *Half Horse*, pp. 136-37, from Joseph M. Field, "Mike Fink: 'The Last of the Boatmen'" (1847).

46. *Ibid.*, p. 19.

47. *Ibid.*, p. 110.

48. *Ibid.*, p. 229.

49. A rich array of articles, poems, and reminiscences about Sam Patch in Rochester newspapers and magazines, dating from 1828 to the present, is available at the Rochester Public Library. Through the extreme kindness of Miss Emma B. Swift, Reference Librarian, transcripts of this material were furnished me. I have also copies of accounts in Paterson, New York, Boston, Worcester, and Buffalo newspapers, and photostats of a handbill and playbills in the Harvard Theatre Collection. Miss Irene Janes of the Paterson Free Public Library and Miss Ruth Russell of the American Antiquarian Society did me favors. Professors Walter Blair and Louis C. Jones materially assisted me in gathering Patchiana. The following references proved of value:

J. Earl Clauson, *These Plantations* (Providence, R.I., 1937), pp. 70-72; Henry J. Finn, *American Comic Annual* (Boston, 1831), pp. 216-20; Edward R. Foreman, ed., *Centennial History of Rochester, New York* (Rochester, 1934), vol. 4, p. 79; Robert Grieve, *An Illustrated History of Pawtucket, Central Falls, and Vicinity* (Pawtucket, 1897), pp. 100-1; John W. Haley, "The Old Stone Bank" *History of Rhode Island* (Providence, 1939), III, 196; Thomas W. Haliburton, *Sam Slick, the Clockmaker* (Philadelphia [n.d.]), pp. 37-38 (cf. *The American Joe Miller* [Philadelphia, 1847], pp. 49-50, "Antipodean Diver"); Nathaniel Hawthorne, "Rochester," in *Tales, Sketches, and Other Papers* (Boston and New York, 1833), pp. 17-18; Francis Hodge, *Yankee Theater: The Image of America on the Stage 1825-1850* (Austin: University of Texas Press, 1964), pp. 226-31; William Dean Howells, *Their Wedding Journey* (Edinburgh, 1884), pp. 119-26; Jonathan F. Kelley, *Dan Marble: A Biographical Sketch* (New York, 1851), pp. 88, 91, 93-94, 133; Charles P. Longwell, *Historic Totowa Falls* (Paterson, N.J., 1942), pp. 36-40; Jenny M. Parker, *Rochester: A Story Historical* (Rochester, N.Y., 1884), pp. 184-91; Robert C. Sands, "Monody on Samuel Patch" (1831), in Rufus W. Griswold, *The Poets and Poetry of America* (Philadelphia, 1858), pp. 257-59; Seba Smith, *The Life and Writings of Major Jack Downing* (Boston, 1834), pp. 235-39; Richard H. Thornton, *An American Glossary*, vol. 2 (London, 1912), p. 762, vol. 3 (Madison, Wis., 1939), p. 557; Mrs. Frances M. Trollope, *Domestic Manners of the Americans* (New York, 1901), pp. 252-53; Thomas Ward, "The Great Descender," in *Passaic: A Group of Poems Touching That River* (New York, 1842), pp. 17-41.

I have published accounts of Sam Patch in the following places: "Sam Patch, Jumping Hero," *New York Folklore Quarterly* 1 (1945): 133-51; "The Story of Sam Patch," *American Mercury* 64 (1947): 741-47; "Sam Patch" in John A. Garraty, ed., *The Unforgettable Americans* (New York: Channel Press for the Society of American Historians, 1960), pp. 183-89; "The Wonderful Leaps of Sam Patch," *American Heritage* 18 (1966): 12-19. The present version is taken from the *American Mercury.*

50. Useful sources for the history of Mose are Herbert Asbury, *The Gangs of New York* (New York, 1928), pp. 32-37, and *Ye Olde Fire Laddies*

(New York, 1930), pp. 177-84; T. Allston Brown, *A History of the New York Stage* (New York, 1903), vol. 1, pp. 282-84, Thomas Gunn, *Mose Among the Britishers: The B'hoy in London* (Philadelphia: A. Hart, 1850) [a twenty-page booklet of hand-colored lithographs]; Alvin Harlow, *Old Bowery Days* (New York, 1931), pp. 193-201; J. N. Ireland, *Records of the New York Stage* (New York, 1867), vol. 2, p. 419; William K. Northall, *Before and Behind the Curtain* (New York, 1841), pp. 91-92; George C. D. Odell, *Annals of the New York Stage* (New York, 1970), vol. 5, pp. 372-74; Harry T. Peters, *America on Stone* (New York, 1931), pp. 306-7. Resources of the Harvard Theatre Collection which have yielded valuable information include files of clippings for B. A. Baker and F. S. Chanfrau and playbills for various Mose plays. *A Glance at New York,* the only extant Mose play, was published as No. 216 in Samuel French's Standard Drama (New York, n.d.). The Harvard Theatre Collection has a typescript and a manuscript prompt copy. The Louisville playbill announcing Mose's coming is dated October 31, 1856, and another reporting his success in Louisville carries a November 6 date. Full documentation is in my article "Mose the Far-Famed and World-Renowned," *American Literature* 15 (1943): 288-300.

51. Reprinted in Richard M. Dorson, *Jonathan Draws the Long Bow* (Cambridge, Mass.: Harvard University Press, 1946), pp. 95-96.

52. Thus in David Humphreys' *The Yankey in England* (n.p., n.d.), p. 44: "Original! A character little known here. A full-blooded Yankey."

53. Lawrence Labree, *Ebenezer Venture* (New York, n.d.; first acted 1841), p. 7; J. K. Paulding, *The Bucktails (ca.* 1815), in Allan G. Halline, *American Plays* (New York, 1939), p. 90; Samuel Low, *The Politician Outwitted* (New York, 1789), p. 7; A. B. Lindsley, *Love and Friendship* (1809), pp. 36-37.

54. Royall Tyler, *The Contrast* (Boston, 1920), p. 56; J. S. Jones, *The Silver Spoon* (Boston, 1911), p. 39.

55. Paulding, *The Bucktails,* in Halline, *American Plays,* p. 93.

56. Humphreys, *The Yankey in England,* p. 31.

57. Paulding, *The Bucktails,* in Halline, *American Plays,* p. 108.

58. C. A. Logan, *Vermont Wool Dealer* (New York, 1884), p. 6.

59. S. S. Steele, *The Brazen Drum* (New York and Philadelphia, n.d.; first acted 1842), p. 10.

60. Logan, *Vermont Wool Dealer,* p. 18.

61. Labree, *Ebenezer Venture,* p. 11; M. M. Noah, *She Would Be a Soldier* (New York, 1819), p. 19.

62. The convention of inquisitive question and reluctant answer has been ably treated by Walter Blair in "Inquisitive Yankee Descendants in Arkansas," *American Speech* 14 (February 1939): 11-22.

63. J. H. Hackett, *Jonathan in England,* adapted from George Colman's *Who Wants a Guinea?* (New York, n.d.), p. 20.

64. J. S. Jones, *The Green Mountain Boy* (Boston, n.d.), p. 9.

65. J. G. Burnett, *Blanche of Brandywine* (New York, 1858), pp. 37-38.

66. Oliver E. Durivage, *The Stage-Struck Yankee* (New York: Samuel French, *ca.* 1845), p. 7.

67. Jones, *The Silver Spoon,* p. 59; H. J. Finn, *Montgomery* (Boston, 1825), p. 16; Morris Barnett, *Yankee Peddler* (New York, n.d.), p. 6.

68. Labree, *Ebenezer Venture,* p. 8; J. S. Jones, *Captain Kyd* (Boston, n.d.), p. 20; A. W. Curtis, *A Change of Base,* in *The Spirit of Seventy Six and Other Plays* (Boston, 1869), p. 104.

69. Steele, *The Brazen Drum,* p. 34.

70. Howard Mumford Jones, in his Introduction to Richard M. Dorson, ed., *Davy Crockett: American Comic Legend* (New York: Rockland Editions, 1939), p. xii.

71. Jones, *Captain Kyd,* p. 33.

72. Jones, *The Silver Spoon,* p. 55.

73. J. S. Jones, *The People's Lawyer* (New York, n.d.), p. 24.

74. J. T. Trowbridge, *Neighbor Jackwood* (New York, 1857), p. 10; M. M. Ballou, *Miralda* (New York, n.d.), p. 28.

75. Marston Balch, "Jonathan the First," *Modern Language Notes* 46 (May 1931): 281-88.

76. Tyler, *The Contrast,* p. 54.

77. *Ibid.,* pp. 59, 77, 58-59.

78. *Ibid.,* p. 109.

79. Barnett, *Yankee Peddler,* p. 5.

80. N. M. Ludlow, *Dramatic Life as I Found It* (St. Louis, 1880), p. 433.

81. See for instance, W. K. Northall, *Life and Recollections of Yankee Hill* (New York, 1850), p. 19.

82. For interesting contemporary accounts of some of these actors, see G. H. Hill, *Scenes from the Life of an Actor* (Boston, 1853); Falconbridge, *The Life and Times of Dan Marble* (New York, 1851); and Mary E. Owens, *Memories of John E. Owens* (Baltimore, 1892). For notices of the Yankee plays, consult the indexes in George C. D. Odell, *Annals of the New York Stage* (New York: AMS Press, 1970), 15 vols. A full discussion of Yankee actors is in Francis Hodge, *Yankee Theater* (Austin: University of Texas Press, 1964).

A somewhat longer version of this material appeared in my article "The Yankee on the Stage," *New England Quarterly* 1 (1940): 133-51.

The Later National Period:

The Economic Impulse

1. Roger D. Abrahams, *Deep Down in the Jungle* (Hatboro, Pa.: Folklore Associates, 1964), p. 77.

Cowboys

1. Edward Everett Dale, *Cow Country* (Norman: University of Oklahoma Press, 1965), p. 25.

2. Wilson M. Hudson, *Andy Adams, His Life and Writings* (Dallas: Southern Methodist University Press, 1964), p. 212.

3. N. Howard "Jack" Thorp, "Banjo in the Cow Camps" (1940), reprinted in N. H. Thorp, *Songs of the Cowboys*, ed. Austin E. and Alta S. Fife (New York: Clarkson N. Potter, 1966), pp. 13-14.

4. *Ibid.*, p. 32.

5. *Ibid.*, p. 124, n. 20.

6. *Ibid.*, p. 114.

7. Margaret Larkin, *Singing Cowboy* (New York: Alfred A. Knopf, 1931), p. 163.

8. N. Howard Thorp, *Songs of the Cowboys* (Estancia, New Mexico: News Print Shop, 1908), pp. 24-26, reprinted in Austin and Alta Fife, eds., *Songs of the Cowboys*.

9. John A. Lomax, *Adventures of a Ballad Hunter* (New York: Macmillan Co., 1947), pp. 56-58, quoted in Austin and Alta Fife, eds., *Songs of the Cowboys*, p. 113; Charlie Siringo, quoted in Wayne Gard, *Sam Bass* (Boston and New York: Houghton Mifflin Co., 1936), p. 237.

10. Austin and Alta Fife, eds., *Songs of the Cowboys*, p. 241.

11. Gard, *Sam Bass*, p. 178; Charles L. Martin, *A Sketch of Sam Bass, the Bandit* [1880] (Norman: University of Oklahoma Press, 1956), pp. 24, 136.

12. Gard, *Sam Bass*, pp. 197-98.

13. *Ibid.*, p. 219; Martin, *Sketch of Sam Bass*, p. 125.

14. Gard, *Sam Bass*, p. 239.

15. *Ibid.*, pp. 177-78, 191.

16. See J. Frank Dobie, "The Robinhooding of Sam Bass," *Montana 5,* no. 4 (1955): 34-42.

17. Gard, *Sam Bass*, p. 174.

18. *Ibid.*

19. Austin and Alta Fife, eds., *Songs of the Cowboys*, p. 148.

20. "Cow Boy's Lament" in Austin and Alta Fife, eds., *Songs of the Cowboys*, pp. 153-54.

21. Austin and Alta Fife, eds., *Songs of the Cowboys*, pp. 167-70.

22. Austin and Alta Fife, *Heaven on Horseback* (Logan: Utah State University Press, 1970), pp. 44-47.

23. Andy Adams, *Why the Chisholm Trail Forks and Other Tales of the Cattle Country,* ed. Wilson M. Hudson (Austin: University of Texas Press, 1956). The other fictional sources are *A Texas Matchmaker* (1904), *The Outlet* (1905), and *Cattle Brands* (1906), while four tales are taken from an unpublished manuscript and one from the *Breeder's Gazette* (1905).

24. Some were reprinted by Thorp in his autobiography, *Pardner of the Wind,* written in collaboration with Neil M. Clark (Caldwell, Idaho: Caxton Printers, 1945), pp. 212-27.

25. J. Frank Dobie, "The Traveling Anecdote," in *Folk Travelers: Ballads, Tales, and Talk,* ed. Mody C. Boatright, Wilson M. Hudson, and Allen Maxwell, Publications of the Texas Folklore Society no. 25 (Dallas: Southern Methodist University Press; Austin, 1953), pp. 10-12.

26. Adapted by Stan Hoig, *The Humor of the American Cowboy* (Lincoln: University of Nebraska Press, 1958), pp. 70-72, and by Austin and Alta Fife, eds., *Songs of the Cowboys,* by N. Howard (Jack) Thorp, pp. 148-49, from John H. Callison, *Bill Jones of Paradise Valley, Oklahoma* (Chicago: M. A. Donohue & Co., 1914).

27. Dale, *Cow Country*, p. 140. Adapted by Stan Hoig, *Humor of the American Cowboy*, pp. 181-82. This is also known as a lumberjack tale; see Wright T. Orcutt, "The Minnesota Lumberjacks," *Minnesota History* 6 (1925): 17.

28. Charles M. Russell, *Trails Plowed Under* (New York: Doubleday, Doran & Co., 1940), p. 34.

29. Thorp and Clark, *Pardner of the Wind,* pp. 200-1.

30. Dale, *Cow Country,* p. 141. Stan Hoig, *Humor of the American Cowboy,* p. 128, cites a variant from Frank M. King, *Wranglin' the Past* (Pasadena, Cal.: Trail's End Publishing Co., 1935), p. 97.

31. Dale, *Cow Country,* pp. 141-42; adapted by

Hoig, *Humor of the American Cowboy*, p. 141.

32. From "American Cattle Ranching," in the *Breeder's Gazette* [Chicago], February 5, 1885, p. 194, reprinted in Clifford P. Westermeier, ed., *Trailing the Cowboy: His Life and Lore as Told by Frontier Journalists* (Caldwell, Idaho: Caxton Printers, 1955), p. 307.

33. Thorp and Clark, *Pardner of the Wind*, p. 199.

34. *Ibid.*, pp. 209-11; adapted by Hoig, *Humor of the American Cowboy*, pp. 161-62.

35. "The Cowboy and the Folding Bed," *Field and Farm*, June 30, 1894, p. 6; reprinted in Clifford P. Westermeier, ed., *Trailing the Cowboy* (Caldwell, Idaho: Caxton Printers, 1955), p. 308.

36. Bulah Rust Kirkland, in J. Marvin Hunter, ed., *The Trail Drivers of Texas*, 2nd ed. (Nashville, Tenn.: Colasbury Press, 1925), p. 548.

37. E. C. Abbott ("Teddy Blue") and Helena Huntington Smith, *We Pointed Them North* (Norman: University of Oklahoma Press, 1939), p. 230.

38. Russell, *Trails Plowed Under*, p. 6.

39. Thorp and Clark, *Pardner of the Wind*, pp. 221-26, "Terrapins." In his *Type and Motif-Index of the Folktales of England and North America* (The Hague: Mouton & Co., 1966), Ernest W. Baughman assigns the following motifs to this tale: X1091.1* (a) and X1322* (a), "Man drives turtles as he would cattle"; X1091.1* (aa), "Man drives turtles three hundred yards the first day"; X1091.1* (ab), "Man has to bed his turtles underground when winter comes"; X1091.1* (ac), "Rival puts diving turtle on log at ford; all turtles dive, drown." In addition to Thorp's *Tales of the Chuck Wagon*, Baughman cites a turtle-herding tale from James R. Masterson's *Tall Tales of Arkansaw* (Boston, 1942), p. 331, reprinted in Vance Randolph, *We Always Lie to Strangers* (New York: Columbia University Press, 1951), pp. 143-44.

40. Owen Wister, *The Virginian* [1902] (New York: Macmillan Co., 1925), chap. 16, "The Game and the Nation—Last Act."

41. Baughman, motif X1091.1* (b), citing Earl C. Beck, *Lore of the Lumber Camps* (Ann Arbor: University of Michigan Press, 1948), p. 337.

42. Frank Bacon, *Lightnin'* (New York: Grosset & Dunlap, n.d.), p. 139.

43. Baughman, motif X1091.1* (c), citing Randolph, *We Always Lie to Strangers*, pp. 256-57.

44. V. H. Whitlock (Ol' Waddy), *Cowboy Life on Llano Estacado* (Norman: University of Oklahoma Press, 1970), p. 77.

45. John R. Craddock, "The Legend of Stampede Mesa," in J. Frank Dobie, ed., *Legends of Texas* (Hatboro, Pa.: Folklore Associates, 1964; first published 1924), pp. 111-15.

46. Paul Patterson, *Pecos Tales* (Austin: Texas Folklore Society, 1967), pp. 94-95.

47. See e.g., Philip Ashton Rollins, *The Cowboy* (New York: Charles Scribner's Sons, 1922), chap. 4, "Cowboy Character," pp. 65-102; Ramon F. Adams, *The Cowman and His Code of Ethics* (Austin, Texas: Encino Press, 1969), 33 pp.; "The Cowman's Code of Ethics," in Ramon F. Adams, *The Old-Time Cowhand* (New York: Macmillan Co., 1961), pp. 53-61; Douglas Branch, *The Cowboy and His Interpreters* (New York: Cooper Square Publishers, 1961), chap. 9, "This Man the Cowboy," pp. 146-61; C. L. Sonnichsen, *Cowboys and Cattle Kings* (Norman: University of Oklahoma Press, 1950), "The Code," pp. 42-55; Austin and Alta Fife, eds., *Ballads of the Great West* (Palo Alto, Cal.: American West Publishing Co., 1970), "Code of the Cowboy," pp. 21-24.

48. Adams, *Cowman and His Code of Ethics*, p. 6.

49. Rollins, *The Cowboy*, p. 66.

50. *Ibid.*

51. Sam P. Ridings, *The Chisholm Trail. A History of the World's Greatest Cattle Trail* (Guthrie, Okla.: Co-operative Publishing Company, 1936), chap. 19, "Tales of a Cow-Camp and Breaking in a Cowboy," pp. 303-24.

52. Baughman, type 1890, *The Lucky Shot*, motif X1124.3 (type 1890A, *Shot Splits Tree Limb*, motif X1124.3.1); type 1917, *The Stretching and Shrinking Harness*, motif X1785.1.

53. Warren Roberts, "The Sheep Herder and the Rabbits," *Journal of the Folklore Institute* 3 (1966): 43-49.

54. Baughman, type 1881, motif X1133, "Lie: the hunter in danger"; absurd misunderstandings are J1750-1849.

55. For recollections of Billy the Kid see, e.g., Thorp and Clark, *Pardner of the Wind*, "Billy ('The Kid') Bonney," pp. 168-93; George W.

Coe, *Frontier Fighter: The Autobiography of George W. Coe, Who Fought and Rode with Billy the Kid* (Albuquerque: University of New Mexico Press, 1951); Charles Siringo, *A Texas Cowboy* (New York: William Sloane Associates, 1950), chaps. 21, 22, 27; J. Frank Dobie, *A Vaquero of the Brush Country* (London: Hammond, Hammond & Co., 1949), pp. 159-63.

56. Baughman, type 2200, "Catch Tales."

Lumberjacks

1. Elizabeth M. Bachmann, "Minnesota Log Marks," *Minnesota History* 26 (1945): 134.

2. Wright T. Orcutt, "The Minnesota Lumberjacks," *Minnesota History* 6 (1925): 19.

3. Stewart Holbrook, *Holy Old Mackinaw* (New York: Macmillan Co., 1938), p. 230, n. 1.

4. Robert E. Pike, *Tall Trees, Tough Men* (New York: W. W. Norton & Co., 1967), p. 62.

5. Malcolm G. Laws, *Native American Balladry*, rev. ed. (Philadelphia: American Folklore Society, 1964), p. 146.

6. Richard M. Dorson, "Folksongs of the Maine Woods," *Folklore and Folk Music Archivist* 8, no. 1 (Fall 1965): 14-15; Fanny H. Eckstorm and Mary W. Smyth, "The Pursuit of a Ballad Myth," In *Minstrelsy of Maine* (Boston and New York: Houghton Mifflin Co., 1927), pp. 176-98.

7. Dorson, "Folksongs of the Maine Woods," pp. 24-26.

8. Franz Rickaby, *Ballads and Songs of the Shanty-Boy* (Cambridge, Mass.: Harvard University Press, 1926), pp. 36-37. The bracketed line, forgotten by Rickaby's singer, is from Eckstorm and Smyth, *Minstrelsy*, p. 31.

9. John I. Bellaire, "Silver Jack," *Michigan History Magazine* 25 (1941): 21-22. Cf. the sixteen-stanza version in E. C. Beck, *They Knew Paul Bunyan* (Ann Arbor: University of Michigan Press, (1956), pp. 88-91, "Lumberjack's Revival or Religion in Camp."

10. John E. Nelligan, "The Life of a Lumberman," as told to Charles M. Sheridan, *Wisconsin Magazine of History* 13 (1929): 8.

11. *Ibid.*

12. Walker D. Wyman, *The Lumberjack Frontier* (Lincoln: University of Nebraska Press, 1969), p. 81.

13. Michael G. Karni, "Otto Walta, Finnish Folk Hero of the Iron Range," *Minnesota History* 40 (1967): 391-402.

14. Roy Swanson, "A Swedish Immigrant Folk Figure: Ola Värmlänning," *Minnesota History* 29 (1948): 105-13.

15. Wyman, *Lumberjack Frontier*, pp. 81-82.

16. Roger E. Mitchell, *George Knox: From Man to Legend,* Northeast Folklore no. 11 (1969) (Orono: University of Maine Press, 1970), p. 72.

17. *Ibid.*, pp. 36-37.

18. *Ibid.*, pp. 22, 23, 25, 35.

19. *Ibid.*, p. 33.

20. Samuel P. Fowler, ed., *Salem Witchcraft* (Salem, Mass., 1861), pp. 285-86.

21. Nelligan, "Life of a Lumberman," p. 132.

22. Gerald Averill, *Ridge Runner* (Philadelphia: J. B. Lippincott Co., 1948), p. 93.

23. Dorothy Dill, "Lumberjack Stories," *Michigan History* 41 (1957): 327-34.

24. Nelligan, "Life of a Lumberman," p. 285.

25. John I. Bellaire, "The Greatest 'Jack' Battle of the Ages," *Michigan History* 24 (1940): 339-44.

26. *Milwaukee Journal*, January 23, 1949, reprinted in Robert E. Gard and L. G. Sorden, *Wisconsin Lore* (New York: Duell, Sloan & Pearce, 1962), p. 84.

27. Holbrook, *Holy Old Mackinaw*, p. 125.

28. James Cloyd Bowman, "Life in the Michigan Woods," *Michigan History Magazine* 21 (1937): 282.

29. Bellaire, "Silver Jack," pp. 14-22; Holbrook, *Holy Old Mackinaw*, pp. 119-23. Bellaire and Holbrook disagree on the dates and number of times Driscoll went to prison.

Miners

1. John Spargo, review of *Coal Dust on the Fiddle* by George Korson, *Journal of American Folklore* 57 (1944): 91; Benjamin Botkin, reply to Spargo, *ibid.*, p. 139.

2. Duncan Emrich, "Songs of the Western Miners," *California Folklore Quarterly* 1 (1942): 221. Cf. George G. Korson, *Coal Dust on the Fiddle: Songs and Stories of the Bituminous Industry* [1943] (Hatboro, Pa.: Folklore Associates, 1965), pp. 237-38.

3. Korson, *Coal Dust*, pp. 108-9. Printed in the *United Mine Workers Journal*, 1898.

4. Emrich, "Songs of the Western Miners," pp. 223, 224.

5. Korson, *Coal Dust*, pp. 130, 132.

6. George G. Korson, *Minstrels of the Mine Patch* (Philadelphia: University of Pennsylvania Press, 1938), pp. 189-91.

7. Korson, *Coal Dust*, p. 260. The priest was the Reverend James P. Henny, pastor of St. Mary's Church, Mendota, Wisconsin.

8. Korson, *Coal Dust*, p. 262, "The Cherry Fire"; Korson, *Minstrels*, p. 201, "The Twin-Shaft Disaster"; *ibid.*, p. 194, "The Mines of Locust Dale."

9. Korson, *Minstrels,* p. 286, "Sing Ho! For Anthracite."

10. Ibid., p. 203, "The Miner's Doom."

11. Korson, *Coal Dust,* p. 124, "That Little Lump of Coal."

12. Quoted in *ibid.,* p. 393.

13. Korson, *Minstrels,* pp. 219-20, "What Makes Us Strike?"

14. Arthur H. Lewis, *Lament for the Molly Maguires* (New York: Harcourt, Brace & World, 1964), p. 11.

15. J. Walter Coleman, *The Molly Maguire Riots* (Richmond, Va.: Garrett & Massie, 1936), p. 28, suggests these two views.

16. Marvin W. Schlegel, *Ruler of the Reading: The Life of Franklin B. Gowen* (Harrisburg, Pa.: Archives Publishing Co., 1947), p. 290.

17. Wayne G. Broehl, Jr., *The Molly Maguires* (New York: Random House, Chelsea House, 1968), p. 28.

18. *Ibid.*

19. Allan Pinkerton, *The Molly Maguires and the Detectives* (New York: G. W. Carleton & Co., 1878), p. 78. Reprinted by George G. Korson, *Songs and Ballads of the Anthracite Miner* (New York: Frederick H. Hitchcock, 1927), pp. 189-91; Korson, *Minstrels,* pp. 255-57; Broehl, *Molly Maguires,* pp. 28-29, reprints of texts from *Irish Nights,* no. 6 (Dublin, *ca.* 1903).

20. Korson, *Minstrels,* pp. 189-91.

21. *Ibid.,* p. 192.

22. Lewis, *Lament for the Molly Maguires,* pp. 42-44.

23. Korson, *Songs and Ballads,* p. 134.

24. Richard M. Dorson, *Bloodstoppers and Bearwalkers: Folk Traditions of the Upper Peninsula* (Cambridge, Mass.: Harvard University Press, 1952), pp. 215-16; William Ivey, "'The 1913 Disaster'; Michigan Local Legend," *Folklore Forum* 3:4 (July 1970): 100-14.

25. Korson, *Minstrels,* pp. 257-59. I have not cited all the stanzas.

26. Schlegel, *Ruler of the Reading,* p. 109.

27. Korson, *Minstrels,* p. 255.

28. Broehl, *Molly Maguires,* pp. 166-67.

29. *Ibid.,* p. 177.

30. Korson, *Minstrels,* pp. 267-68; *Songs and Ballads,* p. 196. Fourth stanza omitted.

31. Korson, *Minstrels,* pp. 266-67.

32. Broehl, *Molly Maguires,* p. 224.

33. Schlegel, *Ruler of the Reading,* p. 145, quoting the *Philadelphia Times,* June 22, 1877.

34. Lewis, *Lament for the Molly Maguires,* pp. 269-70. J. Walter Coleman identifies Kelly the Bum as Thomas Kelly (*Molly Maguire Riots,* p. 165), as does Korson, in *Black Rock: Mining Folklore of the Pennsylvania Dutch* (Baltimore: Johns Hopkins University Press, 1960), p. 341.

35. Korson, *Minstrels,* pp. 245-47. Korson does not name his informant.

36. *Ibid.,* pp. 251-52.

37. Quoted in Lewis, *Lament for the Molly Maguires,* p. 302. Cf. Korson, *Minstrels,* p. 308.

38. Korson, *Minstrels,* pp. 307-8, "Was the Imprinted Hand in the Mauch Chunk Jail a Hoax?"

39. *Ibid.,* p. 303. Schlegel, *Ruler of the Reading,* p. 162, also makes Fisher the cell marker.

40. Rosemary Scanlon, "The Handprint: The Biography of a Pennsylvania Legend," *Keystone Folklore Quarterly* 16 (1971): 97-101.

41. Julia Johnsen, *Capital Punishment* (New York: H. W. Wilson, 1939), and Harry Elmer Barnes and Negley K. Teeters, *New Horizons in Criminology,* 3rd ed. (Englewood Cliffs, N.J.: Prentice-Hall, 1959), p. 315, cited in Broehl, *Molly Maguires,* pp. 358 and 397, n. 42.

42. Korson, *Black Rock,* pp. 342-47.

Oil Drillers

1. Mody C. Boatright, *Folklore of the Oil Industry* (Dallas, Texas: Southern Methodist University Press, 1963), p. 130.

2. Hartman Dignowity, "Nicknames in Texas Oil Fields," in J. Frank Dobie, ed., *Texas and Southwestern Lore,* Publications of the Texas Folk-Lore Society no. 6 (Austin, 1927), p. 98.

3. Boatright, *Folklore of the Oil Industry,* chap. 11, "The Driller."

4. Frederick R. Pond, "Language of the California Oil Fields," *American Speech* 7 (1932): 261-72.

5. *Ibid.,* pp. 261-62.

6. Mody C. Boatright and William A. Owens, *Tales from the Derrick Floor: A People's History of the Oil Industry* (Garden City, N.Y.: Doubleday & Co., 1970), p. 145.

7. Mody C. Boatright, *Gib Morgan, Minstrel of the Oil Fields* (Dallas, Texas: Southern Methodist University Press, 1945), p. 65.

8. *Ibid.,* p. 66.

9. Lalia Phipps Boone, *The Petroleum Dictionary* (Norman: University of Oklahoma Press, 1952), defines these technical terms.

10. Boatright, *Gib Morgan,* p. 68.

11. *Ibid.,* p. 77.

12. See, besides Pond, "Language of the California Oil Fields," p. 262, these articles in J. Frank Dobie, ed., *Follow de Drinkin' Gou'd,* Publications of the Texas Folklore Society no. 7 (Austin, 1928): John Lee Brooks, "Paul Bunyan: Oil Man," pp. 45-54, and Acel Garland, "Pipeline Days and Paul Bunyan," pp. 55-61.

13. Brooks, "Paul Bunyan," p. 53.

14. Garland, "Pipeline Days," p. 59.

15. James A. Clark and Michel T. Halbouty, *Spindletop* (New York: Random House, 1952), p. 66.

16. *Ibid.,* p. 75.

17. *Ibid.,* p. 89.

18. *Ibid.,* p. 83.

19. Boatright, *Folklore of the Oil Industry,* p. 145.

20. Paul H. Giddens, *Early Days of Oil* (Princeton, N.J.: Princeton University Press, 1948), p. 32.

21. Herbert Asbury, *The Golden Flood: An Informal History of America's First Oil Field* (New York: Alfred A. Knopf, 1942), chap. 4, "Coal Oil Johnny," draws from *Coal Oil Johnny: The Story of His Career as Told by Himself* (Franklin, Pa., 1902), which refutes John H. McLaurin, *Sketches in Crude Oil* (Harrisburg, Pa., 1896).

22. Boyce House, *Oil Boom* (Caldwell, Idaho: Caxton Printers, 1941), p. 92.

23. *Ibid.,* pp. 140-41.

24. *Ibid.,* pp. 137-38.

25. Boyce House, *Were You in Ranger?* (Dallas, Texas: Tardy Publishing Co., 1935), p. 78.

26. Clark and Halbouty, *Spindletop,* pp. 75-76.

27. Asbury, *Golden Flood,* p. 118; House, *Were You in Ranger?* p. 78, and Boatright, *Folklore of the Oil Industry,* p. 140; Boatright, *Folklore,* p. 140; House, *Were You in Ranger?* p. 78; Asbury, *Golden Flood,* pp. 114-15.

28. *Golden Flood,* p. 114.

29. House, *Were You in Ranger?* p. 78.

30. *Ibid.,* p. 15.

31. Boatright, *Folklore of the Oil Industry,* pp. 143-44.

Railroaders

1. Norman Cohen, "Railroad Folk Songs on Record," *New York Folklore Quarterly* 26 (1970):

91-113; Ann M. Carpenter, "The Railroad in American Folk Song," in Wilson M. Hudson, ed., *Diamond Bessie and the Shepherds,* Publications of the Texas Folklore Society no. 36 (Austin: Encino Press, 1972), pp. 103-19; B. A. Botkin and Alvin Harlow, eds., *A Treasury of Railroad Folklore* (New York: Bonanza Books, 1953), pt. 5, "Blues, Ballads and Work Songs," pp. 435-66; Sterling Sherwin and Harry K. McClintock, *Railroad Songs of Yesterday* (New York: Shapiro, Bernstein & Co., 1943).

2. Fred J. Lee, *Casey Jones, Epic of the American Railroad* (Kingsport, Tenn.: Southern Publishers, Inc., 1939), p. 206.

3. *Ibid.,* p. 222.

4. Howard W. Odum and Guy B. Johnson, *The Negro and His Songs* [1925] (Hatboro, Pa.: Folklore Associates, 1964), p. 207.

5. John A. and Alan Lomax, *American Ballads and Folk Songs* (New York: Macmillan Co., 1934), pp. 39-41.

6. *Ibid.,* pp. 37-38.

7. *Ibid.,* p. 35.

8. *Ibid.,* p. 36.

9. John A. and Alan Lomax, *Folk Song U.S.A.* (New York: Duell, Sloan & Pearce, 1947), p. 250.

10. Odum and Johnson, *The Negro and His Songs,* p. 208.

11. Lomax and Lomax, *Folk Song U.S.A.,* p. 250.

12. Freeman H. Hubbard, *Railroad Avenue* (New York: McGraw-Hill Book Co., 1945), p. 17.

13. *Ibid.,* p. 10.

14. Lee, *Casey Jones,* p. 286.

15. *Ibid.,* pp. 287-88.

16. James J. Geller, *Famous Songs and Their Stories* (New York: Macaulay Co., 1931), pp. 231-32.

17. Accounts of Casey Jones in the mass media can be found in *Time,* May 15, 1970, p. 88; *Collier's,* August 12, 1939, p. 264; *New Yorker,* April 29, 1950, pp. 23-24; *Life,* January 26, 1942, pp. 61ff.; *Reader's Digest,* April 1967, pp. 25-32.

18. Frank Clyde Brown, ed., *North Carolina Folklore Collected During the Years 1912-1943,* vol. 2, *Folk Ballads from North Carolina,* eds. Henry M. Belden and Arthur Palmer Hudson (Durham, N.C.: Duke University Press, 1952), p. 513.

19. John Harrington Cox, *Folk-Songs of the South* (Hatboro, Pa.: Folklore Associates, 1963), pp. 221-30. *Kentucky Folklore Record* 3 (1957): 99, has still another variant: "I want to die with the engine I love, One Hundred and Forty-four." [!]

20. Josiah H. Combs, *Folk-Songs du Midi des Etats-Unis* (Paris: Les Presses Universitaires de France, 1925), pp. 200-3.

The Master Workman versus the Businessman

1. Carl Sandburg, *The American Songbag* (New York: Harcourt, Brace & Co., 1927), p. 366.

2. Stewart H. Holbrook, *The Story of American Railroads* (New York: Crown Publishers, 1947), p. 442.

3. Duncan Emrich, "Casey Jones, Union Scab," *Western Folklore* 1 (1942): 292-93; and William Alderson, "On the Wobbly 'Casey Jones' and Other Songs," *ibid.*, 373-74.

4. *Songs of the Workers,* 28th ed. (Chicago: Industrial Workers of the World, July 1945), pp. 46-47.

5. Ed Cray, *The Erotic Muse* (New York: Oak Publications, 1969), p. 170, quoting Mack McCormick, "The Damn Tinkers," *American Folk Music Occasional,* No. 1 (1964), p. 12.

6. Indiana University Folklore Archives, collected in Kokomo, Indiana, 1969. The archives has two close variants. Cray cites parodies in William Wallrich, *Air Force Airs* (New York: Duell, Sloan and Pearce 1957), pp. 31-33, 35, 71, 155. Donald Davidson comments on parodies of Casey Jones in his essay "The Tradition of Irreverence," in *Still Rebels, Still Yankees,* 2nd ed. (Baton Rouge: Louisiana State University Press, 1972).

7. Indiana University Folklore Archives, collected in Cincinnati, Ohio, 1952.

8. Richard M. Dorson, "Paul Bunyan in the News, 1939-1941," *Western Folklore* 15 (1956): 26-39, 179-93, 247-61.

9. Kenneth W. Porter, "The Business Man in American Folklore," *Bulletin of the Business Historical Society* 18 (1944): 113-30.

10. *Ibid.*, p. 119, quoting Sandburg, *American Songbag,* pp. 304-5.

The Contemporary Period:

The Humane Impulse

1. Yosal Rogat, review of *On the Democratic Idea in America* by Irving Kristol, *New York Review of Books,* September 21, 1972, p. 8.

2. Carlynn H. Langley, "Notes on Status in the Counter Culture," August 1970, University of Texas Folklore Archives.

3. Steve Russell, "Operation of the S-X Factor in Headlore," January 1970, University of Texas Folklore Archives.

4. Edwin A. Prince, "Stories and Sayings of the Drug Underground," December 1968, University of Texas Folklore Archives.

5. Anne Hershberg, April 1968, University of California Folklore Archives.

6. Steve Russell, December 1968, University of Texas Folklore Archives.

7. Carol Gurdlach, January 5, 1970, University of Texas Folklore Archives.

8. Steve Russell, "Operation of the S-X Factor in Headlore," September 1969, University of Texas Folklore Archives.

9. Marvin Isaacson, June 1968, University of California Folklore Archives.

10. Carol Gurdlach, January 1970, University of Texas Folklore Archives.

11. Steve Russell, "Operation of the S-X Factor in Headlore," January 1970, University of Texas Folklore Archives.

12. *Ibid.,* December 1969 (two texts).

13. *Ibid.,* January 1970.

14. Pat Quarles, November 1964, University of California Folklore Archives.

15. John Durham, "Druglore," December 1969, University of Texas Folklore Archives.

16. Richard M. Dorson, *Jonathan Draws the Long Bow* (Cambridge, Mass.: Harvard University Press, 1946), p. 55. See motif K219.5, "Man cheats devil by giving him sole instead of soul," Ernest W. Baughman, *Type and Motif-Index of the Folktales of England and North America,* Indiana University Folklore Series no. 20 (The Hague: Mouton & Co., 1966).

17. Steve Russell, December 1969, University of Texas Folklore Archives.

18. Marvin Isaacson, June 1968, University of California Folklore Archives.

19. Tom Wolfe, *The Electric Kool-Aid Acid Test* [1968] (New York: Bantam Books, 1969), pp. 134-37.

20. Michael Pearce, March 1969, University of California Folklore Archives.

21. Anne Hershberg, April 1968, University of California Folklore Archives.

22. Sherry Sonnenschein, March 1968; Anne Hershberg, May 1968; Tim Melchior, May 1968; Pat Quarles, October 1964 (see motif K630, "Escape by giving narcotic to guards" [Baughman]); Tim Melchior, May 1968; Anne Hershberg, April 1968; all from University of California Folklore Archives.

23. Sherry Sonnenschein, March 1968, University of California Folklore Archives; Edwin A. Prince, December 1968, University of Texas Folklore Archives; Judy Place, March 1969, University of California Folklore Archives.

24. Edwin A. Prince, December 1968, University of Texas Folklore Archives.

25. Steve Russell, January 1970, University of Texas Folklore Archives.

26. Carol Gurdlach, January 1970, University of Texas Folklore Archives.

27. Steve Russell, September 1969, University of Texas Folklore archives.

28. Tanya Reuvekamp, May 1968, University of California Folklore Archives.

29. *Ibid.*

30. Steve Russell, January 1970, University of Texas Folklore Archives.

31. Pat Quarles, December 1964, University of California Folklore Archives.

32. Marvin Isaacson, May 1968, University of California Folklore Archives.

33. Steve Russell, January 1970, University of Texas Folklore Archives.

34. Arnold Schraer, November 1969, University of California Folklore Archives.

35. John Durham, December 1969, University of Texas Folklore Archives.

36. Arnold Schraer, November 1969, University of California Folklore Archives.

37. Matthew Dickey, March 1969, University of California Folklore Archives.

38. *Ibid.*

39. Tim Melchior, May 1968, University of California Folklore Archives; Tanya Reuvekamp, May 1968, University of California Folklore Archives; *ibid.;* Tim Melchior, *loc. cit.; ibid.;* Mona K. Stevens, April 1970, Indiana University Folklore Archives (from Indianapolis); John Durham, January 1970, University of Texas Folklore Archives; Tim Melchior, *loc. cit.; ibid.;* Mona K. Stevens, May 1970, *loc. cit.;* Tanya Reuvekamp, *loc. cit.;* Joan Gordon, May 1968, University of California Folklore Archives; *ibid.,* June 1968; *ibid.,* May 1968; Sherry Sonnenschein, March 1968, University of California Folklore Archives; Bob Zuckerman, March 1968, University of California Folklore Archives; Tim Melchior, *loc. cit.;* Tanya Reuvekamp, *loc. cit.; ibid.; ibid.*

40. Arvalea Nelson, May 1968, Berkeley. Given in my *American Folklore and the Historian* (Chicago: University of Chicago Press, 1971), pp. 162-63.

41. For Barney Beal, see my *American Folklore* (Chicago: University of Chicago Press, 1959), pp. 124-28, and *Buying the Wind: Regional Folklore in the United States* (Chicago: University of Chicago Press, 1964), pp. 40-54.

42. *San Francisco Examiner,* July 10, 1967, p. 20; December 22, 1967, p. 3; February 26, 1970. *San Francisco Chronicle,* September 5, 1968, p. 2; July 22, 1970, p. 1.

43. Richard A. Gaultz, June 1968, University of California Folklore Archives.

44. The above from John Durham, December 1969, University of Texas Folklore Archives.

45. Olive Spitzmiller, "The Head Community as Deviant Subculture," *Folklore Annual of the University Folklore Association,* no. 1 (Austin, Texas: Center for Intercultural Studies in Folklore and Oral History, 1969), p. 6.

46. Pat Quarles, January 1965, University of California Folklore Archives.

47. *Ibid.,* December 1964.

48. *Ibid.,* October 1964.

49. Philip N. Bliss, January 1968, University of California Folklore Archives.

50. Anne Hershberg, January 1965, University of California Folklore Archives.

51. Miriam J. Harris, January 1968, University of California Folklore Archives.

52. Judy Perani, May 1965, University of California Folklore Archives.

53. Mona K. Stevens, May 1970, Indiana University Folklore Archives (2 variants).

54. Robert W. Newman, April 1964, University of California Folklore Archives.

55. Steve Chance, May 1971, Indiana University Folklore Archives.

56. Baughman, *Type and Motif-Index,* p. 105.

57. John Northland, March 1969, University of California Folklore Archives.

58. Peter Rubin, n.d., University of California Folklore Archives.

59. Leigh Lightfoot, March 1969, University of California Folklore Archives.

60. Tanya Reuvecamp, May 1968, University of California Folklore Archives.

61. Carol Zajchowski, March 1969; Carol Durgin, March 1969; Carol Zajchowski, March 1969; all from University of California Folklore Archives.

62. Stuart Kew, March 1969; Alan Freebury, March 1969; Stuart Kew, February 1969; all from University of California Folklore Archives.

63. Claudia Woodward, December 1965, University of California Folklore Archives.

64. Peter Rubin, n.d., University of California Folklore Archives.

65. Douglas Lipton, March 1969, University of California Folklore Archives.

66. Jeff Dodge, February 1968, University of California Folklore Archives.

67. Dianna Laris, March 1969; Douglas Lipton, March 1969; Stephanie Nicoletti, February 1969; all from University of California Folklore Archives.

68. Joan Gordon, May 1968; Barbara Kirshenblatt-Gimblett, January 1966; both from University of California Folklore Archives.

69. Barbara Mapps, 1969, University of California Folklore Archives.

70. Joan Gordon, June 1968, University of California Folklore Archives.

71. Gracia J. Allen, January 1969, University of California Folklore Archives.

72. Nancy Takiguchi, March 1968, University of California Folklore Archives.

73. Fern Schneider, January 1969, University of California Folklore Archives.

74. Madeline Fine, July 1969, University of California Folklore Archives; John Durham, January 1970, University of Texas Folklore Archives.

75. Fern Schneider, March 1969, University of California Folklore Archives.

76. *Ibid.*

77. Matthew Dickey, March 1969, University of California Folklore Archives.

78. *Ibid.*

79. Fern Schneider, March 1969, University of California Folklore Archives.

80. *Ibid.*

81. *Ibid.*, February 1969.

82. J. Edward Walsh, June 1969, University of California Folklore Archives.

83. Dorson, *American Folklore,* p. 73.

84. Victoria Brady, June 1968, University of California Folklore Archives.

85. Brian Johnson, Fall 1965, University of California Folklore Archives.

86. Michael Fayer, May 1968, University of California Folklore Archives.

87. Victoria Brady, May 1968; Michael Fayer, May 1968; Ruth Borker Maltz, November 1969; all from University of California Folklore Archives.

88. Michael Fayer, May 1968; Victoria Brady, May 1968; both from University of California Folklore Archives.

89. Brian Johnson, Winter 1965, University of California Folklore Archives.

90. Michael Fayer, May 1968, University of California Folklore Archives.

91. Victoria Brady, May 1968, University of California Folklore Archives.

92. Tim Melchior, May 1968, University of California Folklore Archives.

93. *Ibid.*

94. *Ibid.*

95. Michael Fayer, May 1968, University of California Folklore Archives.

Bibliography

Abbott, E. C. ("Teddy Blue") and Helena Huntington Smith. *We Pointed Them North*. Norman: University of Oklahoma Press, 1939.

Abrahams, Roger D. *Deep Down in the Jungle*. Hatboro, Pa.: Folklore Associates, 1964.

Adams, Andy. *The Log of a Cowboy*. Boston and New York: Houghton Mifflin Co., 1931.

——. *Why the Chisholm Trail Forks and Other Tales of the Cattle Country*. Edited by Wilson M. Hudson. Austin: University of Texas Press, 1956.

Allsopp, Fred W. *Folklore of Romantic Arkansas*. 2 vols. New York: Grolier Society, 1931.

Armstrong, Edward A. *The Folklore of Birds*. London: William Collins' Sons & Co., 1958.

Asbury, Herbert. *The Gangs of New York*. New York: Peter Smith, 1928.

——. *The Golden Flood: An Informal History of America's First Oil Field*. New York: Alfred A. Knopf, 1942.

——. *Ye Olde Fire Laddies*. New York: Alfred A. Knopf, 1930.

Averill, Gerald. *Ridge Runner*. Philadelphia: J. B. Lippincott Co., 1948.

Bacon, Frank. *Lightnin'*. New York: Grosset & Dunlap, n.d.

Beck, Earl C. *Lore of the Lumber Camps*. Ann Arbor: University of Michigan Press, 1948.

——. *They Knew Paul Bunyan*. Ann Arbor: University of Michigan Press, 1956.

Belden, Henry M., and Arthur Palmer Hudson, eds. *Folk Ballads from North Carolina*. Frank C. Brown Collection of North Carolina Folklore, vol. 2. Durham, N.C.: Duke University Press, 1952.

Bernstein, Barton J., ed. *Towards a New Past: Dissenting Essays in American History*. New York: Pantheon Books, 1968.

Bishop, George. *New England Judged: The Second Part*. London, 1667.

Blair, Walter, and Franklin J. Meine, eds. *Half Horse, Half Alligator*. Chicago: University of Chicago Press, 1956.

Boatright, Mody C. *Folklore of the Oil Industry*. Dallas, Texas: Southern Methodist University Press, 1963.

——. *Gib Morgan: Minstrel of the Oil Fields*. Dallas, Texas: Southern Methodist University Press, 1945.

—— and Donald Day, eds. *Backwoods to Border*. Austin: Publications of the Texas Folklore Society, no. 18, and Dallas: Southern Methodist University Press, 1943.

——, Wilson M. Hudson, and Allen Maxwell, eds. *Folk Travelers: Ballads, Tales, and Talk*. Austin: Publications of the Texas Folklore Society, no. 25, and Dallas: Southern Methodist University Press, 1953.

—— and William A. Owens. *Tales from the Derrick Floor: A People's History of the Oil Industry*. Garden City, N.Y.: Doubleday & Co., 1970.

Boone, Lalia Phipps. *The Petroleum Dictionary*. Norman: University of Oklahoma Press, 1952.

Botkin, B. A., and Alvin Harlow, eds. *A Treasury of Railroad Folklore*. New York: Bonanza Books, 1953.

Brand, John. *Observations on Popular Antiquities*. 2 vols. Edited by Henry Ellis. London, 1813.

Briggs, Katharine. *Pale Hecate's Team: An Examination of the Beliefs on Magic Among Shakespeare's Contemporaries and His Immediate Successors*. New York: Humanities Press, 1962.

Broehl, Wayne G., Jr. *The Molly Maguires*, 1964. Reprint. New York: Vintage/Chelsea House, 1968.

Brown, Charles E. *Whisky Jack Tales*. Madison, Wis.: State Historical Museum, 1940.

Brown, T. Allston. *A History of the New York Stage*. Vol. 1. New York: Dodd, Mead & Co., 1903.

Burr, George Lincoln, ed. *Narratives of the Witchcraft Cases. Sixteen Forty-eight to Seventeen Six*. 1914. Reprint. New York: Barnes & Noble, 1959.

Callison, John H. *Bill Jones of Paradise Valley Oklahoma*. Chicago: M. A. Donohue & Co., 1914.

Child, Francis James. *The English and Scottish Popular Ballads*. 5 vols. Boston: Houghton Mifflin Co., 1882-98.

Clark, James A., and Michel T. Halbouty. *Spindletop*. New York: Random House, 1952.

Clarke, Mathew St. Clair [anon.]. *The Life of David Crockett, the Original Humorist and Irrepressible Backwoodsman, An Autobiography*. New York: A. L. Burt Co., n.d.

Coe, George W. *Frontier Fighter: The Autobiography of George W. Coe, Who Fought and Rode with Billy the Kid*. Albuquerque: University of New Mexico Press, 1951.

Coleman, J. Walter. *The Molly Maguire Riots*.

Richmond, Va.: Garrett & Massie, 1936.

Combs, Josiah H. *Folk-Songs du Midi des Etats-Unis.* Paris: Les Presses Universitaires de France, 1925.

Cox, John Harrington. *Folk-Songs of the South.* 1925. Reprint. Hatboro, Pa.: Folklore Associates, 1963.

Cray, Ed. *The Erotic Muse.* New York: Oak Publications, 1969.

Dale, Edward Everett. *Cow Country.* 1942. Reprint. Norman: University of Oklahoma Press, 1965.

Danckaerts, Jasper, and Peter Sluyter. *Journal of a Voyage to New York.* Brooklyn, N.Y., 1867.

de Tocqueville, Alexis. *Democracy in America.* Translated by Henry Reeve. New York and London: Oxford University Press, 1947.

Dobie, J. Frank. *A Vaquero of the Brush Country.* London: Hammond, Hammond & Co., 1949.

———, ed. *Follow de Drinkin' Gou'd.* Publications of the Texas Folklore Society, no. 7. Austin, 1928.

———, ed. *Legends of Texas.* Publications of the Texas Folklore Society, no. 3. Austin, 1924. Reprint. Hatboro, Pa.: Folklore Associates, 1964.

———, ed. *Texas and Southwestern Lore.* Publications of the Texas Folklore Society, no. 6. Austin, 1927.

Dorson, Richard M., ed. *America Begins: Early American Writing.* 1950. Reprint. Bloomington: Indiana University Press, 1971.

———. *America Rebels: Narratives of the Patriots.* New York: Pantheon Books, 1953.

———. *American Negro Folktales.* New York: Fawcett, 1967.

———. *Bloodstoppers and Bearwalkers: Folk Traditions of the Upper Peninsula.* Cambridge, Mass.: Harvard University Press, 1952.

———. *Buying the Wind: Regional Folklore in the United States.* Chicago: University of Chicago Press, 1964.

———. *Davy Crockett, American Comic Legend.* New York: Rockland Editions, 1939.

———. *Jonathan Draws the Long Bow.* 1946. Reprint. New York: Russell & Russell, 1969.

Fife, Austin and Alta. *Heaven on Horseback.* Logan: Utah State University Press, 1970.

Gard, Robert. *Johnny Chinook.* New York: Longmans, Green & Co., 1945.

Gard, Wayne. *Sam Bass.* Boston and New York: Houghton Mifflin Co., 1936.

Gardner, Emelyn E. *Folklore from the Schoharie Hills, New York.* Ann Arbor: University of Michigan Press, 1937.

Geller, James J. *Famous Songs and Their Stories.* New York: Macaulay Co., 1931.

Giddens, Paul H. *Early Days of Oil.* Princeton, N.J.: Princeton University Press, 1948.

Goodman, Paul. *Growing Up Absurd.* New York: Vintage Books, 1960.

Gunn, Thomas. *Mose Among the Britishers: The B'hoy in London.* Philadelphia: A. Hart, 1850.

Halline, Allan G., ed. *American Plays.* New York: American Book Co., 1935.

Harlow, Alvin. *Old Bowery Days.* New York: D. Appleton-Century Co., 1931.

Hill, G. H. *Scenes from the Life of an Actor.* Boston, 1853.

Hodge, Francis. *Yankee Theater: The Image of America on the Stage 1825-1850.* Austin: University of Texas Press, 1964.

Hoig, Stan. *The Humor of the American Cowboy.* Lincoln: University of Nebraska Press, 1958.

Holbrook, Stewart. *Holy Old Mackinaw.* New York: Macmillan Co., 1938.

———. *The Story of American Railroads.* New York: Crown Publishers, 1947.

House, Boyce. *Oil Boom.* Caldwell, Idaho: Caxton Printers, 1941.

———. *Were You in Ranger?* Dallas, Texas: Tardy Publishing Co., 1935.

Hubbard, Freeman H. *Railroad Avenue.* New York: McGraw-Hill Book Co., 1945.

Hudson, Wilson M. *Andy Adams, His Life and Writings.* Dallas, Texas: Southern Methodist University Press, 1964.

———, ed. *Diamond Bessie and the Shepherds.* Publications of the Texas Folklore Society, no. 36. Austin, Texas: Encino Press, 1972.

Hunter, J. Marvin, ed. *The Trail Drivers of Texas.* 2nd ed., rev. Nashville, Tenn.: Colasbury Press, 1925.

Hyatt, Harry M. *Folk-Lore from Adams County, Illinois.* 2nd ed. N.p.: Memoirs of the Alma Egan Hyatt Foundation, 1965.

Ireland, J. N. *Records of the New York Stage.* 2 vols. New York, 1866–67.

Keith, George. *The Presbyterian and Independent Visible Churches in New-England and Else-Where, Brought to the Test . . . With a call and warning from the Lord to the people of Boston and New-England to repent. . . .* London: printed for T. Northcott, 1691.

King, Frank M. *Wranglin' the Past.* Pasadena, Cal.: Trail's End Publishing Co., 1935.

Kittredge, George Lyman. *Witchcraft in Old and New England.* Cambridge, Mass.: Harvard University Press, 1929.

Korson, George G. *Coal Dust on the Fiddle: Songs and Stories of the Bituminous Industry.* Philadelphia: University of Pennsylvania Press, 1943.

———. *Minstrels of the Mine Patch: Songs and Stories of the Anthracite Industry.* Philadelphia: University of Pennsylvania Press, 1938.

———. *Songs and Ballads of the Anthracite Miner.* New York: Frederick H. Hitchcock, 1927.

Larkin, Margaret. *Singing Cowboy.* New York: Alfred A. Knopf, 1931.

Laws, Malcolm G. *Native American Balladry.* Rev. ed. Philadelphia: The American Folklore Society, 1964.

Lee, Fred J. *Casey Jones, Epic of the American Railroad.* Kingsport, Tenn.: Southern Publishers, 1939.

Levinge, Captain R. G. A. *Echoes from the Backwoods.* London, 1849.

Lewis, Arthur H. *Lament for the Molly Maguires.* New York: Harcourt, Brace & World, 1964.

Lomax, John A. *Adventures of a Ballad Hunter,* New York: Macmillan Co., 1947.

——— and Alan. *American Ballads and Folk Songs.* New York: Macmillan Co., 1934.

——— and Alan. *Folk Song U.S.A.* New York: Duell, Sloan & Pearce, 1947.

Macfarlane, Alan. *Witchcraft in Tudor and Stuart England.* New York: Harper & Row, Publishers, 1970.

Martin, Charles L. *A Sketch of Sam Bass, the Bandit.* 1880. Reprint. Norman: University of Oklahoma Press, 1956.

Mather, Cotton. *Late Memorable Providences Relating to Witchcrafts and Possessions.* London: printed for Thomas Parkhurst, 1691.

———. *Magnalia Christi Americana: Or, the Ecclesiastical History of New-England* [1702].

2 vols. New York: Russell & Russell, 1967.

———. *The Wonders of the Invisible World. Being an Account of the Tryals of Several Witches Lately Executed in New-England.* 1692. Reprint. London, 1862.

Mather, Increase. *Remarkable Providences Illustrative of the Earlier Days of American Colonisation* [reprint of *An Essay for the Recording of Illustrious Providences,* 1684]. London: John Russell Smith, 1856.

Meine, Franklin J., ed. *The Crockett Almanacs.* Chicago: Caxton Club, 1955.

Northall, William K. *Before and Behind the Curtain.* New York, 1841.

Odell, George C. D. *Annals of the New York Stage.* 15 vols. New York: AMS Press, 1970.

Odum, Howard W., and Guy B. Johnson. *The Negro and His Songs.* 1925. Reprint. Hatboro, Pa.: Folklore Associates, 1964.

Owens, Mary E. *Memories of John E. Owens.* Baltimore, 1892.

Paine, Albert Bigelow. *Mark Twain, A. Biography.* 3 vols. New York: Harper & Brothers, 1912.

Patterson, Paul. *Pecos Tales.* Austin: Texas Folklore Society, 1967.

Peters, Harry T. *America on Stone.* New York: Doubleday, Doran & Co., 1931.

Pike, Robert E. *Tall Trees, Tough Men.* New York: W. W. Norton & Co., 1967.

Puckett, Newbell N. *Folk Beliefs of the Southern Negro.* Chapel Hill: University of North Carolina Press, 1926.

Randolph, Vance. *Ozark Superstitions.* New York: Columbia University Press, 1947.

———. *Sticks in the Knapsack and Other Ozark Folk Tales.* New York: Columbia University Press, 1958.

Reich, Charles. *The Greening of America.* New York: Bantam Books, 1971.

Rickaby, Franz. *Ballads and Songs of the Shanty-Boy.* Cambridge, Mass.: Harvard University Press, 1926.

Rossman, Michael. *The Wedding Within the War.* Garden City, N.Y.: Doubleday & Co., 1971.

Russell, Charles M. *Trails Plowed Under.* New York: Doubleday, Doran & Co., 1940.

Sandburg, Carl. *The American Songbag.* New York: Harcourt, Brace & Co., 1927.

Schlegel, Marvin W. *Ruler of the Reading: The Life of Franklin B. Gowen.* Harrisburg, Pa.: Archives Publishing Co., 1947.

Shackford, James A. *David Crockett, The Man and the Legend.* Edited by John B. Shackford. Chapel Hill: University of North Carolina Press, 1956.

Sherwin, Sterling, and Harry K. McClintock. *Railroad Songs of Yesterday*. New York: Shapiro, Bernstein & Co., 1943.

Sikes, Wirt. *British Goblins*. Boston, 1881.

Siringo, Charles A. *A Texas Cowboy*. New York: William Sloane Associates, 1950.

Sitwell, Sacheverell. *Poltergeists*. London: Faber & Faber, 1940.

Smith, John. *Travels and Works*. 2 vols. Edinburgh: John Grant, 1910.

Thomas, Keith. *Religion and the Decline of Magic*. New York: Charles Scribner's Sons, 1971.

Thorp, N. H. *Pardner of the Wind*. Written in collaboration with Neil M. Clark. Caldwell, Idaho: Caxton Printers, 1945.

————. *Songs of the Cowboys*. Edited by Austin E. and Alta S. Fife. New York: Clarkson N. Potter, 1966.

Westermeier, Clifford P., ed. *Trailing the Cowboy: His Life and Lore as Told by Frontier Journalists*. Caldwell, Idaho: Caxton Printers, 1955.

Whitlock, V. H. (Ol' Waddy). *Cowboy Life on Llano Estacado*. Norman: University of Oklahoma Press, 1970.

Wister, Owen. *The Virginian*. 1902. Reprint. New York: Macmillan Co., 1925.

Wolfe, Tom. *The Electric Kool-Aid Acid Test*. New York: Bantam Books, 1969.

Wyman, Walker D. *The Lumberjack Frontier*. Lincoln: University of Nebraska Press, 1969.

Index

Abbott, "Teddy Blue," 145-6

Abrahams, Roger, 255; *Deep Down in the Jungle,* 126

Adams, Andy, 140-1, 149; *Log of a Cowboy,* 129-31

Adams, Ramon, 150

Adderton, Humphrey, 52

adultery, in Puritan society, 29-30

Allen, Ethan, 59

Allen, John, 42-3

Amateis, Edmond, 248

American Federation of Labor, 213

amphetamines, and the youth culture, 260, 261, 284

Anansi the Spider, 300

anecdotes: of cowboys, 141-2; of druglore, 262-3; of frontier society, 58-9, 66-7; of invoking the Devil, 13; of Mike Fink, 84-8; in newspapers, 58, 61, 63, 83; of the skow-maker, 64-6

Anglicans, in Virginia, 12, 15

antinomianism, heresy of, 29

Arkins, James, 50

Arnold, Benedict, 213

Asbury, Herbert: *Gangs of New York,* 63, 106; *Ye Olde Fire Laddies,* 106

Ashley-Henry expeditions, 81, 90

Asmodeus! or, The Iniquities of New York, 101

Atkinson, John, 43

Autry, Gene, 140

Averill, George, 181

"Avondale Mine Disaster, The," 194-5, 198-9, 202

Baker, Benjamin A.: *Glance at New York, A,* 99-101, 102, 107

Balch, Marston, 118

ballads: of businessmen, 249-50; of coal miners, 186, 187-90, 194, 198-9, 202; collecting of, 133-4; English and Scottish, 23; Irish, 208-9; lumberjack, 156; of Mike Fink, 89-90; the Molly Maguires, 193-4, 203, 204-6, 207-8; of railroaders, 235, 236, 238-42, 244-6, 249; of Sam Patch, 96; sea chanteys, 124; transatlantic crossings, 194, 208-9; of the Wobblies, 244

"Barbara Allen," 127

Barnes, Harry Elmer: *Criminology,* 212-13

Barnett, Morris: *Yankee Peddler,* 116, 119, 120

Bass, Sam. *See* Sam Bass

Baughman, Ernest W.: *Type and Motif-Index of the Folktales of England and North America,* 54-5

Beacon, Joseph, 25

Beal, Barney, 184, 283-4

"Bear and the Swallows, The," 77-9

Beddaford, John, 44

"Been on the Cholly So Long," 240

Bell, Andrew, 193

Bellaire, John, 182

Bennett, Emerson: *Mike Fink: A Legend of Ohio,* 83-4

Benson, Martha, 156, 157

Bermuda settlers, judgments against, 31

Berrigan brothers, 274

bestialities, judgments against, 30

Big Toolie, 222, 227, 246

"Billings," 150-3

Billy the Kid, 62, 151, 153

Bishop, Bridget, 38

Bishop, George: *New England Judged,* 52

black folk songs, and "Casey Jones," 238-40

black folklore, 125-7; Devil in, 50

Blair, Walter, 90

Blanchard, Louis, 170, 174

Blankenship, Tom, 72

Blockheads, The (anon.), 118

bloodstains and bleeding corpses, in providences, 22-3

Blue, Jimmy, 227-8

Boatright, Mody: *Folklore of the Oil Industry,* 214-15; *Gib Morgan, Minstrel of the Oil Fields,* 214, 216-22, 224-6, 227, 230, 234, 235; *Tales from the Derrick Floor,* 215

Boccaccio, Giovanni, 31

Boone, Lalia: *Petroleum Dictionary,* 219

Boorstin, Daniel J., 12

Botkin, Benjamin, 124, 186; *Treasury of Railroad Folklore, A,* 235

Bowman, Robert L., 211

Brady, "Diamond Jim," 250

"Breaking the News," 142

Brer Rabbit, 126, 300

Brewster, Margaret, 53

Bridger, Jim, 218

Briggs, Katharine: *Pale Hecate's Team,* 12, 13

Broady, Joe, 242

Brooks, John Lee, 226-7

Brown, William, 44, 47, 48

Bryan, William Jennings, 249

"Bucking Broncho," 134, 136

Buffalo Bill, 238

"Buffalo Range, The," 243

"Buffalo Skinners, The," 243

Bunyan, Paul. *See* Paul Bunyan

Burnett, J. G.: *Blanche of Brandywine,* 113-15, 119

Burroughs, Rev. George, 38, 180

"Bury Me Not on the Lone Prairie," 140

businessmen, in folklore, 249-50

"C & O Wreck, The," 242
Calvin, John, 51; *Institutes,* 12
Campbell, Alexander, 204, 210, 212
"Canady-I-O," 243
Cargill, Melissa Dianne, 284
Carnegie, Andrew: *Gospel of Wealth, The,* 250
Cartwright, Peter, 84, 92
"Casey" Jones, 235-41; death of, 235-6; as
 phallic hero, 245-6
"Casey Jones" (ballad), 238-41
"Casey Jones—The Union Scab," 244-5
Cassedy, Ben, 88, 91
Chandler, Colie, 237
Chanfrau, Francis S., 61, 99-100, 102, 104,
 106-7
Chanfrau, Hen, 99, 106
Chaplin, Charlie, 128
character types: nicknames for, 59; Yankee,
 108-10
"Charley Snyder," 239
Chaucer, Geoffrey, 15
Chesselden, John, 50
Chicago Seven, 274
Child, Francis James, 23, 185
Chilton, Thomas, 68
"Chinese Fire Alarm," 302
Chisholm Trail, 128-9
churches, early colonial, 12; Devil's attacks on,
 22
Civil War, 57, 59, 123-4; and cowboy folklore,
 128-9
Clark, Neil M., 131
Clarke, Mathew St. Clair, 68
coal miners, folklore of, 128, 185-213; ballads,
 186, 187-90; disasters, 187-8, 194-5, 198-9,
 202; heroes, 187-9, 213; Molly Maguires,
 190-3, 194-5, 202-13
"Coal Oil Johnny," 230-2
"Coat-Hanger Chime," 300
codes: cowboy, 130, 131, 148, 150-3; oil driller,
 215, 216; railroader, 236
Cole, Ann, 35
Coll, Manus "Kelly the Bum," 208, 211, 213
Collins, Joel, 137
Constitutional Convention, 57
Corey, Giles, 23-4
"Cosmos," 302
Cotton, John, 15, 16, 30, 49, 50
counterculture folklore, 253-310; draft dodgers,
 304-9; druglore, 255, 259, 260-303; oral
 legends, 259; traditions, 259-60
cowboy folklore, 128-53; cattle drives, 128-30;
 city visits, 143, 145; cowboy code, 130, 131,
 148, 150-3; death, casualness toward, 142;
 drinking, 142-3; eating habits, 143; folktales,
 140-53; heroes, 134, 136; humor in, 141-3,
 145-8; oral narratives, 130-1, 140; "putting
 the leggins on," 152-3; and Sam Bass, 132,
 133, 136-40; songs, 130, 131-40; supernatural legends, 148-9
"Cowboy's Lament, The," 132, 139-40, 142,
 243
Cox, John, 145
Creasy, William, 87
Creek Wars (1813-14), 66
Crockett, Davy. *See* Davy Crockett

Crockett, John, 66
Crockett almanacs, 58, 68, 76, 77, 80, 219;
 keelboatmen in, 81-2, 84
Crockett's Free-and-Easy Song Book, 76

Dale, Edward Everett, 143
Danckaerts, Jasper, 31, 35
Darley, Felix O. C., 58
Darling, John, 218
Davis, Angela, 274
Davis, James, 80
Davy Crockett, 60-1, 64-80, 82, 85, 87, 110,
 218; almanacs, 58, 68, 76, 77, 80, 81-2,
 84; "Bear and the Swallows," 77-9; coonskin
 trick, 70, 72; death of, 66, 90-1; dramatiza-
 tions of, 68; Dutchman stories, 69-70; and
 folk tradition, 67-71; in Haiti, 80; hunting
 stories, 68-9; vs. Mike Fink, 84-5; oral legends, 62-3; peg-leg trick, 74; in popular literature, 76; as raconteur, 75-6; in Texas, 80;
 Autobiography, 70, 76; *Life and Adventures
 of Colonel David Crockett,* 65, 67-71
Day, Holman, 154
De Carvalho, Silvio Deolindo, 73-4
"Dead Bird," 302
Denisoff, Serge: *Great Day Coming,* 127
Devil, the, 48-51; appearances of, 41, 48-50;
 as clown, 50; covenants with, 13, 14, 15, 24,
 32-5, 41, 50-1, 177-80; and divine judgments, 28; Indian covenant with, 14; in Indian
 folklore, 49-50; as King Philip, 16; and Knox,
 George, 177-80; multiple forms of, 12, 13,
 49, 50; personalized, 12, 13; outwitting the,
 268; Puritan belief in, 15-16; thunder, use of,
 22; and witches, 13, 14, 16, 32-5; 41. *See
 also* supernatural folklore; witches and witchcraft
dialect tales: Dutch, 69-70; French, 84
Dill, Dorothy: "Lumberjack Stories," 181
Disney, Walt, 60, 247
"Dodgin' Joe," 133
"Dog Kelly," 142
Dorson, Richard M., 65, 69, 73-4, 106, 125;
 folk song collecting, 156-65; and the Paul
 Bunyan myth, 247; *Bloodstoppers and Bearwalkers,* 180-2; *Jonathan Draws the Long
 Bow,* 63
Downer, Robert, 44-5, 46, 47
Doyle, Michael, 203-6 *passim*
draft dodgers, folklore of, 304-9; legends, 255
drama, folklore in, 59-60, 61-2; Yankee plays,
 110-21
dramatizations: of Mike Fink, 91; of Mose the
 Bowery b'hoy, 99-107; of Sam Patch, 98; of
 Yankee character types, 118-20
"Drawing Pictures," 303
Driscoll, "Silver Jack," 166-8, 182-4
druglore, 255, 259, 260-303; anecdotes, 262-3;
 busts, 269-70; cops and dopers, 260-70;
 cops as heads, 270-7; and draft dodgers, 308;
 freakout legends, 288-91; games, 300-3;
 graffiti, 295-7; "heads" in, 260-1; heroes in,
 259, 262, 263, 266-7, 269, 278-81, 238-8;
 jokes, 297-300; local legends, 291-5; and
 Owsley, A. S., 278-81, 283-8; paranoia in,

262, 274-6, 278, 289-90; supernatural
motifs, 267
Duffy, Thomas, 207-9
Dugan, John, 182
Dundes, Alan, 255
Durocher, Oliver, 184
Dutch Protestants, 13, 16, 31
Dyer, Mary, 51, 52

Easy Rider, 260
Eckstorm, Fanny Hardy: *Minstrelsy of Maine,*
161
Eliot, Edmond, 46-7
Eliot, Rev. John, 29, 30
Endicott, John, 52, 53
England: fairy beliefs, 14-15; providence manu-
scripts, 18; witchcraft in, 45, 46
esoteric and exoteric traditions, in folklore, 256
ethnic folklore, 124, 125-7
Eulenspiegel, Tyl. *See* Tyl Eulenspiegel
Evelyn, John, 41
extractive industries, legends of, 124, 126

fairy beliefs, 14-15
"fakelore," 170, 246-8
Fanning, Nathaniel: *Narrative of the Adventures
of an American Navy Officer,* 59
Faust tradition, 50, 180
Feboldson, Febold, 247
Field, Joseph M.: "Mike Fink: 'The Last of the
Boatmen,'" 86, 89, 90, 91
Fife, Austin and Alta, 131, 140; *Ballads of the
Great West,* 243; *Heaven on Horseback,* 140
Fink, Mike. *See* Mike Fink
Finn, H. J.: *Montgomery,* 115, 119
Fisher, Miles Mark: *Negro Slave Songs in the
United States,* 126
Fisher, Tom, 211-12
Fisk, "Jubilee Jim," 249-50
Fitzgibbons, Jimmy, 181-2
"Flaming Groovy," 301
folk beliefs: black, 50; drug busts, 274-5; English
models for, 11-14; fairy beliefs, 14-15; oil
discoveries, 214-15; and supernaturalism, 12;
swallows, 77, 79
folk humor, 57-8, 70; cowboy, 141-3, 145-8;
of the frontier, 17; Yankee comedians, 63.
See also tall tales; trickster heroes
folk songs: black, 235, 238-40; coal mining,
185-90; collecting of, 156-65; cowboy, 130,
131-40; lumberjack, 155-68; occupational,
127; railroader, 235, 236, 238-42, 244-6,
249; simulated, of the left, 127-8; slave, 126
folklore: and anecdotes, derived from, 64-6;
anticapitalism of, 249-50; after the Civil War,
123-7; businessmen in, 249-50; contemporary, 253-310; in drama, 59-60, 61-2; English

models for, 11-14, 57; esoteric and exoteric
traditions, 256; and "fakelore," 170, 246-8;
of frontier society, 57; in graphic arts, 58, 61;
homosexual, 256; immigrant, 123, 124-5;
and the industrial age, 124, 244; motifs, 54-5;
occupational, 127-51; in printed sources, 58,
61; urban, 125, 126-7. *See also* occupational
folklore; druglore
folklore collecting: cowboy ballads, 133-4; folksongs, 156-65; supernatural tales, 177-9;
in the youth culture, 255, 257, 258-60
folklore studies: coal mining, 185-6; of immigrants, 125; "secondary ethnocentrism," 186;
of the youth culture, 255
folklore theory, of providences, 17-18
Forbes, Col. John, 80
Fort, Dr. Joel, 257
Foster, Stephen, 298
Fournier, Joe, 184
Fox, George, 51
Free Speech Movement (Berkeley), 253, 257,
258, 283
French Canadian lumberjacks, 174-6, 182
Friar Rush, 28
Friels, Charley, 180
frontier: democratic values, 66-7; humor, 117;
oral narratives, 67-8

games, of the drug culture, 300-3
Garcia, Jerry, 286-7
Gardner, Emelyn E., 43-4
Gary, Ind., 123-4; Greek immigrants in, 125
gay liberation movement, 256
generic names. *See* nicknames
George, Henry: *Progress and Poverty,* 249, 250
ghosts and apparitions, 12; of coal miners, 202;
of the murdered, 25-6; in Puritan folklore,
23-6; rules of behavior, 25
Gib Morgan, 214, 216-22, 224-6, 227, 235,
246
"Git Along Little Dogies," 140
Glanvil, Joseph: *Collections of Relations,* 27
Gleason, Ralph, 293
Glover, Goody, 38, 39
Goldsmith, Richard, 20-1
Goodwin, John, 38
Goodwin children, bewitching of, 38, 39-40
Gowen, Franklin, 191-3, 202, 212, 213
graffiti, in druglore, 295-7
"Grand Round-up," 132
Grant, Pompey, 161-2
graphic arts: folklore in, 58, 61; heroes in, 58,
61, 97, 101; and the Paul Bunyan theme,
247
Grateful Dead, 278, 281, 285, 286-7
Gray, Roland Palmer: *Songs and Ballads of the
Maine Lumberjacks,* 155

Greensmith, Goody, 35
Greenway, John: *American Folksongs of Protest,* 127
Grey, Zane, 140
Grimes, A. W., 138
Grimm brothers, 31
Gunn, Thomas: *Mose Among the Britishers,* 101
Guthrie, Woody, 127, 202

Hackett, James H., 76
Hackett, J. S.: *Jonathan in England,* 112-13, 120
Hair, 253-4, 262
Hale, John, 33-4, 40
Hamilton, Alexander, 249
Hannay, John, 26
Hans Breitmann ballads, 69
"Hard-Working Miner, The," 187
Harlow, Alvin F.: *Treasury of Railroad Folklore, A,* 235
Harris, Joel Chandler, 126
Harris, Thomas, 52
Harry Emigrant, 59-60
hashish, 265
Hawthorne, Nathaniel, 63, 98
Hell's Angels, 255, 259, 260
heroes: character types, 58-9, 61-2; coal miners, 187-9, 213; comic, 57, 59, 60, cowboys, 134, 136; as democratic figures, 60-1; draft dodgers, 304-9; dramatizations of, 59-60, 61-2, 68; druglore, 259, 262, 263, 266-7, 269, 278-81, 283-8; of frontier society, 60-3; in graphic arts, 97, 101; hippies, 299-300; Jonathan the Yankee, 116-17; lumberjacks, 61, 168-84; as master workmen, 124, 127-8; mock-heroes, 96-7; Mose the Bowery b'hoy, 102-4; narrator heroes, 218-19; nicknames for, 59; as outlaws, 62, popularity of, 62; railroaders, 235-42; of the Revolutionary War, 57, 58-60; synthetic, 246-8; as tricksters, 64-5, 70-5, 84-7, 259, 262, 263; urban, 99
Herskovits, Melville, 186
Hibernians, Ancient Order of, 204, 205-6
Hill, George H., "Yankee," 61, 120-1
Hill, Joe, 244
hippies, 297-300
Hoffman, Abbie, 62
Holbrook, Stewart, 184
homosexual folklore, 256
"How the Man Came Out of a Tree Stump," 79
Howells, William Dean, 63, 98
Hudson, Wilson M.: *Why the Chisholm Trail Forks,* 141
"Hugh McGeehan," 207
Humphreys, Moses. *See* Mose the Bowery b'hoy
Huntsman, Adam, 74
Hutchinson, Anne, 16
Hyatt, Harry M.: *Folk-lore from Adams County, Illinois,* 51

Illinois: "Egypt" area, 72-3; witchcraft tales, 35
image magic, in witchcraft, 38
"Imagery Telepathy," 303
immigrant folklore, 123, 124-5; dialect stories, 69-70; Irish, 193-4; and "memory culture," 125
"In the State of Arkansas," 243
Indians, North American, 19; and alcohol, 22; Devil folklore, 49-50; divine judgments against, 29; massacres, 22; powaws, 14, 50, 211; supernatural beliefs, 14
Industrial Workers of the World ("Wobblies"), 244
industrialism, and folklore, 124
Ives, Burl, 127

Jackson, Andrew, 66, 74, 93, 249
"Jam on Gerry's Rock, The," 156, 158-62
Jefferson, Thomas, 249
Jesse James, 62
"Jimmie Jones," 239
"Jimmy Kerrigan's Confession," 203, 204-6
John Henry, 242
Johnny Appleseed, 238
Johnsen, Julia: *Capital Punishment,* 212
Johnson, Edward, 14, 15, 31, 49, 50
Johnson, Guy B.: *Negro and His Songs, The,* 239, 240
jokes, in druglore, 297-300
"Jolly Lumberman, The," 243
Jonathan the Yankee, 60, 61, 63, 108-21; dialect of, 117, 118; dramatizations of, 62, 63, 87, 110-21; as hero, 116-17; inquisitiveness of, 112-13; as lover, 115-16; nicknames for, 117
Jones, Bill, 142
Jones, David, 194
Jones, Frank, 241
Jones, Howard Mumford, 116
Jones, John Luther, "Casey." *See* "Casey" Jones
Jones, John P., 203, 204, 205, 210
Jones, J. S.: *Green Mountain Boy, The,* 113, 120; *Captain Kyd,* 119; *People's Lawyer, The,* 120; *Silver Spoon, The,* 115-16
Jones, Ralph, 52, 53
Josselyn, John, 49
judgments, 12, 15-16; against bestialities, 30; against critics of the Puritans, 30. *See also* providences

Kahler, Mrs. Howard Sr., 213
Karni, Michael, 170
keelboatmen, 81. *See also* Mike Fink
Keemle, Col. Charles, 89
Keith, George: *Presbyterian Churches in New England,* 52-3
Kelly, Edward, 203-6 *passim*
Kembal, John, 43, 45, 46
Kennedy, Mrs. John F., 295
Kerrigan, Jimmy "Powderkeg," 202-6, 213
Kesey, Ken: and the Merry Pranksters, 260, 269, 279, 286-7, 295; *One Flew Over the Cuckoo's Nest,* 289
Kildee, John, 182
King Philip's War, 53
Kirshenblatt-Gimblett, Barbara, 255
Kittredge, George Lyman: *Witchcraft in Old and New England,* 12, 38, 43, 45

kleshmaker anecdotes, 65
Knapp, Elizabeth, 35-6
Knights of Labor, 189, 213
Knox, George, 176-80
Kornbluh, Joyce: *Rebel Voices,* 127
Korson, George, 185-6, 187, 190, 206, 208,
    213, 214, 235; *Black Rock,* 185; *Coal Dust
    on the Fiddle,* 185; *Minstrels of the Mine
    Patch,* 185, 186; *Songs and Ballads of the
    Anthracite Miners,* 185

Laddie, Art, 181
latrinalia, 295-7
Laughead, William B., 168, 247
Lawler, Michael "Muff," 206
Laws, Malcolm, 155
Leary, Timothy, 295-6
Lee, Fred J., 237, 238, 241
legends: bust-avoiding, 255; of the counter-
    culture, 255; of Davy Crockett, 72-4; of the
    Devil, 49; draft-dodging, 255; of druglore,
    270-3; English models, 11-14; of locality,
    291-5; of marijuana, 291-2; Molly Maguires,
    209-12; occupational, 124; as oral repetition,
    17; of Owsley, A. S., 278-81, 283, 287-8;
    and popular literature, 76; Quaker, 52-3;
    railroaders, 236-7; "sick" legends, 288-9;
    supernatural, 148-9
Leighton brothers, 238
Leland, Charles Godfrey, 69
Levinge, Capt. R. C. A., 76
Lewis, Arthur H., 190, 212
Lightnin' Bill Jones, 148
Lincoln, Abraham, anecdotal techniques of,
    65, 68
Linda, the Cigar Girl, 100, 104-6
"Little Brown Bulls, The," 156
"Little Joe, the Wrangler," 134, 141
Locke, "Yankee," 98
Logan, C. A.: *Vermont Wool Dealer,* 120
Lomax, Alan, 127, 239, 240
Lomax, John, 185, 239, 240; *Cowboy Songs,*
    131
Louisiana Purchase, 57
Lovell, Don, 131
LSD (lysergic acid diethylamide), 259, 260-1;
    draft dodgers' use of, 308, and Owsley, A. S.,
    278-81, 283-8; in "Russian Roulette," 302
lumberjack folklore, 153-84; bosses of lumber-
    camps, 180-2; fights, 181-4; heroes, 61, 168-
    84; in Maine, 155, 156-8, 161, 176-80, 250;
    in Michigan, 155, 161, 166-8, 180-2, 184;
    in Minnesota, 170, 172-4; nicknames, 154-5;
    songs, 155-68
"Lumberman's Alphabet, The," 155, 162-6

Macfarlane, Alan: *Witchcraft in Tudor and
    Stuart England,* 12, 13

machismo, 172, 181, 246, 260
Magarac, Joe, 247
Maine: folksong collecting, 156-65; lumberjack
    folklore, 155, 156-8, 161, 176-80, 250;
    witchcraft tales, 35, 44
Manifest Destiny, doctrine of, 57
Marble, Dan, 61-2, 121; *Sam Patch,* 98
marijuana, 259, 260-1; legends, 291-2; "Smoke
    to Death," 302
Martin, Mary, 23, 29-30
Martin, Susanna, "Goody," 13, 42, 44-5, 46-8
Massachusetts Bay Colony. *See* Puritans
master workmen, legends of, 124, 127-8, 243-
    4
Masterson, Bat, 129
Mather, Cotton, 14, 15, 16; on witchcraft, 34,
    36-8; *Late Memorable Providences Relating
    to Witchcraft,* 32; *Magnalia Christi Americana,*
    12-13, 18, 19, 21-3, 26-9, 33-50 *passim;*
    Wonders of the Invisible World, 19, 41
Mather, Increase, 15; on providences, 12; on the
    Quakers, 52; *Illustrious Providences,* 18, 19-
    20, 28, 33, 52
Mather, Mysterious Dave, 142
Mather, Richard, 18
McDermott, Fr. Daniel, 208, 209-10
McGehan, Hugh, 204
McGovern George, 310
McKinley, Pres. William, 249
McParlan, James, 190, 193, 205, 206, 213
Meine, Franklin, 90
memorats, 43
Michigan, Upper Peninsula, 168; dialect stories,
    69; Italian Hall fire, 202; lumberjack folklore,
    155, 161, 166-8, 180-2, 184
"Michigan-I-O," 243
Mike Fink, the keelboatman, 59, 60, 61, 67, 80-
    92; anecdotes, 84-8; as ballad maker, 88-90;
    vs. Davy Crockett, 84-5; death of, 90, 91;
    dramatizations of, 91; in the Louisville court,
    88; newspaper accounts, 83, 84, 85, 86, 91;
    nicknames for, 83; oral legends, 62-3; post-
    humous popularity, 91-2; as sharpshooter,
    84-5, 90-1; and the sheepowner, 86-7; as
    trickster, 84-7; and wife, Peg, 87
Miller, Perry, 11-12
mind-expanding drugs. *See* LSD
"Miner Boy, The," 187
"Miner's Life for Me, A," 187
"Mines of Avondale, The," 194
Minnesota: lumberjack folklore, 170, 172-4;
    Swedish immigrants, 172-3
Mitchell, Roger E.: *George Knox,* 176, 178,
    179-80
Mix, Tom, 140
Molly Maguires, 128, 186, 190-3; 194-5, 202-
    13; ballads of, 193-4, 203, 204-6, 207-8;
    Black Thursday, 203, 207-8, 210, 212-13;

legends, 209-12; origins of, 193; supernatural tales, 210-12
Monroe Doctrine, 57
Moody, John, 30
More, Henry, 27
Morgan, Gib. *See* Gib Morgan
Morse, William, 26
Mose in California!, 100, 102
Mose the Bowery b'hoy, 58-63 *passim*, 99-108; as clown, 102; dramatizations of, 99-107; as guardian of the Bowery, 104; heroism of, 102; oral tradition of, 106-7; in popular culture, 100-1; posthumous stories, 106-7; sayings of, 102
Mose, Joe and Jack, 102
Mose's Dream, 100
Mother Hicks, 44
Motherfuckers, The, 262
motifs, in religious folklore, 54-5
motorcycle gangs, 255, 259, 260
Mouffreau (Mouffron), Joe, 174-6, 182
Mountain Girl, 286-7
"Muff Lawler, the Squealer," 207, 213
Muir, Alec, 180
Münchausen tradition, 75, 76, 148, 151, 218, 225
Murphy, Jim, 138, 285
Mysteries and Miseries of New York, The, 100, 102, 107
myths and mythologizing: of cowboys, 134, 140, 141; of the Molly Maguires, 190-1; motifs, in providences, 19; in the Revolutionary War, 59, 60

"Nachul-born Easman," 239-40
Nasreddin, Hodja, 300
"Neil Hornback," 89-90
Nelligan, John E., 169-70; "Life of a Lumberjack, The," 180-2
Neville, Morgan: "Last of the Boatmen, The," 91
"New Mexico Cowboy in London, A," 143
New York As It Is!, 100, 102, 104
New York Folklore Quarterly, 63
Newton, Eddie, 238, 240, 241
Newton, Stan: *Paul Bunyan of the Great Lakes*, 168-9
nicknames: frontier heroes, 59; Jonathan the Yankee, 117; Mike Fink, 83; oil drillers, 216-17
Nimrod Wildfire, 68, 76
Nixon, Pres. Richard M., 310
Northall, William K., 107
Norton, Henry A., 241
Norton, John, 52
Nutmeg, the Yankee peddler, 59

occupational folklore, 127-51; coal miners, 128, 185-213; cowboys, 128-53; lumberjacks, 153-84; oil drillers, 214-34; railroaders, 235-51; sexual symbolism in, 246; tragic note in, 124
Odum, Howard W.: *Negro and His Songs, The*, 239, 240
oil drillers, folklore of, 214-34; boom towns, 214, 230; cable tool vs. rotary drillers, 216-18; code of, 215, 216; gushers, tales of, 227, 228-9; land prices, 229-30; McClesky legends, 232-4; nicknames for, 216-17; sudden wealth, 230-4; tall tales, 219, 220-2, 224-6; terminology, 219-21
"Ol' John Brown," 239
"Old Chisholm Trail, The," 127, 133-4, 140, 155
Old Continental, 59-60
Old Prairie the settler, 59
"Old Raw Head," 26
"Old Time Cowboy," 137
Old Stormalong, 220
Olympic Theater (N.Y.C.), 99, 100, 101, 106, 107
"Only a Miner . . . Cowboy . . . Brakeman," 243
Opossum the frontier roarer, 59
oral folk tradition, and Davy Crockett, 67-71
oral narratives: of cowboys, 130-1, 140; of Davy Crockett, 62-3; of the Devil, 49-50; of the frontier, 58-9, 66-8; and legends, 17; of Mike Fink, 62-3; of Mose the Bowery b'hoy, 106-7; narrator as hero, 75-6; in newspapers, 58, 63; oil drilling, 215; of the youth culture, 259
Owens, John E., 121
Owsley, Augustus Stanley III, 278-81, 283-8; life of, 284-5; oral legends of, 278-81, 283, 287-8
Ozark folklore, 289, 294; coonskin trick, 72; Devil, appearances of, 50; folk beliefs, 79; tall tales, 148; witchcraft tales, 35, 38, 39

paranoia tales, in druglore, 262, 274-6, 278, 289-90
Parrington, Vernon Louis, 246
"Pat Dolan," 193-4
Patch, Sam. *See* Sam Patch
Paul Bunyan, 61, 168-70, 184, 216, 217, 220, 221, 238; in the oil fields, 226-9; as synthetic hero, 147-9
Paulding, James K.: *Lion of the West*, 68, 76
Peache, Bernard, 43, 45, 47
Pecos Bill, 221, 247
Philip, King, prince of the Wampanoags, 16, 29
Pinkerton, Allan, 193, 194
poltergeists, 12, 26-8
Pond, Frederick, R., 218
Poole, Matthew, 12
Porter, Don, 158, 161
Porter, John, 158, 162-5
Porter, Kenneth W., 249
powaws, 14, 50, 211
Powderly, Terence V., 189
Powell, Morgan, 211
Pressy, John, 43, 45, 47
printed sources: anecdotes in, 58, 61, 63, 83; and the Crockett legend, 67; folklore in, 58, 61; and Mike Fink, 81, 83-4, 91-2; and the Paul Bunyan theme, 247-8; and Sam Patch, 94
providences, 12, 17-31; bloodstains and bleeding corpses, 22-3; divine judgments, 28-31; folklore theory of, 17-18; function of, 16; ghosts and apparitions, 23-6; histories of, 18-19; mythological motifs, 19; poltergeists, 26-8; thunder and lightning in, 19-22; and

witchcraft. *See also* witches and witchcraft; Puritans

Pugh, Red, 143

Puritans, 12-13; and adultery, 29-30; covenant theology, 14, 17; Devil beliefs, 15-16; folklore of, 15-51; and heresy, 29; and judgments, 15-16; supernatural beliefs, 18. *See also* providences

Putnam, Ann, 24

Putnam, Thomas, 23, 25

Quakers, 15, 16, 27, 40; beliefs, 51; divine judgments, use of, 53-4; legends, 52-3; Puritan treatment of, 51-2

railroader folklore, 235-51; code, 236; legends, 236-7; and Sam Patch, 138; songs and ballads, 235, 236, 238-42, 244-6, 249

Randolph, Vance, 38, 79

Rappolt, Dr. Richard, 286

Raudenbush, Jacob, 211

Raymond, Daniel, 250

Read, Allen Walker, 295

Reagan, Ronald, 295

Reed, Alvin, 149

Reed, Perley I., 118

Reeder, Louise, 105

Reich, Charles: *Greening of America, The,* 286, 287

religious folklore, 11-51; motifs in, 54-5; providences, 17-31; witchcraft, 32-48

Revolutionary War, 57, 59; heroes of, 58-60

Ridings, Sam: *Chisholm Trail, The,* 150-3

Ring, Jervis, 45

Ring, Joseph, 46, 49

"Rip Van Winkle," 143-5

Robb, John S., 84

Roberts, Leonard: *Up Catskin and Down Greasy,* 124

Robeson, Paul, 127

Robin Goodfellow, 28

Rockefeller, John D. Sr., 220

Rogers, Roy, 140

Roman Catholic churches, in colonial America, 12

Roosevelt, Teddy, 142

Rosenfield, Jim, 302

Rowlandson, Mary, 15

Rubin, Jerry, 62

Russell, Charles M., 129; *Trails Plowed Under,* 141, 142-3, 145, 146

"Russian Roulette," 302

Salem Village, Mass., 20; witchcraft trials, 13, 16, 19, 23-4, 25, 33, 40-1, 42-3, 44, 45-8, 180

Sam Bass, 132, 133, 136-40, 285

Sam Patch, 59, 60, 61, 63, 92-8; death of, 94-5; dramatizations of, 62, 98; as mock-hero,

96-7; newspaper accounts, 94; Niagara Falls jump, 92-4; in popular sayings, 98; posthumous appearances, 95-6

Sandburg, Carl, 244

Sands, Robert, 96

Satan. *See* Devil, the

Saunders, Wallis, 235, 237-41 *passim*

Sausaman, John, 16

Schmidt, "Moonlight Harry," 181

Schmoker, Chris, 232

Schoharie Hills, N.Y.: folklore, 294; witchcraft in, 25, 43-4, 45

Seeger, Pete, 127

Seibert, T. Lawrence, 238, 240, 241

Sewall, Samuel, 23, 25

Shakespeare, William, 15

Shanty, John, 248

Sheridan, Charles, 169-70

Shiva's Head Band, 289

Short, Beanie, 124

Short, Mercy, 48-9

sidehill gougers, 110

"Silver Jack," 166-8, 243

Simpson, Aleck, 120

Siringo, Charlie, 137

sisu, quality of, 172

skowmaker anecdotes, 64-6

Slave Songs of the United States, 126

slavery, 57

Slocum, Seth, 230-1, 232

Simms, William Gilmore: "How Sharp Snaffles Got His Capital and Wife," 79

Smith, Abraham "Oregon," 218

Smith, John, 31

Smith, Philip, 36-7

Smith, Seba: "Jack Downing letters," 96

"Smoke to Death," 302

Smyth, Mary Winslow: *Minstrelsy of Maine,* 161

Snelling, Job, 71-2, 110

Soulouque, Emperor, 80

Spargo, John, 185-6

specters, witches' uses of, 41-2

spectral ships, 18, 19

Spirit of the Times (New York), 58, 68, 100, 108

Stage-Struck Yankee, The, 115

Steele, John Washington, 230-2

Steele, S. S.: *Brazen Drum, The,* 116, 119

Steen, Cornelius, 239

Stoughton, William, 25

"Streets of Laredo, The," 139-40, 243

Strickie, the boa constrictor, 222, 224

"Strobe Lights," 302

supernatural folklore: collecting of, 177-9; in the drug culture; Faust figures in, 180; and folk beliefs, 12; of Indians, 14; legends, 148-9; Molly Maguires, 210-12; Puritans, 18. *See also* witches and witchcraft

Swanson, Roy, 174
Sweigert, William T., 285

tall tales, 151, 153; of cowboys, 147-8; of Davy
    Crockett, 70; of oil drilling, 219, 220-2, 224-
    6
Taylor, Billy, 181-2
Teeters, Negley K.: *Criminology,* 212-13
Tennessee: Beanie Short legends, 124; and
    Davy Crockett's career, 64-5; ghost tales,
    25-6
Thomas, Keith: *Religion and the Decline of
    Magic,* 12, 13
"Thomas Duffy," 207-8
Thompson, Hunter, 255
Thompson, Stith: *Motif-Index of Folk Literature,*
    54-5
Thorp, N. Howard "Jack": *Pardner of the Wind,*
    131, 146; *Songs of the Cowboys,* 131-4, 140;
    Tales of the Chuck Wagon, 140, 141, 146-7
Thorpe, Thomas Bangs: "Big Bear of Arkansas,"
    69, 80-1
thunder and lightning, in providences, 19-22
"Tiger's Tooth and Panther's Paw," 302-3
"Tin-Can Star Show," 301-2
Tin Pan Alley songs, 235, 236
Tituba, 33
transportation industry, legends of, 124, 126
Trembly, Capt. Alfred W., 284
Trevisard, Alice, 44
trickster heroes: Davy Crockett, 64-5, 70-5;
    drug users, 259, 262, 263, 266-7, 269, 299-
    300; Mike Fink, 84-7; Yankee, 59, 74-5, 108
Turner, Frederick Jackson: "Frontier in
    American History, The," 58, 66-7
Turner, William: *Compleat History of . . .
    Providences,* 12
Turner brothers, 72
Turney, Ida Virginia: *Paul Bunyan, the Work
    Giant,* 247
Twain, Mark, 72, 142; "Golden Arm, The," 153
"Twirling Incense," 301
Tyl Eulenspiegel, 28, 300
Tyler, Royall: *Contrast, The,* 111, 118-19, 120

UFOs, 18
Uncle Remus stories, 126
"Unfortunate Rake, The," 140
unions, coal mining, 186, 189-90, 213
University of California (Berkeley), 254-5, 257-9
urban folklore, 125, 126-7

Värmlänning, Ola, 172-4
Vietnam war, and draft dodgers, 305
Votur, James, 180

Waite, Bobby, 166
Waite, Walter, 188
Walta, Antti, 172
Walta, Otto, 170-2

Walton, George, 27
Ward, Thomas, 96
Warren, William, 120
"Way Out in Idaho," 243
Webb, Sim, 235, 237
Weil, Dr. Andrew, 257
Wenner, Jann, 286
Wetmore, Alphonso: *Pedlar, The,* 59-60, 91,
    119
"What Makes Us Strike?" 189-90
White, Steward Edward, 154
Wickham, William H., 232
Wignell, Thomas, 120
Wilde, Asa, 151
William of Orange, King, 53
Williams, Thomas W., 194
Winters, Buck, 142
Winthrop, John, 12, 15-16, 30
Wisbey, Herbert, 63
Wister, Owen: *Virginian, The,* 147-8
witches and witchcraft, 32-48; Black Mass, 46;
    covenant with Devil, 13, 14, 16, 32-5; 41;
    cows, affinity with, 43-4; "documents," 43;
    English and American, 13; image magic, 38;
    invisibility, power of, 41-2; learned tradition
    on, 46, 49; magic books, 39; and Mather,
    Cotton, 34, 36-8; memorats, 43; "nightmare"
    witches, 45; in the Ozarks, 35, 38, 39; reme-
    dies against, 33, 38, 44, 45; Sabbaths, 46;
    Salem trials, 13, 16, 19, 23-4, 25, 33, 40-1,
    42-3, 44, 45-8, 180; in the Schoharie Hills
    (N.Y.), 25, 43-4, 45; specters, use of, 41-2;
    stereotyping of, 13; victims' symptoms, 35,
    38; white witches, 14, 33. *See also* Devil, the;
    supernatural folklore; Puritans
Wobblies (International Workers of the World),
    244
Wolfe, Tom: *Electric Kool-Aid Acid Test, The,*
    260, 269, 285
women's liberation movement, 256
Wonderful Leaps of Sam Patch, The, 97-8
Wood, William, 49
Woodstock festival (N.Y.), 253
Woodsworth, Samuel: *Forest Rose, The,* 119-20
Workingmen's Benevolent Association, 189, 193
World's Fair (1939), 248
"Wreck of the Old 97, The," 242
"Wreck of the Six-Wheel Driver, The," 239
"Wreck on the C & O, The," 242

Yankee Blade (Boston), 58
Yankee figures: actors, 119-21; antecedents of,
    118-19; as character types, 59, 108-10;
    comedians, 63; dramatizations of, 110-21;
    jokes of, 298-9; peddlers, 58, 59, 71; as
    trickster heroes, 59, 74-5, 108
Yankee Jonathan. *See* Jonathan the Yankee
"Young Hunting," 23

"Zilch," 300-1